As members of the one human family and as believers, we have obligations to the common good, to justice and to solidarity.

—Pope John Paul II
The Umayyad Mosque
Damascus, May 2001

The author extends his thanks to the volunteers who have worked over many months' time to collect, edit, and format material for this handbook. In particular, credit is due to Frederic Hunter, Andrea Stanton, and Steven Schlesser.

Front Cover, inset: A calligraphic design by Mamoun Sakkal based on the poem "Ashiqun min Falastine" (Lover from Palestine), 1966, by the Palestinian poet Mahmoud Darweesh.

How to Use This Book

THE ARAB-AMERICAN HANDBOOK IS DESIGNED to offer readers a varied menu of information about Arab-Americans, Arabs, Muslims, and the Arab and Muslim Worlds. The *Handbook* opens with an easy-to-read, test-your-knowledge quiz that challenges misperceptions about Arabs and Muslims. This is followed by detailed answers and explanations. The author is Nawar Shora, an Arab-American attorney who has given hundreds of consciousness-raising lectures on which this quiz is based.

An Informed Views section follows. Here guest essayists provide insightful and scholarly articles about the Arab and Muslim worlds. Readers will be able to learn about many Middle Eastern places, peoples, and philosophies. They will find analyses of current events—such as 9/11 and the war in Iraq; explore media portrayals of Arabs; and read descriptions of how it feels to be Arab or Muslim in America and beyond.

Finally, the *Handbook* offers a Reference section, designed to provide readers with further resources about Muslims: timelines, thumbnail sketches of Muslim countries, and a glossary of terms. It ends with an index, and information about the guest essayists.

We hope that *The Arab-American Handbook* will give readers a deeper understanding and appreciation of Arabs, Arab-Americans, and Muslims.

—The Editors

For my grandparents . . .

And my grandchildren.

The

Arab-American
Handbook
A Guide to the Arab,
Arab-American
& Muslim Worlds

By Nawar Shora

 Cune

The Arab-American Handbook:
A Guide to the Arab, Arab-American, and Muslim Worlds
© 2010 Nawar Shora
Cune Press, Seattle 2010
Second Edition
3 5 7 9 8 6 4
ISBN (hardback) 978-1885942470 (10 digit) 1885942478 $34.95
ISBN (paper) 978-1885942142 (10 digit) 1885942141 $19.95

Library of Congress Cataloging-in-Publication Data
Shora, Nawar.
The Arab-American handbook :
a guide to the Arab, Arab-American & Muslim worlds / By Nawar Shora.
p. cm.
ISBN 978-1-885942-47-0 (hardback)
1. Arab-Americans--Handbooks, manuals, etc. 2. Arabs--Handbooks, manuals,
etc. 3. Muslims--Handbooks, manuals, etc. I. Title.
E184.A65S56 2009
973'.04927--dc22
2009036788

Calligraphy by Mamoun Sakkal (www.sakkaldesign.com). Illustrations by Ali Farzat (www.alifarzat.
com). Editing by Frederic Hunter. Timelines by Steven Schlesser. At a Glance by Andrea Stanton.

Cune Press, an independent book publishing company founded in 1994. PO Box 31024, Seattle, WA
98103. Thanks to the Salaam Cultural Museum for its encouragement and support.

Select titles in the Bridge between the Cultures Series:

www.cunepress.com | www.cunepress.net

Contents

1
Section One

An easy-to-read, test-your-knowledge quiz that challenges misperceptions about Arabs and Muslims. This is followed by detailed answers and explanations.

Contents (Section One)

1. A Quiz . . . and More

For Your Information

Points to Ponder

Illustrations

A Map

Calligraphy by Mamoun Sakkal

(For More Mamoun Sakkal Calligraphy, see page 299)

Drawings by Ali Farzat

(For More Ali Farzat Drawings, see page 300)

A Note to the Reader

THIS HANDBOOK AIMS TO INFORM YOU about Arabs, Arab-Americans, and Muslims. It is designed for civil servants (in the military, law enforcement, border patrol, or homeland security) as well as the general public. *The Arab-American Handbook* provides general, apolitical information: cultures, demographics, history, languages, and religions.

You may choose to read the book in its entirety, or instead use it as a reference book and skip between the sections of greatest interest to you. *The Arab-American Handbook* is so named because Arabs, Arab-Americans, and Muslims are often lumped together by a public that assumes they are all adherents of Islam. Distinctions among these groups will be made throughout the book. Please note that statistics provided in this edition are up-to-date as of November 2009.

It's my hope that readers will walk away with a newfound understanding and appreciation of Arabs, Arab-Americans, and Muslims—the people, the cultures, the languages, the habits. Most important: I hope to demystify these groups and to lower the level of fear, mistrust, and apprehension.

Nawar Shora, JD
Washington, DC

Introductory Quiz

THIS BOOK IS GUIDED BY A BASIC FORMULA that summarizes the root of the many challenges we face as a society:

Lack of Understanding + Lack of Communication = Lack of Trust

Trust is the key factor to unlock a clearer future for all of us. Once we secure trust between the public, the government and those minority communities most affected by 9/11 (including Arabs, Arab-Americans, Sikhs, South Asians, Iranians, Turks, and Muslims as a religious group), we can achieve a great deal together, making valuable progress towards genuine trust. The more accurate—and more positive—illustration of the above formula is:

Understanding + Communication = Trust

This handbook will target the first element of *understanding*. Often, distrust of others comes from the fact that we believe them to be different from ourselves. Chief Joseph of the Wallowa Native Americans said: "We fear that which we do not understand." The less Americans know about Arabs and Muslims, the greater the likelihood of hostility between them.

I have been doing diversity-awareness training for eight years and have reached thousands of individuals in that time. Often the best way to start is to catch people off guard, to quiz them on how much they actually know about a subject. That is what I tend to do in my presentations. My quiz is never graded, however, and the answers remain anonymous. It is intended used as a teaching tool and a vehicle for discussion.

So let's take the quiz!

It's made up of ten straightforward questions. If you are unsure of your answers, mark something down, even if it's only a guess. If you feel completely stumped, check with a friend, a colleague, or a family member—this won't be considered cheating. As each of the answers will be explained to you later, there is no need to do any research to seek out the right answers.

Take fifteen minutes on average to complete the quiz—though you may take more time if you need to. Remember that questions six and seven ask you to name a character, and not an actor. In question ten, there is at least one Arab-American in each category. Now go ahead and start. Good luck!

1. On a scale from one to ten, with one being least and ten being most, how much do you know about Arabs, Arab-Americans, and Muslims?

2. True or False: All Arabs are Muslim, and all Muslims are Arab.

3. What is the world's most populous Muslim country?

4. What is the first thing that comes to mind when you hear the term 'Arab'?

5. True or False: Arab-Americans were responsible for the Oklahoma City bombing.

6. Name one or more positive Arab *characters* in television history.

7. Name one or more positive Arab *characters* in movie history.

8. True or False: Arab-Americans were responsible for the 9/11 attacks on the US.

9. Do you believe a negative stereotype exists of Arab-Americans in the United States?

10. Circle the Arab-American public figure(s) in each of the following categories:

A. Shakira   Christina Aguilera   Britney Spears

B. Ralph Nader   Al Gore   Ross Perot

C. <u>Salma Hayek</u>   Shannon Elizabeth   Denise Richards

D. <u>Debbie Gibson</u>   Paula Abdul   Tiffany

E. <u>Doug Flutie</u>   Jeff George   Drew Brees

F. <u>Shaggy</u>   Fred Flintstone   Homer Simpson

In the next sections, you will learn the correct answers to the quiz, and will discover the most common questions and comments I receive after administering it in my own presentations.

Chapter One

Arabs & Muslims

A Discussion of the Introductory Quiz

THIS FIRST CHAPTER OF THE HANDBOOK USES the answers to the Introductory Quiz as a framework for presenting some basic information about Arabs and Muslims.

Topics to be discussed:
- Basic knowledge about Arabs, Arab-Americans, and Muslims.
- Immigrant behavior and mannerisms.
- Perceptions of Arabs, Arab-Americans, and Muslims.
- Domestic and international population statistics on Arabs and Muslims.
- What makes a country an Arab country?

Points to Remember:
- Arabs are a multiracial, religiously diverse, heterogeneous group of people.
- Muslims believe they are followers of the third and final Abrahamic faith, continuing from Judaism and Christianity.
- Muslims live all over the world, although their largest populations are in South and Southeast Asia.
- Arabs live in what is commonly referred to as the Middle East (though Southwest Asia is technically more correct) and North Africa.
- Learn the Three Factor Test to determine an Arab country:
  - A cultural and historical link;
  - One majority religion, Islam, although not always the only one practiced;
  - One majority language, Arabic, with many different dialects, although not always the only language spoken.

Question One
On a scale from one to ten how much do you know about
Arabs, Arab-Americans, and Muslims?

OF THE THOUSANDS OF INDIVIDUALS WHO have taken the quiz, most respondents
rank themselves as one, two or three. Some label themselves four, five or six.
Few assign themselves eight or more, including people who are familiar with Arabs
and Muslims.

Indeed, the majority of individuals who have taken this quiz believe that they
know little about Arabs, Arab-Americans, Arab culture, or Muslims. Such honest
self-appraisal is good news, although it would be preferable if all quiz takers knew
enough to give themselves a top grade! However, it's far better to recognize one's lack
of knowledge, than to believe that one knows more than one actually does. Ignorance
or lack of knowledge is regrettable, but not dangerous. The false perception of
knowledge, on the other hand, is dangerous.

Here is an example. In an informal survey conducted in a university setting,
25% of those who graded themselves seven or higher, believed that Arab-Americans
were involved in the Oklahoma City bombing—a bombing that killed 168 people,
many of whom were children—of April 1995. This, of course, is plain wrong. It was
heartland Americans who committed this crime. Such false knowledge plants seeds of
misunderstanding, bigotry, and hatred. We will address this problem in more detail,
when discussing question seven about positive Arab characters in movie history.
Why respondents believe they know so little:

Many quiz respondents realize they don't know much about this topic. Here are the
reasons they give for their lack of knowledge:
* We don't learn about these people in school.
* We aren't sure why we should learn about them.
* We don't know about them because they don't play a significant role in our
  society.
* We don't know about them because they don't know about us.
* We don't know about them because they choose to stay away from the rest of us.
* We don't know about them because the media taught us everything we know.

Let's address some of these explanations.

We do not learn about Arabs, Arab-Americans, or Muslims in school.

This is true for two reasons. First, most of the history and culture we learn about in school is rooted in Judeo-Christian and Anglo-European traditions. A study by the Center for Middle Eastern and North African Studies of eighty textbooks showed that materials about Arabs and Muslims in them tended to rely on stereotypes, based on overly simplistic or inaccurate information. In addition, textbooks rarely presented facts and/or perceptions from the perspective of Arabs and/or Muslims themselves.[2] As a result, a large group of immigrants, whose cultures have helped shape American society, are thus ignored and denigrated. Arabs and Muslims have been part of America even before the United States became a nation. They played a significant role in shaping world history, and in positively influencing American society.

The second reason is this: generally, the US educational system tends to ignore the rest of the world. Most students learn little world geography, investigate few societies other than their own, and study few foreign languages. Two National Geographic Society surveys, one done in 2002, the other in 2006, confirmed this state of affairs. They showed that American men and women, aged 18 to 24, knew little about either world or domestic geography (these studies will be discussed later).

When I was in high school, my fellow students and I rarely had to consult a world map. Our course work hardly ever scratched the surface of the world beyond our own shores. While many of our institutions of higher learning have excellent departments of Middle Eastern and Islamic studies, their curricula are not integrated into other departments. Unless students make a determined effort to learn about Arabs—the people, their history and culture, or to study Muslims—their faith and their diversity as a community, they literally "will not learn about them in school."

We aren't sure why we should learn about them.

Many respondents wonder, almost defensively, why such an understanding is necessary or useful.

Here's why. First, given the terrorist activities the United States and its allies now face, we as a society (including those in all areas of government, especially law enforcement or security careers) need to learn to understand Arabs, Arab-Americans, and Muslims, and not on the basis of the false perceptions mentioned earlier. For example, understanding something about Islam will help us discern how extremists manipulate and misinterpret it when seeking to justify terrorism.

Secondly, understanding what Islam is will help thwart false perceptions, and end the intolerance and hatred bred by fear, and spread on both sides in the name of religion.

A third reason is that knowledge about Arabs and Muslims will curb the targeting of innocent people, based solely on dress, appearance, preconceptions, or stereotypes.

What will happen as we gain a better understanding of Arab and Muslim communities, both here and abroad? Tensions will be reduced. We will come to realize that these people have the same goals as do most Americans. They want peace, prosperity, and better lives for their children. Such understanding would make it possible not only to make Americans feel safer, but to work together for a better world.

We don't know about them because they don't play a significant role in our society.

In fact, Arabs and Muslims have played important roles throughout US history. They continue to do so today. Many Americans are unfamiliar with the range of societal roles played by Arab-Americans and American Muslims. Among those of Arab descent are Ralph Nader; White House press corps legend Helen Thomas; General John Abizaid, former commander of the United States Central Command; and acclaimed actor and multiple Emmy award winner, Tony Shalhoub. American Muslims include famous entertainers Ice Cube and Dave Chappelle, poet Pamela K. Taylor, and legendary athletes, Kareem Abdul Jabbar and Muhammed Ali. This question will be addressed more fully when we discuss question ten about significant Arab and Muslim figures in American society.

We don't know about them because they don't know about us.

Millions of Muslims and Arabs do know about us because they are *us*! Most Arabs in this country are Arab Americans. Of the three to four million of them, about 83.3% are United States citizens. 46% were born here. Over half of foreign-born Arabs are naturalized citizens.[3] A sizable percentage of the 16.7% of non-citizen Arabs come here to study at universities throughout the United States.[4] Others come on business, as tourists or to visit relatives.

Many Arabs and Muslims living elsewhere are very familiar with the United States and Americans, and with many aspects of American popular culture. They watch our movies. They listen to our music. Moreover, for decades, American foreign policy has played an important role in Arab politics, most acutely since 9/11, and the war on Iraq in 2003.

This handbook mentioned "false perceptions." Our music and movies may tend to present false impressions of American life as being violent, sex-obsessed, and characterized by too much freedom and too little discipline. As a result, Arabs who suppose that armed criminals hang out on every American street-corner or that most American teenage girls are single mothers, are sadly ill-informed. They are like those Americans who see the world in terms of "us" and "them," who suppose that "we" are light-skinned and democratic and Christian, whereas "they" are dark-skinned and extremist and Muslim.

If some Arabs have false perceptions about America, many others, especially the elites, follow US politics very closely, by reading and watching our news media via the internet or satellite television. They know about us more than we know about ourselves, and for three main reasons:

Firstly, US culture reaches across borders. Its delivery systems are dominant. So is its language. English is increasingly taught in schools all over the world.

Secondly, individuals outside the United States study the cultures and languages of other peoples, because they believe that such study enhances their world awareness and their prosperity. For example, only 9% of Americans speak a language other than English. By contrast, in eighty-five countries where English is not the native tongue, it is the premiere influential second language of trade, tourism, and hip youth culture. This is the case in Arab countries such as Egypt and Jordan, and in Muslim countries such as Pakistan and Malaysia.

Thirdly, like many people around the globe, Arabs and Muslims understand the need to learn about different countries and cultures, because these provide insights into other nations' political and economic policies. Because of globalization, cultures are becoming more intertwined. Present US dominance in cultural globalization, politics and economics requires others to learn about it.

Question Two
True or False: All Arabs are Muslim . . . and all Muslims are Arab.

FALSE! BECAUSE THE TERMS "ARAB" AND "Muslim" are often used interchangeably in conversation and sometimes in media reports, many people now believe that the two groups are one and the same. However, not all Arabs are Muslims. Nor are all Muslims Arabs. Let's analyze the distinctions.

Who are the Arabs and what makes an Arab country?
Arabs are a multiracial, religiously diverse, heterogeneous group of approximately three hundred million people living in, or originating from, Southwest Asia and North Africa.

> ### FYI – Terminology: Middle East
> *We should note that the Arab World and the Middle East are not the same. Geographically speaking, the Arab World lies in Southwest Asia and North Africa. "Middle East" is a term coined by the British, to distinguish what was, for them, an area between the "Far East" and the "Near East." The Middle East includes non-Arab countries such as Turkey, Israel, and Iran.*

The Arab World is generally considered to include the members of the League of Arab States (the Arab League). There are twenty-two countries in the Arab League reaching across North Africa into parts of the Middle East. They are: Algeria, Bahrain, the Comoros Islands, Djibouti, Egypt, Iraq, Jordan, Kuwait, Lebanon, Libya, Mauritania, Morocco, Oman, Palestine, Qatar, Saudi Arabia, Somalia, Sudan, Syria, Tunisia, the United Arab Emirates, and Yemen. (For more on countries, see page 272.) Although Sudan is considered an Arab country, its population in the north is mainly Arab, while that of the south is comprised mainly of non-Arabic speakers. Other countries in the region have large percentages of Arabs and native Arabic speakers but are not generally considered to be Arab countries.

The majority of Arabs live in the continent of Africa. A woman from Morocco might describe herself as a Moroccan, as an Arab (if she is not Berber), and as a North African. All three descriptions are apt, and all are true at the same time.

So what exactly makes an Arab country? Why is Tunisia an Arab country, but not Iran? Why is Syria an Arab country, while its neighbor Turkey is not? Why is Bahrain an Arab country, but not Israel? The answer cannot solely be geographical, because Arab and non-Arab countries are found in the same region.

Let's look at an analogy more familiar to Americans. The Arab World is linked together—in much the same way as Latin America is—through three dominant factors: (1) a cultural/historical link; (2) a majority religion, though not the only one practiced; and (3) a majority language, often with many different dialects, although not the only one spoken. Each factor helps to distinguish countries as Arab. A country

FYI – Morocco
In 1777, Morocco became the first country to recognize the United States of America as a sovereign and independent nation.

is not Arab unless all three factors are present.

The cultural and historical link dates back many centuries. Our civilization was born when people first organized in cities in what is today the Arab World. These people shared similar cultures, spoke related languages, believed in similar mythologies and methods of warfare. They had many social factors in common: everything from attire to cuisine to types of dancing.

It was religion and language that shaped the Arab World. What ultimately united the land and people of what we know today by that name was the spread of Islam. It came from the Arabian Peninsula and moved across the Fertile Crescent, that territory beginning at the Mediterranean, stretching between the Tigris and Euphrates rivers, and ending at the Persian Gulf. When the Prophet Mohammad died in 632 AD, the religion could have lost its following. However, under the guidance of the first four caliphs (or successors to Mohammad), the religion spread across the entire region. Within thirty years, the Muslims had conquered Persia (Iran), Iraq, Syria, parts of North Africa, and the Byzantine (Eastern Roman) empire.

Throughout the Arab World, there are significant minorities of various faiths. For example, Lebanon is roughly 50% Christian. Morocco and Tunisia have small minorities of Jews. Members of the Coptic Christian Church are an important group in Egypt.

Language also served as a unifier. As the Arabs spread throughout North Africa and Southwest Asia, so did the Arabic language. Its interface with the original local languages is believed by some to have caused the evolution of dialects and regional accents.

Minority populations living in the Arab World also speak Armenian, Kurdish, Aramaic, Berber, Assyrian, Amharic and other languages. From country to country, the spoken Arabic varies quite a bit.

FYI – The Three Factor Test for determining Arab countries

1. Cultural and historical links to each other.
2. One majority religion, although not the only one practiced.
3. One majority language, with many different dialects, although not the only one spoken.

Arabic accents are quite diverse. A Moroccan speaking to an Omani in Arabic is similar to a Texan speaking to a Highland Scot in English. Both are speaking the same language, but because there are different word usages and pronunciation, the speakers may have a challenging time understanding one another. Speaking Modern Standard Arabic is the way around this.

FYI – Are there two Arabic languages?

No. But Modern Standard Arabic (the formal version of the language that evolved from the Classical Arabic in which the Quran is written) is taught in schools, used in formal settings, in business contracts, and in most Arab Parliaments. Spoken Arabic is the less formal, colloquial version of Arabic, commonly used in everyday situations. Some would argue that it has evolved into a multitude of dialects across the Arab World.

Educated Arabs can understand Modern Standard Arabic, but they may have a hard time expressing themselves in it.

While Arabic accents and dialects vary greatly from country to country, the similarities between dialects can be divided into six regional groupings.

FYI – Afghanistan

Although Afghanistan is 99% Muslim, it is not an Arab country because Arabic is not one of its primary languages. However, many Arab and Muslim fighters who entered Afghanistan during the Soviet / Afghan war of the 1980s stayed and joined the Taliban, a group that adhered to a strict and fanatical version of Islam. The Taliban took control of Afghanistan after the Soviets pulled out and ruled it during the 1990s. Among these fighters was Osama bin Laden, a Muslim from Saudi Arabia, whose family is originally from Yemen. The bin Ladens run a multinational construction company, based in Saudi Arabia. This company has made them very wealthy. Osama bin Laden created an international terrorist network now known as Al-Qaeda. Al-Qaeda means "the base" and refers to the "database" of fighters assembled during the guerilla wars against the Soviet presence in Afghanistan.[5]

North African Arabic, the everyday language spoken in Algeria, Morocco, and Tunisia shares many similarities, such as the inclusion of French words within it, as a result of French colonial occupation.

Egyptian Arabic has its own unique identity, but it is commonly understood by other Arabs because Cairo—Egypt's capital city—was for decades, the Hollywood of the Arab World, and the greatest producer of popular songs and singers.

East African Arabic, the language spoken in Sudan, Djibouti, Somalia, the Comoros Islands, and by the minority Arabic-speaking populations of Eritrea and Ethiopia, shares some similarities, including an intermixture of African languages.

Levantine Arabic is spoken in Jordan, Lebanon, Palestine, and Syria. While the accents vary, the vocabulary remains largely the same throughout.

In the case of Iraqi Arabic, there is a slight geographical division. The southern part of Iraq, which is close to the Arabian Peninsula, shares accents with the countries of the Gulf region, whereas the Arabic of northern and western Iraq is more closely related to Levantine Arabic.

The Arabic of the Arabian Peninsula—that spoken in Saudi Arabia, Kuwait, Bahrain, Qatar, the United Arab Emirates, Oman, and Yemen—generally shares similarities, while retaining its own individual, at times very distinctive, accents.

Most individual cities across the Arab world have their distinct and easily recognizable accents.

Let's now apply the three criteria to some other countries in the region. Iran does share some cultural and historic similarities with the Arab World: history, attire, certain cuisine, traditions, and customs. So Iran partially meets the cultural/historical criterion. It is also among the ten most populous Muslim countries in the world, and thus meets the religious criterion. Ethnically different from Arabs, Iranians are Aryans while Arabs are Semites. Iranians speak Farsi (known in English as Persian), not Arabic. Therefore, Iran is not an Arab country.

How about Israel? Although it shares some cultural/historical traits in terms of food, dance, and history, it does not qualify under either the majority religion criterion (which is Judaism) or the language (which is Hebrew). While there are Arabs living in Israel, it is not an Arab country.

What about Greece? Well, it shares a lot of history and culture with the Arabs—since both peoples were ruled by the Ottoman Turks. Is it Gyro or Shawarma?   Is it Baklava or Baqlawa? Is it a Kalamtianos dance or a Dabke? Eastern Orthodox Christianity is the majority religion in Greece, not Islam, and the language there is Greek. Thus, it is not an Arab country.

Emigrant Arabs and Arab-Americans
As already mentioned, three to four million Arab-Americans live in the United States.

FYI – Arab-Israelis or Palestinians with Israeli Citizenship
Roughly 20% of Israel's population is Arab and non-Jewish (typically Christian or Muslim). Some identify themselves as Palestinians with Israeli citizenship while others see themselves as Arab-Israelis. Beyond the 20%, some ethnic Arabs are Sephardi or Mizrahi (Eastern) Jews. The term Sephardi originally referred to Jews of the Iberian Peninsula prior to the Spanish Reconquista. More recently, it has come to include Jews of Arab and Persian backgrounds who have no historical connection to present day Spain and Portugal. The term Mizrahi generally refers to Jewish people from the Middle East.

About 83% of them are US citizens. While most of the Arab World is Muslim, the Arab-Americans are overwhelmingly Christian (77%). More specifically, 42% of these Christians are Catholic, 23% Eastern Orthodox (belonging to Antiochian, Greek, Russian, or Syrian Orthodox dominations), and roughly 11% are Protestant. Only 23% of Arab-Americans are Muslim.[6]

Arab-Americans live in every state in the nation and hold positions across society. They are taxi drivers and grocers, firefighters and law enforcement officers, doctors and lawyers, nurses and dentists, businessmen and stockbrokers, designers and entertainers. Arab-Americans are woven into the fabric of American life and history.

Who are Muslims and what do they believe?
Arabs—over three hundred million people located in mostly Southwest Asia and North Africa—constitute about 20% of the world's 1.4 billion Muslims. Terminology note: These people are called Muslims—not Mooslims, Mohammedans, Mohamidans, Islamics, Mussulman, Musselman, and Mussulmaun. Employing the name of the Prophet to refer to Muslims (e.g. Muhammadans) is wrong and is similar to referring to Christians as Jesusites. Muslims do not worship Mohammad. Muslims are followers of Islam. Muslims believe in one God and regard their religion as a continuation of Judaism and Christianity. All three are seen as continuations of one another, or different branches on the same tree.

When I was growing up, my mother always taught me, "To be a good Muslim, you must first be a good Jew and a good Christian." That one sentence explains the heart of Islam. Islam continues the Abrahamic faiths. Throughout its teachings, Islam refers

© 2009 Ali Farzat

FYI – The Faith of Arab-Americans

42% – Catholic
23% – Eastern Orthodox (belonging to Greek, Russian, or Syrian Orthodox denominations)
11% – Protestant
23% – Muslim [7]

to the "people of the book," meaning Muslims, Christians, and Jews, those whose monotheistic faith descends from Abraham. It does not matter whether you call the Divine Being, God, Yahweh, or Allah. It is the same Being who created the heavens and the earth, who supports good over evil, and whom believers hold as the highest power of all.

Islam originated in 610 AD when forty-year-old Mohammad, a deeply-spiritual native of Mecca, was meditating in a cave, as he often did. The Archangel Gabriel appeared before him and commanded Mohammad to recite what Muslims believe is the word of God. Over the next twenty years, Mohammad received many such revelations from Gabriel. These recitations were later compiled into the 114 chapters, or *suras*, of the *Quran*.

The *Quran* is the Muslim holy book, the same way that the New Testament is the holy book of Christianity and the *Torah* (Old Testament) the holy book of Judaism. Muslims believe the *Quran* to be the word of God. The term "Quran" is derived from the Arabic verb *iqra*, meaning to read or to recite, which is what the Archangel Gabriel commanded the illiterate Mohammad to do: to recite God's message. Muslims consider Mohammad to be the human messenger of God—and in the tradition of Biblical prophets.

FYI – Arabs in Latin America

Estimates vary as to the number of people of Arab descent in Latin America. Some say there are ten million; others put the figure as high as thirty million. These are the descendents of immigrants who arrived from what was then Ottoman Syria in the late nineteenth century. For example, of Honduras' population of six million, roughly 200,000 are of Arab descent.[8] About 25% of the population of San Pedro Sula, Honduras' second largest city, descend from Arabs.[9] The family of Latin America's richest businessman, Carlos Slim Helú of Mexico, came originally from Lebanon. In June 2007, Señor Helú surpassed Bill Gates as the wealthiest person in the world. Two former Ecuadorian presidents, a president of Argentina, a prime minister of Belize, a minister of education of El Salvador, and a minister in Brazil were of Arab descent.[10] Latin Americans of Arab descent constitute a vital and highly-visible part of society, occupying as they do a larger proportion of the population than in the United States.

There are the five pillars, or five required religious practices, in Islam:
1. Belief in one God, whose Messenger is Mohammad
2. Prayer five times a day (at set times)
3. Charity
4. Fasting during the holy month of Ramadan (if one is able to)
5. Pilgrimage to Mecca (if one is able to)

Moreover, there are six articles of faith:
1. Belief in God
2. Belief in the Angels
3. Belief in the Holy Books
4. Belief in the Day of Judgement and the Afterlife
5. Belief in the Prophets
6. Belief in Destiny

Islam does not have any religious leader, such as the Pope, nor any ordained council. It is meant to be a religion of personal reflection and action, a direct relationship between each individual and God, unmediated by a priestly caste. Even during the time of the prophet, the message was received and interpreted in various ways.

Prayers at mosques are led by an *imam*, who, ideally, should be the congregation member who is most well-read in the community. People often turn to Islamic teachers or to imams (of their own mosque, or of larger mosques around the world) for help in interpreting the religion for themselves. Unfortunately, some of the individuals to whom they turn are ignorant of Islam. Or worse still, they might take verses of the *Quran* out of context, for political or for personal gain, thereby spreading deformed versions of this humanistic faith. Although this is a phenomenon that happens in all religions, following 9/11, the media has tended to focus on Islam alone, and on the most violent and extremist interpretations of it by these so-called religious leaders.

As with all other Scriptures, it is important not to isolate passages of the *Quran* out of context. Such passages become vague and unclear, if judged independently of other qualifying sections. The *Quran* itself addresses this very issue by saying, "Some verses are precise in meaning, they are the foundation of the Book, and others ambiguous. Those whose hearts are infected with disbelief follow the ambiguous part, so as to create dissension… No one knows its meaning except God."[13] Taking verses out of context from the *Quran* can lead to a grave misinterpretation of the religion. Extremists, who come to be considered Islamic scholars or leaders, turn people astray by doing this. Many non-Muslim individuals, including Western scholars and religious or political leaders, do the same thing too in order to denigrate Islam.

Here, for example, is a passage from the *Quran* often misquoted and misinterpreted to portray Islam as a violent faith: "When the sacred months are passed, slay the idolaters wherever you find them, and seize them, beleaguer them and lie in wait for them with every kind of ambush. But if they convert and observe prayer and pay

FYI – Wahhabism

"Wahhabism" is a term we often now hear in the media. It refers to a tiny sect of Islam, founded in the eighteenth century in what is present-day Saudi Arabia, by one Mohammad Ibn Abd al-Wahhab. His heterodox religious movement only gathered strength and influence thanks to its alliance with Mohammad Bin Saud, founder of the present ruling Saudi royal family and of the Kingdom of Saudi Arabia. The followers of al-Wahhab and those of Ibn Saud managed between them to unite the tribes of the region. Consequently, much of Wahhabi fundamentalist ideology became woven into Saudi society and culture. Al-Wahhab was the severest of fundamentalists, who believed that any evolution of Islam beyond the narrowest and most literal interpretations of Mohammad's teachings was blasphemous. Wahhab and his followers focused more on the differences between them and mainstream Muslims than on the similarities. The Wahhabis saw fit to label most other Muslims, as well as all other faiths, as lost in jahila ("ignorance"), the term Prophet Mohammad used to describe the pagan tribes of the Arabian Peninsula. Wahhabis regard themselves as the chosen ones, deeming other Muslims, as well as all Christians and Jews, as damned unbelievers. Because of Saudi oil wealth, the Wahhabi fundamentalist message has been spread through the financing of its schools and publications, which are free. As a movement, Wahhabism is a recent and intolerant phenomenon. It runs counter to Islam's central principles of tolerance, coexistence and the pursuit of knowledge and scholarship.[11]

the obligatory alms, then let them go their way for God is forgiving and merciful."[14] Taken out of context, it appears that God orders Muslims to act brutally. However, this verse refers to a specific historical incident, and the disavowal of a peace treaty, breached by the pagan enemies of Mohammad. In other verses of the *Quran*, God maintains, "Whoever killed a human being, except as punishment for murder or other villainy in the land, shall be deemed as though he had killed the whole of mankind."[15] Additionally, the *Quran* says, "Do not burn a plant, nor cut down a tree, nor kill an old man, nor a young child, nor a woman ... nor monastery dwellers."[16] While there are sections addressing matters of violence within the *Quran*, as there certainly are in the Bible, it is important to remember that the term "Islam" is derived from the word *salaam,* which means peace. But as with every faith, individuals tend to read and interpret what they choose from its scripture.

Another false notion about Islam is that Muslims do not believe in Christianity and Judaism, and order the "conversion by the sword" or eradication of Christians and Jews. Muslims honor Moses and Jesus, and believe in the Immaculate Conception. In fact, the Virgin Mary is mentioned more times in the *Quran* than she is in the *Bible*—thirty-four times in the *Quran* as opposed to only nineteen times in the *Bible*.[17] There is an entire chapter of the *Quran* dedicated to Mary. "Those who believe, and

FYI – Sharia

Sharia is often labeled as Islamic law, though some would argue that it is more precisely an evolving body of law inspired by the Quran *and the Sunna (or the Teachings of the Prophet Mohammad). Islam can be interpreted to provide instruction for most aspects of life. Sharia is formed from two main fields: religious guidance, as well as judicial guidance on far-ranging issues that include marriage, divorce, child custody, and inheritance.*[12]

Point to Ponder
Key Language: "Allah" is not the Muslim God

Allah is the Arabic word for "God." Because the Prophet Mohammad spoke in Arabic, and the Quran *was sent to him in Arabic, "Allah" has become incorrectly interpreted by non-Arabic speakers as connoting the "Muslim God." However, it is important to note that all Arabic-speakers use the word to refer to God, regardless of whether they are Muslim, Christian, Jewish, atheist, or otherwise. In Aramaic, the original language of the Bible, the term for "God" is "Allaha," which is only one letter away from the Arabic "Allah."*

those who follow the Jewish scriptures, and the Christians who believe in God and the Last Day, and work righteousness, shall have their reward with their Lord; on them shall be no fear, nor shall they grieve."[18]

Other misguided people look for absurd examples to invoke a fear of Islam. The religious holiday of *Eid*, a term that literally means "celebration" in Arabic, has been written in reverse to spell "die." A small number of individuals actually believe that transliterating an Arabic word and rearranging the letters demonstrates how Islam is embedded with violence. Such absurdities are baseless and counterproductive to the greater good.

We are beginning to hear the newly-coined terms *"Islamists"* and *"Islamofascists,"* to mean "violent extremists." These terms, while widespread, are misleading. Many people find it troublesome that a word derived from "Islam" is applied to organizations they consider radical and extreme. However, the terms "Islamist" and "Islamism" are used in publications within Muslim countries to describe domestic and transnational organizations seeking to implement Islamic law. The English website of Al Jazeera, for example, uses these terms frequently. Similarly, *"jihadi"* is a poor choice to refer to a violent extremist, because *jihad* (struggle) is justified by faith. Instead, use the term "violent extremist" when discussing such a person. By using religious sounding language, one further arms the extremists and helps justify their causes as religiously motivated and supported. In reality, they are not and can be disarmed of such influence by taking away the religious sounding terms.

Women in Islam

Another area of Islam that is regularly misinterpreted and incorrectly practiced concerns the relationship between the sexes. Islam preaches equality between women and men. Arabic, the original language of the *Quran*, is not gender-neutral, meaning that many words have both a masculine and feminine form. As such, the *Quran* makes itself clear. For example, when discussing the believers, a verse would mention both believing men and believing women, faithful men and faithful women, pious men and pious women.

Nowhere in the *Quran* does a verse indicate that one gender is superior to the other. The *Quran* asserts, for example, that women and men were created from a single soul. "O mankind! Be careful of your duty to your Lord who created you from a single soul

FYI – Sunni and Shia Islam

In recent years, the public has started to hear more about Sunni and Shia Islam. People hear buzzwords and news highlights and sometimes get confused. Put simply, Sunni and Shia are two denominations in Islam, similar to Catholic and Protestant in Christianity. There are distinctions and differences in interpretations, traditions, and beliefs, but they are still under the same umbrella of Islam.

All Sunnis do not hate all Shias, and all Shias do not hate all Sunnis. Similar to how all Catholics don't hate all Protestants and vice versa. Even during the conflict in Northern Ireland, the rest of the world knew better than to expand the perception of hostility to Christendom at large. The same reasoning applies with Sunni and Shia and what takes place in Iraq.

Simply put, the split in the faith took place after the death of the Prophet and revolved around who was best suited to succeed the Prophet and lead the people. One group that later came to be known as Sunni, wanted to nominate the leader, or Caliph, *based on who they believed to be best suited. The other group, later known as Shia, believed it was the wish of the Prophet to continue the succession through the bloodline. Both groups have evidence to support their claims.*

Sunnis make up an estimated 90% of the Muslim population and are found all over the world. Shias make up an estimated 10% and are located heaviest in Azerbaijan, Bahrain, Iran, Iraq, Yemen, and parts of Afghanistan, Lebanon, Syria, and Turkey, but can also be found globally. Sunni is derived from the religious term sunna *which speaks to the teachings of the Prophet. Shia is derived from* Shiat Ali *translated to mean those who are on the side of Ali. Ali was the Prophet's son-in-law.*

and from it its mate and from them both have spread abroad a multitude of men and women. Be careful of your duty toward God in whom you claim (your rights) of one another, and towards the wombs (that bore you). Lo! God has been a Watcher over you."[19] This is quite different from women being created from the rib of a man or that men were created first, both of which can imply that women are somehow inferior to men.[20]

Islam advocates that men and women have exactly the same responsibilities and duties. The *Quran* teaches that men and women must be paid equally. Passages express, "Men and women have equal rights of earning"[21] and "I shall not lose sight of the labor of any of you who labors in My way, be it man or woman; each of you is equal to the other."[22] It is noteworthy that Mohammad's wife Khadija was a successful businesswoman, the primary breadwinner in the family. Islam also stresses the importance of educating both sexes. Acquiring as much knowledge as possible throughout one's lifetime is considered a virtue. According to the *Hadith*, Mohammad said that seeking knowledge is mandatory for every Muslim, man and woman.

Islam does not condone or suggest the oppression of women in any way. The religion, instead, champions the independence and overall respect of women. Prior to the existence of Islam, Jewish, Christian, and pagan tribes in what is present-day Saudi Arabia captured many women as slaves and sexual objects. Islam liberated slaves of all kinds and made concerted efforts to raise women from their objectified existence. The Prophet Mohammad was anxious to emancipate women. They were among his

Point to Ponder
Buzzword: Jihad

Jihad is commonly thought of as Muslim holy war against non-Muslims. Although popularized by violent extremists and the media, this usage is incorrect. The concept of jihad does exist in Islam and means "struggle" in Arabic.

Within the context of Islam, there are two forms of jihad: greater jihad and lesser jihad. Greater jihad is meant to be the daily and personal struggle to be a better person, to resist temptation, to serve God, and to help one's fellow human beings. For example, when one fasts during the holy month of Ramadan, it is considered part of his struggle, his jihad.

Lesser, sometimes called defensive, jihad is meant to be a military stand against enemies of the religion whose goal is to attack the religion and threaten it and its followers with annihilation. A good friend of mine, Hanaa Rifaey, explains it best: If the concept of lesser or defensive jihad existed in Judaism, then Jewish uprisings against the Nazis in World War II would have been a fitting example. In my view, the most recent true example of lesser or defensive jihad occurred in the eleventh century when Salah El-Din (Saladin) fought the Crusaders. Some people have asked if jihad played a role in the Soviet/Afghan war, but I hesitate to label that war as jihad because it had tribal and international dimensions and thus was not a purely defensive religious struggle.

Keep this in mind: When violent extremist groups like Al-Qaeda characterize their acts of violence as jihad, they are misapplying the concept and hijacking the term and the faith. Their actions are not in defense of Islam. It is in no way threatened by annihilation. Violent extremists attack innocent civilians. By initiating such action, they contradict Islam and the foundations of lesser or defensive jihad. If we use their terminology, we are empowering them and incorrectly justifying that they are indeed involved in a religious duty. (To further confuse the situation, "Jihad" is also sometimes used as a gender-neutral first name in Arabic.)

FYI – Hadith and Quran

The Hadith is a collection of the teachings and sayings of the Prophet Mohammad organized and written by a specific group of his companions roughly two hundred years after his death. It is considered to compliment the Quran. The Arabic text of the Quran is believed to be the only word of God. As each text has been translated into a multitude of languages around the world, transliteration of Arabic names and some terms has proved to be challenging. "Quran," "hadith," "Mohammad" are considered now to be the standardized English spellings of each. "Quran" is pronounced core-ann. "Hadith" is pronounced ha-deeth. "Mohammad "is pronounced mo-ham-mad.

first converts.[23] Islam gives women rights of inheritance and divorce, which women in the West did not enjoy until the nineteenth century. Islam preaches modesty of both men and women. In an effort to de-objectify themselves in the period of early Islam, converted women began wearing looser clothing and covering their hair, so as no longer to be judged by their bodies, but only their work and words.

In that early period, wearing the *hijab*, or head covering, for women became a symbol of empowerment, and it is so regarded by many women today. A recently converted woman stated that, because of wearing looser clothing and the *hijab*, "Men treat me as a person, as a professional, not as a sex object."[24] It is important to note that Islam does not require women to cover their hair outside of prayer; this is a personal choice. Women covering their hair predates Islam. Judaism encouraged the practice and even today many Orthodox Jewish women cover at least their shoulders for prayer services. In many Catholic countries today, women cover their hair when attending church.

This section explains the theoretical equality of the sexes in Islam. Unfortunately, as in other aspects of the religion, gender equality is an area in which both political and religious leaders have manipulated Islam so as to make it patriarchal and oppressive to women. In other words, they have made it conform, not to Islam, but to ancient tribal practices. Laws that hinder the independence and equality of women, such as Saudi Arabia's laws forbidding women to drive are very much against the equality that Islam preaches. The fact that women often do not enjoy equal rights in Arab societies has social, rather than religious, roots.

Acclaimed author, professor, and former nun Karen Armstrong adds some pertinent and relevant information about the position of women in religions. She states that whenever a religion was born, the position of women took a turn for the worse.[25]

Professor Armstrong states, "Most of these religions had an egalitarian ethos, but they were and have remained essentially male spiritualities. Confucius, for example, seemed entirely indifferent to women; Socrates was not a family man. In India, the Jain and Buddhist orders were irenic forms of the ancient Aryan military brotherhoods, and though nuns were permitted to join, in a second-class capacity, many felt that the presence of women was inappropriate. Even the Buddha, who did not usually succumb to this type of prejudice, declared that women would fall upon his order like mildew on a field of rice."[26]

Armstrong continues: "This chauvinism infects the spirituality of the faithful, male and female alike. Male Jews are supposed to thank God daily for not creating them women; every Christmas, Christians sing 'Lo! He abhors not the Virgin's womb,' as though Jesus's tolerance of the female body was an act of extraordinary condescension on his part."[27]

Let's look at the issue of polygamy. Polygamy has existed throughout the world for many centuries—in the Far East, in Africa, in the Arab World, and even in the United States where Mormons were polygamous up until about a century ago. (Some fundamentalist Mormons in southern Utah and northern Arizona still practice polygamy.) Polygamy became established in these societies for multiple reasons. As societies modernize, polygamy tends to disappear. In his time and place, Mohammad's restriction against a man's having more than four wives was, in fact, an advance, a protection for women and their children. Moreover, in that time, women who did not have the protection of a man and his household were lost in the societies where they lived. As Arab countries modernize, polygamy is disappearing. Very few modern Muslim men can own a house and a car, pay for their children's education, and offer equivalent accommodation to multiple wives.

Let's examine polygamy in Islam. Can a Muslim male marry up to four women? Yes, this is technically allowed. However, it is not often practiced today. Polygamy in

Islam originated in the early days of the religion's existence during a time of war and ongoing battles between local and regional tribes. Because many men died in battle, the female to male ratio was much higher than usual. Consequently, the surviving men were expected to protect and care for the women. In order for the widows to live in the same household with men to whom they were not related, they had to be married. Mohammad also entered into multiple marriages to unite the tribes.

The *Quran* explains, "If you deem it best for the orphans, you may marry their mothers—you may marry two, three, or four. If you fear lest you become unfair, then you shall be content with only one, or with what you already have. Additionally, you are thus more likely to avoid financial hardship."[28] In a sense, polygamy in Islam was meant to be a form of welfare, not to provide men pleasure. *Harems*, where a ruler or a rich man has many wives, is an aberration under Islam.

Today, polygamy exists only in rare situations. When it does occur, it is usually through a selfish interpretation of the religion by men. In the Arab World, it is considered backward for a man to take multiple wives, and is very much looked down upon. Men sometimes take additional wives thinking that it legitimizes what is essentially taking a mistress.

Questions sometimes arise about the treatment of women in mosques. For instance, why do women and men sometimes enter through different doors? Why do they not pray among one another? Sometimes women are seated behind the men. Does that symbolize women as lesser than men because they are in the rear? Firstly, women are not always behind men in mosques. Depending on the design of the mosque, women are sometimes situated on the second floor, above the men, physically elevated, refuting the notion that they are subordinate. Moreover, in the mosque, a house of God, Muslims are meant to worship; nothing else. How many reading this handbook have been in a church or house of worship and, instead of listening to the minister or priest, were checking out someone in the congregation? Everyone who visits a mosque to worship is meant to do so without distraction.

Global Muslim Population

Islam is the world's second most practiced religion after Christianity. The Muslim world numbers roughly 1.4 billion people, although worldwide estimates have ranged from 1.0 to 1.6 billion. Most Muslims live not in the Arab World, but in South Asia and the Indian subcontinent. More Muslims live in South Asia than in the entire Arab World. South Asia includes India, Pakistan, Afghanistan, Nepal, Bhutan, Bangladesh, Sri Lanka, and Singapore. While none of these countries is Arab, each is either majority Muslim or has high numbers of Muslims within its population.

As with the "Christian World," it is difficult to describe the "Muslim World" geographically because Muslims live in every part of the world, on every continent. Islam has spread across the world. The highest concentrations of Muslims are in Africa and Asia.

We can confirm that none of these South Asian countries is Arab by simply applying

the three factor test: (1) cultural/historical link; (2) dominant religion of Islam, although not the only one practiced; (3) dominant language is Arabic with many dialects, although not the only one spoken. Let us use Pakistan as an example. Because of the Silk Road and the constant commerce it carried between the Arab World and

FYI – Muslims in Latin America

Islam is among the fastest growing religions in Latin America. Estimates of Muslims there reach about five million, many of them recent converts. Others are descendents of Muslims who came to the region many decades ago. as slaves from Africa. While the people integrated into Latin American life, many retained their religion.

South Asia, there are aspects of culture and history that overlap between it and the Arab World. However, those aspects do not constitute a strong cultural or historical link. Pakistan's dominant religion is Islam; in fact, it is one of the top ten most populous Muslim countries. Therefore, the second factor is met. Finally, the third factor, often the most determinative, is language. The Pakistani national language is English, which is used in the Constitution, corporate business dealings, and universities. The official language is Urdu, although it is only spoken by roughly 8% of the population.[29] Most Pakistanis actually speak Punjabi.[30] Pakistan hosts a number of other languages and dialects as well, as do many parts of South Asia. Arabic, however, is not spoken at all. Although many Muslims who are Pakistani may be able to read Arabic because they

learned it to read the *Quran*, an ability to read Arabic does not equate with an ability to speak or fully grasp the language.

The United States is home to roughly seven to eight million Muslims, few of them Arab. The two largest groups of American-Muslims are African-Americans and South Asians. Best estimates are that 33% of mosque-attending American-Muslims are of South Asian descent and another 30% are African-American.[31] Islam continues to be one of the fastest growing religions in the world, including in the United States. That is due both to high birthrates among Muslims as well as conversion to the religion.

In short, Arabs and Muslims are two separate heterogeneous groups that overlap, but are not one and the same. Muslims are followers of the monotheistic religion of Islam that has many similarities to Judaism and Christianity. Arabs are a multiracial and diverse people who are rooted in the Arab World, which spans North Africa and Southwest Asia. Arabs practice a variety of faiths, including Islam, Christianity, and Judaism.

Question Three
What is the world's most populous Muslim country?

ANSWERS TO THIS QUESTION OFTEN REFLECT what Muslim countries are being discussed in the media: Iraq, Saudi Arabia, or Afghanistan. Sometimes the answer is "Africa." Africa, of course, is not a country, but a continent of fifty-three independent nations. Israel is, surprisingly, another common answer, though it is predominantly Jewish, not Muslim.

The correct answer is Indonesia, a nation of islands located in South East Asia, between Australia and Malaysia. With roughly 240 million people, Indonesia is the world's most populous Muslim country. Ninety percent of Indonesia's population is Muslim.[32] Ethnically, Indonesians are not Arabs, but overwhelmingly native people of these islands, including Javanese, Madurese, and Sundanese (not Sudanese, who are predominantly Arab).[33] Muslim merchants and traders brought Islam from the Arab World and introduced certain cultural influences to Indonesia.

The top nine most populous Muslim countries are: Indonesia, Pakistan, Bangladesh, India, Turkey, Iran, Egypt, Nigeria, and China. Of these, only Egypt is an Arab country.[34] Algeria, Morocco, and Sudan come next on this list.[35] As you can see, only four out of the top twelve most populous Muslim countries are also Arab.

FYI – China

Islam in China dates to as early as 650 AD, less than twenty years after the death of the Prophet Mohammad. An envoy, sent by Uthman, the third caliph, and led by the prophet's uncle, Sa`ad ibn Abi Waqqas, was received by Yung Wei, the Tang emperor who ordered the construction of the Memorial mosque in Canton, China's first mosque. During the Tang Dynasty, China had its golden day of cosmopolitan culture. This facilitated the introduction of Islam. The first major Muslim settlements in China were composed of Arab and Persian merchants. Today, it is estimated that 1% to 2% of the population of China is Muslim.

Chapter Two

What an Arab Looks Like

Stereotypes Here and Abroad

THIS SECOND CHAPTER OF THE HANDBOOK looks briefly at both conscious and unconscious bias.

Topics to be discussed:
- Stereotypes about Arabs and Muslims.
- What does an Arab *look* like?
- Why do *they* hate *us*?
- Arab culture, advances, and inventions.

Points to Remember:
- Arabs are a very diverse people and span the spectrum in appearance.
- Arabs are responsible for a significant number of historical advances and have made serious contributions to global society.
- It is important to remember that, due to the transliteration of Arabic names, the same word in Arabic may be spelled a variety of different ways in English.
- Sikhs are neither Arab nor Muslim. Instead, they are followers of the fifth largest religion in the world, Sikhism.

As with all stereotypes, though some seeds of truth may make up a small part of the overall picture, they are generally inaccurate.

Question Four
What comes to mind when you hear the term *Arab?*

THIS IS MY FAVORITE QUESTION. It is so simple, yet so insightful. Take a minute and think about your answers. What is the first thing that comes to mind when you hear the term *Arab?*

What does an Arab look like?
When I ask this question in classes, often people who have no idea will start describing me. I am just under 5'8", with olive-toned skin, dark hair, and a thin beard (think Russell Crowe in the movie *Gladiator,* only shorter, darker, and not as suave). For example, people would respond, "Arabs are short." Well, no, that *I* am short does not mean that all Arabs are short.

So what *does* an Arab look like? The typical reaction tends to be dark, brown, or olive-skinned, with dark hair, dark features, and men with thick facial hair. You say "Arab" and people have a certain image that pops into their heads. Similarly, and just as incorrect, you say "Latino" and one thinks of a certain image. Arabs cut across the racial spectrum because they are a multiracial, heterogeneous group. There are Arabs of every combination of skin tone, eye color, hair color and texture, and size and shape. While olive tones and dark hair and eyes tend to be the most common physical attributes found among Arabs, you will also find redheads, blondes, blue eyes, green eyes, white skin, black skin, and everything in between.

If a man is wearing a turban, it rarely means he is Arab. In the United States, more often, this is a sign that he is a Sikh. Sikhism (pronounced Sik-ism), the world's fifth largest religion, was founded by Guru Nanak more than five hundred years ago in the Punjab region of present-day Pakistan and northern India. Sikhs number approximately twenty-four million people worldwide and roughly one million in North America.[36]

This reminds me of a good story about stereotypes. I once had a police officer genuinely and in all seriousness ask me, "Where's your turban?" I paused, looked at her with a big smile, and asked her back, "Where's your cowboy hat?" Immediately, she started laughing and the absurdity of her question was suddenly clear to her.

Nicknames and Transliteration of Names

Nicknames for Arabs are an interesting area of the culture. Here in the United States we shorten names (for example, Mike as short for Michael or Jen as short for Jennifer). Arabs will often be nicknamed "father of..." (*Abu*) or "mother of..." (*Imm* or *Um*). This nickname is given once a person has his or her first child. In my family, you might call my father *Abu Kareem*, as my older brother was the firstborn in our family. If a person does not have children, he or she may still have a similar, friendly nickname. For example, my nickname growing up was *Abu Nour*, meaning "Father of Light." This was because my name, Nawar, which means "bright one," is derived from *Nour*, the Arabic word for light. Arab names also use "*ibn*," "*bin*," and "*bint*," meaning "son of" and "daughter of," respectively. This is similar to many English surnames: Richardson is derived from Son of Richard. In Arabic, it would be *Bin* Richard.

Mohammad is the most popular name in the world. As a sign of respect to the Prophet, as well as a blessing for that child, many Muslims give their son the first or middle name of Mohammad. It is not uncommon for parents to name one son (or even each of their sons) Mohammad. However, none of the sons would actually go by that name but rather by the second name. As with most Arabic names, Mohammad can be spelled a variety of ways in English, Mohammed, Mohamed, Muhamed, Mahamed. Variations of Mohammad are also extremely popular; these include Ahmed, Mahmoud, Mehmet, and Hamid. Similarly, many women in the Western world have the names Mary or Maria, and variations include Mary Pat, Mary Jane, Marybeth, Maria Martha, Rosa Maria, and so forth.

Muslim names often refer to "worshiper" as in "Worshiper of God"—Abed Allah. Since there are ninety-nine callings of God in Islam, any one can be part of a name. For example, Abed Al-Latif means "Worshiper of The Pleasant One"; Abed Al-Azziz means "Worshiper of The Mighty One." Frequently, these extravagant names are shortened to simply Abed (worshiper) or a combination of the names such as Abed Allah (worshiper of God) becoming Abdallah.

Many Arab last names start with *Al* or *El*, meaning "the." This can be rendered several ways in English. Members of the El Rifaey family, for instance, might use Elrifacy, El'Rifaey, El-Rifaey, or even simply Rifaey. For the sake of simplicity, Arabs frequently drop the *Al* or *El* when immigrating to the United States. However, when they say their names aloud, the *Al* or *El* is still present. Arabic names often have meaning. The same way Native American names have distinct meaning, so do Arabic names. For example, "Fadi Al Tayeb" means "The saviour and good one."

In regard to question four (What is the first thing that comes to mind when you hear the term "Arab"?), people answer in three distinct ways: extreme negatives, broad neutrals, and extreme positives. In the following section, I will elaborate on each of these categories. As the overwhelming majority of answers I receive are broad neutrals, let's begin here.

Arabs: **Broad Neutral Answers**

Often these neutral answers are clearly derived from varied media portrayals. For example: "sand," "rich," "turban," "Bedouin," "oil," "sheik," "harem," "taxi driver," "7-Eleven," "Slurpee," "Middle East," "fez," "gas station attendant," "Islam," "Saudi Arabia," "camels," and "Aladdin."

"Sand," "rich," "oil," and "Bedouin" are all stereotypes about Arabs. Some people imagine the Arab World as a giant desert, with cities and villages scattered randomly throughout. Though a conventional image of many people, this is, of course, a very incomplete picture of the region. There are vast deserts in the Arab World, and in parts of those deserts Bedouins and nomads live. However, supposing that this predominates would be like saying that the United States is made up of country towns run by cowboys.

The topography and climate of the Arab World are as diverse as its people. There are beaches, dense forests, mountains that are snowcapped year-round, large metropolises, and every imaginable climate. Moreover, not every Arab country possesses oil. There are potentially more oil reserves in Alaska than in Saudi Arabia. The stereotype of the oil-rich Arab leads to assumptions of the financially rich Arab. There are rich Arabs just as there are rich Americans and other rich people all over the world. The notion that all Arabs are rich is no more accurate than supposing that all African-Americans are athletic, that all Asians are smart, and that all Caucasians are successful.

FYI – Bedouins

The word "Bedouin" is derived from the Arabic word badawi, *a generic name for a desert dweller. "Bedouin" is a term generally applied to Arab nomadic groups, who are found throughout most of the desert belt extending from the Atlantic coast of the Sahara via the Western Desert, Sinai, and Negev to the eastern coast of the Arabian desert. The term is occasionally used to refer to non-Arab groups as well, notably the Beja of the African coast of the Red Sea.*

Bedouins were traditionally divided into related tribes, each led by a sheikh. Traditionally, they herded camels, sheep, and goats while riding on highly prized horses, moving according to the seasons for grazing lands. For centuries up to the early twentieth century, Bedouins were known for their fierce resistance to outside government and influence. Some notable Bedouin groups in Africa include the Baggara of Sudan and Chad, the Chaamba of Algeria, and the Beni Hassan of Mauritania.[37]

These positive stereotypes may contain a kernel of truth but are untrue when applied without distinction to the entire group.

As regards the first thing that comes to mind being Islam, remember that people often confuse Muslims and Arabs and make the mistake of equating the two. While there is overlap between Muslims and Arabs, they are nonetheless distinct. Furthermore, while most Arabs are Muslim, only about 20% of Muslims are Arab.

"Sheik" and "harem," other responses, are aspects of the seductive allure of Arab culture. They come out of popular stories such as *1001 Arabian Nights, Aladdin and the Magic Lamp,* flying carpets, and the legend of *Scheherazade.* Moreover, there is the image of the dominant patriarchal figure with a harem of willing, scantly clad (yet veiled) women at his beck and call. Such sheiks and harems do not actually exist.

"Taxi driver," "gas station attendant," the convenience store 7-Eleven and its popular Slurpee beverage are other neutral responses based on respondents' personal experiences, or from pop culture depictions of Arabs in the United States. Are there Arab taxi drivers, gas station attendants, and 7-Eleven employees? Absolutely! Do most Arabs living in the United States fit into one of those three categories? Absolutely not! Arab-Americans tend to be a highly educated group contributing to a very diverse workforce. Of Arab-Americans, 84% have achieved at least a high school diploma, more than 40% have a bachelor's degree or higher (compared to only 24% of the general public), and 15% have a post-graduate degree, nearly twice the national average of 9%. Of the school-age population, 13% are in pre-school, 58% in kindergarten through twelfth grade, 22% in college, and 7% pursuing graduate studies.[38]

Arab-Americans work as taxi drivers, grocers, doctors, lawyers, comedians, actors, firefighters, police officers, FBI agents, soldiers, chefs, bus drivers, researchers, business people, teachers, engineers, and as many other professionals representing every walk of life in American society. While 5% of Arab-American adults are unemployed, about 73% of them are in the labor force, about three quarters employed in managerial, professional, technical, sales, or administrative fields. Nearly half as many work in service jobs (12%) compared to Americans overall (27%). Most Arab-Americans work in the private sector (88%); 12% are government employees.[39]

"Saudi Arabia" and "Middle East" are common responses because some people assume that Saudi Arabia represents the whole of the Arab World. But Saudi Arabia is merely one of its twenty-two diverse Arab countries. Each country is different. Few Arabs in the region share similarities to those living specifically in Saudi Arabia. While "Middle East" is a common response, that colonial term, used regularly but incorrectly as synonymous to the Arab World, represents the nations in Southwest Asia, many of them Arab. However, the Arab World stretches across North Africa.

"Camels" is another common response. Horses are rarely mentioned, although Arabian horses are known to be some of the purest and fastest in the world. Famous for needing little water and thus well-adapted to desert regions, camels do exist in the Arab World. They have played a vital role in the history and the shaping of the region. But so have horses.

Some respondents mention the fez, a headdress, usually red in color, that actually comes from ancient Turkey. It was popularized in parts of the Arab World in the nineteenth century as a status symbol of gentlemen of the Ottoman Empire. Today, one might see an older man wearing a fez, but it is a rarity outside of the tourist industry, where bellhops and porters wear traditional clothing for show.

Arabs: Extreme Negative Answers

The second most common category of answers are the extreme negative ones. Sometimes experience serves as a basis for judgment. Other times, unfortunately, these negatives are simply hateful epithets used to hurt or attack one's background. Examples of the extreme negatives include: "terrorist," "sand nigger," "camel jockey," "rag head," "diaper head," "suicide bomber," and "America-hater."

Epithets

"Sand nigger," "camel jockey," "rag head," and "diaper head" are all commonly heard, hateful racial epithets directed at Arabs or those perceived to be Arab. These degrading terms are based on ignorance and hatred. "Sand nigger" is an extension of the racial epithet often given to African-Americans, but "sand" is added to make a distinction for Arabs.

"Camel jockey" goes back to the false belief that camels populate the Arab world to the extent that each person owns his or her own camel. While the term does not sound derogatory, it is used in a fashion to humiliate and degrade. Similarly, mispronouncing Arab as "Ay-rab" is considered very offensive. Like the derogatory label "whitey," a variant of "white," "Ay-rab" has been used in an insulting manner and has become a racially charged insult.

"Rag head" and "diaper head" refer to the stereotypical image of Arabs wearing turbans. Some Arabs do wear various kinds of turbans. However, believing that all Arabs wear turbans is as untrue as the stereotype that all Americans wear baseball caps or cowboy hats. These two unfortunate epithets are also used by some to refer to individuals from Southeast Asia.

Next let's explore the stereotype that all Arabs hate America. As an Arab-American and a patriot, I find this stereotype particularly disheartening and discouraging. Remember, most Americans are not "purely" American. The term Arab helps define what kind of American I am. We have Anglo-Americans, African-Americans, Asian-Americans, Latino-Americans, and so forth. America is a nation of immigrants. Except for Native Americans, we—or our ancestors—all came from somewhere else.

Do some Arabs hate the United States? Yes, absolutely. Do most Arabs or even a large percentage of them hate us? Absolutely not. They may resent our foreign policy, but not our country. In fact, they idealize us. US culture dominates global culture today, even for the Arab World. Generally speaking, Arabs love things American. They want to wear our clothes, drink our soft drinks, eat our food (including fast food), drive our cars, listen to our music, watch our movies, and learn English, which has become the international language. However, a small percentage of highly conservative, traditional, perhaps puritan, Muslims regard US pop culture as sharing similarities to pagan cults of the past that worshiped money and sex.[40] This is not unlike some of the growing puritan movements within Western culture.

A survey conducted by the Pew Forum on Religious and Public Life in 2007 shows that most Muslims in America were happy and fit, dare I say, normally within our society.[41] Apart from that, do many Arabs and Muslims resent the US government specifically for its foreign policy? Of course. They resent the war in Iraq. They resent the perception that, in the Arab-Israeli conflict, the United States portrays itself as both an honest broker of peace and a "special friend" to Israel. They resent the perception—whether true or not—that we are global bullies. Generally, Arabs make a clear distinction between the American people and the nation, on one hand, and the US government and foreign policy on the other. Despite the fact that we the people elect the government, Arabs distinguish between the policies with which they disagree and Americans as individuals.

Ask any US citizen who has traveled to the Arab World as a civilian how they were treated and whether they felt any overt hatred. I'll bet their experience was positive, non-confrontational, and, in fact, friendly and hospitable. Generally, Arab culture tends to be one heavily based on generosity, hospitality, and respect.

Terrorism

"Terrorist" is the most common extreme negative answer. It is also the most challenging to address because peoples' emotions are linked to the word. "Terrorist," one who terrorizes, bombs innocent people, and kills women and children, is a scary word, used so much that we have become desensitized to its meaning. This term is clearly associated with horrible things in recent history: the attacks on the World Trade Center and the Pentagon on September 11, 2001; the 1993 World Trade Center bombing; the USS Cole Bombing; and the attacks on US embassies in Kenya and Tanzania in 1998. All were terrible acts carried out by Arabs who proclaimed themselves Muslims.

The fact that individual Arabs were responsible for these acts of terrorism does not mean that all Arabs are responsible for them, nor that all Arabs condone them. Terrorists are not only Arab or Muslims; they come in every imaginable shape and creed: pure-bred American ultra-conservatives who perpetrated the 1995 Oklahoma City bombing; Catholics of the Irish Republican Army; white supremacists who lynched blacks in the American South; African guerrillas combating apartheid in South Africa and White Afrikaner Dutch Reformed extremists trying to maintain it; the Janjaweed in Darfur. The acts of a few individuals of any group do not represent the group as a whole. There are bad Arabs, just as there are bad individuals in every ethnic or religious group. It is not only unfair to stigmatize all Arabs and Muslims. More importantly it is also an inefficient and unproductive form of law enforcement. Terrorism is not and has never been exclusive to Arabs and Muslims.

In the past decade, with all the terrorism that has taken place, the one largest group of victims of terror has been Muslims. When a bombing takes place in Pakistan, our media will often mention the innocent Westerners killed and forget about the local population. They are innocent victims too. Terrorism is a global dilemma that supersedes any one group, any one religion, any one people.

A Bit of History

Traditional terrorism is associated with nineteenth-century, bomb-throwing revolutionaries and ethno-nationalists operating within the declining Russian, Ottoman, and Hapsburg empires. Prior to these came a series of historical acts that, in today's standard, would qualify as terrorism, ranging from Guy Fawkes, who failed in his attempt to kill King James I of England in 1605 and instate a Catholic monarch, to *La Terreur* in 1794, where radicalized rival factions during the French Revolution took out their rage on monarchs, clergy, and the public.

Terrorism intensified and became a global phenomenon, however, in the years following 1945. The Jewish Irgun in Palestine, the EOKA movement in Cyprus, and the FLN in Algeria can all be classified as the first wave of post-war, anti-colonial terrorism. Because these organizations were understood as having led to the foundation of new states by the 1960s, terrorism was seen as an effective instrument to be used by other aggrieved individuals. As many analysts have observed, terrorists use instruments of violence out of weakness. They lack the power to effect change. Some strategists have called this "displacement." That is, states and state-supported NGOs, such as Al-Qaeda, realize that they are incapable of winning or even waging a "regular" or a "conventional" war.[42]

Terrible undertakings are constantly acted out in the name of religion—and not only by Muslims in the name of Islam. In the past few years, a number of horrible attacks took place in the false name of religion. In 2001, the FBI arrested two high-ranking members of the Jewish Defense League for plotting to blow up the largest mosque in Los Angeles, California, the offices of the Muslim Public Affairs Council, and the office of Congressman Darrel Issa, who is of Christian Lebanese descent.[43] In 2002, twenty thousand Hindus attacked and killed some six hundred Muslims in the Gujarat region in India.[44] In 2004, a mob of Buddhists attacked and vandalized six Christian churches in Sri Lanka.[45] There are so-called "bad apples" in every religion or faith, and from every background or ethnicity. It is up to the rest of us to right their wrongs, to educate and reach out to each other.

The other primary extreme negative response is "suicide bomber." Like "terrorist," this term is charged by real-life circumstances. The 9/11 hijackers were suicide bombers, and we are, unfortunately, hearing regular news accounts of suicide bombings in Israel, Palestine, Afghanistan, Pakistan, and Iraq. Violent extremist suicide bombers, whether they are Arab or not, have reinterpreted aspects of Islam to legitimize and even prize such actions. However, suicide is a major taboo in Islam. Karen Armstrong, a theologian and expert on Islam, summed it up best in an interview with *Newsweek* magazine after 9/11:

Newsweek: "We have all heard that suicide bombers believe they will go straight to heaven and enjoy a paradise of milk and honey, with seventy-two beautiful virgins for every martyr. Is there any religious basis for this?"

Armstrong: "It is completely illegitimate. The *Quran* and Islamic law forbid suicide in the strongest terms. You may not wage a war against a country where Muslims are allowed to practice their religion freely. You may not kill children or women in any war. It's a cheapened version of it to imagine these martyrs as thinking that they're buying a first-class ticket to heaven where they'll enjoy all of these virgins.

Martyrdom is something done to you and you must never take anyone else with you. But what annoys me somewhat [is that] none of these questions were asked in 1995 after eight thousand Muslims were killed by Christian Serbs. We knew enough about Christianity that to say Christianity condoned the massacre, was illegitimate. The trouble is that most Western people just don't know enough about Islam to make that correct judgment."[46]

The idea of martyrdom in Islam is the same as in other religions: dying at the hand of enemies for the adherence of your faith. Martyrdom does not include ramming a plane into a building and killing oneself and thousands of others. Moreover, the whole idea of acquiring seventy-two virgins is either completely negated or explained in an equivocal context. The following excerpt explains in detail:

"Another point of contention for many Christian leaders," writes Karen Armstrong, "is Islam's presentation of Heaven as a seductive, sensuous garden of delights, where believers are promised seventy or seventy-two virgins, also called *houris*, and one can drink from rivers of wine. The fact of the matter is that the idea of heaven in the Islamic tradition is still a contentious point that has been debated for hundreds of years. Syro-Aramaic scholars, who are some of the most respected scholars of Islam, approach this issue from a linguistic perspective. Many Aramaic scholars maintain that the word *houri* is derived from the word *hur*, which means clear or pure [or free]. The three or four verses of the *Quran* that detail the idea of houris as fair maidens fail to conform to the passages before and after them, in that these passages describe fruits and beauty and other aesthetic wonders. Linguistic experts, Muslim as well as non-Muslim, believe that these verses are about fruit or intellectual purity.

"Other scholars believe that 'houri' may indeed be translated correctly as 'fair maiden,' but that this representation is allegorical [or figurative], as is every other description of Heaven in the *Quran*. After all, what use would anyone have for low-hanging fruit, palaces, and rivers of wine? And how would it be possible to describe the flavor of chocolate to one who has never tasted it? Heaven, these scholars maintain, is a place where needs are fulfilled and sorrow is no more. The allegories of the houri, the fruit, and opulence are symbolic representations of a world where physical and spiritual needs are finally fulfilled, as opposed to the world in which we live right now."[47]

I hope this helps shed some light about any confusion regarding suicide bombings as well as the constant intrigue over the supposed Islamic promise of seventy-two virgins.

Arabs: Extreme Positive Answers
Now let us switch to the most infrequent group of answers, the extreme positives. These responses put a smile on my face because often the rest of the class is completely unaware of them. Examples of these include: "zero," "algebra," "first alphabet," "the code of law," "numerals," "astronomy," and "civilization."

Let us start with the advances in mathematics. The term "algebra" is derived from the Arabic term *al-jabr*, which means "the reunion of broken parts." It uses variables

FYI – Arab Christians and Jews

Historically, many Jews and Christians were ethnically Arab. They worked together with Arab Muslims and coexisted in the Islamic empire—the equivalent of a global superpower. This is still true today with ethnically Arab Jews and Christians living all over the world. While there are occasional tensions and negative examples, it is still possible to walk down a street in Damascus and find mosques, churches, and synagogues. In a number of historical examples, it is worth noting Jews preferred to live in Muslim societies rather than Christian ones because they were better treated.

and is defined as: "a mathematical system using symbols, esp. letters, to generalize certain arithmetical operations and relationships. (Ex.: x + y = z.)" Arabs also made advances in trigonometry, fractions, and geometry.

Another great historical achievement is the zero. As defined by the *Merriam-Webster Dictionary*, zero is, "The arithmetical symbol 0 or null denoting the absence

Point to Ponder
Nothingness

By around 300 BC, the Babylonians had started to use a basic numeral system and utilized two slanted wedges to mark an empty space. However, this symbol did not have any true function other than as a placeholder. The use of zero as a number was a relatively late addition to mathematics. It is alleged that Indian mathematicians introduced it as early as 628 AD, after which it made its way westward. Then under the Arab Muslim beacon, Andalusia, the zero was introduced to Europe. It is speculated that the origin of a base-10 positional number system used in India is traced to China. Because the Chinese Hua Ma system is also a positional base-10 system, Hua Ma numerals—or numeral system similar to it—may have been the inspiration for the base-10 positional numeral system that evolved in India.

This numeral system had reached the Middle East by 670 AD. Muslim mathematicians working in what is now Iraq were already familiar with the Babylonian numeral system, which used the zero digit between nonzero digits, so the more general system would not have been a difficult step. In the tenth century AD, Arab mathematicians extended the decimal numeral system to include fractions, as recorded in a treatise by Abu'l-Hasan Al-Uqlidisi in 952-953.

of all magnitude or quantity."[48] Without the concept of zero many calculations would be impossible to make. The term zero is derived from the Arabic word *sifr*, from *zefira*, and was carried over from India to the West by the Arabs. As successful merchants, Arabs traveled across the known world, spreading ideas and possessions, and bringing other such effects back with them.

It is unclear exactly what role Arabs played in developing the numeric system. However, today Arabic numerals are the most widely used system in the world. These were probably developed in the Indian subcontinent. However, it was the Arabs who spread this system through their mercantile trade. As a result, these numerals have come to be known as Arabic numerals. This system is used everywhere in the world.

Sometime near 770 AD in Baghdad, (which was a cultural and intellectual hub, where Arab, Greek, Persian, and Indian scholars coordinated their academic efforts), an Indian scholar introduced a predecessor of the current numbering system, the concept of one symbol representing one number, to which the Arab scholars later assigned their own numbers.[49]

Some theorists believe the Arabic numerals were based on trigonometry and angles, with each numeral representing each number, based on how many angles exist in each symbol. For example, number two would have two angles, number seven would have seven angles, and so forth.[50] This concept makes logical sense because, for centuries, the Arab World excelled in discovering and broadening new ideas in mathematics.[51]

Now that we have learned to blame Arabs for not only algebra, but also fractions, it's time to move on to a safer subject: the first alphabet. Although ideas were put on

Point to Ponder
Mathematical Advances

Abu Abdullah Mohammad Ibn Musa al-Khwarizmi (780 – 845 AD) was a mathematical pioneer and author whose work was essential to the development and advancement of mathematics.

He was born in the town of Khwarizm in what is now Uzbekistan. His family moved soon afterward to an area near Baghdad where he accomplished most of his work in the period between 813 and 833. Though his native language was Farsi, al-Khwarizmi published most of his scientific works in Arabic, the scientific language of his time and place. He developed the concept of the algorithm in mathematics, and the word "algorithm" itself comes from an English corruption of his last name. Al-Khwarizmi also made major contributions to the fields of algebra, trigonometry, astronomy, geography, and cartography.

Al-Khwarizmi's systematic and logical approach to solving linear and quadratic equations gave shape to the discipline of algebra, a word that is derived from the name of his 830 book on the subject, Hisab Al-Jabr Wal-Muqabala. *While his major contributions were the result of original research, he also did much to synthesize the existing knowledge in these fields from Greek, Indian, and other sources, stamping them with his unique mark of logic and rigor. He appropriated the place-marker symbol of zero. He is also responsible for the use of Arabic numerals in mathematics that forever changed the way the world thinks about numbers.*

clay tablets for thousands of years in the form of pictographs and cuneiform writings, the first actual alphabet is widely believed to have come from a city-state in present-day Syria called Ugarit. This took place at approximately 1400 BC. An original piece of the clay tablet lies in the National Museum of Damascus, in Syria.

The code of law is another very important accomplishment. We often think correctly of the Roman Emperor Justinian as the father of the civil code, circa 529 AD. However, the father of the codification of law, the basis for written, organized laws of justice in society was the Babylonian King Hammurabi (who ruled an area that comprises present-day Iraq) in roughly 1700 BC. Moreover, the very first written law is attributed to the Mesopotamian king, Urukagina, in the twenty-fourth century BC.

One of the positive results of Arab advances in science is astronomy. During the peak of the Muslim Arab empire from the eighth through the thirteenth centuries, great advances were made in astronomy. Knowledge of the stars was important to these Muslim Arabs to help them track time in order to identify hours for prayer. Additionally, they needed proper navigation skills in order to direct their prayer toward Mecca. This was one of the driving forces behind a number of broad advances

Point to Ponder
Old Arabs?

It is very important to note that the people of many of these ancient cultures, such as Mesopotamia, did not necessarily speak Arabic. However, they were the historic ancestors of today's Arabs. They were all people of the land.

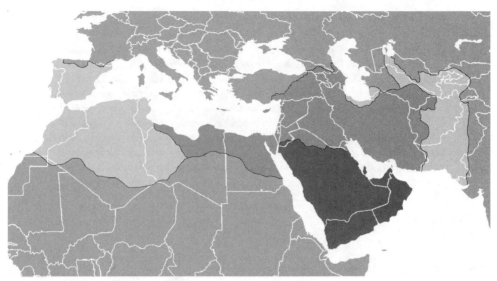

Map of the expansion of Arab/Muslim Empires

FYI – Where is Mesopotamia?

Ancient Mesopotamia rests in present-day Iraq and Syria. It was one of many great empires that have controlled this part of the world over the past six thousand years.

within astronomy, including the compass, the astrolabe, nautical maps, and seaworthy lanterns. The Arab influence on astronomy is evident when looking up at the stars. What are Rigel and Betelgeuse on Orion's Belt? They are transliterations from the Arabic of *rijl* (foot) and *beit el jouz* (house of two). How about Saiph? It means *sword* in Arabic. Many more names derived from Arabic exist in astronomy.

Finally, there is the achievement of the broader concept of civilization—specifically, the Islamic civilization that contributed so much to the world and ushered in the Renaissance. While Europe was experiencing its Dark Ages, the Arab and Muslim Worlds were at the peak of their golden age, which lasted from approximately the seventh century until the fifteenth century. The reach of this golden age spanned from present-day Spain and Portugal all the way to Central Asia. During this period, Arabs translated previously lost Greek and Roman works of science and literature, and expanded their findings. They made a range of advances in global society that still make an impact today.

Some additional advances and contributions from the Arab Muslims include:
• Alcohol (derived from Arabic *al kuhoul*)[52]
• Algorithms[53]
• Backgammon[54]
• Crystallized sugar[55]

FYI – The Umayyad Empire and the Umayyad Mosque

The Umayyads (also known as Umawiy depending on the transliteration of the term from Arabic into English) were an Arab Muslim dynasty responsible for one of the greatest and largest empires in history. At its peak, the empire stretched from the borders of China, throughout North Africa, and into Southern Europe. Their rule was based in Damascus where they built the great Umayyad Mosque, which was replicated throughout their empire. Interestingly, the mosque is situated on land that has always been sacred. Initially built as a pagan temple, it was later dedicated as a Roman temple to the sun god and still later expanded as a church. With the rise of Islam, Muslims worshiped next to their Christian brethren at this church. Once the numbers grew so much, the Caliph asked permission from the Christian community to purchase the land and expand it into a great mosque. In return for the right to purchase, he also built a new church in Damascus.

- Compass[56]
- Coffee[57]
- Cotton[58]
- *El Taleb*, which means "the yearning one" or "the student." It is the Arab equivalent to *The Kama Sutra*. The Arabs had a hedonistic view of sex, viewing it as for pleasure as well as procreation.[59]
- Hookah[60], also known as Hubbly-Bubbly, Argilla, Nargilla, or Chi Cha
- Hydrolics[61]
- Introduction of varied fruits and cultivation to Europe[62]
- Lute (the predecessor of the guitar)[63]
- Medical advances, including eye surgery and anesthesia[64]
- Navigation Maps[65]
- Pendulum[66]
- Syrup[67]
- Universities[68]
- Translation and preservation of Greek and Roman literature[69]

Of course, this is only a summary of some of the advances and inventions that led to a thriving civilization within the Arab and Muslim world. The Arabs also learned and spread advances from other civilizations. They successfully absorbed and honed talent from all over the known world. Arabs took paper from the Chinese and, while learning from the Chinese, seem to have been the first to use gunpowder for propulsion in battle. Similar to the United States' present global dominance, the Arab Muslim world was the dominant global power for roughly eight hundred years. The world spoke Arabic and people came from all over to learn, research, and absorb knowledge in the Arab World. In the way that our modern-day university system hosts students from all over the world, so did universities in Cordoba, Cairo, Damascus, and Baghdad. In numerous cases, non-Arabs or non-Muslims made advances in the intellectual haven of the Arab/Muslim golden age. Jews, Hindus, and Christians lived and studied in peace with their Muslim hosts. Furthermore, Indians, Persians, and Italians lived and studied with their Arab colleagues.

Chapter Three

Racial Profiling

Morality vs Effectiveness

THIS THIRD CHAPTER OF THE HANDBOOK explores the problems that arise when racial profiling is used as a tool for minimizing risk.

Topics to be discussed:
- The concept of profiling based on race
- The Oklahoma City bombing
- The Anthrax Killer
- The DC Sniper

Points to remember:
- Learn through analogy the practical flaws within racial profiling.
- There is no such thing as "suspicious" appearance, only suspicious behavior.
- False perception of knowledge is dangerous. As an example of this, let's examine public reactions to the Oklahoma City bombing of April 19, 1995.

Question Five
Were Arab-Americans responsible for the Oklahoma City bombing?

I N A SURVEY BASED ON THE QUIZ in this book conducted in 1999 among underclassmen on the campus of a large southeastern American university, 25% of those who ranked their knowledge of Arabs, Arab-Americans, and Muslims as seven or higher on the survey based on the quiz thought Arabs were responsible for the Oklahoma City bombing. They were not! In the Oklahoma City bombing, the worst case of terrorism on US soil in American history prior to 9/11, the culprits were two young, white, Christian, former military men: Timothy McVeigh and Terry Nichols. The misperception that Arabs committed this crime may be understandable. Muslim terrorists had attacked the World Trade Center two years earlier. Because of this, many initial news stories speculated that Islamic terrorists had staged the attack. However, the misperception this generated strongly suggests that it is not lack of knowledge that is dangerous. Rather it is the false perception of knowledge that proves dangerous and needs to be rectified.

Suspicious Behavior, Not Suspicious Appearance
What was the upshot of this misperception? Some media and so-called "experts" labeled the attack the work of Arab or Muslim terrorists. In the absence of concrete facts, news reports jumped to conclusions. *USA Today* headlined: "Bomb Consistent With Mideast Terror Tactics."[70] Pundits surmised that the level of horror in the act meant that Middle Easterners must be responsible because such were their traits. As a result, a backlash immediately erupted. Within the first three days, over 222 hate crimes, attacks, and incidents against Arabs and/or Muslims were reported.[71] Suhair Al Mosawi was a twenty-six-year-old Shiite Muslim and refugee from Iraq now living in Oklahoma City. The day of the bombing, a mob is said to have surrounded her home and someone threw a brick through a window. Frightened by the event, Mrs. Al Mosawi, who was seven months pregnant, felt terrible pains in her abdomen, began bleeding uncontrollably, and a few hours later gave birth to a stillborn boy. A news story later reported, "His name will not be listed among the victims of the bombing."[72]
    A similar situation arose after the now famed "Anthrax Killer" terrorized the mail

the following month, in December 2001. The terrorist portrayed himself as a Muslim or Arab by sending messages that included such phrases as "Death to America, Allah is Great." Even so, profile authorities suspect that the responsible individual is a Christian, middle-aged, white male, with a military background. Should men fitting that description be racially profiled in post offices? No, of course not.

Experts stress that behavior, not appearance, is the effective determinant. Rafi Ron, a leading Israeli expert on aviation security, with more than thirty years of experience, was consulted by Logan Airport in Boston, Massachusetts, after September 11, 2001. His task: to improve security. When presented with the idea of profiling Arabs and Muslims, he allegedly scoffed at the thought. In November 2003, Ron and I both spoke at Northwestern University's Center for Public Safety's annual conference on racial profiling. During the question and answer session, a law enforcement officer asked Ron for an unmistakable clarification about this hypothetical situation: if he had a white guy and an Arab guy both acting in the same suspicious manner, should they each be treated in the same way? Should race not be a considered factor? Ron reiterated one of the main points of his speech: race should not matter. Instead,

suspicious behavior should be the focus.

If the emphasis has to be on what is suspicious behavior, not appearance based on one's perception of a person's race, national origin, or religion, what exactly is that suspicious behavior? Unfortunately, it is not that simple to specify. "Suspicious" is far too often a subjective term. What may be suspicious to one person could seem completely benign to another. Is a person reading a book in a different language instantly suspicious? No. Is it suspicious to hear people speaking in a foreign language that is very unfamiliar to your ears? No. Is it suspicious to see someone praying in a way you have never seen before? No. Is it suspicious if someone looks like what we imagine a terrorist to look like? No. What if that person has a dark complexion, olive or brown skin and sports a beard or a turban? No, none of those factors alone is suspicious. This last person could simply be an observant Sikh male.

One needs to look at suspicious behavior as opposed to what one may perceive as a suspicious appearance, religion, or ethnicity. Now try these questions: Is a person wearing a ski mask inside a bank suspicious? How about a guy wearing heavy trousers in Hawaii that might conceal a gun? Maybe you get the idea. While it may be difficult to encapsulate what is suspicious, there is no such thing as a suspicious race or religion, only suspicious behavior.

Another example of failed racial profiling concerns John Allen Muhammed who perpetrated the October 2002 Beltway sniper attacks in the Washington, DC, area. The suspect's racial profile was a white, Christian, former military male. While the authorities succeeded in calling out the gender, the terrorist turned out to be an African-American Muslim. Many DC area news outlets were reluctant to label him a "terrorist," as if a legitimate terrorist had to be a foreigner or linked to a particular religion. But Muhammed terrorized the community. People all over the Washington, DC, metro area stretching for hundreds of square miles were genuinely terrorized and panicked. Drivers would run from their cars into the nearest building. Others would fill gas at stations while kneeling beside their vehicles. Fear consumed many.

In combating terrorism, ultimately people need to keep two goals in mind: First, look to suspicious activity and behavior, not to appearance and ethnicity. Second, law enforcement and the government need to engage the Arab and Muslim communities both inside and outside the United States in order to build relationships and trust. A healthy, open, trusting relationship will benefit everyone. Building and maintaining *trust* is the key underlying principle. Trust is the pathway to the solution: trust from and in the community, trust from and in the government, and trust from and in law enforcement.

Chapter Four

Media

From Aladdin to Saladin

T HIS FOURTH CHAPTER OF THE HANDBOOK probes the power of media to influence our understanding of Arabs and Muslims.

Topics to be discussed:
- The branding of Arabs and Muslims in television shows and movies.
- The media's power over and influence on our beliefs and perceptions.

Points to remember:
- Most media portrayals of Arabs and Muslims are negative.
- These portrayals tend to shape our perceptions and to provide us with incorrect and ultimately detrimental attitudes.

Question Six
Name one or more positive Arab *characters* in television history.

Iɴ ᴅᴇᴀʟɪɴɢ ᴡɪᴛʜ Qᴜᴇsᴛɪᴏɴs Sɪx ᴀɴᴅ Sᴇᴠᴇɴ, we will be taking a close look at how television and movies have portrayed Arab, Muslim, and Arab-American characters in entertainment vehicles. From time immemorial, stories have shaped perceptions of peoples and places, of great heroes and great villains, as well as characters who possess both laudable and regrettable traits. In our time, these stories come to us as movies and television shows and, because they come in a visual form, they have enormous impact on attitudes and perceptions, and deeply influence them. In a sense, they teach us our attitudes. So it is useful to analyze what they are teaching.

While the following discussion has its light-hearted aspects, it's vitally important in terms of suggesting how we come to possess the attitudes we have. While fun and

interesting, these questions are also meaningful, not simply a quiz of your knowledge of Hollywood and television. Pop culture and our media are responsible for much of our education, ideas, and misperceptions about these groups. So it is vital to address them thoroughly.

Arab Characters in Television

Let's address Question Six first: Name one or more positive Arab characters in television history. The names I usually hear include: Hadji, Fez, Apu, Klinger, Danny Thomas, and Jeannie.

Hadji was a character on the 1964 cartoon hit, *The Real Adventures of Johnny Quest*, and first appeared on the show entitled "Calcutta Adventure." He was clearly South Asian, likely Indian, perhaps even a Sikh. He wore a turban, a religious obligation for Sikh males, and his last name was *Singh*. Although, not all people named Singh are Sikhs, all Sikh males have the name Singh somewhere in their names, be it as part of their first, middle, or last name.

A very popular recent character is Fez from the comedy show, *That 70's Show*. F.E.Z. apparently stands for Foreign Exchange Z(s)tudent. According to the actor who plays Fez, Wilmer Valderamma (actually Latino, born in Miami to a Venezuelan father and Columbian mother), the character is meant to symbolize the "foreign kid," with his ethnicity ambiguous. It is not clear whether he is Latino, Middle Eastern, Arab, or South Asian. Ultimately, whether he is an Arab character or not, he is still a positive character.

Apu Nahasapeemapetilon, or simply Apu to most people, is the lovable character on the cartoon *The Simpsons*. Apu, in many ways the token foreigner on the show, often brings in varied issues about being from a different culture or an outsider in our western culture. Apu is neither an Arab nor a Muslim, but Indian. The show clearly identifies him as a follower of India's Hindu faith. Even though he is a walking stereotype, with his Quickie Mart and heavy accent, the character is actually a positive one, helping to add a certain flavor of diversity to the show.

Corporal (later Sergeant) Maxwell Q. Klinger from the 1970s hit sitcom *M*A*S*H**, the famed sitcom about military medics during the Korean War, was of Lebanese descent, as was the actor portraying him, Jamie Farr. While he was a comedian who did not want to be in the war, Klinger was still a positive figure. He was not some raving lunatic with an AK-47 screaming how he was going to kill heathens for his religious beliefs. The show was a comedy and the Arab-American character was a positive one that many viewers related to and admired.

Danny Thomas, a well-known television actor-producer of some years back, was also of Lebanese descent. He was one of the first Arab-American lead characters in *Make Room for Daddy* (also known as *The Danny Thomas Show*), the hit ABC show from 1953 through 1971. Another character on the show was the lovable Uncle Tunoose, who would make references to "the old country." These characters were significant as the first to portray positive Arab-American characters leading normal and fulfilling lives as part of American society.

Incidentally, through his work at the American Lebanese Syrian Associated Charities (ALSAC), Danny Thomas helped start St. Jude Children's Research Hospital, now the world's sixth largest charity hospital.

Although played by a blue-eyed American blonde, Jeannie, the Genie from *I Dream of Jeannie*, the comedy that ran from 1965 through 1970, suggested that Arabs come in all shapes and sizes, with all types of appearances, facial features, and skin tones. Most people did not realize that Jeannie's character was technically Arab, supposedly born in 64 BC in Mesopotamia, which includes present-day Iraq and Syria. The term "genie" is a derivation from the Arabic word *jin-ny*, meaning spirit.

A more recent character is Sayid, one of the survivors on the ABC drama *LOST*. Sayid is an Iraqi, a former member of the Republican Guard under the command of Saddam Hussein. Though early in the series other characters made negative comments based on stereotypes about Arabs and Muslims, such as accusing him of being behind the plane crash, Sayid is an extremely positive character on the show. This strikes a powerful chord with the viewers as it helps to humanize someone they have perceived as the enemy. He is no longer viewed through the lens of his ethnicity or faith.

Had the question been reversed, asking for negative Arab characters in television history, there would be many from which to choose. One of the worst offenders was *JAG* on CBS. Fairly regularly, the antagonist was the ultimate negative stereotype, the "brown," scruffy, dirty Arab trying to harm the innocent, blond, American woman. In a John Wayne-ish manner, the hero of the show always swooped in to save the day.

Following 9/11, it became the fad to do shows about combating terrorism. They capitalized on people's fears (and in many instances added to levels of paranoia). Such shows rarely lasted more than a single season and included *Threat Matrix* on ABC, *The Grid* on TNT, and *The Agency*, *The Unit*, and *Navy: NCIS* on CBS. Each of those shows often had the antagonist as an Arab.

Every so often other shows delve into the large pool of ignorance for story ideas. For example, on NBC's *The West Wing*, which was largely well-written, an early episode involved Syria shooting down an American civilian jetliner, resulting in US President Bartlet and his staff discussing carpet-bombing Damascus. In reality, Syria has never attacked the United States in any capacity. In later seasons, the writers sometimes concocted fake Arab nations to create a potential attack-defense situation.

One 2004 *West Wing* episode focused on the Abu Ghraib scandal in Iraq. Based loosely on real events, its ultimate message was that war between Islam and Christianity is brewing. Consequently "we" must heighten our awareness of Arabs and Muslims. Arab-Americans were seen as equally suspect. The episode went so far as to portray Arab-Americans en masse as assassins roaming freely in our cities. It blurred the line between fact and fiction. Having former New York City Mayor Rudy Guiliani appear as himself sent a confusing message, blurring the line between what aspects were pure entertainment and which were reality replayed. Considering the negative messaging at the time about Arabs and Arab-Americans, the show sent a frightening and dangerous message about a sub-community in society.

However, other shows that are usually neutral, occasionally portray positive aspects of Arabs, Arab-Americans, or Muslims. The ABC comedy *The George Lopez Show*, the first mainstream sitcom to feature a majority Latino cast, addressed a very important issue for the Arab-American community in one episode: employment discrimination. In the episode, George and others at George's small airplane plant deliberated about whether, on one hand, Hosni, an Arab-American employee, ought to be fired because he was Arab or, on the other, should be judged based on his personality and work ethic. Although Hosni lost his job, the episode broke barriers and addressed important issues. For it, the American-Arab Anti-Discrimination Committee awarded George Lopez and his show the 2003 Annual Tolerance Award.

As a summation of this section, it is worth noting just how strong an impact television makes on children, on us, and all who watch it. Our perceptions and behavior are highly influenced and shaped by what we experience through the media. Studies have shown that images in the media—especially television—can change how we think about and relate to other people. While children and adolescents are particularly likely to be influenced, none of us are immune. If we were, no one would pay to run commercials!

Having said that, it should come as no surprise that much of what we know—or believe we know—about Arabs comes from the various forms of media, television shows, both print and electronic news, films, and so on. Oftentimes, this information is skewed, one-sided, or simply focuses on the negative. We know that bad news sells, so we shouldn't be surprised that our information sources often focus on bad news. We rarely hear positive stories about Arabs or Muslims living in the United States or anywhere else in the world in any media. Consequently, it is sadly not surprising that so many people take the most recent story of a horrible bombing in Iraq or violent protest against the US embassy in Pakistan to be reflective of all Arabs or Muslims. These biases are not limited to domestic US media. International media also use the widely accepted "if it bleeds, it leads" news strategy. It is important that we recognize existing media biases in order to better decipher fact from fiction or exaggeration, and to understand that stereotyping entire communities of people based on the publicized actions of a few is incorrect.

Question Seven
Name one or more positive Arab characters in movie history.

ALTHOUGH NOT A MOVIE *character*, many respondents—mostly women—name Omar Sharif, a Lebanese-Egyptian who grew up in Egypt to become a successful actor in the Arab film world before crossing over to Hollywood. There, Sharif played a number of memorable characters including the title role in *Dr. Zhivago*, Nicky Arnstein opposite Barbra Streisand in *Funny Girl*, as well as Sherif Ali ibn el Kharish in *Lawrence of Arabia*. (Curiously, Alec Guinness, an Englishman, and Anthony Quinn, a Mexican-American, also played prominent Arab characters in the latter film.)

Arab Characters in Movie History
The usual responses include: characters from *Aladdin*, *The Siege*, *The Mummy* series, *The Scorpion King*, *Hidalgo*, "the guy with the fez in Indiana Jones," *Robin Hood: Prince of Thieves*, and *Lawrence of Arabia*.

Disney's *Aladdin* is by far the most common response, often given with almost childlike enthusiasm. For that reason it may be worthwhile to examine *Aladdin* in some detail to show how media prejudice works. Released in 1992, *Aladdin* proved to be a blockbuster hit and winner of two Academy Awards. Aladdin was portrayed as the brave peasant hero who rids the empire of the evil Jafar. On the surface, this movie is an innocent children's cartoon with good triumphing over evil. When put under a magnifying glass, however, it turns out to carry a freight of negative stereotypes.

Interestingly, the movie received criticism for its depictions of Arabs. In a *Des Moines Register* editorial, for example, Professor Joanne Brown of Drake University stated that *Aladdin*'s villains displayed "dark-hooded eyes and large hooked noses...perhaps I am sensitive to this business of noses because I am Jewish." She noted how distressed she would be if Disney created a feature-length cartoon, portraying folk-tale Jews as Shylock, the miserly Jewish money-lender in Shakespeare's *Merchant of Venice*.[73]

Aladdin also featured songs that were full of blatant bigotry. For example, the opening song included these lyrics: "Oh, I come from a land, from a faraway place, where the caravan camels roam, where they cut off your ear, if they don't like your face, it's barbaric, but hey, it's home."[74]

As with most cartoons, the character of Aladdin was modeled on a real person: Tom Cruise. Since Arabs come in all colors and shapes, it's possible for an Arab Aladdin to resemble Cruise. However, the protagonists Aladdin and Jasmine were fair-skinned and spoke perfect American English. By contrast, villains and buffoon bystanders had brown complexions, large, droopy eyes, beards, and big, crooked noses. Their English was heavily accented. In addition, throughout *Aladdin*, Arab culture was belittled. Arabic names were mispronounced and Arabic street signs were rendered as meaningless gibberish and squiggles.[75]

Two years later, Disney released a successful direct-to-video item, *The Return of Jafar*, a sequel to *Aladdin*. Following reactions to *Aladdin*, Disney instituted a "policy of prior consultation," promising that films representing minority cultures would be reviewed and critiqued prior to postproduction. However, neither American-Arab Anti-Discrimination Committee nor any other Arab-American organization reviewed the sequel. As before, bigotry and negative stereotypes filled *The Return of Jafar*. This time the public sent numerous letters criticizing Disney.

The pressure had some effect. In 1996, when Disney released the third movie in the series, *Aladdin and the King of Thieves*, producers consulted with experts and the Arab-American community and made positive changes. Aladdin and Jasmine had darker complexions than in the first two films and the accents of the characters were addressed. Moreover, neutral bystander characters were shown as good human beings.[76]

The Siege (1998) starring Denzel Washington, Bruce Willis, Annette Bening, and Tony Shalhoub opens with a terrible bombing in New York City. The imposition of martial law results. Arabs, Arab-Americans, and Muslims are soon rounded up and placed in makeshift camps in sports stadiums. The film vilifies Arab immigrants, US citizens of Arab descent, and Muslims, and throughout it anti-Arab voiceovers are present. At its core it proposes that most, if not all, Arabs, Arab-Americans, and Muslims are terrorists and should be treated with grave suspicion. Before the detonation of a super-bomb, director Edward Zwick shows terrorists going through the Islamic pre-prayer holy cleansing process, creating a direct—but wholly false—link between the Islamic prayer process in Islam and terrorism. Unfortunately, Zwick ignored recommendations from Arab and Muslim experts. Tony Shalhoub's portrayal of an Arab-American FBI agent was the one positive Arab-American character in the movie. However, as Professor Jack Shaheen notes in his book, *Reel Bad Arabs*: "Though Shalhoub's character is a good one, it can never offset all those scenes that show Arab Muslims murdering men, women, and children."

The *Washington Post*'s Sharon Waxman makes a valid point through analogy: a nefarious rabbi exhorts his extremist, ultra-Orthodox followers to plant bombs against Arab sympathizers in America. Innocents are killed and maimed. The FBI starts rounding up Orthodox Jews and putting them in camps. Or how about this: a Catholic priest has molested an altar boy. The church refuses to hand him and other offenders over to police. The FBI starts rounding up clerics in an attempt to ferret them out.

These provocative story lines—unlikely, perhaps, but not entirely implausible—would certainly spark an outcry from Jewish and Catholic interest groups. The question is: Would Hollywood choose to portray them in the first place?[77]

The positive aspect of *The Siege* juxtaposes a general who uses force and coercion, shooting first and asking questions later, against a coolheaded FBI agent who wants to engage Arabs and Muslims. Ultimately levelheaded and inclusive thinking triumphs. The angry general is arrested for crimes against humanity, for torturing and killing a suspect.

In general, *The Mummy* series—*The Mummy* (1999), *The Mummy Returns* (2001), and the prequel, *The Scorpion King* (2002)—is demeaning to Arabs, specifically Egyptians. *The Mummy*, filled with bumbling, dirty, evil Arabs, has been called a "masterpiece of bigotry."[78] The movie faces off slimy and filthy towel-heads against handsome, noble-looking Englishmen and Americans. *The Mummy Returns* was just as bad except for Israeli-born actor Oded Fehr's characterization of Ardeth Bey, an heroic Bedouin.

The Scorpion King, on the other hand, is a bit more positive in its portrayals. The movie depicts the rise of the leader known as the Scorpion King in pre-Pharaonic Egypt, well before the Arab emergence. Still, the film's comic relief, a sidekick character named Arpid, says *shukran* ("thank you," in Arabic) and *la*, which means "no."

FYI – The Real Scorpion King
Although the movie was not meant to be a true story, evidence exists that the king who first united the tribes and ruled ancient Egypt was known as King Scorpion.

Here are some other movies worth noting: The 1962 Oscar winning classic *Lawrence of Arabia*—with Peter O'Toole as the title character, Alec Guinness as Prince Faisal, Anthony Quinn as Auda Abu Tayi, and Omar Sharif as Sherif Ali Ibn El Kharish—may have been plagued with historical misinformation. It suggested that Lawrence "saved" the Arabs during World War I. (Arabs tend to regard Lawrence's crucial contribution as being his ability to supply them arms and equipment.) But the movie's portrayal of Arabs showed them demonstrating honor, valor, courage, and hospitality. Moreover, the Hollywood stars of the day were all playing Arabs. Imagine, if you will, the stars of *Ocean's 11*—George Clooney, Brad Pitt, and Matt Damon—all playing Arab characters in an upcoming movie.

Hidalgo (2004) featured Arab characters ranging from positive to neutral to negative. Omar Sharif played a patriarch sheik who fights in the name of love and honor.

Syriana (2005)—a powerful thriller revolving around the life of a CIA undercover officer, Arab and American politicians, power brokers, and the roots of terrorism—explored high-level politics and corruption between the Arab World and the United States. It offered fair portrayals, with George Clooney in an Oscar-winning role, bad

Arabs and good Arabs, and everyone in between. In my non-law enforcement view, this film does a great job looking into how a terrorist is created and managed.

Robin Hood: Prince of Thieves (1991) features Morgan Freeman playing a Saracen warrior indebted to Robin Hood for saving his life. Wearing appropriate garb, carrying a scimitar (the weapon of choice for Arab warriors at the time), the character displays honor, courage, strength, valor, respect, and humility, and prays as a Muslim. The movie alludes to the superior technology of the Arab World at that time. Robin Hood looks through the telescope and is puzzled by how close the advancing soldiers appear.

FYI – Salah-el-Din (Saladin) 1138 – 1193

Salah-el-Din (literally Righteousness of Faith) was born to a Kurdish family in present-day Tikrit, Iraq. Known as a great military leader, he led the Muslim resistance to the European Crusaders, eventually recapturing Palestine from the Crusader Kingdom of Jerusalem. At the height of his power, he ruled over Egypt, Syria, Iraq, and most of the Arabian Peninsula. Notable beyond his military skills were his chivalry and honor. Whenever he had the upper hand in a battle, he would accept a peaceful and just surrender. He would offer enemies a chance to live among Muslims in peace or pay a tax and earn their freedom. He strove for peace with the Crusaders and had high respect for his opponents. At one point Salah-el-Din sent his personal physicians to aid the English King Richard the Lionheart, when he fell ill. Although Salah-el-Din gained riches from his victories, when his treasury was opened after his death, there was too little money to pay for his funeral. This was because Salah-el-Din had throughout his life given his wealth to the poor and needy. His tomb lies in Damascus and is a major tourist attraction.

The 13th Warrior (1999) told the story of Ahmed Ibn Fahdlan (Antonio Banderas) and is based on the historical records of the real-life Ibn Fahdlan, who kept detailed accounts of his endeavors with Norse warriors. The character, full of honor, courage, and humility, wears the traditional garb of the time, alters the large Viking sword into a scimitar, and prays as a Muslim.

Kingdom of Heaven (2005) by far the best movie of its generation in its portrayals of Arabs, Muslims, and Salah-el-Din (Saladin), showed how the twelfth century Crusades, like most great wars in history, may have had religion as the justification, but ultimately were about power and land. Loosely based on the life of Balian of Ibelin (Orlando Bloom), the movie also focused on the internal struggles for peace or war within the hearts of the Christian Europeans, and the valor and honor of their noble enemy, Salah-el-Din (Ghassan Massoud), who ruled out of Damascus and is buried there. The movie portrayed the Arabs and Muslims of the time as the more advanced, humble leaders who are better organized than their European counterparts.

Traitor (2008) is another movie that took great steps forward in its portrayals of

Islam. Writer/director Jeffrey Nachmanoff aimed for accuracy and reality with this complicated tale about terrorism. Samir Horn, spectacularly played by Don Cheadle, is a former US Special Forces soldier caught in a complex web of good and evil and driven by his faith in God. Horn is an Arab-American and devout Muslim (born in Sudan to a Sudanese father and African-American mother). The movie, unlike anything before it, takes an honest look at terrorism and Islam without vilifying the faith. I was fortunate enough to consult with Nachmanoff and two producers, Anjalika Mathur Nigam and Jeff Silver on the project and am pleased with the overall storyline and its execution.

In *Reel Bad Arabs*, which was the primary resource for this chapter of the *Handbook*, Jack Shaheen reviewed more than nine hundred films. He created a "Best List." How many films do you think he assigned to that list? Only twelve. Shaheen considers that offerings on the television front are not much better.

Shaheen ends with a poignant suggestion, "Writers and producers ought to show us as true Americans: devout fathers and mothers, military veterans, teens catching flyballs, and families walking on the beach. Show us as we are."[79] As was demonstrated, had Question Seven asked for any *negative* characters, we could have easily found such examples. I flippantly mention qualifiers such as a number of Chuck Norris movies, from *Invasion USA* to *The President's Man* and *The President's Man 2: Line in the Sand* (formerly *The President's Man 2: Holy War*) to *Delta Force, Operation Delta Force 2*, and *Delta Force 3*. Although Norris did not appear in *Operation Delta Force 2* and *Delta Force 3*, he did do *Delta Force 2*, where the bad guys were Columbian drug lords. But not to worry, *Operation Delta Force 2* and *Delta Force 3* still had the villainous Arabs. Chuck Norris just happened not to star in them. Arnold Schwarzenegger's movie *True Lies* was horrible in its portrayals and messaging—the villain again being the negative stereotypical Arab with curly black hair, big nose, and scruffy dirty beard. *Rules of Engagement* not only vilifies and attacks an entire existing Arab country (Yemen), but also denigrates a cross-section of that society, as we see women, children, and the like all ultimately guilty of unbelievable violence and terror.

This exercise demonstrates that all groups, all faiths, all ethnicities tend to be stereotyped by television programs and movies. For most groups, however, there are positive portrayals. But when it comes to Arabs and Muslims, it is very hard to find the positive side of the coin. That's why it's important to recognize that our popular culture not only dominates globally, but also makes an impact on each and every one of us, shaping our beliefs and perceptions.

Chapter Five

Arabs & Arab-Americans

Not as close as one would think.

THIS FOURTH CHAPTER OF THE HANDBOOK EXPLORES the history of majority - minority interaction and looks at the distinction between Arab-Americans and Arabs beyond US borders.

Topics to be discussed:
- Labeling others and historical maltreatment of minorities
- Arabs vs. Arab-Americans
- Negative stereotypes in our society

Points to remember:
- Profiling based on one's race is ineffective and counterproductive.
- The dangers of self-perceived knowledge.
- All Americans—hyphenated or not—are Americans.
- Arabs and Arab-Americans are not the first, nor will they be the last, groups to be targeted within our society.

Question Eight
Were Arab-Americans responsible for the 9/11 attacks on our country?

EVEN TODAY, YEARS AFTER THE September 11, 2001, attacks, people still answer this question as true. It is false.

Arabs or Arab-Americans?
This book has already addressed the differences between Arabs and Muslims, now it's time to distinguish between Arabs and Arab-Americans.

Arab-American is a hyphenated term. The word "Arab" defines what type of Americans they are. If assimilation were total, we would not still be using hyphenated terms in our society. But we have not reached that point. We still define each other—and ourselves.

None of the 9/11 terrorists were Arab-American. All were Arab visitors to the United States. Not immigrants, who were trying to become US citizens. They did not have green cards. They were here on student visas, visitor visas, or employment visas.

Did US citizens provide material support for the 9/11 terrorists in the form of hosting, logistical support, and so forth? The investigation never clearly stated whether these men acted alone or with support from others. If they did in fact get support from others, we still do not know if that support came from Arab-Americans.

An important point of clarification may be useful. Generally speaking, and as discussed earlier, hospitality is common and traditional within Arab culture. Some or all of the 9/11 terrorists may have requested aid when they first arrived in the United States. They may have asked to stay a few nights at the home of relatives (close or distant) or of friends (or friends of friends). They may have sought assistance with basic needs. If this happened, unaware of the terrorists' plans, Arab-Americans would have willingly helped anyone to whom they had a connection. Unfortunately, if this did in fact take place, the terrorists took advantage of a cultural characteristic they knew they could manipulate.

Question Nine
Do you believe a negative stereotype about Arab-Americans exists in the United States?

D O NEGATIVE STEREOTYPES ABOUT Arab-Americans exist in the United States? Absolutely. Do negative stereotypes also exist against Arabs? Yes. What about Muslims? Also yes. Are Arab-Americans, Arabs, and Muslims the only groups facing problems due to negative stereotypes? Of course not.

Do *You* Face a Stereotype?
Are Arabs, Arab-Americans, and Muslims the first groups to face negative stereotypes in our society? No! Will they be the last such groups? Unfortunately no.

Since the time of the early settlers, America has been plagued by a deep strain of nativism, which *Webster's New English Dictionary* defines as "the practice or policy of favoring native-born citizens as against immigrants." This has led to discrimination, first against what are now termed Native Americans, then against African-Americans, Irish, Italians, Jews, Chinese, and Japanese. The most recent groups targeted for discrimination are Mexican and Latino immigrants, as well as Arabs, Muslims, and Arab-Americans following the 9/11 attacks.

Moreover, since its emergence as a pre-eminent world power after World War I, America has also exhibited a seeming need always to envision an enemy lurking just over the horizon. After German Nazism came Soviet communism. Once the Soviet empire collapsed, a "new world order" was hailed, only to be erased by fears of Japanese economic might, the rise of modern China, Latino immigration, and then what some of the American chattering classes have decided to term "Islamo-fascism," which as mentioned previously, is an inaccurate, improper term to refer to a violent extremist movement to which some Muslims subscribe.

Let's briefly examine this pattern of discrimination. Native Americans were seen as obstacles to the fulfillment of "Manifest Destiny," a nineteenth century notion that American settlers should expand across the continent. Native Americans were commonly regarded as savages back then, fit to have their land expropriated and be herded into reservations, their way of life destroyed. White-skinned Christian immigrant groups—Irish, Italians, and the Swedish (in the upper Midwest)—faced discrimination because of their differentness. Majority Protestants felt strong prejudice against Catholics. American anti-Semitism dates back to the colonial era. Jews faced exclusion from businesses, universities, and social clubs until well after World War II. Alarmed by the bugaboo of a "Yellow Peril," Congress enacted the Chinese Exclusion Act in 1882, initially only as a ten-year ban. Extended indefinitely in 1902, it was repealed only in 1943 when China was needed as an ally against Japan in World War II. Following the Pearl Harbor attack, 120,000 Japanese and Japanese-Americans were interned as a knee-jerk reaction to the attack, and because of fears that Japanese immigrants would aid a Japanese invasion of the West Coast of the United States. More recently, nativist feeling has been directed against immigrants, especially illegal aliens, crossing the border from Mexico. Suspicions have also been aroused against Arabs, Muslims, and Arab-Americans.

Among the greatest sufferers of American prejudice have been African-Americans, whose ancestors were brought from Africa to America as slaves. The original American constitution counted a slave as three-fifths of a person. The civil rights struggles of the past forty-five years are well known. Although much progress has been made, racial discrimination still exists. Ask a young black man in New York City how easy it is for him to hail a taxicab. In its 2009 Annual Religion and Public Life Survey, the Pew Forum noted that 58% of Americans believe that Muslims face a lot of discrimination, second only to homosexuals (64%). As for violence, an alarming 38% believe that Islam encourages violence more than other religions, whereas only 45% believe Islam is no more likely than other faiths to encourage violence.

Pew also confirms that people who know a Muslim are less likely to see Islam as violent. Apparently too few people know a Muslim, since 45% of Americans see Islam as "different" than their own belief. Even Pew errs in stating, ". . . the Muslim name for God is Allah." As we mentioned earlier, "Allah" is merely the Arabic term for God. Arab Christians and Arab Jews both call God, "Allah."

Although plagued by many forms of discrimination based on power, wealth, education, family status, and even religion, the Arab World does not have overt discrimination based on race. Of course, there exist different forms of individual bigotry, but on a societal level racial prejudice is much less prevalent.

In sum, Arabs, Arab-Americans, and Muslims are not the first groups, nor will they be the last, to be stigmatized and stereotyped in our nation. Unless we learn how to get over our fear of one another, however, we will never quite learn how to deal with one another's differences.

Overcoming ignorance is the key. To quote Yoda, the Jedi master from George Lucas' *Star Wars*: "Ignorance leads to fear . . . fear leads to anger . . . anger leads to hate . . . hate leads to suffering."[80] This quotation paraphrases Supreme Court Justice Louis D. Brandeis from 1927. "But they knew that . . . fear breeds repression; that repression breeds hate; that hate menaces stable government; that the path of safety lies in the opportunity to discuss freely supposed grievances and proposed remedies; and that the fitting remedy for evil counsels is good ones."[81]

Chapter Six

Who's Who in Arab-America

From the heart pump to the ice cream cone.

THIS SIXTH CHAPTER OF THE HANDBOOK LOOKS at the civic and cultural contributions of Arab-Americans to American society.

Topics to be discussed:
- Famous Arab-Americans
- Contributions made to different parts of society by Arab-Americans

Points to remember:
- Arab-Americans have played a role in every segment of our society.
- Most people know Arab-Americans in their community, but may not realize it.
- Americans of Arab descent are as "American" as everyone else.
- Lebanon is the country of origin of the highest number of Arab-Americans in the United States.

Question Ten
Circle any Arab-American public figures in the following categories.

BEFORE EXAMINING QUESTION TEN, here's a related one. Can you think of any famous or influential Arab-Americans? (Don't consider those already discussed.) Because image and perception shape attitudes, it is important to recognize Arab-American individuals making positive contributions in our society.

Arab-American Contributions:

Here are some notable Arab-Americans and other Western Arabs:

Joseph Abboud – famous fashion designer.

General John Abizaid – former commander of the US Central Command.

Mohammed Abu-Ghazaleh – CEO and Chairman of Del Monte Produce.

F. Murray Abraham – Oscar winner, Best Actor for *Amadeus*, 1985.

Spencer Abraham – former US Senator from Michigan, US Secretary of Energy.

Ahmed Ahmed – Egyptian American comedian (Axis of Evil).

Paul Anka – legendary musician and lyricist.

Yasmine Bleeth – motion picture and television actress.

Don Bustany – legendary radio personality and co-founder of several radio shows, including Top 40.

Dr. Michael DeBakey – Houston-based pioneer surgeon, inventor of the heart pump

Yamilia Diaz-Rahi – international model, *Sports Illustrated* cover girl.

Emelio Estefan – singer Gloria's husband/manager, of Cuban Arab descent.

Robert George – White House Santa for seven administrations.

Carlos Ghosn – CEO of Nissan and Renault automobile companies.

Khalil Gibran – great twentieth century Arab-American poet/philosopher, died 1931.

Sammy Hagar – former lead singer of Van Halen.

Joseph Haggar – founder, Haggar clothing, largest manufacturer of men's slacks.

Najeeb Halaby – former head of Federal Aviation Administration and CEO of Pan-American Airlines, died 2003. His daughter Lisa married Jordan's King Hussein, taking the name Queen Noor.

Tony Ismail – president and founder of Alamo Flags, largest US flag retailer.

Assad Jebara – businessman and designer of Zana-di Jeans.

James Jebara – first jet ace.

Steve Jobs – Co-Founder of Apple, Inc. is the son of two grad students, an American mother, and a Syrian Father, Abdulfattah John Jandali.

Aaron Kader – Palestinian/Mormon comedian (Axis of Evil).

Casey Kasem – the voice of numerous cartoon voices, including some in Scooby Doo and Batman & Robin, as well as co-founder and host of Casey's Top 40.

Candice Lightner – founder of Mothers Against Drunk Driving (MADD).

Ed Masry – lead lawyer in the Erin Brockovich case.

Christa McAuliffe – notable teacher, victim of NASA space shuttle *Challenger* tragedy.

Wentworth Miller – Rising actor, star of Fox's Prison Break.

George Mitchell – former US Senator from Maine, former senate majority leader, chairman of Disney Board of Directors, negotiator of Irish peace agreement, investigator of steroid use in baseball.

Kathy Najimy – comedian/actress.

Jacques Nasser – former CEO of Ford Motor Company.

Dean Obeidallah – Palestinian/Sicilian comedian (Axis of Evil) – Maz Jobrani, who is not Arab-American, rather Iranian-American is also part of the Axis of Evil Comedy Tour.

Bobby Rahal – Indy 500 race car champion.

Nick Rahall II – congressman from West Virginia.

Diane Rehm – Nationally syndicated radio personality.

Boris Said – multitalented professional race car driver.

Lucie Salhany – first woman to head a TV network (Fox).

Tom Shadyac – film director (*Ace Ventura*, *Nutty Professor*, and *Liar, Liar*) .

George Shaheen – founder of Accenture (formerly Anderson Consulting).

Jack Shaheen – Author, professor, and subject matter expert on Arab portrayal in the media.

Donna Shalala – first Arab-American to hold a cabinet post, longest-ever serving Secretary of Health and Human Services, former President of New York's Hunter College, former Chancellor of the University of Wisconsin, present President of the University of Miami.

John E. Sununu – US Senator from New Hampshire.

John H. Sununu – former White House Chief of Staff, former Governor of New Hampshire, father of the present New Hampshire Senator.

Vic Tayback – Mel on the sitcom *Alice*.

Danny Thomas – former actor, comedian, and founder of St. Jude Children's Hospital.

Helen Thomas – Dean of the White House Press Corps.

Point to Ponder
The Origin of the
Ice Cream Cone

At the 1904 St. Louis World's Fair, there were fifty ice cream booths, all of them serving ice cream in glass dishes. Next to one of these worked a pastry maker, Ernest Hamwi, who had emigrated from Syria in 1903. Mr. Hamwi was selling zalabia, *a crisp, wafer-like pastry baked on a flat waffle-iron and served thin, sprinkled with sugar. This waffle was popular throughout the Arab World as well as in France and Scandinavia, known as* rosenkuken *in Germany,* gaufre *in Belgium.*

The ice cream booth next to Mr. Hamwi ran out of clean dishes. To be of help, he quickly rolled one of his warm wafer waffles into the shape of a cone. As it cooled, the wafer set in the shape of a cone. When the vendor placed ice cream in it, the ice cream cone was born. Soon it was on its way to becoming a great American institution.[82]

Frank Zappa – father of alternative music.

NFL legends Don Shula and John Elway are also part Arab.

Finally, perhaps most importantly, Ernest Hamwi, the inventor of the ice cream cone, an Arab-American of Syrian decent. Where would Americans be without the ice cream cone?

Now let's address the correct answers to Question Ten: Circle Arab-American public figures in various categories.

Arab-American Contributions to American Life

The list of names includes public figures, known to Americans, who hail from Central and South America.

While some three million people of Arab descent live in the United States, in North, Central, and South America as a whole there are closer to ten million Arabs. They are more fully integrated into their societies than their cousins in the US. They are comparable to Italian and Irish communities in the US who long ago became part of the proverbial melting pot.

Of these young pop stars, who is the Arab-American: Shakira, Christina Aguilera, or Britney Spears? The correct answer is Shakira, who is half Columbian, half Lebanese. "Shakira," is derived from the Arabic term "shuker," which means gratitude. Shakira's two heritages coexist. She is proud of both. On her first English language CD *Laundry Service*, she sings in English, Spanish, as well as Arabic (which may explain why you may not understand all of the songs!). In some of her music videos she also belly dances, an Arab style of dancing.

Who is the Arab-American former presidential candidate: consumer advocate Ralph Nader, Former Vice President Al Gore, or self-made billionaire Ross Perot? The answer is Ralph Nader, who is of Lebanese descent. His role in enacting seatbelt laws saved many lives and made an impact on all Americans. His mother, Rose Nader, authored a Middle Eastern cookbook, *It Happened in the Kitchen*, which included wise sayings of Ralph's father, Nathra Nader.

Who is the Arab-American movie starlet: Salma Hayek, star of such films as *From Dusk 'til Dawn*, *Desperado*, and *Frida* (which she produced and for which she was nominated for an Academy Award); Shannon Elizabeth, most famous as the exchange student in the *American Pie* movies; or Denise Richards, Bond girl in *The World is Not Enough* and *Wild Things*? Remember, there is at least one Arab-American in each category; in some instances there are two. In this question two out of three of your choices are Arab-American, so your chances were relatively high to get one right. The correct answers are Hayek and Elizabeth. Hayek (both her first and last names are Arabic) is half Lebanese and half Mexican. Elizabeth was born in Texas but is of Syrian descent through her father's side.

Who is the Arab-American 1980s pop star (you may think this is easy, but it could be a trick question): Debbie Gibson, teen queen most famous for her hit single "Only In My Dreams"; Paula Abdul, music video dancer/choreographer, recently in the spotlight again through her appearances as a judge on the television show *American Idol*, and famous for such hits as "Cold Hearted Snake," "Straight Up," and "Forever Your Girl"; or Tiffany, most famous for touring malls throughout the United States in

Point to Ponder
Arab Jews

People sometimes find it confusing that someone like Paula Abdul can be of both Syrian and Jewish descent. Here's how. Damascus, Syria's capital, is one of the oldest cities in the world, perhaps the world's oldest continuously inhabited city. Its archeological sites date back to 6000 BC. Jews have lived in Damascus since ancient times. Some still live there—and in other Arab countries.

Other famous Jews of Arab origin include Max Azria, the fashion designer and founder of BCBG, who is originally from Tunisia; Paul Marciano, co-founder of GUESS, who is of Moroccan descent; famed fashion designer Isaac Mizrahi of Syrian ancestry; and American Idol sensation, Elliot Yamin, the son of an Iraqi Jewish father. Last but certainly not least, Jerry Seinfeld, famed comedian and American pop culture figure, is the son of a Hungarian father and a Syrian mother. Who knew?! [83]

FYI – Lebanon

You may have noticed that most of the Arab-Americans mentioned were originally from Lebanon. Most Arab immigrants to the United States do come from Lebanon, followed by Egypt, Syria, and Palestine. Some claim themselves as Syrian-Lebanese because the region was historically known as "Greater Syria" until the French and British carved up the remains of the Ottoman Empire after World War I.

order to reach the public with her music? Again, there are two correct answers: Paula Abdul and Tiffany. Paula Abdul (Abdul is an Arabic name) is half Syrian-Jewish/half Canadian. Born in Oklahoma, Tiffany is of Syrian descent. She was named Tiffany Renée Darwish (Darwish is an Arabic name). She's credited with discovering New Kids on The Block; they opened for her in 1987!

Who is the Arab-American NFL quarterback: Doug Flutie, Jeff George, or Drew Brees? Here again, we have two correct answers. Doug Flutie is most famous for the miracle Hail Mary at Boston College in 1984, which clinched the Heisman Trophy for him. Of Syrian-Lebanese descent, Flutie has also led the Buffalo Bills and the San Diego Chargers in the NFL. Jeff George, also of Lebanese descent, has played with the Washington Redskins, Atlanta Falcons, and Chicago Bears.

Which cartoon character was voiced by an Arab-American? Was it Shaggy, the slinky, scruffy, hippie friend of Scooby; Fred Flintstone of *The Flintstones*, most famous for bellowing out his wife's name, "Wilmaaaa!"; or the ever genius Homer from *The Simpsons*, with his "Do'h's" and philosophies? While a lot of people often guess Homer, the answer is actually Shaggy. The person who voiced Shaggy is none other than esteemed radio personality and Top 40 host Casey Kasem, originally from Lebanon.

As you can see, there are many Arab-Americans who have made a positive impact on our society, be it in entertainment, sports, politics, medicine, or business.

Congratulations! You have completed the quiz. Let's hope it was helpful.

Chapter Seven

Norms & Mores

Cultural and Demographic Affairs

T HIS SEVENTH CHAPTER OF THE HANDBOOK tries to give the reader a sense of the substance of Arab-American culture, built up from details as diverse as style of dress, hospitality, and sex.

Topics to be discussed:
- General social norms and mores
- Demographics of the Arab-American community
- The myth and mystery of Arab sexuality
- Contemporary Arab dress

Points to remember:
- All norms and mores concerning a community are ultimately generalizations. They are not true for every single member of that community.
- Generally, Arabs tend to have a more intimate, more formal, and very hospitable culture.
- Although they tend to keep to themselves, they also blend in with the greater society.
- Current Arab attire stretches across the spectrum, everything from traditional robes, dresses, and handmade traditional clothes, to every version of "Western" clothing.

ARAB CULTURE IS OBVIOUSLY VERY DIFFERENT from American culture. Part of the challenge of American multiculturalism is that the culture is larger and more varied than what we tend to experience on a daily basis. So it is critical to have a multicultural understanding. That way we can avoid the fear and sometimes the hate that unfortunately tends to come with a lack of understanding. Therefore, it is important to identify and understand what is different in Arab culture. On that note, this section will cover Arab social norms and mores in order to provide information about how Arabs or Arab-Americans may behave, in particular during social interaction.

General Arab and Muslim Cultural Norms and Mores

In general, Arab culture revolves around family, respect, and hospitality. Being gracious and courteous not only with family and friends, but also with strangers, is one of the strongest aspects of Arab culture. Should you have a meeting with an Arab or Muslim, you need to know the following cultural idiosyncrasies so that you are seen as courteous.

When an Arab enters the room, stand up, look him/her straight in the eye and greet him. Shake his/her hand and, unless told otherwise, refer to him/her by his/her title and last name (Mr., Ms., Dr., and so forth). Formality is standard with first encounters.

Some conservative Muslims do not shake the hands of someone of the opposite sex. (For example, Iraq's Prime Minister Nouri al-Maliki refused to shake hands with the American Secretary of State Condoleeza Rice.) If you are a man, and a woman refuses your hand, apologize and move on. Persons may avoid shaking hands by touching the right hand to the heart, and it is considered polite for you to do the same. This gesture symbolizes a greeting of an open heart to you. However, do not assume because the person appears to be conservative (e.g., a woman wearing a head scarf or a man wearing a skull cap or *kufi*) that the person does not shake hands. It could appear more insulting if you do not offer your hand to a person who does shake hands than if you offer your hand to a person who does not.

Make small talk for the first minute or so. Be sure to ask how the person is doing. Feel free to talk about the weather, the surrounding neighborhood, or other neutral subjects. Do not bring up politics, religion, or conditions that may relate to the government in the person's native country. However, weather-related conditions that have been in the headlines are fine to ask about (e.g, storms, an earthquake). Arabs, for the most part, do not speak about politics with strangers, though political discussions with close friends and family are a norm. This hints at the dichotomy of the private versus public in Arab culture.

If you do not know the Arab individual well, be careful in complimenting his family, wife, children, and so forth. This could be construed as inappropriate and is safer to avoid. Should a conversation come up discussing the successes of a family member, such as a son's new job or a daughter's recent soccer win, give generalized statements of support such as "That's wonderful news." This is preferable to, "Wow, she/he is doing so well!" Some Arabs are consumed with jealousy, which is why it is best to not focus specific praise.

Be energetic and animated! In general, Arabs regard Americans as stiff and cold. Such attributes are generally read as signs of being dismissive. Keep in mind that just as we have certain stereotypes about their culture, they too have some about ours.

When seated, be sure not to cross your legs in a manner that exposes the sole of your shoe. This may be interpreted to mean that you are pointing at a person with your feet, a grave insult in certain Arab populations.

When speaking with a person, be sure to make frequent eye contact with him/her. Be an active listener—smile and nod while the person speaks. Do not fidget at your desk or computer. Do not turn your back to the person. These are all signs of being dismissive and rude.

Point to Ponder
Their stereotypes about us

So Aladdin *and* Lawrence of Arabia *have influenced our perception of Arabs. What do you believe has shaped their perceptions of us? Again, it's the great and powerful mass media. If I were to choose dominant pop culture images of the United States in Arab and Muslim pop culture, I would narrow it down to three images:*

1. Cowboys – The broad concept of the Old West, six shooters, and John Wayne or Clint Eastwood on horseback.
2. 90210 – Those five frightening numbers may have affected and misinformed an entire generation, and lead them to believe that we all live like those in that zip code, that we all sleep together, live in lavish mansions, and drive convertibles.
3. Baywatch – Two names: David Hasselhoff and Pamela Anderson.

Questions about religious behavior are considered offensive. Stay away from questions about personal religious practice and participation in mosques. Moreover, as previously mentioned, a follower of the religion of Islam is a Muslim. (This is pronounced Muss-lim with an SSS sound, not Muz-lim or Moz-lem. In some dialects, these last translate as "oppressive" and would not start the meeting off well). Also, avoid other incorrect terms such as "Islamite" or "Mohammedan." If the purpose of your visit is to ask questions relating to a mosque or religious habits, be very respectful and as proper as possible in your demeanor.

Should you be meeting with more than one person, avoid referring to each person by "he" or "she," and instead by "Mr." or "Mrs." (For example, not "He said…" but "Mr. Ibrahim said"). This reiterates the formality within the culture.

When referring to a person in his presence, do not use hand gestures. To call someone over to you, do not motion with your index finger. Pointing is considered as rude in the Arab World as it is here. If you need to gesture, use your entire open hand or arm.

The Arab World gauges personal space differently than do Americans. As a result, Arabs will sometimes get very close to an individual during conversation. Americans sometimes see this person as being aggressive or hostile. However, Arabs communicate as closely as possible. Personal space, our so-called comfort zone in US culture, is roughly ten to twelve inches from nose to nose. In Arab culture it tends to be much closer, roughly six to eight inches, nose to nose. If you feel crowded, feel free to step back or ask the person to take a step back. They should not be offended, as chances are they do not even realize what they are doing.

Generally, Arab culture is far more intimate in all facets of society. For example, people often hug and kiss friends and family each time they see one another. (In some parts of the Arab World these signs of affection may be displayed to same sex only). By contrast, some non-Arab Muslim cultures can be very shy when it comes to personal space. Thus, while many Arabs (Muslim or not) may be very intimate, many non-Arab Muslims, such as Pakistanis, may do very little touching, hugging, and kissing in public. Please remember that these are cultural generalizations and have exceptions.

When persons are leaving, stand up just as you did when they entered the room. Look them in the eye and shake their hands (if they accepted your hand upon first meeting you). Thank them for coming. Once again, formality is imperative.

When visiting an Arab's home, be sure to immediately introduce yourself and explain your reasons for stopping by. Some conservative women (Muslim or not) may not allow a man to enter the house if a male relative is not home, and vice versa. If this is the case, leave your card or contact information and ask when would be a better time to return. In future occasions it may be better to go as a pair, with a man and a woman.

Many Muslim households remove shoes at the door, as rooms with carpeting or rugs are used for prayer. Japanese culture does the same, although for different reasons. If you do not feel comfortable removing your shoes, ask if there is somewhere you could sit and talk without having to remove your shoes.

As hospitality is so highly regarded in Arab culture, most Arabs will try and make you feel at home by offering food and drinks. These are usually sweets (perhaps some baklava or chocolate) and tea or coffee. Even if you do not want to eat or drink anything, accept something small in order to not be seen as insulting your hosts. You are not required to eat or drink the item once it is accepted.

An important aspect of giving compliments must be emphasized. Make no exaggerated compliments. Due to the overt hospitality in Arab culture, bear in mind that if you strongly compliment or admire an Arab's possession, that person may feel obliged to give you that possession as a gift, even if it is dear to him. Material compliments should be sincere, but never over the top.

When interacting with Muslims, show proper respect for the *Quran*. If you do not need to handle the *Quran*, do not do so. If you do handle the *Quran*, do not write on it, place anything on top of it, or place it on the floor. Treat it as you would any other holy book, with respect. It is common for Muslims to have Qurans in numerous places in the home, in their cars, or even in luggage or purses.

It is also common for Muslims and Arabs (irrespective of their faith) to use religious language in everyday conversation. They do it in greetings, business dealings, and regular social interactions. Even Muslims who are not speaking Arabic may use certain Arabic phrases or statements throughout their conversation. A reference to God is always near the conversation. For example, a regular "Hey, how's it going?" conversation could go something as follows:

Person A: *Greetings and salutations and peace be upon you and the mercy of God.*
Person B: *And peace be to you too and the mercy of God.*
Person A: *How have you been?*
Person B: *Thanks be to God, I am doing well. And you?*
Person A: *Thanks be to God, I am well too.*

There are a select few religious buzzwords in Arabic that may be stated in English as part of the conversation. *Inshallah*— "God willing"—is used often in everyday conversation. *"Would you like to grab lunch?"* *"Yes, God willing,"* is not atypical. *Bismillah al Rahman al Raheem*—"In the name of God most merciful, most gracious," (sometimes limited to only *Bismillah*, "In the name of God") is often used as a short prayer before eating or starting an act. *Hamdillah* or *Hamdulillah*—"Thank God"—are also used regularly in everyday conversation. Thanking God after a meal or most events is accepted as normal. *Mashallah*—"By the will of God"—is usually used as a reaction to something positive taking place. For example, if Person A shares with Person B the fact that her child earned straight A's in school, Person B can reply *Mashallah*.

Arabs tend to be a very proud and courteous people. Arab culture is filled with pride, honor, and self-respect. This is partly due to the great history from which Arabs come. Do your best to be respectful. In circumstances that may involve humiliation, Arabs will prefer to save face and be discreet about it. Keep in mind that the family is a very important part of Arab culture. In some cases an Arab or Arab-American may prefer to hold an interview in the presence of the family.

Generally speaking, Arab families tend to be patriarchal. The father, or sometimes the grandfather, usually holds a position of power and authority over the family. Very high levels of respect exist for the family patriarch. In addition, the elderly are held in high esteem.

These points are very important as they will help the individual break the ice. Once that ice is broken, trust can be secured. Once both individuals learn to trust one another, there is no limit as to what can be gained.

It should also be noted that while countries like Saudi Arabia require women to cover up in public, irrespective of their beliefs or faith, other Muslim countries, such as Turkey, forbid veiled women or men with beards from working in any government or public buildings. However, that typically is not an image we see of Muslim countries.

FYI – La la la la laa!

Many of you may have seen images of Arab women, celebrating at weddings, going "La la la la laa!" *with their hands over their mouths. This is called ululating, and it is cultural. It is a tradition that traces back to old times when the women would celebrate by sounding off for the bride, then serenading her with a spontaneous poem.*

FYI – Rhythm

Here's an Arab joke: Put three Arabs in a room, and it becomes a party. Generally, Arabs tend to share a sense of rhythm and soul. Often when Arabs are applauding, random clapping becomes one unified sound. It highlights the common rhythm often found in Arab culture.

Traditional and Current Arab Dress

What is traditional Arab dress? Well, many Arabs today wear some form of modern Western dress, from plain jeans and tee-shirts to three-piece suits to the latest fashions from Paris or Milan. Others wear various forms of traditional attire, often due to the climate and custom.

Men in Saudi Arabia and the Gulf States tend to wear traditional headwear that includes a *ghutra*, a large, diagonally folded cotton square, plain white, or checkered with black or red. This is held in place by an *igaal*, which looks like a fancy rope border around the top of the head and acts as a weight over the cloth.[84] Men and women in the Levant region, (the area including Syria, Lebanon, Jordan, Palestine, and parts of Iraq) do not usually wear the *ghutra*. Instead, they wear a *kufi* , *kufiyeh*, or *hut-ta*—usually a checkered cloth, black and white or red and white, worn not as a headpiece, but more often as a shawl or scarf. This is not a political statement,

© 2009 Ali Farzat

although some have tried to make it so, and one wearing it is simply expressing their culture or being fashionable.

Men in North Africa do not traditionally wear any form of headscarf or turban, although you may find local and traditional influences and exceptions. Occasionally you may see older North African men wearing a fez or *sheysheh*, usually as part of wedding attire. The fez is a remnant of the Ottoman Empire, which ruled that whole region into southern Europe for close to eight hundred years. In other parts of the Arab World, the fez is known as the *tarboosh*.

Some Arab men wear the *thawb* or *gallabeya*, a simple, ankle-length shirt of wool or cotton. While part of culture and tradition, this garment is also practical for those who live in the heat and/or desert where the *thawb* flows freely in the wind and helps cool the person. Other men wear a flowing, floor-length outer cloak, known as a *bisht* or *abaya*. These are made of wool or camel hair in black, beige, brown, or cream tones. Perhaps because of Americans' familiarity with Scottish kilts, I am sometimes asked whether the men wear anything underneath these long garments. The answer is yes—the material is usually thick enough that it cannot be seen through, but men tend to wear undershirts of some form and underwear at the very least. Occasionally loose, short pants are worn underneath. Traditionally, these clothing styles were very practical and comfortable in an often-harsh climate. In the strong winds of the desert, air could keep one cool. The head coverings (worn in public by both men and women) protect wearers from the strong sunlight.

Women's attire also ranges across the spectrum. Women across the Arab World wear modern attire, including business suits, skirts, shorts, and formal gowns. Others will be dressed more traditionally in the *abaya* or even more conservative garb such as the *burqa*.

Women in Islam are expected to be modest (as are men) and are required to cover up during prayer. Depending on the region and their personal preference, some women choose to wear a veil or *hijab*. In Saudi Arabia, they are expected to always wear it in public. In other countries, women in public choose a more conservative veil that is tight around the head and worn along with an overcoat. Still, others choose different color veils, and mix and match with modern attire. Beyond veils, women in the Arab World may also wear traditional long flowing dresses called *gallabeya*. Similar to the *abaya*, this is related to the men's version but not the same. In some localities women will wear a *burqa* or *niqab*, which also covers the face. Note that this is a cultural and political interpretation of the faith.

Remember, all Americans do not wear cowboy hats, large belt buckles, or ball caps. But for those who do, it is merely an expression of themselves and their culture through their attire.

Images of Arab Sexuality

A subject that must be explored at least briefly is the image of Arab sexuality. *The Thousand and One Nights* and the adventures of *Scheherazade* are famous and, to some, sexually enticing. They have been translated into numerous languages over the centuries. Although these works in particular date back to the tenth century, many parts were a mixture of Arab, Persian, and Indian folk tales combined by Arab authors to become known ultimately as *The Arabian Nights*.

The durability of these ancient folk tales suggests that the Arab possesses a certain allure, in particular the Arab woman. The concept of a harem is also appealing and intriguing, perhaps particularly to societies where polygamy is outlawed. Additionally, because little is known about the Arabs, the sexual side is treated with anticipation and uncertainty. A record of Internet searches about Arabs suggests that images of Arab sexuality hold an unusually high attraction and curiosity. Interestingly enough, the most searched phrase associated with the term "Arab" on the Internet is *Arab sex*.[85] Of the most searched terms associated with the term "Arab," over 40% are in one way or another related to sex, including *Arab nude, Arab girl, Arab gay, Arab porn, Arab woman*, and *sexy Arab*.[86] This is very interesting, as there seems to be an attraction and curiosity toward the unknown world of the Arabs.

After discovering that the top Internet search term associated with Arab was "Arab sex," I decided to search a variety of other terms to see if sex was always the most searched term. After all, the online porn industry is one that exceeds six billion dollars annually and is constantly growing. I searched Italian, Finnish, German, Mexican, Korean, French, and American.[87] All had sex somewhere in the top twenty, but none had it as the top term:

Italian: *learn Italian*
Finnish: *Finnish sauna*
German: *learn German*
Mexican: *Mexican recipe*
Korean: *travel Korean*
French: *learn French*
American: *American Idol*

After doing a number of searches, most came up with "learn _____," as in "learn Russian," or "learn Japanese." The only other term to have "sex" as the highest searched phrase was "Indian." Interestingly enough, the two cultures, although different, do share some history and tradition. More importantly, similar to Arab culture, Indian culture is treated with that same sort of alluring mystery.

It is ironic that although there is a stereotype of Muslims being sexually repressed, Arabs are still represented as exotic sexual beings. Depending on where you are in the Arab World, the degree to which public displays of affection are accepted varies greatly. Dating, though it is most definitely taking place among the younger generations, is generally not discussed openly. Physical affection and sex are expected to be limited to married couples. Depending on the country, violations can be punished by law. Once a couple is married, they are encouraged to explore their sexuality and please one another in private.

In most instances, when conducting a security search of an Arab or Muslim, it is best to ask if the person would prefer someone from the same gender to do the search. A conservative Muslim, man or woman, would expect this. If a woman wearing a veil must be searched, this should be done by another woman, and in private. If her veil needs to be removed, it should also be in private where strange men cannot see her.

Some Arab countries are beginning to accept expressions of sexuality in public. Lebanon seems to lead that charge and has become very "Westernized" in that respect. A colleague of mine used to say that the reason Italians and Spaniards are known as great lovers is because the Arabs were in those lands for more than eight hundred years. In other words, it's in their blood. The point is that the passionate and exotic image of Italians and Spaniards holds true for Arabs.

By the Numbers – Statistical Breakdown of Arab-Americans
The following is critical statistical information about the Arab-American community.

- There are approximately three million Arab-Americans.[88]
- Most Arabs in the United States are American citizens. [89]
- 59% of Arab-Americans were born in the United States.[90]
- 21% of those not born in the United States are naturalized citizens[91]
- 19% are not yet citizens[92]

- 29% Lebanese[93]
- 14.5% Egyptian[94]
- 9% Syrian[95]
- 7% Palestinian[96]
- 4% Jordanian[97]
- 4% Moroccan[98]
- 3.5% Iraqi[99]
- 10% from Algeria, Bahrain, Comoros Islands, Djibouti, Kuwait, Libya, Mauritania, Oman, Qatar, Saudi Arabia, Sudan, Tunisia, the United Arab Emirates, or Yemen[100]
- 20% "Arab"[101] – Country of origin not specified
- 35% live in California, Michigan, and New York[102]
- 48% live in twenty metropolitan areas[103]
- Those Arabs living in Fairfax County in Virginia, along with Macomb and Wayne counties in Michigan, make up 2% to 3% of the entire Arab-American population.[104]
- The metropolitan areas with the largest Arab-American populations are Los Angeles, Detroit, New York City, and Washington, DC, respectively.[105]

- 42% Catholic[106]
- 23% Eastern Orthodox[107]
- 12% Protestant[108]
- 23% Muslim[109]

- 84% have at least a high school diploma (the national average is 80%)[110]
- 41% hold a bachelor's degree or higher (the national average is 24.4%)[111]
- 15% hold graduate degrees[112]

- 73% of Arab-Americans aged sixteen and older hold some form of employment (higher than the national average of 71%).[113]
- 42% of working adults are employed in professional or managerial fields (higher than the national average of 34%).[114]
- 77% work in the private sector[115]
- 12.4% are government employees[116]
- 5.9% are unemployed[117]

- Average income of $52,318 for Arab-Americans in 2005 was higher than the national average of $50,046.[118]
- Among the various Arab groups, Syrian, Lebanese, and Egyptian families had higher median incomes than others, near $60,000 per year.[119]

Chapter Eight

Arabs in US History

Historical, Geographical, and Linguistic Affairs.

THIS EIGHTH CHAPTER OF THE HANDBOOK TRACES the history of Arabs in North and South America.

Topics to be discussed:
- Early Arab voyages to the New World
- History of Arab-Americans, including slavery
- World Geography
- Arabic influence on the English and Spanish languages

Points to remember:
- Evidence suggests Arabs arrived at our shores as early as the 1500s.
- There have been two primary waves of immigration: the first in the late nineteenth century and the second in the mid-twentieth century through the present.
- There are approximately one thousand English and French words and several thousand Spanish words derived from Arabic. You probably know more Arabic than you realize.

Early Arab & Muslim Americans

ARABS AND MUSLIMS HAVE BEEN COMING to what is today the United States since the late 1500s. They have fought and died in every US war dating back to the Revolutionary War. Some historical experts believe that the first Arab settler in North America was a shipwrecked passenger who landed on the island of Okracoke just off the coast of North Carolina in the mid-1600s.[120] According to the authors of *The Arab Americans*, "Family tradition holds that the Wahab family of Okracoke Island, thirty miles off the coast of North Carolina, descends from the first Wahab sent as an emissary of the 'King of Arabia' in the mid-seventeenth century to establish the Muslim religion in the New World."[121] Shipwrecked with a load of Arabian horses on the outer banks of North Carolina, Wahab established "Wahab Village," which today is the site of an inn that is still run by the Wahab family.

Other records show that the first Arab in North America was an Andalusian. (Remember Andalusia was Arab Spain, which existed for roughly eight hundred years). He was known only as Esteban, his Christian name. Like many other Muslims and Jews, Esteban converted to Christianity to avoid being expelled by the Spanish government after 1492. Esteban reached what is now Florida in 1528.[122] He learned the dialects and customs of many of the Native American tribes along the Gulf of Mexico. In 1539 he led the Conquistadors into the present states of New Mexico and Arizona in search of the "Seven Cities of Cibola." The Native American Pueblo peoples understandably did not welcome the intrusion. Esteban himself was killed by the Zunis, whose descendants today remember him in the form of a Kachina in their religious tradition.[123]

Others believe that Christopher Columbus's navigator was an Arab. (Apparently, he was not very good though, as they were trying to get to India!) In fact, the Pinzon brothers, the owners and captains of the Nina and the Pinta, were Andalusians. The Pinzon family was related to Abuzayan Muhammad III (1362 – 66), the Moroccan sultan of the Marinid dynasty (1196 – 1465). Arabs made many advances in navigation and navigational tools. They were skilled and successful sea travelers and merchants.

Another of the early arrivals was a Chaldean priest, Father Elms from Mosul, Iraq. He arrived in the Americas in 1668 and traveled here for fifteen years, journeying through the booming Spanish-American communities and ending in Mexico.[124]

Many victims of the slave trade triangle brought to the New World against their will were Arabs and/or Muslims from Africa. (Remember that most Arabs are also

African; most Arabs live in the continent of Africa). Arab slaves? Absolutely. Muslim slaves? Absolutely. Consequently, a great number of Arabs were slaves. An estimated 20% to 30% of the slaves brought to the United States were Muslim. Slaves with names such as Omar Ibn-Said, Job Ben-Solomon, Paul Labman Kibby, Prince Omar, and Ben Ali were brought here as slaves.[125] While the vast majority of slaves were forced to practice Christianity, many kept Islamic traditions that you can still find today in several African-American churches along the eastern seaboard and in the Deep South. However, many of the worshipers don't recognize the origin of those traditions. Some of them include avoiding pork products, facing east to pray (and in some cases building the church so that the structure faces east), using prayer rugs, and naming children traditional Muslim names such as Mohammed, Jamal, Zainab, and Aisha.

FYI – Andalusia – Muslim Spain

In 711, the Umayyad (or Ummawiy) empire based in Damascus, Syria had stretched to the borders of India and China eastward and spanned North Africa westward. An oppressed Christian chief, Julian, went to Musa Ibn Nusair, the governor of North Africa, pleading for help against the tyrannical Visigoth ruler of Spain, Roderick. Musa responded by sending the young general Tariq Bin Ziyad with an army of 7,000 troops to face the Visigoths. The name Gibraltar is derived from Jabal Tariq, which is Arabic for "Mount Tariq," named after the place where the Muslim army landed.

The Muslim invasion, and subsequent administration of Iberia, freed the Spanish population of Jews from Visigothic oppression. It was said that immediately after the invasion, the Jewish population of Toledo opened the gates of the city, welcoming the Arab Muslims. Though prevailing warriors, the Muslims were full of honor and chivalry. They gave the Goth Spaniards an opportunity to surrender each of their provinces, to which most agreed. This was a tactic seen again and again in battles where Muslims gained the upper hand. They would often offer peace and the right to live among them, if the opposing army laid down its arms and accepted peace (never forcefully converting Christians or Jews, as they are "People of the Book.") Salah El-Din (Saladin), the great Muslim leader who regained Jerusalem from the Crusaders, was famous for such acts of kindness and chivalry.

And so Andalusia flourished for about 800 years, until January 2, 1492, when Ferdinand and Isabella expelled all the Jews and Muslims and the Arab influence withered. Andalusia was Arab, it was Muslim, and it hosted the peaceful and fruitful coexistence of Jews, Christians, and Muslims where a great civilization thrived in science, literature, and architecture that helped usher in the rebirth (Renaissance) from the Dark Ages in Europe.

In 1790, the South Carolina House of Representatives allowed Moors, subjects of the Emperor of Morocco, to be tried in court according to the laws of its citizens, and not under slave codes. Like others forced into slavery, these Arabic-speaking people, over generations, lost ties with their former culture.[126]

Larger numbers of Arabs began settling in the United States toward the end of the nineteenth century, attracted like most other immigrants by economic and educational opportunities. Today, the majority of Arab-Americans are descendants of the first wave of primarily Christian Syrian and Lebanese immigrants. This wave began in the mid-to-late nineteenth century and lasted through the early twentieth century. As a direct result of this wave of immigration, 77% of Arab-Americans today identify themselves as Christian, despite the majority of Arabs worldwide being Muslim.

Immigration to the United States was restricted following World War I. The second wave of Arab immigrants did not begin until after World War II. This second wave also primarily consisted of Syrians and Lebanese, though Palestinians, Jordanians, Yemenis, Iraqis, and Egyptians also made their way to the States. These first two waves of immigrants came largely from rural areas and had limited amounts of formal education. In the 1970s, political tensions in the Middle East were high and the United States began loosening immigration laws. Consequently, the immigration trends from the Arab World began to diversify: more Arab Muslims began immigrating, as well as Arabs from urban areas and with higher educational backgrounds.[127]

Today, Arab-Americans are present in each state of the union, in every field of employment, from factories to hospitals to Hollywood. By now you have learned that Arab-Americans have fought and died in every war and military conflict, from the Revolutionary War to the conflict in Iraq. An Arab-American is responsible for the creation of the ice cream cone, the first artificial heart, and the American Top 40 Countdown.[128]

Arab and Muslim Influence on the United States
Although often not openly recognized, the Arab World and the Muslim faith have influenced much in our American culture. So much of what is today labeled as "American" traces its roots to the Arab Muslim world. Let me explain:

The Spanish who settled in the southern part of the North American continent transported designs, materials, and food inspired by Arab Muslims, who ruled and influenced Spain for over eight hundred years.[129] Typical "southwestern" architecture, such as enclosed patios, fountains, and arches were brought here by way of Arab Muslim Spain: Andalusia.

Some Native American historians believe that certain Native American jewelry (specifically types of Navajo jewelry) was originally influenced by Spanish-Arab-Muslim Mudejars.[130] The squash blossom necklace looks like an inverted crescent and was apparently influenced by a design adopted from Muslim ornaments of the crescent. The crescent moon is the symbol of Islam as the cross is the symbol for Christianity and the six-sided star for Judaism.[131]

Who would have thought that the all-American image of the cowboy was actually

FYI – Mudejars
Mudejars *were Arab Muslims who stayed after the fall of Andalusia in 1492, when most Muslims and Jews left or were forced out. Those who remained were forced to convert to Christianity. However, many Muslims (*Mudejars, *also called* Moriscos, *"little Moors")* and Jews (*Moranos*) observed their faiths in secret, pretending to be Christian in public. Most also took Christian names.*

influenced by Arabs and Muslims? The Mudejars were skilled horsemen and brought over the saddle, spurs, and even the boots to the United States.[132] Donald Chaves, a New Mexican author and cowboy historian, has stated that the pointed-toed, high-heeled, and high-topped boots that Americans identify as cowboy boots were designed by Muslims in Andalusia. Moreover, the intricate stitching is reminiscent of the decorative Arab designs.[133]

Geography and the World

In November of 2002, the National Geographic Society published what ultimately was an embarrassing report about the United States' younger generation. A survey conducted in nine countries asked fifty-six questions about geography and current events. Those surveyed were ages eighteen to twenty-four, the prime age for the military, and the results were troubling, to say the least. Bear in mind that, at the time the survey was administered, the US military had been in Afghanistan for approximately a year. In addition, although we had not yet begun fighting Operation Iraqi Freedom, thousands of soldiers had been stationed in the vicinity of Iraq since Operation Desert Storm from the early 1990s. The United States passed with a "D" average, barely ahead of Mexico, which came in last place.[134]

Findings from the survey included the following:

• 87% of Americans surveyed could not find Iraq on a map. (The same was true for Iran.)
  • 83% could not find Afghanistan on a map. (We had already been there for a year.)
  • 76% could not find Saudi Arabia on a map.

• 70% could not find New Jersey on a map. (I know we pick on it, but come on.)
• 49% could not find the state of New York on a map. (The nation's third most populous state.)
• 11% could not find the United States on a map. (Even though our nation takes up half a continent.)

In April 2006, the National Geographic Society conducted a second survey of geography and Americans.[135] Sadly, the numbers are still disappointing. In fact in certain cases, they were worse:

• 88% could not find Afghanistan. (At this point, the United States had been there more than four years.)
• 63% could not find Iraq or Saudi Arabia.
• 75% could not find Iran.
• 50% could not find New York State.

Why am I sharing this? We, as Americans, need to be aware of ourselves and our surroundings. The results of these surveys are not only disappointing, but also frightening. One of the basic steps to reach a better understanding of those who are different from us is to learn about their existence and their homeland as they would about ours. Because of this study, I always bring a world map with me to class so that I can point out the countries I talk about. For your edification, feel free to review a world map at www.cia.gov/library/publications/the-world-factbook/reference_maps/pdf/political_world/pdf.

Arabic in Your English, Spanish & French
There are approximately one thousand words in the English language derived from Arabic. The same is true for French. Moreover, because the Iberian Peninsula (present-day Spain and Portugal) was Arab for over eight hundred years (Andalusia), there are literally thousands of Spanish words that are ultimately derived from Arabic. Therefore, chances are that you speak more Arabic than you realize. It is good to learn about these words in order to further understand our culture.

Listed below are a few words with their Arabic origins and meanings. For some of these words, Arabic is not the original root, but it was through the spread of the Arabic language that the words made it to English. Also remember, "al" is merely the Arabic word for "the."[136]

Admiral:	*amir al*	Ruler of; originally "amir al-bahr," ruler of the sea.
Alchemy:	*alkimia*	Greek "chemia," a pouring together.
Alcohol:	*al-kuhoul*	Powder of antimony, used to color the eyebrows.

Alcove:	*al-gobbah*	Vault, arch, dome.
Alfalfa:	*al-fac, facah*	The best fodder.
Algebra:	*al-jabr*	The reunion of broken parts, from "jabara," reunite.
Almanac:	*almanakh*	Almanac or calendar.
Amber:	*'anbar*	Grey amber.
Arsenal:	*dar as-sina' ah*	Workshop, literally, house of skill or trade.
Azure:	*lazward*	Sky blue, from Persian word *lazhward*.
Candy:	*qandi*	Made of sugar.
Calibre:	*kaleb*	Mold or cast.
Cipher:	*sifr*	Cipher, nothing.
Coffee:	*qahwa*	Coffee.
Cotton:	*qutun*	Cotton.
Crimson:	*qermez*	Crimson, from Sanskrit *krmija*.
Elixir:	*el iksir*	The philosopher's stone.
Gazelle:	*gazal*	Gazelle.
Jar:	*jarrah*	Water vessel.
Julep:	*julab*	Persian *gulab*, rose water.
Lemon:	*laymoun*	Lemon.
Magazine:	*makhzan*	Storehouse.
Mattress:	*matrah*	Mattress, foundation, place where anything is thrown.
Muslin:	*Mawsil*	Mosul, a city in Iraq where the first muslin was made.
Ream:	*rizmat*	Bale, a packet, especially a ream of paper; from "razama."
Saffron:	*za'faran*	Saffron.
Sahara:	*sahra*	Desert.
Sash:	*shash*	Turban.
Satin:	*Zaitun*	Medieval name of Chinese city, Tsinkiang
Sherbet:	*sherbet*	*sharaba*, to drink.
Sheriff:	*sharrif*	Honorable one—because it was the honorable one who enforced the law.
Sofa:	*soffah*	Cushion or saddle.
Sugar:	*sakkar*	Persian *shakar* and Sanskrit *carkara*, candied sugar.
Syrup:	*sharab*	*Shariba*, drink.
Tariff:	*tar'if*	Explanation, information, a list of things, especially of fees to be paid; from *arafa*, to inform.
Zenith:	*semt-ar-ras*	Zenith, literally *way of the head*.
Zero:	*sifr*	Cipher.

FYI – Yalla

Literally Ya Allah, which means "oh God." It has become a colloquial term meaning, "Let's go." In certain situations, there have been examples of non-Arabic speakers adopting and using the word.

With regard to the Spanish language, Gerald Erichsen, an active online Spanish editor and translator, has written, "It is not 'real' Arabic you are speaking, but rather words that come from Arabic. After Latin and English, Arabic is probably the biggest contributor of words to the Spanish language, and a large portion of English-Spanish cognates (words that the two languages share) that do not come from Latin come from Arabic."

"The etymology of English words," Erichsen continues, "goes beyond the scope of this article, but the introduction of Arabic words into Spanish began in earnest in the eighth century, although even before then some words of Latin and Greek origin had roots in Arabic. People living in what is now Spain spoke Latin at one time, of course,

FYI – Who were the Moors?

"Moor" was another term for Arabs, mostly from North Africa. When the Romans entered Africa in 46 BC, they saw local people and called them Maures, from the Greek adjective mauros, meaning dark or black. It is from these meanings that the term "Moor" is derived. Because the inhabitants of North Africa had darker skins, the Romans and later the Europeans called them Moors, i.e. the Darks.[138]

but over the centuries Spanish and other Romance languages such as French and Italian gradually differentiated themselves. The Latin dialect that eventually became Spanish was highly influenced by the invasion of the Arabic-speaking Moors in 711. For many centuries, Latin/Spanish and Arabic existed side by side, and even today many Spanish place names retain Arabic roots. It was not until late in the 15th century that the Moors were expelled. By then literally thousands of Arabic words had become part of Spanish."[137] As an example of place names, Guadalajara is derived from the Arabic term Wadi Al-Hijara or *Valley of the rocks.*

Note: For more on the importation of Muslims from Africa to the US as slaves, see Muslims in American History by Jerald F. Dirks.

Conclusion

I N THE POST-9/II WORLD, Arabs, Arab-Americans, Muslims, and those perceived to be such have been mislabeled and sometimes victimized because of their national origin, ethnicity, faith, and even appearance. We must remember that Arabs and Muslims are part of the fabric that was woven together to create our United States. Arabs and Muslims, therefore, are embedded in our great history and culture.

If we inherently alter our way of life and ultimately try to choose between security and liberty, then we will have changed the foundation of this nation and the terrorists will have won. A healthy balance between liberty and security has made the United States a global success. If we change the essence of our liberty and all that our nation has stood for over the past several centuries, we will have lost the war, regardless of how many battles we win. The vision of our founding fathers will have died and the United States' stance as a beacon of freedom and opportunity across our world will have mutated into a frightened society. It is critical to note that one of the greatest and most powerful empires in history, the Roman Empire, was not destroyed by an army. It did not collapse from an invading force. Rather, it deteriorated and disintegrated from within. We as a nation and as a society cannot afford to go down a similar path and ultimately make a similar mistake. No matter how terrible our challenges may appear, we must remain steadfast in the face of adversity and controversy. We must learn from history and maintain our courage. Otherwise we are bound to make the same mistakes.

I hope this handbook has been helpful and achieved the goal I set out for it as an introductory guide to the Arab, Arab-American, and Muslim communities. I hope it shed some much-needed light on the subjects at hand and, for lack of better terms, that it humanized and demystified these communities so that you could better understand them.

I hope this handbook has stimulated your thirst for information and will allow you to go about your responsibilities in your professional and personal life with added insight about these communities, that it will make you want to learn more about them from accurate sources. I hope that you are now able to tell who is an Arab and what they are all about, both physically and that which exists beneath the surface; that you are not so quick to judge or label or even blame or hate; and that you now have developed a new appreciation for Arabs, Arab-Americans, Muslims, and their respective cultures.

You now know that Arabs come in many different appearances and "colors," that they practice many different faiths, and that they are not one large homogenous cohesive unit, but a diverse and multi-hued, heterogeneous, multiracial people, whose origins extend as far east as Oman, as far west as Mauritania and Morocco, as far south as Sudan, and as far north as Algeria, Tunisia, Syria, and Iraq.

You now know that most Muslims are not Arab but rather from South Asia and South East Asia, that Muslims currently live all over the world. You also now know that Muslims believe that Islam is a continuation of the holy faiths of Moses and Jesus, Judaism and Christianity, respectively. You now know what is the real meaning of *jihad*, and who Allah really is to any Arabic speaking person. You also now know some basic cultural norms and mores and methods. Hopefully these can help break the proverbial ice and, in certain cases, melt an entire glacier.

Ultimately, when all is said and done, the goal was to provide a thorough and detailed introduction to these communities. In the post-9/11 world, they have been at the center of a lot of attention, much of it negative and speculative. Perhaps now these communities can be better understood. The formula once again is simple:

Understanding + Communication = Trust

Lack of trust is our greatest challenge. Once we achieve trust between the communities and their government, together we can achieve so much. I see this handbook as a civil servant of some sort trying to take necessary steps to improve communication and understanding, and therefore ultimately to gain and maintain trust. I hope this book has helped with understanding and will lead to better trust. The next step of communication falls partly on your shoulders.

I choose to end with a brief section of *Quotes & Notes*. It is made up of various quotations from history and other sources that apply to this handbook. For some of the quotations, I felt the need to elaborate and provide my own input, influence, or explanation. I hope you will appreciate them and learn from them as much as I.

Quotes

People are unreasonable, illogical, and self-centered. Love them anyway. If you are kind, people may accuse you of selfish motives. Be kind anyway. If you are successful, you may win false friends and true enemies. Succeed anyway. The good you do today may be forgotten tomorrow. Do good anyway. Honesty and transparency make you vulnerable. Be honest and transparent anyway. What you spend years building may be destroyed overnight. Build anyway. People who really want help may attack you if you help them. Help them anyway. If you find serenity and happiness, others may be jealous. Be happy anyway. Give the world the best you have and you may get hurt. Give the world your best anyway. You see, in the final analysis, it is between you and God; it was never between you and them anyway.
—Mother Teresa

We will not be driven by fear into an age of unreason.
—Edward R. Murrow

This quote by the famed journalist signifies my belief that more information, more knowledge, and more understanding is needed and necessary to combat the growing fear, confusion, and hate.

We can easily forgive a child who is afraid of the dark. The real tragedy of life is when men are afraid of the light.
—Plato

We must scrupulously guard the civil rights and civil liberties of all citizens, whatever their background. We must remember that any oppression, any injustice, any hatred, is a wedge designed to attack our civilization.
—President Franklin Delano Roosevelt, 1940

President Roosevelt's sentiment applies to Arab and Muslim-Americans today.

They that can give up essential liberty to obtain a little temporary security deserve neither liberty nor security.
—Benjamin Franklin, 1759

In 1759, when Franklin spoke, the United States was not yet a nation. Liberty would become a founding pillar of this country. We should understand that liberty and security are not mutually exclusive.

Are you a politician asking what your country can do for you or a zealous one asking what you can do for your country? If you are the first, then you are a parasite; if the second, then you are an oasis in the desert.
—Khalil Gibran, 1925

Gibran was one of the most famous Arab-Americans of the twentieth century. This particular quote was later reworked and attributed to President John F. Kennedy as part of his famous "Ask not what you can do for your country..." speech.

True servants of the Compassionate (God) are those who walk the earth in humility and when ignorant people address them, they reply with words of peace.
  —The Holy Quran, 25:63

In valor, there is hope.
  —Publius Cornelius Tacitus, 55-120 AD

Before today, I used to criticize my companion if my religion was not the one which he followed. But my heart changed to accept every image, so pastures for the carefree lovers and convents for the monks. A house of idols and the idol house at Taa'if, the tablets of the Torah *and the mushaf of the* Quran. *I follow the religion of love wherever it takes me, so all religion is my religion and belief.*
  —Ibn 'Arabi, *Dhakhaairul-A'laaq*

This is from Ibn 'Arabi, the twelfth century Arab philosopher. His intent is self-explanatory and provides a deeper look inside the mind of this famed Arab and Muslim intellectual. What his thought states is true Islam, the understanding and continuation of Judaism and Christianity.

Excellence is the result of caring more than others think is wise; risking more than others think is safe. Dreaming more than others think is practical and expecting more than others think is possible.
  —Anonymous

And I believe that it is in you to be good citizens. And what is it to be a good citizen? It is to acknowledge the other person's rights before asserting your own, but always to be conscious of your own. It is to be free in thought and deed, but it is also to know that your freedom is subject to the other person's freedom. It is to create the useful and the beautiful with your own hands, and to admire what others have created in love and with faith. It is to produce wealth by labor and only by labor, and to spend less than you have produced that your children may not be dependent on the state for support when you are no more. It is to stand before the towers of New York, Washington, Chicago and San Francisco saying in your heart, "I am the descendant of a people that built Damascus, and Biblus, and Tyre and Sidon, and Antioch, and now I am here to build with you, and with a will." It is to be proud of being an American, but it is also to be proud that your fathers and mothers came from a land upon which God laid His gracious hand and raised His messengers.
  —Khalil Gibran, 1926

This quote, part of a poem dedicated and entitled, "To Young Americans of Syrian Origin," summarizes the Arab-American community and its experience. I am tremendously moved and emotionally affected each time I read it. I am here to build with you…and with a will.

You belong to two great civilizations—keep the best of the Arab culture and take the best of the American culture—and you will have achieved a balanced success.
  —Zayada Shora

I quoted my mother several times in this book, and for good reason. Like her mother before her, she is full of practical wisdom. Her quotes about Islam, culture, and life have always been a guide for my life. I hope the achievement of this book speaks to the balanced success she mentioned.

Wise men speak because they have something to say. Fools because they have to say something.
  —Plato

Resources

Islam:
Acts of Faith: The Story of an American Muslim, the Struggle for the Soul of a Generation, by Eboo Patel.
Covering Islam: How the Media and the Experts Determine How We See the Rest of the World, by Edward Said.
Islam: A Short History, by Karen Armstrong.
Jihad: The Trail of Political Islam, by Gilles Kepel.
Muslims in American History, A Forgotten Legacy, by Jerald F. Dirks.
No god but God: The Origins, Evolution, and Future of Islam, by Reza Aslan.
Peace Be upon You, The Story of Muslim, Christian and Jewish Coexistence, by Zachary Karabell.
The Koran, Edited by N.J. Dawood.*

*It must be noted that the *Quran* was born into the Arabic language the same way the *Bible* was in Aramaic. No one wholly understands everything in it and it is beyond anyone to truly "translate" what God's words mean. This is at best an interpretation. Additionally, Arabic is a far more complex language than English and thus translation becomes more difficult. If one were to truly grasp The Quran, they would need to read it and understand it in Arabic.

Lost History: The Enduring Legacy of Muslim Scientists, Thinkers, and Artists, by Michael H. Morgan.
Unholy War: Terror in the Name of Islam, by John Esposito.
What Everyone Needs to Know About Islam, by John Esposito.

Arabs:
Arab Voices Speak to American Hearts, by Samar Dahmash-Jarrah.
Guilty: Hollywood's Verdict on Arabs After 9/11, by Jack G. Shaheen.
Orientalism, by Edward Said.
The House of Wisdom: How the Arabs Transformed Western Civilization, by Jonathan Lyons.
The Prophet, by Kahlil Gibran.
Reel Bad Arabs: How Hollywood Vilifies a People, by Jack G. Shaheen.

DVDs:
A Dream in Doubt
Reel Bad Arabs
Secrets of the Koran
When the World Spoke Arabic: The Golden Age of Arab Civilization

Notes

[1] Barlow, Elizabeth, ed., *Evaluation of Secondary-Level Textbooks for Coverage of the Middle East and North Africa*, Center for Middle Eastern and North African Studies, Ann Arbor, MI; Middle East Studies Association, Tucson, AZ, 3rd edition, 1994.

[2] *Id.*

[3] "We the People of Arab Ancestry," US Census Bureau, March 2005. (Note: Although the census found an estimated 1.2 million Americans of Arab ancestry, those numbers are believed to be widely underrated and the three million population is a more accepted estimate.)

[4] *Id.*

[5] *CIA World Factbook*, Afghanistan, http://www.cia.gov/cia/publications/factbook/geos/af.html.

[6] *Id.*

[7] *Id.*

[8] "Saudi Aramco World: The Arabs of Honduras," http://www.saudiaramcoworld.com/issue/200104/the.arabs.of.honduras.html.

[9] *Id.*

[10] *Id.*

[11] "Wahhabi," *The Columbia Encyclopedia,* 6th ed., Columbia University Press, New York, 2001–04, www.bartleby.com/65/.

[12] http://i-cias.com/e.o/sharia.html.

[13] *The Holy Quran*, (111:7).

[14] *Id,* (9:5).

[15] *Id,* (5:32).

[16] From a Hadith of the Prophet Muhammed. Terrorism, Al Muhaddith, http://www.muhaddith.org/Islam_Answers/Terrorism.html.

[17] "Jesus and Mary in the Quran," http://www.submission.org/jesus/Mary-Jesus.html.

[18] *The Holy Quran*, (2:62).

[19] *Id,* (4:1).

[20] "The Koran's Spirit of Gender Equality," http://www.qantara.de/webcom/show_article.php/_c-307/_nr-19/_p-1/i.html.

[21] *The Holy Quran*, (4:32).

[22] *Id,* (3:195).

[23] Armstrong, Karen, "The Eve of Destruction," http://www.countercurrents.org/armstrong150204.htm.

[24] *Arab Culture and Society*, American-Arab Anti-Discrimination Committee, http://www.adc.org/index.php?id=1172.

[25] Armstrong, Karen, "The Eve of Destruction," *Guardian Unlimited*, January 15, 2004.

[26] *Id.*

[27] *Id.*

[28] *The Holy Quran*, (4:3).

[29] CIA World Factbook.

[30] *Id.*

[31] www.usinfo.state.gov.

[32] CIA World Factbook, 2004.

[33] *Id.*

[34] "Facts about Arabs and the Arab World," American-Arab Anti-Discrimination Committee.

[35] http://www.aneki.com/muslim.html.

[36] Sikh American Legal Defense and Education Fund, www.saldef.org.

[37] http://en.wikipedia.org/wiki/Bedouin.

[38] US Census Bureau, Census 2000, Summary File 4.

[39] *Id.*

[40] Belt, Don, "The World of Islam," *National Geographic*, January 2002, p. 85.

[41] http://perresearch.org/pubs/483/muslim-americans.

[42] Cooper, Barry, *Unholy Terror: The Origin and Significance of Contemporary, Religion-based Terrorism*, March 2002.

[43] "Jewish militant faces bomb trial," June 15, 2004, BBC News.

[44] "Hindu hardliners 'led Gujarat attacks'," March 6, 2002, BBC News.

[45] "Armed guards for Sri Lanka church," January 27, 2004, BBC News.

[46] "Understanding Islam," Interview with Karen Armstrong, *Newsweek*, October 29, 2001.

[47] Khawaja, Sobat, ed., "Islam: The Moral Code Re-Examined," www.proislam.com, March, 3, 2003.

[48] *Id.*

[49] Nawwab, Ismail I.; Speers, Peter C.; and Hoye, Paul F., eds, *ARAMCO and Its World: Arabia And The Middle East*, edited by, Islam and Islamic History Section, Arabian American Oil Company, Washington, DC, 1980.

[50] M Erhayiem, http://www.arabicnumerals.cwc.net/.

[51] http://www.fact-index.com/a/al/al_khwarizmi.html.

[52] http://www.arab2.com/articles/a/A-is-for-Arabs-George-Rafael.html.

[53] *Id.*

[54] *Id.*

[55] *Id.*

[56] *Id.*

[57] *Id.*

[58] *Id.*

[59] *Id.*

[60] *Id.*

[61] *Id.*

[62] *Id.*

[63] *Id.*

[64] http://www.mediamonitors.net/sherri24.html.

[65] *Id.*

[66] *Id.*

[67] *Id.*

[68] *Id.*

[69] "The impact of the Arab Culture on European Renaissance," http://www.isesco.org.ma/pub/Eng/Arabiculture/page4.html.

[70] *USA Today*, cover story, April 20, 1995, p. 1 A.

[71] ADC 1995 Report on Anti-Arab Racism.

[72] *Chicago Tribune*, April 25, 1995, p. 20.

[73] *Id.*

[74] Shaheen, Jack G., *Reel Bad Arabs*, 2001, p. 51.

[75] *Id.*

[76] *Id.*

[77] Waxman, Sharon, *The Washington Post*, November 6, 1998, p. 1.

[78] Hoffman II, Michael, *Hoffman Wire*, Associated Press, May 14, 1999.

[79] *Id.*

[80] Star Wars, Episode I – Yoda quote.

[81] Whitney v. California, *274 US 357 (1927)*.

[82] Waffle Classic - The Original Ice Cream Cone.

[83] http://en.wikipedia.org/wiki/Mizrahi_Jews.

[84] Royal Embassy of Saudi Arabia website, Traditional Dress and Jewelry.

[85] http://inventory.overture.com/d/searchinventory/suggestion/, as of June 2005.

[86] *Id.*

[87] *Id.*

[88] "We the People of Arab Ancestry," US Census Bureau, March 2005. (Note: Although the census found an estimated 1.2 million Americans of Arab ancestry, those numbers are believed to be widely underrated and the three million population is a more accepted estimate.)

[89] El-Badry, Samia, "Arab-Americans are Well-Educated, Diverse, Affluent & Highly Entrepreneurial," *Arab-American Business*, November 2001.

[90] *Id.*

[91] *Id.*

[92] *Id.*

[93] "We the People of Arab Ancestry," p. 3.

[94] *Id.*

[95] *Id.*

[96] *Id.*

[97] *Id.*

[98] *Id.*

[99] *Id.*

[100] *Id.*

[101] *Id.*

[102] *Id.*

[103] *Id.*

[104] *Id.*

[105] *Id.*

[106] "Arab-Americans are Well-Educated, Diverse, Affluent & Highly Entrepreneurial," www.arabamericanbusiness.com/issue1_nov2001/sr_badry.html.

[107] *Id.*

[108] *Id.*

[109] *Id.*

[110] "We the People of Arab Ancestry," p. 11.

[111] *Id.*

[112] "Arab-Americans are Well-Educated, Diverse, Affluent & Highly Entrepreneurial," www.arabamericanbusiness.com/issue1_nov2001/sr_badry.html.

[113] "We the People of Arab Ancestry," p. 12.

[114] *Id.*

[115] "Arab-Americans are Well-Educated, Diverse, Affluent & Highly Entrepreneurial," www.arabamericanbusiness.com/issue1_nov2001/sr_badry.html.

[116] *Id.*

[117] *Id.*

[118] "We the People of Arab Ancestry," p. 15.

[119] *Id.*

[120] El-Badry, Samia and Shabbas, Audrey, *Arab World Studies Notebook*, Middle East Policy Council, The Arab-Americans.

[121] *Id.*

[122] *Id.*

[123] *Id.*

[124] *Id.*

[125] *Id.*

[126] *Id.*

[127] Samhan, Helen Hatab, "New Census Figures Show Continued Growth of the Arab-American Community," *Arab-American Business.* July 2002.

[128] "Arab American Demographics," Arab American Institute. www.aaiusa.org/demographics.html.

[129] McIntosh, Phyllis, "Islamic Influence Runs Deep in American Culture," Washington File, August 24, 2004.

[130] *Id.*

[131] *Id.*

[132] *Id.*

[133] *Id.*

[134] http://archives.cnn.com/2002/EDUCATION/11/20/geography.quiz/.

[135] "Study: Geography Greek to young Americans," http://www.cnn.com, April 2006.

[136] *Webster's Deluxe Unabridged Dictionary*, Dorset & Baber, New York, 1983, http://www.adc.org/index.php?id=1172.

[137] Erichsen, Gerald, *Spanish's Arab Connection*, http://spanish.about.com/cs/historyofspanish/a/arabicwords.html.

[138] Clark, Yvonne, "Moors and Arabs," http://www.africawithin.com/moors/moors_and_arabs.html.

2 Section Two

In the Informed Views section guest writers provide personal essays as well as scholarly articles about the Arab and Muslim worlds.

Contents (Section Two)

2. Informed Views

I. Glimpses of the Muslim World

Chapter One

Glimpses of the Muslim World

Scenes from Muslim Ports of Call
by Frederic Hunter

AT SUNSET, THE CRUISE SHIP PULLED AWAY FROM the pier in Muscat, Oman. Two tugboats assisted its departure. Half of the crew members attended to their work. The others threw prayer rugs onto the decks and knelt in the direction of Mecca. The tugs bobbed in the waves of the harbor, and the devout crew members bobbed in the process of their prayers.

As the tugs shifted their positions, moving away from the pier, the men at prayer shifted their positions in order to stay aligned with Mecca.

The guard on the third floor of the Yemen National Museum sat as still as a statue in a hard-backed chair. The guard's garment, black as the Dark Ages, robed her slight, unmoving body all the way down to her worn black leather shoes. Black gloves hid her hands. Dark cloth covered her head, masking it except for her black eyes.

I walked about the architecture exhibits, examining the models of various dwellings typical of these highlands of the mountainous Arabian peninsula. The model of a typical dwelling of the Sana area showed a four-story building similar to the one the guard and I were in: beige stone on the lower floors giving way to beige brick on the upper ones; painted designs over the doorways and above the windows; and semicircular pediments of carved limestone, each one different and set with stained glass.

The legend both in English and Arabic explained that the first floor of a typical house served as a granary, storerooms, and stables. On the top floor, a sitting room was located. There the men of the house would meet male friends, and at separate times, the women of the house would entertain women friends.

I bent over the exhibits, my hands clasped behind my back, and walked about them. I had the urge to approach the black-veiled, unmoving figure in the chair and, maintaining the hands-behind-back stance, peer at this exhibit. For surely the figure was a cultural artifact of Yemen.

Of course, I did not. I examined the exhibits, and the guard examined me. Every now and then I glanced at her. Her dark eyes, framed by dark skin and black veil, would meet mine.

But I felt no connection. She could see me: my lanky, gray-haired American frame, my long-sleeved sport shirt, my slacks, my hands with the gold band on the left one, my manner of approaching the exhibits. But I saw nothing of her: only two dark eyes robbed of context by the veil.

I felt as I had before in this country, that I did not know what I was seeing.

At two o'clock in the afternoon businessmen paced about the hotel lobby, waiting for transportation. Hotel personnel—all men—leaned against the counters marked "Concierge," "Reception," and "Cashier."

A group of tourists was also there. Some relaxed on leather couches. Others stood near their hand luggage, shifting their weight back and forth, chatting in twos and threes. The tourists were waiting for folkloric dancers who would give them some depiction of Yemeni culture.

A figure entered from the outside, clothed in black from head to foot. A black veil hung from the crown of her head. She was obviously a modern woman, entering a hotel with self-possession and without a chaperone.

There was no crash of cymbals and no blare of trumpets. But everyone in the lobby was aware of her, this unexpected depiction of Yemeni culture. She drew the eyes of the tourists and businessmen and even the hotel personnel as she walked across the lobby, her step demure. She gazed at the floor, looking neither right nor left.

At sunset on the docks of Salalah in Oman, five men were praying. The air was humid and warm, and there was no sound except that of the cruise ship pulling away from the dock.

The men all faced the same direction: north/northwest toward Mecca. One man stood in front of the others. Then they knelt on the prayer rugs. They bowed their foreheads to the ground. They sat back on their heels, still praying, and one of the men adjusted his leg, as if to avoid a cramp.

The men were alone on the dock, five small, sunset-reddened figures in the expanse of asphalt, praying as the light went from the sky.

At the airport in Sana, eight or nine Muslim women sat waiting to be called for their flight. The chairs they occupied were arranged in series of eights: four chairs on each side facing each other. Small tables stood between the second and third chairs. On these, travelers could rest small items of luggage.

Chadors cloaked the heads and bodies of the Muslim women in black cloth. Black gloves covered their hands and black veils masked their faces. Only their eyes and a framing of olive skin around them were visible.

It was so crowded in the waiting room that at first we had to stand. Then two seats became available opposite our friend Elisabeth. Donanne and I took seats.

Next to Elisabeth and across from us sat one of the veiled women. It was hard to make any judgments of her from the kind, lively eyes that watched us. But guessing from her girth, she appeared to be middle-aged and was content with her life. Elisabeth tried to strike up a conversation with her. Pushing a map before the woman, Elisabeth indicated the route of her travels.

The veiled woman observed Elisabeth as if she were a jabberer from that curious corner of outer space where unknown foreigners talk at you in airports. Then she looked at me.

Hailing from the same outer space, I pointed to myself. I tapped my chest with my hands. "I am from California," I said, pronouncing my words with both unusual clarity and unusual volume. "I am going to al-Hudayah." The woman's dark eyes measured me. "Where are you going?" I asked.

The woman's eyes narrowed. Was she frowning? She glared at another veiled woman. This woman, thin, wrapped in her chador as if it were a protective covering, sat beside me across the small table on which her packages lay. Her veiled scrutiny was unmistakably hostile.

I looked at the "friend" across from me. "Are you," I asked, pointing to her, "going to Cairo?" Her mystified look left me bereft of other possible destinations.

Then she spoke. She offered a brief burst of unintelligible gutturals—not the English I had hoped to hear.

"Riyadh?" Donanne asked her. "Are you going to Riyadh?"

More gutturals and I recognized among them something that sounded like Riyadh. Suddenly we were all smiling at one another. And just as suddenly etiquette forced me to surrender my seat to the woman who had originally occupied it.

Withdrawing, I watched Donanne and Elisabeth continue a sign-language conversation with the veiled women.

Donanne formed her arms as if they were cradling a baby and pointed at the Arab woman. In return, she smiled and held up four fingers. She indicated the heights of her children in stair steps. Donanne reciprocated. All the while the thin Arab woman, the one who used her chador as armor, looked on with uncertainty.

Soon the women were comparing jewelry. In the souks we had visited, Muslim women crowded jewelry stores. Following local custom, they wore much of the family wealth on their person in the form of gold.

Our "friend" scrutinized a gold bracelet brought from America. She shook her head and waved her hands along a horizontal plane. By her standards, the (quite lovely) bracelet was no good.

Donanne showed her a necklace—made of coral and "white metal," presumably silver—that we had bought only a few hours before. The woman placed her hands across it. Then she looked at Donanne, placed her hands before her and put both thumbs up.

Everyone laughed, and Donanne felt she had made a friend of an Arab woman whose face she had never seen.

We were given royal dispensation to enter Jiddah. Tourists are not welcome in Saudi Arabia, so we were a study group. The women wore scarves over their heads and over their bodies chadors, black high-necked outer garments that reached almost to their ankles.

It was a little like dress-up for adults. Some of the women even bought face-coverings: pieces of black cloth with eye-holes that fastened behind the head with

Velcro. The women also bought sheer black veils to cover the crowns of their heads.

Once masked and veiled, our "study group" women were difficult to distinguish from Saudi women shopping in the souk. One of our men lost track of his veiled wife, then saw and went to her. When he touched her shoulder, she spoke sharply to him in Arabic. The woman he had touched was not his wife.

While the Saudi women were dressed in black, their husbands wore white robes with red-and-white headcloths. Usually the children had on Western clothes. It was charming to see a white-robed Saudi man pushing a stroller and keeping two other young children in tow while his wife floated from store window to store window, seeing what was on display.

We were told you could ride horseback into Petra, in southwest Jordan. You could even take a horse-drawn cart.

But we wanted to walk through the narrow corridor of cliffs. And we wanted to do it alone—before the mounts and the carts of our companions forced us to eat their dust. So we hurried into the mile-long passageway. In some places it seemed no wider than our arm span. They all laughed, those who rode or were driven. But let them. Walking in, I believe, is the only sensible way to enter Petra, the ancient Nabatean-Roman trade entrepôt carved into the red rock of Jordan. The cliffs close you in, but they open your imagination. Each step takes you closer to a mystery. With each step, anticipation of what's ahead builds.

As you near the entrance into Petra, the trek rewards you with glimpses of an immense colonnaded façade. But it's not a building. It's an elaborate rock carving from which a building has been made. Beyond the cliffs open into a wide valley filled with carved monuments.

After an hour the carts and the horses were anxious to return. Suddenly they were gone. The two of us who had walked in had the valley to ourselves. We climbed about the monuments for another hour in the heat and silence of early afternoon.

Returning alone, we felt a strange satisfaction. Petra was a secret for hundreds of years. The narrow shade-cooled corridor we were passing through had protected the "rose-red city" against visitors in the past and kept its secret well. But not from us.

The buildings of greater Cairo stretch all the way out to the pyramids now.

When I first saw them in the early '60s, I was en route to a posting in central Africa. They stood then on the edge of the desert. I climbed Cheops, wondering about the *fellahin* who had moved those mammoth blocks of stone under the relentless sun.

I had a sense of being alone with the Sphinx. I beheld it for a long time, feeling that we were connected personally. (And why shouldn't we be? We were alone on the edge of emptiness.)

Nowadays, apartments crowd virtually up to the feet of the Sphinx. Visiting the great pyramids of Giza, you no longer feel alone with them in an unpeopled desert. Instead, you stand "alone" at the edge of a busy parking lot in a high-rise suburb.

Should such a fate befall great monuments?

We had tea at the hotel in Cairo. It was the end of the trip. A couple sat nearby, looking out across the hotel garden that had once been the playground of a pasha.

We heard the woman say, "You know, I'm not really sure what to make of what I've seen on this trip. I mean, you see women veiled head to foot and you think, how dreadful! It infuriates you that the men of Muslim society—you assume it's the men who do it—force women to move about outdoors like black blobs, without any possibility to express their individuality."

The man with her nodded and sipped his tea.

"Then in Jiddah when we actually put on the veil, I must say, I thought: Hmm, this is rather nice. I didn't have to worry all the time about how I looked, what I was wearing. Men didn't eye me, didn't check out my body.

"Then we get here to Cairo. There are women on the billboards again, smiling enticingly, showing their bodies—not in bikinis, of course—but still displaying. It makes you realize the extent to which we've let sex drive our society."

"Hmm," said the man.

"Do you think a resurgent Islam is really threatening our way of life?"

"I doubt it." The man shrugged. "The media has to write about something." He took another sip of his tea.

"The men praying at sundown. I liked seeing that."

The man nodded.

"Didn't you like seeing that? You pray."

"In my closet."

"Closet religionist."

"That's the way we do it," said the man. "We've all made a tacit agreement that our society has two cultures: a secular mass entertainment culture we can all share and a private culture. We often let the secular culture be driven by sex and greed. And we put matters of faith in the private culture and mention them only to our very closest friends."

"I'm not sure I like that," the woman said. Then she added: "You know, I'm not sure Arabs are as dangerous as we've been led to believe."

The man shrugged.

"I'm just glad we've seen for ourselves," she said. "It makes a difference."

He suggested, "Shall we have more tea?"

"Welcome Home"
by Devon Alisa Abdallah

FOR AS LONG AS I CAN REMEMBER I have wanted to visit to Lebanon, the land of my ancestors, the "homeland." The homeland in all its backward ways and mystique. One must always be proud to be Lebanese. It is the best thing in the world to be. To be Lebanese is to be blessed—the food, the values, family. I learned this at the knees of relatives who had never visited Lebanon.

My great grandparents on my father's aside immigrated from Lebanon to California almost a hundred years ago. Two Abdallah brothers married two Rishwain sisters; they were all from a small mountain village in northern Lebanon and immigrated to the land of opportunity for just that - opportunity, specifically economic opportunity. To this day, the Rishwains and the Abdallahs are intrinsically tied; many of the two families still live in California and in our family's Catholic village in Lebanon.

My jidue, my father's father, never visited. He had wanted to; my grandma and he even mapped out the hospitals closest to our village due to his bad health. But my grandparents never did visit. Civil war broke out, life got in the way, and then my jidue died.

My dad has never visited Lebanon. He is always waiting for it to calm down "over there." I had dreamed of visiting Lebanon, our homeland, with my father: the two of us exploring her rich culture, visiting our village, searching out relatives, sightseeing, eating food we were familiar with and some we were not, just the two of us, a father-daughter team. A few years ago when Lebanon was bouncing back to her former glory, a tourist destination once again, the banking capital of the Middle East, the Riviera of the Arab World, I realized it would not happen. Once again my father was waiting for it to calm down. I knew then there would be no father-daughter adventure; I would make the journey on my own.

Nobody else in my immediate family had ever made the journey "back home." Not my cousins, not my aunties, my dad's sisters. One of my dad's cousins had visited her father's village of Francis, but not her mother's village, the village of Abdallahs. When I went, I would be the sole adventurer, an ambassador for the American Abdallahs. Contemplating the trip, part of me felt a huge responsibility to make sure nothing unpleasant happened, that I had a lovely trip so as to bring back fond memories of Lebanon, her beauty and her people so my nervous family would perhaps visit one day. But I am getting ahead of myself.

I am mixed. I am not white and I am not Lebanese. I am white and I am Lebanese. I am both and I am neither. I identify with both cultures. I wear a white privilege with my light skin, blue-green eyes and European features. At the same time, I have a quintessential Arab last name, one associated with Islam.

If you see me, you will have an entirely different impression of me than if you first read my surname. Most people who see me without knowing my last name or heritage assume I am white and treat me accordingly. I have heard horrible racist jokes and remarks because I am assumed to be one of them. People have physically recoiled when they learned I am of Arab descent as if my Arabness is contagious and will infect them. Unfortunately, I hear the things many people would keep to themselves or refrain from saying in front of a darker skinned person or a "real" Arab. Many people, who do learn of my last name, assume it is my husband's name with some, you can tell, not understanding how a white woman could marry a dirty Arab.

On just seeing my last name, people assume I am olive skinned with brown eyes and black hair; many assume I will have my head covered. I have had numerous double takes when walking into job interviews or other events. When looking for jobs, I am sure my family name will be a disadvantage. Even if people are not blatantly racist, many on a subconscious level feel uncomfortable with a Muslim or an Arab. Phone calls can be interesting too. People speak slowly as if I do not understand English. Muslims, assuming I am Muslim, call me "Sister" and say "Salam Al-lakyum".

My mother's family consists primarily of white Southerners. My parents divorced when I was young, but lived in the same town. While I have been influenced by both parents, culturally my father's Lebanese heritage had greater impact on me. Perhaps because I am my parents' oldest child. Perhaps because I spent more time with my father's family since they are closer and live in one location. My sister and I would visit the family every summer and spend weeks with my grandparents, aunties, cousins and even second cousins.

In California, we would call my grandfather "jidue," the Arabic word for grandpa, have grape leaves rolling contests, eat huge Lebanese meals my grandma and aunties would prepare and spend hours together as a family. More importantly, from a young age I was taught to identify with being an Abdallah, that being Lebanese was an honor. I grew up knowing I was part Lebanese, never really thinking about being white or that others would view me as such.

I was living in Seattle now. As I prepared for my trip, nobody in the family wanted me to visit Lebanon. Not Lebanon in the summer of 2007, two years after former Prime Minister Hariri's assassination, a year after the Israeli-Lebanese war, a time of fighting between the Lebanese Army and Fatah al-Islam in the North, amidst protests and talk of another civil war. But for the first time in years, I had accumulated enough holiday time at work, was not in school and had enough money to visit Lebanon.

My mother was afraid the Israelis would start bombing again. My dad feared I would not be able to keep my mouth shut and Hezbollah would kidnap me. Friends and other family members were sure I would get blown up in a car bomb intended for someone else. Or war would break out... Friends and family kept telling me to be careful.

Of course I told everyone I met I was visiting Lebanon. As my departure date approached, my biggest stress became finding a little black dress. I had nothing to wear in what I envisioned to be wild nights of partying and dancing in Beirut. I had heard stories of how fancy the women in Lebanon dressed.

Thinking about our family village, I realized I did not even know where our family is from. My jidue and all of his brothers are dead. My grandmother, my father's mother, knew only that her husband's family was from the north, a village in the mountains outside Tripoli.

I started doing investigative work Arab style; in other words, I listened to the family gossip. Through the Abdallah grapevine I learned that a relative of mine—a Rishwain —had visited our family village. I phoned the woman, a second or third cousin of mine. From her, I got phone numbers and names of a couple of Abdallahs in Lebanon and the name of our village—Serhel.

It was weeks before I could actually phone my relatives in Lebanon. Part of me was nervous they would not want to see a distant relative from America. I kept telling myself I did not phone due to the time difference between Seattle and Lebanon. I eventually contacted Jeanette Abdallah. She seemed sweet and more than welcoming, but I was still nervous about visiting my relatives and Serhel. Would they really accept me as an Abdallah, as Lebanese? Every person has such feelings when they visit the family homeland, in particular mixed people who often look physically different from their relatives and by some people's standards are not "pure."

As the date of my departure grew closer, my parents insisted I should not go. I had friends stuck in Lebanon during the Israeli-Lebanese 2006 war. I had heard their stories including tales of escaping Lebanon—all in a different manner. I watched the news religiously including Lebanon's The Daily Star and Al Jazeera. I could always avoid the Tripoli if it was too violent.

Perhaps I am stupid, but I was never afraid. I do not think I was naïve. But I knew that I had to go; my very soul depended upon it. I could not explain it to anyone or even myself for that matter. I just knew visiting Lebanon now was something I had to do.

It was ten days before I phoned my relatives. Some of my initial nervousness stemmed from how the family would view me. I wondered, "Would I be a bother?" I will say in Lebanon I was accepted as Lebanese. For the first time in my life I felt as if I fit in. Upon learning my family name the Lebanese insisted I was Lebanese and welcomed me into Lebanon. In fact, when I landed in Beirut the first words out of the Lebanese immigration official's mouth after opening my passport were, "Welcome home."

No Lebanese person I had spoken to either inside or outside of Lebanon had ever heard of Serhel. I could not find it on any map. I phoned Jeanette Abdallah for directions. The Lebanese give directions by landmarks, so I handed the phone over to Husam, the brother of a friend in Seattle with whom I was staying. He spoke with Jeanette in Arabic to get specific directions.

Two days later, Husam and I hopped in the car and headed from Saida to Serhel. Not trusting the taxi drivers, he insisted on driving me.

As we wound through the mountains, I was stunned by the beauty. The air felt so crisp. I almost felt as if I was home - not in the "I am finally home" cheesy sense but as if I were near Seattle. The mountains in Lebanon are not as grand as the Cascades in Washington State and the cedar trees are smaller than the evergreens of the Pacific Northwest. But there is something amazing about smelling sea air from the Mediterranean while winding through a mountain range.

Following Jeanette's directions, we drove through an army checkpoint, took a left and continued to drive. We passed through the "large village" of Tourz, not much more than houses off a paved winding road, and kept going. I was getting excited. My jidue never had a chance to visit where his parents were from. Neither had my dad or his sisters. But I was doing it!

We soon came upon a sign reading "Sereel." Husam stopped; I took a photo. I could not stop smiling! I was here!!! I could not really believe it. Any remaining nervousness about meeting my family dissipated.

In the Serhel square a young woman came up to our car to tell us in perfect English she was Mary Abdallah. "Just park the car where it is." Mary turned out to be an American cousin of mine and the same age as me.

We walked into the apartment building. There I met Jeanette Abdallah who gave me a big hug and called me "honey" all the time. Mary took me upstairs to the apartment of her father, Tony Abdallah.

Tony returned to Lebanon when his wife was taken ill because the health care costs in the States were too high. Mary moved to Lebanon two years ago to help her parents. Mary's mother has since passed and Tony is not in the best of health. We chatted and I was shown an old photo with several of my relatives in it including my jidue, grandma, Tony, Uncle Al. It brought tears to my eyes to realize the closest my jidue had gotten to Lebanon was in an old photo.

We spent the next few hours eating and visiting in Jeanette's apartment and then walking around the village which was quite quaint. The paved mountain road wound through it with roads like long driveways branching off it. Most of the houses sat on the mountainside facing the valley. You could see across the valley to a larger village sitting on the facing mountainside. The views were lovely. The air was fresh and tastes clean, especially after the oppressive humidity of Saida and Beirut. Everywhere grapevines reached over driveways and archways. Olive trees were spattered throughout the village. Husam cut a piece of one for me to take to my dad.

Serhel is unique, a Catholic village; most Christians in Lebanon are Maronites. We visited the little church which has beautiful, brightly painted murals of the Virgin Mary, Jesus, and saints. Behind the church is a shrine where a dead priest, mummified in his full robes and encased in glass, is reputed to dispense miracles.

As we walked through Serhel, Mary pointed out more Abdallah households. I seemed to be related to most everyone in the village. We passed by the old Rishwain house where my great-grandmother lived.

Back upstairs having a final farewell with Tony, my new family kept asking me to spend a few days. I could not believe once I had been nervous about how they would accept me. They even decided that I should meet Tony's son John, Mary's brother, so we could get married. We would not even have to change last names; after all, we are all Abdallahs. I promised next time I would stay a few days. I will be back and I will bring my dad.

When Husam and I started back to Saida, I felt a little sad. I wished I had spent the night with my family. But I know I will return.

I Fight an Iranian
by Scott Davis

October 10, 1987.

I ARRIVED IN DAMASCUS, THE CAPITAL OF SYRIA, LATE SATURDAY NIGHT. I had never been to the Middle East before. I had no friends here, no near or distant relatives, no ethnic connections. On this date, the radical Shiite Muslim group Hezbollah was still holding Americans hostage nearby in Beirut, Lebanon, and the State Department had banned Americans from entering that country. Just a few years earlier, Hezbollah had killed 241 US Marines in a suicide attack in Beirut. And, a few years before that, Shiites in the Iranian capital Tehran had held 52 Americans hostage for 444 days. My country, at this moment, was an ally and arms supplier to Saddam Hussein's Iraq. Saddam had attacked Iran and was spilling Iranian blood in the sand at an alarming rate. Relations between the US and the Shiite Muslims in Beirut and Tehran were tense. In the waters of the Gulf, there had been attacks and counterattacks.

Perhaps it was fitting, then, that my sole guide and protector in this country was a Shiite Muslim wearing a blue business suit. Saleh and I had arrived on the same flight. We met in the line at Customs. Saleh was of Indian extraction, a Ugandan who lived in London. He had come to Damascus on a serious religious mission that would carry me into the arms of the Hezbollah. He was a Muslim fundamentalist. Still, he was a friendly face.

From the airport, we made our way to the al-Boustan Hotel downtown, where all the full-sized rooms were taken. A porter showed Saleh and me a tiny room on the seventh floor. The porter was an old man dressed in a synthetic uniform that was losing its shape, and the room did not look much better. Still, the night manager was asking thirty-two dollars—in hard currency. Saleh scowled when he saw the room. Our inspection complete, the porter led us back to the lobby. It was 2:00 AM and I was exhausted. But Saleh was energized.

"I have thoughts about the price," said Saleh. He spoke to the night manager, a slender, dark-haired man of twenty-five who stood behind the counter. "Such a small room, scarcely with space to breathe. Under the circumstances I think we should pay no more than fifteen dollars." Saleh stood facing the night manager across the polished wooden counter.

"You do us great honor to seek accommodations with us," said the night manager in crisp, perfect English. "You must know, however, that we have our established rates and that it would be irregular and unprincipled of me to deviate from them."

"You have your rates," replied Saleh, "but surely they apply to full size rooms with enough oxygen to sustain a guest for an entire evening."

"The room is small but entirely sufficient. We keep it available for emergencies such as yours, when travelers come to us late at night with no place else to stay and beg us for a small space in which to rest themselves for the evening. And of course we offer the same banquet at breakfast as for our guests in other rooms."

"We are foreigners," said Saleh. "We are guests in your country, your city. We are, in a way, guests in your home. Has not the entire world heard of Arab hospitality? Is it not proper to give us the very best you have, to take the slippers from your own feet to give us comfort?" The night manager glanced down for a moment, then looked back at Saleh.

"You speak well and you must know how my heart has sorrow for your late arrival this evening and your carelessness in the matter of reservations."

"How long does this go on?" I said to the porter. He didn't speak English, but caught my meaning and shrugged. In a few hours Saleh was supposed to be at a Shiite shrine outside town—the burning, spiritual purpose of his visit and a must for this Muslim—yet he seemed to have forgotten.

"Yes," said Saleh. "But let us consider that half the night is gone, which should bring a commensurate deduction in the price of the room."

"As you undoubtedly understand," said the night manager, "I am a person of great authority in this hotel during the evening, but I do not set the rates and I do not have the power to alter them."

"Look," I said. "I'll pay the difference. I haven't slept for two days." Saleh held up his hand for silence.

"You must admit," said Saleh to the night manager, "that it is late and unlikely that anyone else will rent this room for the night. If we do not take it for fifteen dollars, then no one will take it. Under the circumstances, do you feel that your superior would rather you collected fifteen dollars, or nothing?"

I began to carry our bags to the open elevator. The porter held the elevator door. I shoved my passport across the counter to the night manager and tugged on Saleh's sleeve.

"Tonight, since my friend is tired, we will agree to stay in shameful conditions at this inflated price of thirty-two dollars which amounts to robbery, assault, and three sex crimes added in," Saleh smiled. "But in the morning we will speak with your superior to ask for a deduction. And in consideration of your desire to keep your position at this establishment, we will not tell him of the grievous difficulties and aggravations that you have caused to come down upon our heads. And for this favor of silence on our part, we must insist that your porter immediately transform our room into spotless condition, with a suitable bed for my friend, and all the amenities that travelers in our position have a right to expect when they put down one half their year's income for a simple night's lodging."

Saleh placed his passport on the counter, smiled, and followed me to the elevator. By the time the porter had set up a bed for me and Saleh had performed prayers to make up for those missed during the flight it was 4:00 AM. Saleh glanced at his watch and announced his decision to wait up an hour so that he could perform his morning prayers at the proper time. I thought this plan unwise. How could he endure a four-day pilgrimage if he did not get his rest? I offered to set the alarm on my wristwatch.

Saleh agreed and got under the covers. I fiddled with the alarm, and he was asleep before I turned out the lights.

We slept through the alarm, and at 10:00 AM I woke to the sound of traffic on the street below. Saleh was still asleep. He had come a long way for a religious purpose, was trying his best to get everything right, and now he had botched the morning prayer, his first religious duty of the day. I expected him to be agonized with guilt. I shook him. "You've missed your morning prayers," I said softly. "I'm so sorry. It's entirely my fault. I should have properly wakened you." Saleh sprang from bed.

"You and I have paid dearly for breakfast," he announced. "The manager would love to have us miss our meal. We must go quickly."

Saleh had come to Damascus to attend a festival at Sayida Zeinab, a Shiite shrine on the outskirts of town. With casualties rising in the Iran-Iraq war, the shrine had grown ever more popular. The Iranian government gave women all-expense-paid trips to Sayida Zeinab as compensation for the loss of their sons in battle. The temple had minarets, a tiled courtyard, and in the center a small structure with two enormous gold doors enclosing the tomb of Zeinab. The place had cost a mint to restore, but Iran had picked up the tab. In all, it was perfectly sized for an intimate mass meeting.

By the time we arrived, Saleh had missed two prayers. He hurried into the inner sanctum while I sat on low marble steps on the south side of the shrine and rested my head on my knees. The sun was pleasant, and I was beginning to sleep when I sensed movement. I looked up and saw five young men, their faces two feet from mine.

"Who are you?" their leader said in English.

"I am an American. Who are you?"

"We are the Hezbollah." I had no obvious means of escape, so I smiled. "Nice to meet you," I said.

The young men stared at me for a few moments, then one looked at the others and smiled slightly. I had expected snarling terrorists, but I sensed that these particular young men had been raised well by good mothers. They introduced themselves, we shook hands, and they began to teach me the error of my ways. After what I would learn was the customary posturing, I found that they were more interested in watching the movies of Sylvester Stallone than they were of dying for their cause. In fact, they were Lakers fans who rooted for Kareem Abdul Jabar and never missed a game on satellite TV, beamed into Beirut by the Christian stations. Still, I was curious. I had come to Damascus, as opposed to Beirut, specifically to avoid the Hezbollah. What were these guys doing here?

"Where else can we go on vacation?" explained Jamal.

Over the next several days, I noticed that the Syrians seemed to trust the thousand or more Hezbollah who were attending the festival—not. Syrian military helicopters flew continuously over the festival and it followed my Hezbollah companions whenever we walked into the neighboring village. Each day, while Saleh talked theology with the imams, Jamal and Mohammad and I walked in circles around the shrine. Women—

many of them clad head to toe in black gauze *abayas*—had spread blankets on the covered promenade at the edge of the courtyard and sat amidst their bundles while they watched the younger generation walking past. Occasionally someone with a battery-powered megaphone would begin to chant and a group of solemn-faced men, standing in a circle, would do a hopping dance, beating their breasts and sometimes beating their backs with chains.

"Hussein, Hussein," explained Mohammad. "They are having sorrow over Hussein."

I was wearing Levis and was easy to identify as a foreigner. When other pilgrims approached and challenged me, Jamal and Mohammad interceded. "He's OK," they said in rapid Arabic. "He's with us."

After four days of festival going and little sleep, everyone in the temple was exhausted. Saleh was preoccupied with quixotic missions—he was debating theology with austere imams and spent the rest of his time trying to find his shoes (he would lose them in the pile whenever he went into the sanctuary to pray). Late in the evening, foolishly, I ventured out on my own, beyond the protection of Jamal and Mohammad, and was forced to defend myself in halting Arabic to one hostile, suspicious young man after another. I was demonstrating the good intentions of one American, yet the effort tired me and made me irritable. Normally I am a peace-loving guy, especially when outnumbered three thousand to one. Now, however, I was beginning to lose my cool. At ten o'clock I met a young man, an English major at the university in Beirut, a member of the Hezbollah. He offered to shoot me with his AK-47 if only I would come to Beirut to make this pleasure possible. At midnight I met a rude young man who mocked the US Marines killed in Beirut by the Hezbollah suicide bomber, and succeeded in exhausting my last traces of good humor. I was annoyed at these Muslims, tired of playing the compliant American. My survival instincts were still alive, however, so I kept my mouth shut and hurried toward the exit. But where was Saleh? By now he was staying in the nearby village with friends. I needed to say good-bye. I turned back and found him standing below the clock, a look of triumph on his face: he had found his shoes, wedged in a corner beneath a heap of sandals. I congratulated him and excused myself for the evening.

At that moment a dozen grim-faced young men blocked my exit. The men stepped aside to reveal a dark, sinewy man with close-cropped hair, some kind of tough guy, an Iranian—bitter and angry, a man with no light in his eyes, a hollow man. In a few seconds twenty people encircled us, then fifty. The Iranian and I faced each other in a small opening in the center of the crowd. Saleh had been trailing me, and I glanced to my right but I couldn't spot him, then I saw him ten paces behind me, caught in conversation with a religious man wearing spectacles, oblivious to my predicament, unreachable. I looked back at the Iranian.

"*Iranee Amerikee*," shouted the young men. "*Iranee Amerikee. Yala, yala,*" Fight, fight. The shouting became a chant and the chant repeated again and again, growing louder, swelling until it filled the courtyard. It was hot and I was tired, so tired, my head aching, I was losing my grip. Still the chant continued, on and on, insinuating, hypnotic and I began to lose it—noise, color, the pressure of bodies crowding around and, in the center of my vision: the Iranian. He seemed no longer to possess his own mind. He seemed emptied of will, a vessel for the malice of the crowd. I had come to this festival as an observer—it had seemed a good idea at the time. Now, I felt like a child beaten by waves. I was nauseated, shivering, dripping sweat. I was going to pieces—but not the Iranian. The crowd affected him in a different way. It focused him, gave him a center, gave him control. His head was down, his eyes narrowed, and he seemed to grow in stature as I watched. I thought that he was preparing himself for some ultimate test, some act of glory.

A few weeks earlier the United States had entered the Gulf in an effort to protect Kuwaiti tankers from the Iran-Iraq war. The Iranians had objected and had run their torpedo-laden patrol boats into our path. On the preceding Thursday our helicopters had sunk one of these boats, killing Iranian Revolutionary Guards. On Saturday the Iranians responded with sneak attacks. Now it was Tuesday. People on the streets in Damascus watched TV in sidewalk sandwich shops and knew what was happening. They were up-to-the-minute. And now they were waiting for the American response. Especially for Hezbollah and Iranians on vacation, these incidents were fresh evidence of American treachery. Was I an opportunity for revenge?

Many in the audience had been like Jamal and Mohammad, friendly after the first few moments. But this crowd had sucked up the friendly faces. Now, as I watched, the Iranian slowly raised his head, opened his eyes, and stared straight at me. He lifted his head as though to speak and then paused—it was like a knife going through the crowd: silence, utter silence. And then he spoke quick, fierce words. By now Saleh had caught up with me. He translated. "Imam Khomeini says, 'Our war is with the American government, not with the American people.'"

At this moment, preparing to be slaughtered, I did not need a cliché. If I am going to be mauled in Damascus, I thought, at least let's be honest, there is a lot of hate between Iran and America, a lot of unfinished business.

"The hostages in Teheran in 1979 were American people," I replied in English. "So were the Marines in Beirut in 1983. So is Terry Anderson who, right now, today, you've got chained to a radiator somewhere in Lebanon. You have tortured Americans, killed Americans. Isn't this war against my people? If not, then tell me, what is?" Saleh grabbed my arm and cut in. "I must translate," he said and began babbling in Farsi. After a few minutes I tugged on his sleeve and eventually he wound down and turned to me with an explanation.

"I told him that you said you have great love for Imam Khomeini and the utmost respect for Islam, that you have observed the sincerity of the believers at this temple and…"

As Saleh continued to tell me the words that he had put into my mouth, I turned to the Iranian. Suddenly he lunged, his two thick hands gripped my neck, and he was pulling me down. In a flash I realized that I was being sucker-punched—an Islamic sneak attack. I was contemplating a countermove when, instead of a knee to my groin, the Iranian delivered three wet kisses, left cheek, right cheek, left cheek. Then he backed away and, facing me, gave a thin smile and then bowed slightly. The young men, now a hundred strong, cheered. I wiped the slobber from my cheeks. Getting kissed in public was painful enough, but to be kissed by a man, and an ugly one at that, was more than I could bear.

The Iranian grabbed my arm and led me through the crowd with Saleh trailing. We pushed and dodged until we reached a passageway and ran through it to make our escape. On the sidewalk outside the temple the Iranian again smiled and bowed slightly, then disappeared into the gloom.

Termites and Clans
by Jamal Gabobe

I AM AN AFRICAN AND a Muslim.
In February 1993, I returned to Somaliland for the first time since I left with my parents when I was five years old. This time I was there for five weeks, most of which I spent in Somaliland's capital city, Hargeisa. One clear morning at ten o'clock, I began scouting the Shaab area, which is in the western part of Hargeisa, looking for termite mounds.

Two days earlier, I had seen one of these mounds and instantly became curious about its odd shape, the prodigious amount of labor that went into its construction, and the fact that it was made of simple materials: sand mixed with termite saliva. It is difficult to see termites at work, but one can tell the result of their most recent efforts by the wet appearance of the new deposit compared with the rest of the mound.

After twenty minutes of searching, I spotted the reddish top of a termite mound behind some bushes. I waded through the bushes to find a five-foot high structure that looked like a female fertility figure, the kind I had seen in books.

I got my camera out, angled for a good shot, and was just about to press the button when I heard a man's voice declare in Somali, "You better not do that."

I turned around and saw a short, light-skinned man, wearing corduroy pants and smoking a cigarette.

"Are you talking to me?" I asked, also in Somali.

"Yes," he replied.

"Are these termite mounds yours?" I inquired.

"No, they aren't mine," he answered, "but there's a story behind what you're doing."

"What could this story be?"

The short guy puffed his cigarette a couple of times, moved a step closer to me, then asked, "Do you really want to hear it?"

"Yes."

He looked both ways, then said, "You may not believe what I'm about to tell you, but it did happen. There was this guy who was originally from here, but who lived in Saudi Arabia for many years. Two years ago he came back here and, like you, took many pictures of these termite mounds. When he returned to Saudi Arabia, he showed the pictures to the Saudi government. He told them that most Somalis were pagans who worshipped those mounds, and that he was engaged in a project to convert Somalis to Islam, and needed help."

"And what did the Saudis do?" I asked.

"They believed him and gave him a lot of money to carry out his project. He took the money, came back here, bought a lot of real estate, trucks, and cars and kept the rest of the money for himself. He's a rich man today thanks to the Saudis."

"But the Saudis know that Somalis are almost one hundred percent Muslim," I said.

"They must not know it," he answered, "otherwise they wouldn't have given him the money."

I was speechless. A complete stranger was accusing me of planning to cash in on the people of Hargeisa by misrepresenting them to the outside world, and this stranger hadn't made the slightest effort to get to know me first. A snap judgment. I was angry. Why had I listened to him in the first place?

Later that afternoon I went to the Bar Hargeisa to have dinner with two of my acquaintances. Bar Hargeisa occupies a low brick building with a courtyard, and, despite its name, does not serve alcohol—the same way that Somali coffee shops do not serve coffee but tea, although Somalis call them "coffee shops." My acquaintances Hassan and Osman were already there, sitting in the courtyard. Hassan was a grade school teacher with thick glasses and a penchant for explaining things. Osman worked at a clothing store.

I ordered lamb shanks and a side of rice. We ate and talked about the news. Hassan updated us on his marriage plans. Although it was hot, a steady breeze made it more tolerable. There were only a handful of men in the restaurant, since it was already past lunch hour.

Then I told them about my encounter with the short man and the elaborate con game he'd described. Hassan and Osman listened attentively. But as soon as I revealed the name of the alleged con artist, Hassan became angry. "He is a good man. He would never do such a thing," Hassan said.

"Yes, he did do it," replied Osman.

"How do you know he did it?" asked Hassan.

"I've heard it from several people," answered Osman.

"Come on, this whole story was made up by his enemies," said Hassan.

This went on for a while with Hassan insisting that it never happened, and Osman equally adamant that it had. After listening to their assertions and counter assertions, it gradually became clear to me that neither had any proof. Everything they said was based on hearsay. Also, since the one defending the alleged con man was from his subclan, while the one condemning him was not, and since there was no other connection between the con artist and either of them, I came to the conclusion that this was just another case of Somali clan rivalry in action. Neither Osman nor Hassan was interested in finding the truth, only in defending members of their clan and attacking those who were not.

I had seen similar arguments between Somalis abroad, but there was a major difference. If you argued or quarreled with another Somali in London or New York, and decided, as a result, not to see him or have anything to do with him, you stood a good chance of doing just that. But here in the land of Somalis, everyone belongs to a clan. Consequently, even if you succeed in avoiding your antagonist, you cannot escape other members of his clan who may number in the thousands. And clan memories last for generations.

Whenever I think of the Somali tragedy I think of the short guy who accused me of fraud without any evidence. I also imagine how easily the debate between Osman and Hassan could have turned violent. In both cases, one person was unwilling to give the other the benefit of the doubt. It is such an attitude of blind loyalty to one's group and visceral hostility towards everyone else that is at the root of the Somali catastrophe.

Walking Like an Egyptian
By Sara Rashad

I am from LA, but for the last three months I have dreamed of the pyramids. My greatest fantasy has always been to become Princess of the entire Arab world like I was when I played Princess Badr al-Budur in "Aladdin and the Magic Lamp." When I boarded a plane bound for Cairo I thought my fantasies would dissipate. I was wrong.

I slipped into an aisle seat. I was wearing a leopard print dress. My body felt like Cheez Whiz and my mind like Swiss. The man sitting beside me possessed a cow-like voice and his body was attached to the hairiest arms I had ever seen. He was wearing an egg-yolk yellow sports shirt and beige slacks, his pudgy face framed by thick, brown hair. He had a wide grin, and you could stick a quarter between his two front teeth. After a polite nod I stashed the sterilized pillow behind my head and attempted to rest. The pillow quickly became an Arabian Prince with whom I've mingled saliva time and again in my dreams.

Later, I was entertaining another fantasy: a school of sting rays attacked as I was scuba diving with my prince in Ras Mohammed at the Egypt-Israeli border. The stewardess broke my reverie with her lecture on the oxygen mask. I flipped through the pages of Vogue. Christi Turlington and Cindy Crawford on every other page. In swimsuits their breasts popped out like the two step-pyramids at Giza. Split Tooth leaned over my shoulder and stabbed the magazine with his finger. "This one very nice!" Christi in a cobalt blue leather miniskirt and jacket. I handed him the magazine, and he offered me his hand, "My name is Magdee."

"Magdil?"

"No. Magdee! Magdee! I show you." He unlocked his briefcase and grabbed his business card. He handed it to me.

"Magdee?"

"Yes, that is correct. And your name?"

"Sara."

"Ah, Sara! Arabic name in Qur'an!" He pronounced my name correctly on the first attempt, unlike most Americans.

"You Arabic girl?"

"My father is Egyptian."

"You visit him?"

I explained to him that my father was the only one of his family who had emigrated to America. At twenty-one, I was going to Egypt to visit the rest of my family for the first time.

I didn't catch a wink due to Magdee's incessant chatter, and before I knew it we had landed in Cairo. In the airport lobby I strained to see past glass doors smudgy with cigarette smoke. On the other side I saw hundreds of faces with bovine eyes as brown as mine. These images were all too familiar—I had seen them in my dreams. Poking out of the crowd I spotted a slip of crumpled paper waving in the air. The man who was waving it bellowed my name, "Sara Nabil Rashad. Sara Nabil Rashad."

I squeezed through the crowd to find a bulbous mass of flesh accompanied by a head, two arms, and two legs. "Hello. I am Sara Nabil Rashad."

"You?"

"Yes."

He inspected the slip of paper, rubbed his prune-like forehead then continued to bellow my name. He sounded like an auctioneer.

The crowd dissipated, so I made another attempt at convincing him. "Hi! I am Sara Rashad. Nabil is my father. Who are you?"

"OK, Sara!" The auctioneer pushed me away, and a new influx of travelers—robust and pungent—flattened me against a wall. All I could see was the auctioneer's arm waving in the air and his shiny head.

Plowing my way through the frantic crowd, I tugged on the auctioneer's left sleeve until I received his complete attention. "Excuse me, sir! I am Sara Rashad!" I jabbed my fingers into my chest. "Were you sent to collect me?"

"You?" The last thing he was expecting was a woman draped in leopard print. "OK, Sara!" He traipsed his eyes through the airport lobby one last time. "Passport?" I hunted for it in my backpack. He smiled at me, a look of total disbelief. He had the raunchiest teeth I have ever seen.

In the passport control area, white plastic paddle fans sliced two-month-old air. The flies weren't even dizzy. Men lit up cigarettes at the rate of two per minute. The silver-green, gritty tile floor was a storehouse of ash, cigarette butts, and peasant women crouched down to rest. Saudis stood in long, white floor-length gowns—garments that resembled tailored bed sheets. Their wives in black body-bags sat hip-to-hip on the green and blue plastic chairs. They were covered by black muslin except for a tiny slit for eyes. Children bounced on their mothers' stomachs or grabbed at their heels. The medley of Arab dialects, cigarette smoke, and body odor became more powerful minute by minute. My head spun. The auctioneer grabbed my hand, yanking me through the crowd. I tightened my grasp and kept pace.

We arrived at a green-gray room. Another official—especially rude and unintelligent—was speaking on the phone in loud, guttural tones. The auctioneer escorted me to the plastic chairs against the wall. The auctioneer left, and this new, featherheaded official stared at me. I was obviously overdressed for the occasion. He continued to stare. The minutes passed like a snail crossing the street. "Did somebody call for me?"

"I no understand."

"Did Samir Rashad ask you to take care of me?"

"Yes, don't worry. You must sit. OK! No problems!"

"Who called for me?"

"Sami Nagira Mustafa called. Chief of Police." Oh great! Tomorrow's headlines: American woman wearing jungle clothes is arrested in Cairo airport. I asked a dozen more questions and received oblique answers. I was at the man's mercy. I was losing it.

I tried to modulate my breathing. Tears welled up in my eyes. At last, the auctioneer returned with my passport and tossed it on the desk.

"OK! Come with me, Sara!" He grabbed my hand and a few minutes later, in baggage claim, I watched the last of the bags pass on the conveyor belt.

"My bags! They're not here."

"No? They will come," said the attendant. If there were a flood the Egyptians would still be smiling. The conveyor belt already had made four complete cycles. The crew unloaded stray baggage. Still no sign of my maroon suitcases. I filled out paperwork.

The crocodile in my throat continued snapping at my vocal chords. I couldn't speak. I returned the paperwork, then sat in a row of plastic chairs.

"Miss . . . you need taxi?" asked an official. He disappeared into the back office. I stared at the stragglers from my plane and swallowed my tears. There was one man left. He offered me a cigarette. After smoking it, I swung my pack over my shoulder, pulled down my skirt, and recharged my demeanor.

I pushed open the steel double-doors and wandered into a crowd full of waves, smiles, cigarettes, and hand-drawn signs. Hundreds of faces that resembled my own stared back at me. Then I saw an apparition. My father? The man was holding a cardboard sign with my name on it. I pushed my way through the crowd and tossed my arms around the stranger—my father's brother. People lunged toward me from all directions! Somebody prodded my left shoulder. I turned my head to find a five-foot-tall woman supported by a cane, Nanny Zuba! I bent down to hug her. Children galloped toward me and pulled me down to offer their love. A boy close to my age grabbed my backpack and introduced himself as my cousin Basheer. He asked about the rest of my luggage.

"They lost it," I said. Basheer laughed. A security guard approached and informed us that my bags had been found in London and would arrive in two days. We left for home in several cars. The city of Cairo stretched out across the blackness of the sky.

When I finally fell asleep, it was the deepest sleep I had experienced in three months. In the morning I wandered downstairs. A robust woman rushed towards me with a cup of Turkish coffee. Her name was Hoda. She had lived with the family as house maid for over ten years. As I took the first sip, the doorbell rang. Cousins, aunts, uncles, and their children surrounded me, grabbed my cheeks, and showered me with kisses. We sat down on couches. Abdelbaie, one of my nine uncles, teaches about Islam in remote villages throughout Egypt. "Do you know the story of the Qur'an?" he said.

"No," I replied. Everyone else had heard the story many times before. As we spoke, the kids started playing and the women began their own conversations.

"It's your history! You must know it!" He proceeded to describe the creation of the world as it is depicted in the Qur'an.

I had never known the story of the Qur'an. My father has been a ghost throughout most of my life, passing in and out at his convenience, assisting me financially as a way to express his love. We never had a conversation about his past, his life in Egypt, and what brought him to America. That is why I had always dreamed of going to Egypt— to fill in some of these gaps. By being close to people who knew him as a child, who understood his ambitions, I hoped to feel closer to him as well.

During my time there I came to know my father through the men and women of his family—my family, through the crowded city, and through the Egyptian people themselves. The Egyptians I met possessed a vitality which has remained unconquered by famine or foe. In Egypt, you cannot survive without a tenacious sense of humor against the poverty, the corrupt government, the time warp that makes everything happen tomorrow and tomorrow takes a week. Beneath each wizened face lay secrets never whispered. Every Egyptian man and woman was a vessel of a hundred tales that could not be spoken. Still, I learned what I could by documenting every conversation.

For the previous three months I had imagined what Egypt would be like. The reality, it turned out, was different. Egypt was painful, and yet, I now realize, it was my home.

Moon Over Dakar
by Frederic Hunter

OVER THE ATLANTIC OCEAN THE PLANE MOVED through the night sky in the light of a brilliant moon, approaching the coast of Africa. Four years earlier I had flown out of Nairobi after two years' work as a USIS officer in the Congo, unsure if I would ever return to the continent. Now, surprisingly, I was returning to Muslim

North Africa as a tyro foreign correspondent—emphasis on the tyro.

The pilot announced our descent into Dakar. Then he added, "We have great news! Americans have just landed on the moon!" My wife and joined the spontaneous applause. As Americans we could not help feeling proud.

As we crossed the tarmac, the moon shone above us, glowing white in the shape of a melon slice. What were the men up there doing? How did they feel?

"Ce soir," I told the driver who taxied us to the airport hotel, "il y a des hommes sur la lune." I pointed to the moon above us. "Vous avez entendu de ça?"

"Oui, m'sieur," he answered, humoring me. "Vous voulez engagé mon taxi pour demain? Je suis à votre disposition." But we declined his offer to hire his taxi the next day.

From the balcony of our hotel room the next morning we watched sun-sparkled Atlantic rollers lapping at the shore of Africa. But even as they sent balmy air and salty pungency toward us, I was feeling frantic pangs of inadequacy. It was my first day as an Africa Correspondent in Africa. I had perhaps had ideas of becoming a latter day Ibn Batutta, that great traveler, a Maghreb Berber, the quintessential enlightened man, whose Muslim faith undergirded his intellectual curiosity. Ibn Batutta had traveled the Mediterranean world and even as far as China in the 14th century while Europe still lay in the long sleep of the Middle Ages. I had learned of him while taking a masters degree in African Studies at UCLA. Now, big foreign correspondent that I was, I did not have the slightest idea of how to go about scratching up some copy.

I felt trapped in the luxury beach hotel out by the airport. It seemed impossible to chase down any news there. The hotel news kiosk was inexplicably closed. The American Embassy had declared a holiday. The room clerk had not listened to his radio that morning and could tell me nothing. I craned my body far out over the balcony of our room, trying to catch breeze-blown bits of news in French from a radio playing somewhere below us.

I asked myself, "What am I doing in this job?"

Nothing seemed to work in Africa. That, of course, was its charm! And my wife, the daughter of Foreign Service parents, loved that aspect of it. But it was hardly something an Africa Correspondent could report.

We took an ancient bus into Dakar. It stopped often. At the airport there had been plenty of seats, but soon it grew crowded. The passengers laughed and yakked; babies cried. Passengers pressed against one another. No one seemed to respect that which Americans hold so dear: private space. Packing the aisle, passengers began to block the flow of air from the windows. The temperature rose in the bus. The heat released the odors of humanity.

The bus took us through Ouakam, a shantytown of wood and metal scrap, a home to peasants seeking urban survival and a better life, people who had fled servitude to a drought-plagued land. It was a place of the odors of decaying garbage, of cook fires and sweating bodies. Ouakam overwhelmed me: with its laughter, its color, with its communality, its vitality, its open-air sociability—and with its crowding, poverty and dirtiness. The smells, the heat, the closeness in the bus: all these afflicted me. Overload shut down my senses. My head swam. What, I wondered, was wrong with me? I had come to report on Africa and I was woozy with culture shock. Meanwhile, more like Ibn Batutta than I could be, Donanne was grinning, drinking in the sensations, loving them.

Leaving the bus at last, we walked around the center of Dakar, a city of tall buildings and noisy hubbub. Despite the veneer of French culture from its colonial past, it pulsated with Africanness. I was glad to witness that again. My head stopped swirling. I interviewed some people, got their reactions to a man being on the moon. We made arrangements to move the next day to a hotel in the center of town.

Later, standing again on the balcony of our room, I felt better about Africa, better about me. Below me I watched a woman walking in the hotel garden. She moved in clouds of cloth, within a yellow-patterned fabric wrapped about her waist. Above that a pink bodice floated. And above that a blue bandanna of satiny sheen, elaborately tied, ensconced her head. Slowly, sinuously, the woman drifted along, moving with that matter-of-fact African grace.

Observing her, I realized that she was walking into the copy of the first Africa-datelined story I would write. She would lead my American readers across the long bridge they would have to cross to understand who she was. It was that long span from America's ready acceptance of modern technology and astronauts on the moon into traditional Africa where the skills set involved living in a city on nothing a day and finding joy in it, where news of the moon landing was being met with skepticism.

"Allah will not allow men to walk on the moon," people had told me in Dakar. "The moon is sacred. Allah will place in the sky a facsimile of the moon. It will deceive the Americans."

They were saying: "The moon is hot. It will burn up any men who try to land on it."

They were saying, "These American astronauts are demons! They deny the existence of God!" They were saying, "Men on the moon? It is a white man's lie. Haven't they always lied to us?"

I wrote the piece and filed it. That made me a working correspondent.

And looking at the moon, I couldn't help thinking: Wouldn't Ibn Batutta have loved to take that trip!

On the Back of a Donkey
by Hanna Eady

MY GRANDFATHER AND I SHARED THE SAME name. Grandmother called me "Little Hanna." Grandfather was "Big Hanna." The year was 1964, I was eight, and I lived in a flat-roofed house of limestone blocks chinked with mud and plastered with mud inside and out. This was in Buqayah, or what the Israelis called "ancient Peqiin," a remote northern village of Palestinian Christians, Druze, Muslims, and Jews in the Upper Galilee Mountains. Our two churches were small stone buildings: one was an Eastern Orthodox church down by the water mill, and the other a Catholic church on top of the mountain. The Druze worshipped in private, the Muslims did not have a mosque (they were mostly refugees from 1948), and the Jews worshipped in an old temple not far from our house.

It was August, and the night was cold. My grandmother came to my bed and woke me, and I sat up and tried hard not to fall asleep once again. The previous evening I had volunteered, begged my grandfather to take me with him to the small orchard where we grew olives. Some of our trees were very old, hundreds of years old, and some were young and needed a lot of care. I got my wish. "I am up. I am up," I kept saying. I finally opened my eyes and saw nothing but the weak, flickering light of an oil lamp. It was dark and everything was still. Nothing moved except the faint shadow of my grandfather, packing. Everyone else in the house slept. All the children in the village slept, and I thought that all the children in the world slept as well. I was in a different time, *nuss lile,* the midnight hour that the big people talked about. I had never known it before.

In a few minutes I was dressed in worn jeans and a cotton shirt and stood outside the doorway in the dark. I held a knapsack and a large canteen wrapped in cloth soaked in cold water. Our village seemed strange. It was dark and quiet, and the air was still. The village had lost its beat, as if it were dead. My grandfather brought out the donkey, no one in Buqayah had a car, and, in those years, cars came up the narrow road once or twice a day, at most. Donkeys, however, were everywhere. Every family had at least one. Ours was *himar kisrawi,* a donkey from Kisra, a nearby Druze village where donkeys were well-bred, well-fed, and respected. With a weaker donkey, my grandfather would have walked and let me ride, but with a strong healthy *kisrawi* we both rode. My grandfather was a lean, small man, wore a thin shirt, and covered his head with a white *kaffiah.* I wrapped my arms around his waist and rested my face against his back to keep warm. It was two o'clock in the morning.

We left the village behind and soon were passing other donkeys carrying farmers like us, but none with a child. My grandfather recognized these men from a distance. There were few farmers from our village who traveled to the groves so early, and those who did admired one another. "That's Abu Sharif Muhanna over there, and Abu Issa Raddi clearing under his trees, and look at Abu Yosef Abbass's grove. You can tell he tends it every day." We reached a higher point. Grandfather looked up to the constellations in the sky and named a few. "This is Thuraya," he said, the Pleiades, "and over there is the Mizan and al-Aqrab," Libra and Scorpio, "and that, all that," he motioned across the sky, "is Darb al-Tabanat, the women who carry bales of hay on their heads leaving trails behind them," the Milky Way.

We reached the top of the mountain on a dirt track that forked to the west, and I looked down and saw New Peqiin, an Israeli town with bright lights that cut through the darkness. A strange sight. The town looked like it was on fire, or like a star had fallen on it. Light but no smoke. It was like the burning bush of Moses: it burned but was not consumed. "Don't let the settlement fool you with its lights," my grandfather explained, "nobody is awake. They leave their electric lights on to keep their chickens awake so they'll eat and lay a second egg." We turned east to our grove and started working.

My grandfather was a humble man, a good boss. He never rushed me. We worked till eight and then sat down to eat our breakfast of *khubiz raqiqs*—very thin bread dipped in olive oil, with goat cheese and black olives. In a few minutes he got up and went back to work still chewing his food. "Take your time," he said, "and when you're done with your meal join me to finish the upper section. We'll come back for the lower one tomorrow." I looked at my watch, "What!" I thought, "No way we can do it. I thought we were working until nine o'clock today, or maybe he just doesn't know that it's almost nine. I should tell him."

"Grandfather!" I shouted, "it's half past eight." I hoped he would pack and head home, but instead he began working faster than ever. "I know, I know," he said. "It was eight when we pulled out that big white rock just before breakfast." Grandfather never had a watch and told time by looking at the length of his shadow on the ground. The next thirty minutes would be very hot: on top of the mountain we were first to see the sun rise, but we were also first to burn. If he had been alone, Grandfather would have worked into the heat. Today, however, he had mercy. "All right, all right," he said. "Go find the donkey."

As grandfather prepared to go home, I rode the donkey alone for the first time. I knew it was a donkey not a horse, but I could pretend. Instead of saying, "*Haa, haa,*" to him, (the order for a donkey to go), I treated him like a horse: "*Diah, diah,*" I said. I did not poke him with a stick on his neck (like you do to a donkey) but kicked with my heels to make him go faster. I knew that my grandfather was not in a hurry, so I rode a few times around the field before handing my "horse" over to him. Even then, my grandfather motioned me onward. He preferred to walk. About halfway home, grandfather spotted a large rock which he used to mount the donkey. He rode in front of me until we got back to the village.

By that time the other kids were awake, and, in daylight, our village was a familiar place once again: the low, flat-roofed stone houses, the gushing spring water running by the church, and the smell of fresh baked bread. On this day nothing was changed except me. I had returned to the village with the soil of our land between my fingers. Now I was a young man. I spent the rest of the day in the shadow of my grandfather, did not play with the rest of the kids. My grandmother no longer called me "Little Hanna." Now grandfather and I were both big.

Many years later, I remember the night I rode to our orchard with grandfather. I look back and think of what I learned. Grandfather taught me to name the stars, to work the land before breakfast, to ride the donkey by myself.

Tata Olga's Hands
by Lisa Majaj

M Y GRANDMOTHER'S HANDS WERE BROWN as the eggs she boiled in onion skins for Easter, rough like the bark of the jasmine vine that twined its way up the back wall of her chipped-stone house. She ladled *maftoul* in steaming portions, chick peas and onions like islands in the gold brown sauce, hands firm as she hefted the bowl from stove to table. Tomato in one hand, knife in the other, rivulets ran to her wrists. The bread was paper-thin and tore in long strips, dusting her hands with flour. Afterwards she poured tea over mint leaves, stirred a spoon round and round till the sugar dissolved, offered the steaming glass.

When my uncle died, Tata Olga washed his body with a stained white rag, wrung the cloth out fiercely in clear cool water. In the kitchen, bitter coffee boiled in a huge pot over an open flame. Her knuckles were white on the ladle. She carried the tray without wavering, offered tiny cups that mourners tilted between thumb and forefinger. Cigarette smoke hung on the air. All evening she held out her palms.

Tunisia
by Frederic Hunter

W E DROVE SOUTH FROM TUNIS WITH WHEAT fields stretching all around. We did not go along the coast, which is the preferred route, but inland toward Zaghouan. Behind the town enormous mountains rise up and we got to see rural Tunisia, passing huge trucks loaded to the toppling from the harvest. We had liked Tunis. The Hotel Maison Blanche had proved luxurious and reasonable, the trams easy to negotiate, the medina invigorating with narrow passageways fragrant with spices, tight-packed and noisy with passersby jostling, children running, shoppers and merchants bargaining outside stalls and the view from Byrsa Hill where Carthage once stood as magnificent as any I'd ever seen. Now south to Kairouan.

We had the devil's own time finding our hotel. Once settled, we plunged into the medina, smaller than that of Tunis, of course, but equally atmospheric. Just across from the gate into the medina—the Bab ech Chouhada, according to our map—stood a collection of tables, metal chairs surrounding them, with idlers passing the beginning of the late afternoon. We joined them, ordered cokes—the choice was that or coffee—and proceeded to watch the Kairouan world pass in and out of Bab ech Chouhada. The minutes lazed by. The sidewalk café tables began to fill. Finally every one was occupied. First at the table next to ours sat two middle-aged men. Friends joined them, singly or in pairs, a couple of them accompanied by their children. Eventually eight or ten men idled at the table, drinking coffee and holding the children in their laps. The kids seemed to know all the men and the men delighted in them.

After a while it struck me: men and children. My wife was the only woman in the sidewalk café. The Tunisians understood that we were foreigners. We had that look, that sound. It did not bother them that an American woman sat among them. Would it have bothered them if a Tunisian woman had?

We left the café and walked about that section of the town outside the medina's walls. There were sidewalk cafés everywhere and they were all filled with men, drinking coffee, smoking hookahs.

I was delighted. Tunisia was living up to what I'd been led to expect. Few women wearing chadors or the veil. A theoretical equality between women and men. But still a separation of the sexes.

The next morning we visited the great mosque, impressive with its enormous courtyard and its 400-plus columns, no two alike. We drove north to Maktar where we had the impressive Roman ruins to ourselves, got fruit for a roadside picnic at Kesra Nord and on to El Kef. After dinner there we walked up to the *casbah*, a great fort sited high on a rock outcropping. The gate to the fort was closed. We expected as much. Suddenly it opened. The gate keeper beckoned to us. We and two other couples entered the fort. We climbed around the battlements and watched the sun set, the light leave the sky. I admit it. I kept checking on the two couples, both perhaps in their early 30s. They looked like Tunisians. So what were they doing out as couples, acting as naturally together as an American couple? How baffling! I was pleased to see them together. As an American I assumed this was the way men and women were meant to be: together. But why weren't these couples acting as I expected them to act?

The next day we visited Dougga—more Roman ruins—and Bulla Regia, an ancient Roman farming community notable for its underground dwellings. To escape the heat houses were built below the surface of the earth. We visited one. It featured a magnificent mosaic of Venus flanked by centaurs. Arriving there at 3:00, 3:30, we understood the advisability of refuge from the heat. It must have been 20 degrees cooler at the Venus mosaic than it was on earth's surface. And it was still only May.

But what struck me about Bulla Regia was what we encountered there in the first ruin we entered. Some young people, students, were waiting around outside this ruin, presumably for a ride to pick them up. Inside were a young man with a slightly younger girl, late teens. They were sitting on stones, talking. We moved on quickly. But I kept wondering: What? Why? How come? Is this wise? (But who cares about "wise" when you are 18?)

It occurred to me that I had caught myself thinking, not like a reporter (one who accepts things as they are), but instead like a consumer of news reports. (I had, in fact, been a reporter, a foreign correspondent in Africa. The reporter – at least in theory - tells what he saw, what he heard, what he learned. Not what his reading has told him to expect. He is supposed to see with "new eyes." He is not supposed to recycle what he has read about his post before arriving at it. At least not for the paper I worked for.)

As a correspondent in Africa, I conceived of myself as an advocate of sorts for Africans, as an explainer of how they saw the world. I felt then—and still feel—that Africans and their continent were/are badly represented by the press, partly as a result of lingering American racial attitudes and partly out of a lack of compassion for the immense leap they had to make out of a tribal and colonized past into the modern world. As a correspondent I did not see my job as being a decoder of the American angle on every story I covered. Which was how some of my colleagues saw their jobs. (While I was covering Africa, one of my colleagues—an excellent reporter—won a Pulitzer for a series of reports about apartheid in South Africa. What interested me about the series was that, instead of offering new insights into the complexities of that situation, his articles reaffirmed what his editors and the Pulitzer committee already thought about South Africa. I confess I thought: So that's how you win a Pulitzer—by reaffirming existing attitudes.)

And here I was in Tunisia seeing evidence contrary to reports in the books and journalism I'd read and the television news I'd seen. And yet I was still assessing it through the lens of those reports, trying to make what I saw correspond to what I was supposed to see.

If my notions were romantic, this was preferable to thinking that everyone who was different must be an Al-Qaeda terrorist or a suicide bomber. Still those notions partook of the same kind of fantasy thinking engendered by the media.

I don't know why the two couples who toured the El Kef *casbah* with us were together. Nor do I know why those two kids were talking in the ruin in Bulla Regia. Except that things are not as chador black and blazing sun white as I had been led to believe.

The next day we drove back to Tunis. We had dinner at Dar el Jeld, a splendid restaurant in a house in the medina. We sat on a balcony, overlooking the main floor of the restaurant. Eventually three couples, two mature, one young, took seats directly below us. The older men began to gesture as if expounding to one another their accomplishments. Ah ha! I thought. The two young people have agreed to an arranged marriage, a profitable union. The two fathers are showing off for one another. And then I thought: Oops! You're doing it again. Stop! Just enjoy the view!

The Veil
by Lauren M. Connolly

THERE ARE COMPLICATED AND DIVERSE REALITIES for women wearing the Muslim veil. In addition to government mandated and religious reasons, some women wear the veil as a form of protest or as a way to identify themselves within a political, class or cultural structure. The veil can be used to reinforce cultural identities or to create divisions between the classes. These reasons are more complicated than the popular notions that are presented in Western art, literature and media. In order to have meaningful dialogue regarding the veil, the social, political, class and religious issues must also be addressed.

In the memoir, *Reading Lolita in Teheran*, Iranian author Azar Nafisi, discusses how her grandmother "resented the fact that her veil, which to her was a symbol of her sacred relationship to God, had now become an instrument of [political and governmental] power, turning women into political signs and symbols." She notes how her grandmother "refused to leave the house for three months when she was forced to unveil." Now forced to wear the veil herself, Nafisi believes that she is "being compromised by [the government's] insistence that [she] wear the veil under false pretenses... The issue was not so much the veil itself as freedom of choice." For Nafisi, the issue of the veil involves women seeking control over their own bodies by removing it from the political realm.

Through the eyes of Western culture, the veil is viewed as oppressive, backwards, and a tool expressly used for silencing women. Little is understood about the multitudes of reasons why women wear the veil. For the West, the over-simplification of this concept widens the gap between cultures. It ignores the important issues facing women today, such as access to healthcare and education. By overlooking the diverse reasons for veiling, the West uses an overly simplistic perspective to assert its superiority over other ways of life.

A wealth of literature written by Muslim women addresses the many issues confronting them today, including living in a society where the veil is commonplace. Frequently these works confound the dominant Western view of women who live in Muslim countries. Anthologies such as *Veil: Veiling, Representation and Contemporary Art* attempt to address these issues surrounding their portrayal.

French Algerian artist, Zineb Sedira notes in her *Veil* article "Mapping the Illusive," in the West "the unveiled woman is seen as an individual and civilized subject... [compared] to the culturally constructed veiled woman, who is considered anonymous, passive and exotic." This supposedly authoritative construction of Muslim women facilitates the West's assertion of dominance, not only of its own cultural values but to also its political, governmental and military power in the name of saving women from their native culture, religion or homeland.

Today the conflict over the issues of the veil can be connected with the United States' involvement in the conflicts in both Iraq and Afghanistan. Sonali Kolhatkar, who is a citizen of India, but was born and raised in the United Arab Emirates and currently lives in Pasadena, California, is a reporter and activist on Afghan women's issues. In an interview on the radio program *Democracy Now!*, she states that the United States calls the war on Afghanistan, "Operation Enduring Freedom,...[and the Bush Administration claimed that it was] going to liberate the people and particularly liberate the women of Afghanistan." In addition to United States government's claims, Western based non-profit organizations attempt to "free" Muslim women by using the veil as a tool to raise money. Kolhatkar furthers the critique, in an op-ed in *Znet Magazine*, on the actions by organizations, such as the Feminist Majority that "promotes itself...by selling small squares of mesh cloth, similar to the mesh...[on a] traditional Afghan *burqa*." Both the American government and Western non-profit organizations perceive that veiled women come from a "backwards culture." These actions perpetuate these passive perceptions and encourage Western society to look down on women from the East.

Moroccan author Laila Lalami, who is currently on the faculty at the University of California Riverside, continues the critique in *The Nation* article, "The Missionary Position." She states that a "burden of pity" is now imposed on Muslim women caught in the middle between both Muslim "extremists and evangelical and secular supporters of the empire in the West." Lalami states that the West's pity on the East is so pervasive that people ignore "Christian and Jewish women living in similarly constricting fundamentalist settings" and instead focus on Muslim women as being "so oppressed they don't even know that they are oppressed." Images of women wearing the veil have become the singular most popular image to represent Muslim women reinforcing the stereotype in the West today.

In her article "Visibility, Violence and Voice? Attitudes to Veiling Post-11 September" *Veil* contributor Alison Donnell notes that veils, such as the *burqa*, have come to represent the sole emblem of oppression. As a result, the discussion over women's healthcare and education become secondary issues. Even with the post-September 11 attention on Afghanistan, the interest is directed towards Afghan women only in Western terms.

"Multiple functions and values of the veil also need to be acknowledged," states Donnell. "For some women, the veil empowers them by removing their bodies from male scrutiny and the social judgments of beauty and sexuality and they wear it by choice. For others, enforced veiling is a political oppression disconnected from Islam....[but] veiling can also be a conscious drawing attention to oneself...as a political [being]."

The West regards cultures, in which the veil is used, as being static and unchanging. "In the West *harem, veil, polygamy* invoke Islam and are synonymous with female weakness and oppression," observe the artists and editors of *Veil: Veiling, Representation and Contemporary Art*, David A. Bailey and Gilane Tawadros. But the veil or the reasons for wearing the veil are not static. According to Iraqi-born artist and *Veil* contributor Jananne Al-Ani, who lives in London, the use of the veil shifts "according to different historical and political contexts." In Egypt during the early 1900s the veil was removed as a "sign of defiance and feminist resistance." Whereas in Algeria during the 1950s and 1960s the veil was used "as a symbol of Arab resistance to French colonial oppression." The representation of the veil can empower women when used for "political protest and a symbol of a search for [a]...non-westernized identity," comments by Egyptian author and London resident Ahdaf Soueif in her *Veil* article on "Language of the Veil." In addition to the political and historical reasons for wearing the veil, in some counties, poor and working-class women may wear it because the veil solves an economic need to maintain a hairstyle, and others may wear the veil because it is becomes a fashion statement in society.

Westerners should note that there are different kinds of veils. Historically many of the differences between the styles were based on local customs and class. The most common veil consists of a simple headscarf, known as the *hijab*, whereas the *al-amira*, *shayla* and *khimar* may cover the head, neck and shoulders. The *chador*, a more conservative veil worn in Iran, is a full body cloak that keeps the face uncovered. Countries such as Saudi Arabia wear the *niqab*, which covers the face but leaves the eyes uncovered. The most concealing is the well-known Afghani *burqa*, with a mesh fabric to see through.

Veils and veiling can be very different based on the country, culture, interpretation of the Qur'an, social-political affiliations, class placement, and fashion. With the West's continual attempts to infantilize women who live in the East, it is important to break down the many preconceptions of the women behind the veil. It is crucial to remember how much the global community affects something as simple as what women wear and how it is interpreted. The critique on the veil is no different than the debate surrounding equity within women's healthcare, body rights, fashion, in the workplace or in the home.

These women's issues are connected within a larger context, but with the governments of the East and West politicizing the issue, using laws to dictate whether a woman must wear the veil or absolutely forbidding require public discussion. Either of these extremes uses a woman's body as a political statement. While the rights of a woman's body are only casually mentioned within the context of the veil issue, an in-depth critique is necessary. Creating legal statutes on the veil is similar to the government legislating length of a woman's skirt or mandating that she wear one at all.

Chapter Two

Contemporary Issues

Operation Blend In
by Maz Jobrani

MY FAMILY MOVED TO AMERICA IN 1978. When we first arrived, being Iranian wasn't much of an issue. That would change later in 1979 when 66 Americans were taken hostage by Iranian students in Tehran. Suddenly something that was happening on the other side of the world and 10 time zones away from me in California had a huge effect on my life. We went from being an innocuous ally of the United States to its mortal enemy. We went from having a strong currency around the world and being part of the international community to being pariahs. And for me, in the West, I went from a neutral kid playing sports with my friends to a reluctant political pawn in a game that was out of my control.

This was the beginning of an era I call the Italianification of Iranians. Suddenly Iranians in America didn't say they were Iranian, but rather Italian or French or Turkish. In the years to come I would meet many Sharokhs and Hooshangs who had changed their names to Tony or Vince or Leonardo (actually I've never met a Persian Leonardo, but there's still time). One of my friends would say he's Italian and then if the person he was talking to would talk Italian back to him he'd freeze, mumble the few Italian words he knew—"linguini, fettuccini, tortellini" and make a quick exit. "Ciao!"

Since in my youth being Iranian was not cool, I did what any other kid would do, I tried to blend in. I didn't become Italian, but rather turned to being more American. I played baseball, rooted for the Dallas Cowboys (America's Team) and ate hot dogs and apple pies. Sometimes I would eat hot dogs and apple pies while playing baseball with a Dallas Cowboy jersey on. (Well it never got that bad, but you get the point.) Most days, things would be going fine as I would hang with my friends and not really think much about my ethnicity. Operation "Blend In" would usually be going well until…until my dad would show up with his loud Persian accent and blow my cover.

Nothing was more embarrassing than to be hanging with my friends when we were in junior high and trying to act cool around the girls at school only to have my Iranian dad pull up in an expensive Mercedes, pull down the window, and call out my full name "MAZIYAR! Let's go home." I wanted to turn to everyone and say, "I don't know that guy. I think he's trying to kidnap me." To him I wanted to say, "Dad, first of all it's Maz. Secondly, just lightly honk the horn and I'll come. You don't need to reveal that we're FOBs with your thick Persian accent. Didn't you get the memo? It ain't cool to be Iranian."

To make matters worse at one point he bought his friend's Rolls Royce and started to drive us to school in THAT. I was mortified! "Great," I thought, "now everyone's going to think I'm the son of some rich Saudi Sheik. All the oil well jokes will really start to fit." I remember ducking as we drove past some of the other kids in his Silver Shadow (that was the model). The last thing you want to be known as, when you're trying to blend in, is the spoiled rich Persian kid.

As I grew older I came to realize that my dad wasn't doing this loud, accented, yelling thing as a shtick to embarrass me, but rather it was his nature. He had a funny way of being noticed whenever he entered a room. He was always loud. I remember going to buy ice cream with him when I was 12 years old. We entered the ice cream parlor and there was a 14 year-old girl working behind the counter. He started with his silly ways asking the girl if she wanted to marry me. "You would like marry my son Maziyar?" The girl smiled knowing he was joking. I turned red, thinking, "Oh god, here we go again."

Sometimes I would wake to his loud voice, yelling at 6:00 in the morning, as he would talk to family in Iran. He'd speak in the regional Iranian dialect of Turkish. I wouldn't understand what he was saying, but I'd just think, "My god, these phone lines can't be that bad, can they?" Once in a while he'd get me out of bed and put me on the phone to say hi to an aunt or uncle that I barely knew. "Hello!" "Hello!" "How are you?" "Speak up, I can barely hear you." "HOW ARE YOU?" "FINE." "I HOPE TO SEE YOU SOON!" "ME TOO!" "GIVE THE PHONE BACK TO YOUR DAD." "OKAY." I'd get off and think, "The phone lines really *are* that bad." I don't know if this was practice for my dad, but I think that he somehow felt that he had to speak in his phone voice all the time.

I never recall hearing my father whisper. You always knew when he was in the room. He was proud of who he was—a loud, proud, Iranian, macho man! He was the king of the castle and everyone was going to know it. Even when he fell asleep, his snoring yelled. It was that snoring that starts loud and gets louder. The kind where you would think that it should wake him up, but it didn't. As a kid I didn't relate his snoring to any mundane diagnosis like a deviated septum or bad sinuses. Rather I saw it as a sign of his manliness. He was such a proud man that even in his sleep he was going to let you know that he was there and he was the boss. (I actually thought that when I grow up I want to snore like that. It really was like the roar of a lion and I couldn't wait to grow up and have my own roar.)

The loudness is not something I inherited. I do have my moments, when I'm on stage or feeling goofy, but for the most part I'm more subtle, especially in public. Whereas he'd enter a room and you'd know he was there, I enter a room and want to blend in. I don't want to draw any attention to myself and I don't want to impose on people's space. I don't know if that's a more American trait of mine, but it is.

In the past few years my dad had problems with his spine and had to go through

Cune Press was founded in 1994 in Seattle to explore innovative ways of bringing talented new writers to public attention. Our name is derived from "cuneiform." If you would like to know more, please fill out this card and drop it in the mail OR email us: info@cunepress.com.

_____
Name

_____
Email Address

_____
Street Address

_____
Title of the book in which you found this card.

_____
City, State, Zip

_____
Where did you purchase this book?

_____
Phone Number

_____
How did you hear about this book?
Comment?

_____
Fax Number

Visit us on the web at www.cunepress.com

BUSINESS REPLY MAIL

FIRST-CLASS MAIL   PERMIT NO. 457   SEATTLE WA

POSTAGE WILL BE PAID BY ADDRESSEE

CUNE PRESS
PO BOX 31024
SEATTLE WA 98103-9939

NO POSTAGE
NECESSARY
IF MAILED
IN THE
UNITED STATES

surgery. It was a very tough time for the whole family, but also a good time because I got to spend almost every day with him. Whereas as a kid I was embarrassed by his loud voice that revealed my ethnicity, I now found myself wanting to hear him speak. His new favorite word was "Appreciate. Appreciate." "That's my father," I'd say. "We're Iranian."

I guess if there's one thing I've learned from my father it's to be proud of who you are. Say it loud, say it proud—I'm Iranian and there ain't nothing wrong with that!

Stereotypes: What's the Harm?
by Laila Al-Qatami

IN AMERICA WE LIVE IN A SOCIETY IN WHICH our friends, neighbors, co-workers, and fellow citizens tune into mass media sources for their daily dose of news and information. This source of information is readily available 24 hours a day, seven days a week. It's quick and easy and fits into our daily lives. The effect of this is that most Americans tend to believe, either consciously or subconsciously, the images of Arabs, Arab culture and Islam which come from the news media. Americans also watch films, TV shows and the like on a regular basis. Yet, defamation and stereotypical portrayals of Arabs, Arab culture, and Islam have long been a feature of American popular culture and are now increasingly prevalent on mainstream TV news programs.

Numerous authors have written in depth about the prevalence of this defamation and have offered perspectives on the basic types of stereotypical portrayals. The foremost authority on media portrayals of Arabs, Dr. Jack Shaheen, has detailed the Instant Arab kit, often used in films as Arab and Arab Culture equals terrorist, belly dancer, harem, veil, oil, and camels. Such negative images in movies and in the media are rarely countered by positive or neutral images of Arabs and Arab culture in which Arabs are portrayed as people with multifaceted identities. Through repeated exposure to these types of depictions and by failing to seek out alternate, more accurate and more in-depth information, Americans are left with a grossly inaccurate picture of Arabs and Islam. Failing to question the veracity of what we see or hear on TV or in the movies has the same effect.

Additionally, in the seven years I've worked for the leading Arab-American organization, American-Arab Anti-Discrimination Committee (ADC), I've seen a marked increase in outright defamation about Arabs, Islam, or anything remotely associated with Arabs and Islam in the news media. These verbal attacks and outright defamation come not only from members of the media themselves but are also carried out by guests, who range from public officials to individual citizens. When something is said that is false, bigoted, or defamatory, it is rarely challenged or corrected on these types of programs, leading viewers to believe what they are hearing or watching is accurate, when it clearly isn't.

One might ask: "So what if the picture is inaccurate? What's the harm?" I believe that this widespread defamation tends to create a hostile environment which has led to discrimination, and even hate crimes, perpetrated against Arabs, Muslim and those perceived to be. The perception is that anyone who is brown could potentially be an Arab and/or a Muslim, which has unfortunately led to violence and discrimination against Sikhs, Hispanics, and others who are perceived, inaccurately, to be Arab or Muslim.

Because I wanted to counter these negative portrayals and to give voice to the community, I began to work for the American-Arab Anti-Discrimination Committee. Through my work I began speaking out against these inaccuracies and stereotypes. I appeared on numerous mainstream news programs and have worked with many national and international movie directors. For those who had spent a lifetime consuming the popular culture image of Arabs, I was an anomaly, a well-educated, articulate, unveiled Arab woman. I did not fit the stereotype. Many times, I could see the hostility that news figures wanted to express toward me, but they seemed caught off guard when I could respond and challenge their views and stereotypes and correct their misperceptions. Those were the people I could see, right there in front of me, or on the radio with me. But I couldn't gauge the effects on the viewers or listeners. That is, until I read my emails or letters in response to my appearances. By and large the majority of correspondence I received was positive and encouraging. Writers said they learned something from an interview or they saw Arabs a bit differently. I even received a few "fan letters." One came from a sommelier who wanted to write a story about Arabs and Islam, ironically enough, in a leading wine magazine. Others wanted to learn more about the community and Islam. But there were others.

One incident stands out in my mind and is emblematic of the harm of negative stereotypes and their effects. As I was opening the mail in my office one lovely spring day I found a letter which looked suspicious. I gingerly opened the envelope and could see a letter enclosed by a page of pornographic images of women and caricatures of the Prophet Mohammad. But what was inside the letter I'll never know because the intense smell of feces and the large brown stain on the letter stopped me. How could a person hate and detest Arabs so much that they'd send a feces-filled hate letter? It was the moment where I personally came face to face with the harmful effects of negative stereotypes and the hate to which they can lead. It has only encouraged me to continue to give voice to the Arab and Muslim community, and hopefully change perceptions of the community.

Children Are Not Born Bigots
By Susan Burton

GROWING UP IN RALEIGH, NC AS A WHITE, CHRISTIAN, heterosexual, middle class woman, I benefited from privilege that was given to me at birth. Although I experienced and participated in plenty of ridicule as is the case with most children, rarely was my right to belong and participate questioned. (When it was, I was doing something that only boys were supposed to do.) My parents had grown up in the deep South during Jim Crow segregation and were clear that they did not want me to grow up believing that I had the right to exclude any group of people.

There were very few images that challenged the entitlement, hatred and supremacy that I heard in my friends' homes, on TV and saw reflected in our nation's foreign policy. Willie Horton, welfare queens, apartheid, US intervention in Latin America, and AIDS as the "gay disease" were just a few signs of the times. My parents, however, were committed to offering counter stories that told of God's intention for a just world and my responsibility to question the dominant culture.

As I grew up and began using my voice to oppose the death penalty, the first Gulf War, greed, and racism within my community, I realized how much we are invested in the systems that perpetuate injustice in our nation and world. My character and patriotism were questioned on a regular basis. My mother had had this experience and taught me as a small child that a patriot is someone who loves his or her country so much that when it is moving in a dangerous direction that the patriot is willing to challenge the leaders and citizens to change. To illustrate this point she asked, "As your parent who loves you deeply, how could I sit back and let you run into the road when that action could lead to your demise?"

Traveling by Amtrak in NC as a teenager, I saw one very memorable image that reinforced my parent's teachings—a billboard with a racially and ethnically diverse group of children that read, "No child is born a bigot." As an educator, I have the opportunity to lessen the misinformation that leads to discrimination and oppression by introducing young people and adults to those whose identities and lived experiences are different than their own. Mother Teresa's words ring true for me at this time in our world's history: "If there is no peace, it is because we have forgotten that we belong to each other." Relationships are essential to recognizing and honoring the humanity of people whose race, ethnicity, faith, nationality, language, class, and sexual orientation are different from our own. Who are the people in your life who counter the images of the Other based on fear and stereotypes that only serve to divide us? By cultivating these relationships, we can learn how to live peacefully with one another and become counter stories that inspire others to set forth on this journey.

Arab, American, Muslim . . . Marine
By Bill Bazzi

"O'ER THE LAND OF THE FREE, AND THE HOME OF THE BRAVE." These famous words from the Star Spangled Banner hold special meaning for me. America has long been seen as the country of freedom and opportunity, with an extraordinary amount of diversity. For instance, I am a Lebanese American. Time and time again, core American values have been protected by men and women who chose to serve this country. At the age of 18, I decided to serve my country and enter the United Stated Marine Corps. The attacks that took place on September 11, 2001 changed America forever. On a personal level, this tragedy had a profound impact on my life, both as a Lebanese American and as an American Marine. In the aftermath of the attacks, anti-Arab and anti-Muslim tensions spiked dramatically in many parts of the country, leaving me feeling vulnerable as a potential target of misguided discrimination. These attacks were an attack on *all* Americans. I watched the events play out in horror and disgust, just as white Americans, black Americans, and Asian-Americans watched in horror and disgust.

I was activated by the US military after September 11, 2001. Shortly after the attacks, the Pentagon declared "Threatcon Delta" for US forces around the world. Essentially, this system outlined the security measures for US military personnel to take when threatened by a terrorist attack. Soon after, I was designated as a Watch Commander, meaning that I was charge of the Marine security team at the military base where I was stationed.

During a routine check on the gate entries, a woman driving a large SUV, with three children, approached the gate. As she reached the gate's entry, she told the Marine Sentry Guard, "Make sure not to allow any Arabs or Muslims through the base." This call for racial profiling and baseless discrimination was deeply offensive to me on many levels.

Following proper protocol, I approached her vehicle. Having heard her offensive and ignorant statement, I wanted to figure out what made her say such a thing.

"What do Arabs or Muslims look like?" I asked the woman.

"They look like terrorists," she replied.

I told her that she was too late. I explained to her that I am an Arab and a Muslim, and that I was at the gate protecting her and her family. My statement that I was serving my country to protect her, like all other men and women in the military of different ethnic or religious backgrounds, left her flustered, struggling to find a response. She stated that I was "different." After I asked her how I was "different," she still did not know what to say. It was clear to me that my words and presence had quite an impact on her and her children.

In as calm a manner as possible, I told the woman that she should be ashamed of herself. I thought of the three children she had with her, and how they might be influenced by their own mother's prejudices. I asked her to think of her kids before she makes general racist remarks, obviously without possessing much knowledge about Arabs or Muslims. Although the setting was slightly unconventional, I wanted to make sure I left her with what my family taught me and what a good Muslim's duties and beliefs truly are, and how my Muslim upbringing actually influenced me to serve my country. Once again, the woman was speechless, while her three children look at me, focused and engaged in the conversation.

As I cleared the woman and her children to proceed through the gate, I lingered in hope that that this experience will shed some light on the dangers of the misguided perceptions and generalizations that this woman had about Arabs and Muslims. I am an American, just like her. I take tremendous pride in my Lebanese heritage, just as I take pride in serving in the United States military. American ideals are not exclusive to any single ethnicity or religion. They apply to all. My experience with the woman at the entry gate revealed that there are still some people that are unable, or perhaps unwilling, to accept this. However, if we collectively work together, as Americans, to educate and inform people about the truth, America will become more united in the years to come. This experience revealed to me that we still have work to do in this country, to dispel the negative and potentially dangerous stereotypes about Arabs and Muslims that instill hate and only divide our great nation. If each of us work in unison to combat these devastating beliefs, the next generation of Americans stands a better chance of advancing in the ongoing efforts to eradicate racism.

I hope the woman's three children will be part of these efforts.

Move Over
by Barbara Nimri Aziz

"MOVE OVER" IS THE TITLE OF A POEM BY Mohja Kahf. And for me it is a statement that Western feminists need to hear. It is time for Western feminists to step aside and let women from other parts of the world speak. Why is it that feminists who serve as book editors and conference organizers urge me to talk about my victimization at the hands of my brother, husband, or another Arab man? Why won't they hear me explain the injustices of Western actions, for example, in the Gulf War? These women, perhaps more than my Arab brother, are an obstacle to my true liberation.

> We are the spreaders of prayer rugs
> in highway gas stations at dawn.
> We are the fasters at company banquets
> before sunset in Ramadan.
> We wear veils and demin,
> prayer caps and T-shirts.
> We don't know what to do at weddings:
> wear white and cut the cake,
> or red and receive garlands,
> sing rap songs or rap tambourines.
> It doesn't matter.
> We will intermarry
> and co-mingle
> and multiply.
> Oh, how we'll multiply
> the number of Mohammed-loving Muslims
> in the motley miscellany of the land.
> – Move Over by Mohja Kahf

Do you remember the opening passages of Maxine Hong Kingston's *The Woman Warrior*, or Alice Walker's *The Color Purple*, or Nawal el-Saadawi's *The Hidden Face of Eve*? I cannot forget them, and you, too, may remember how each opens with a powerful scene of a woman being abused. Either she is raped, or driven to suicide, or violated in some other way. A coincidence? "Abused Third World Women." Is such a portrayal a fair reflection of reality, or a pre-judgment? By selecting these themes, can publishers of our work influence our voice?

The books I note, and many more like them, were celebrated in the West, especially by feminists. As a result, they appear in many world literature courses and are a must on any women's studies college reading list. Even high school teachers assign these books. Think about receptive young readers eager to learn about the wider world. Often these stories are the first image young people have of Asians, Africans, or Arabs.

Why do so many stories about third world women portray us as victims? I only began to ask myself this question very late in the game because it took me years to break through the conditioning and to say, "Wait a minute. Is this really what I am?" Finally, when I did speak out, Western feminists responded that, "The world must understand what hardships you face." Moreover, they maintain, "These sufferings bond women worldwide. These stories arouse interest where, before, there was none at all. We take pity on you."

Why do we need bonds of suffering to unite us? And why do stories of our suffering seem to dominate what is published, and thereby what is known about us? I am speaking not only about Asian, African, and Arab women but also about those of us identified as Hindu, Muslim, African-American, Nicaraguan, or Bosnian—all so-called third world women.

In the United States, the power centers are the Congress, the judiciary, corporate boards, the clergy—Muslim, Christian, Buddhist, and Jewish—the military, and the press. All these remain entrenched male domains. Before the Western feminist movement began in the 1970s, scholars, journalists, and activists gave little thought to the power of our patriarchy here. Then feminists began to expose social inequities and call for a balance. There were some changes, and some women entered places where they had once been excluded. Yet gains were limited.

So I can't help wondering: is it possible that, because of their frustration over limited success at home, feminists have shifted their attention to women worldwide? Are these women distorting the third world situation to create a winning argument for themselves at home—to make it appear they are really better off, after all? And why the focus on the abuse of third world women at the hands of their patriarchal systems? What about the exploitation of third world women by international corporations, by arms suppliers from the industrial world?

The Arab or Muslim woman is a prime example of the edgy relationship that third world women have with Western women. Recall Taslima Nisrine, the lately celebrated writer in Bangladesh. She was publicly denounced in some circles within Bangladesh because she had criticized some interpretations of the Qur'an. Newspapers worldwide rushed to report how rampaging hoards of Muslim men were out to kill her. What a boon for Western feminists! They could expose the excesses of Islam, and its abuse of women, especially those who aspire to be freethinkers. In the end, Western women offered Nisrine and other Muslim women little real assistance. (Nisrine herself, I was told, was aware that she might be exploited by Western women if she called for their help.) Before this, Nisrine's writing hadn't interested American readers, and her work was not translated into English. But once she fit the stereotype promoted by feminists—sure enough, a collection of her work is being translated for publication by a major house in the United States. Meanwhile, the American public was left with the impression of another ugly incident from the "undeveloped, extremist" third world.

Let's come back to the roles of American women. Where are American women effective today? Few women, regrettably, have risen to positions of power in the Senate or in corporate America. One place they seem to be more influential is the local media and publishing. Feminists have a major impact on what is published about women in the world and thereby on what is taught about other societies in schools and colleges.

The Arab or Muslim woman finds herself defined by experts in women's studies. Repeatedly we find the same simplistic presentations. First, we are perceived as weak. Second, we are seen as victim. Third, our oppressor is typically a male relative. Fourth, we appear uneducated and incapable of managing without outside help—namely support, publicity, and ministering from those already educated and liberated, the capable Western women. Fifth, the Arab or Muslim woman is caged and needs to be released. Everything is set up for the arrival of a fairy godmother.

The pattern I speak about is very real, and I believe that it is by design. It is not a conspiracy in itself. It is rather a natural spin-off of arrogance. These women often exhibit the same patronizing attitude for which they fault the men of their own society. Remember their complaints of how they were criticized by men for their oversensitivity and weakness? Aren't they making the same accusation toward Arab and Muslim women? Western women assume that they are somehow historically better placed to take global leadership of women's issues—that they evolved ahead of others to an advanced stage of social and sexual enlightenment.

The assumptions of Western women are unfounded. There is also a racist element in their attitude. We have repeatedly tried to correct this. But the many objections voiced by women worldwide are unrecorded in the West. Americans and Europeans simply fail to hear third world women when we call out to them, "Wait a minute! We do not all feel the way such and such an author reports we feel. What about my brother? What about my father? What about the strong among us?"

Meanwhile, to verify these Western claims, a select group of third world authors is trotted from one TV round table to another, from one feminist conference to the next, and featured in magazine stories on a regular basis. Take the example of Arab women and the Egyptian writer, Nawal el-Saadawi. Careful research by Amal Amireh, presented at the 1995 Middle East Studies Association conference, pointed out that current editions of el-Saadawi's work in English have been altered to overemphasize violence to women and demonstrate apparent intolerance in Islam. Perhaps against her own wishes, el-Saadawi has found her work used by others to try to illustrate the general oppression of Islam toward women.

The best known books about Arab and Muslim women are, in any case, not by Arab authors, but by American women. Anne Mahmoody's book *Not Without My Daughter* has been made into a successful film. More recently, in the wake of the Gulf War, we have *Price of Honor*, by Jan Goodwin, and *Nine Parts of Desire*, by Geraldine Brooks. Goodwin and Brooks (both journalists) draw on the research of Arab women scholars, and therefore bring an "insider" authority to their claims.

As third world women, we must not be intimidated. We must ask: Why this fascination, this curiosity, this obsession with the lives of Arab and Muslim women, almost to the exclusion of other subjects? And what happens to our male writers?

We have many male novelists of the caliber of Nobel laureate Naguib Mahfouz. Yet few are published abroad and most remain unknown outside the Arab world. Many find themselves overlooked in favor of Arab women writers who are, perhaps, less accomplished. And, when Arab male writers are sought out, it is less for their humanistic creative work and more for their analyses of Middle East political events. But that's another story.

In the end, let us recognize that Western feminism, including its academic dimension, has its cultural context and its political agenda. The women who embrace us and pander to us as victims must step back. Then they must learn to take our strength with our weakness.

The Ordeal of the LA8
by David Cole

In January 1987, before some readers of this handbook were born, while Ronald Reagan was president and the threat of Communism still haunted the American government, seven young Palestinians and a Kenyan woman were arrested and deportation proceedings begun against them. The charge? Alleged ties to the Popular Front for the Liberation of Palestine. Suspicions of Communist ties. Immigration judges refused to deport the LA 8. The government kept hounding them. Finally in October, 2007, it dropped the case. The following article was written by a defense attorney for Khader Hamide, one of those who outlasted almost 21 years of American government harassment.

ON OCTOBER 29, 2007, THE BUSH ADMINISTRATION abandoned a two-decade effort to deport two Palestinian immigrants, Khader Hamide and Michel Shehadeh. Hamide and Shehadeh were two of the "LA 8," a group of college-age students and activists arrested in pre-dawn raids in Los Angeles in January 1987 and placed in deportation proceedings for their alleged ties to the Popular Front for the Liberation of Palestine (PFLP), at the time the second-largest faction of the Palestine

Liberation Organization. The long and twisted history of the case demonstrates what can go wrong when the government treats political activism as a proxy for terrorism.

The initial charges were not for terrorism, but for communist affiliation under the McCarran-Walter Act. When the case began, Ronald Reagan was President, the Berlin Wall was still standing and we were arming Osama bin Laden in his battle against the Soviets in Afghanistan. Shortly after the LA 8 were arrested, William Webster, then head of the FBI, admitted in Congressional testimony that the men had committed no crimes and that if they were US citizens there would be no basis for their arrest. But at the FBI's behest, immigration authorities charged them with distributing PFLP magazines, hosting annual community dinners that celebrated the PFLP, and raising money for humanitarian aid organizations in Palestine.

Because the PFLP had a Marxist-Leninist ideology, the eight were charged as communists. They were the last persons sought to be deported from the United States for alleged communist affiliations.

The eight were held in maximum security conditions. The government argued that they should be detained for as long as it took to deport them. When the immigration judge asked what evidence the government had to show that the eight were dangerous, the government responded that the evidence was classified. The judge could see it, but only behind closed doors, out of the earshot of the eight or their lawyers. The immigration judge, Ingrid Hrycenko, rejected that approach. She required the government to show its evidence to the eight. The government balked, and the eight went free. They remained free for the remainder of the two-decade legal struggle. The evidence, subsequently declassified, contained no evidence of any criminal wrongdoing whatsoever, much less terrorism.

In 1989 Federal Judge Stephen Wilson, a former federal prosecutor and Reagan appointee, declared the initial charges against the LA 8 unconstitutional. He ruled that immigrants enjoy the same First Amendment rights as citizens. Since citizens could not be punished for advocating communism or affiliating with communist groups, he ruled, foreign nationals could not be deported for the same conduct. The Reagan administration appealed, but Congress repealed the McCarran-Walter Act.

Immigration authorities then charged Hamide and Shehadeh under a new immigration law, making material support of terrorist organizations a deportable offense. This immigration law, enacted in 1990, was the first federal law to target "material support" to so-called terrorist groups. It was the precursor to the 1996 criminal material support statute that has been so widely used by the Bush Administration since 9/11. Meanwhile, the government sought the deportation of the other six on technical visa violation charges, but admitted in a press conference that the real reason it sought their deportation was their political affiliations with the PFLP.

In 1994 Judge Wilson halted all the deportation proceedings on selective prosecution grounds, finding that the government had singled out the LA 8 for their constitutionally protected political associations while not seeking to deport similarly situated immigrants who had aided the Nicaraguan *contras* or the Afghan *mujahedeen*.

The Ninth Circuit affirmed. However, the government persuaded Congress to strip federal courts of jurisdiction over selective prosecution claims in immigration cases. In 1999 the Supreme Court upheld that court-stripping statute, and the cases returned to immigration court.

In 2003 the government again amended its case. It charged Hamide and Shehadeh with being retroactively deportable under the Patriot Act. In 2005, when the Real ID Act expanded grounds for deportation still further, the government amended the charges yet again, seeking retroactive application of the new law.

However, in January 2007 immigration judge Bruce Einhorn, in one of his last acts before he left the bench, dismissed the case for prosecutorial misconduct. He ruled that the government had repeatedly failed to comply with the court's orders and had delayed unconscionably in bringing the case to trial. The government initially appealed the decision, but eventually agreed to dismiss all charges.

Why was the Bush Administration able to do what Presidents Reagan, Bush Senior and Clinton could not?

Perhaps this is one case where 9/11 did indeed change everything. The United States recognized that it faced a threat from *real* terrorists and college student magazine distributors no longer seemed such a grave concern.

The case against Hamide and Shehadeh prefigured many of the tactics widely and aggressively employed since 9/11, including reliance on guilt by association and sweeping charges of "material support;" the targeting of immigrants, backed by arguments that they don't deserve the same basic human rights as citizens; and the use of secret evidence. It took the government twenty-one years to recognize that such tactics were a mistake in Hamide and Shehadeh's case. How long before the government recognizes that it is making the same mistakes today?

Iraq, not Eye-raq, please
by Ghassan Rubeiz

D ESPITE THE DELUGE OF INFORMATION ON THE Middle East in the US media Americans remain baffled and confused about basics in politics and culture. It is my guess that most Americans do not know that Kurds are generally Sunnis, that Iranians are not Arabs, that Arabs are not necessarily Muslim and that the Shiite-Sunni divide is largely political rather than religious.

Americans need blame-the-victim theory to justify the crime of occupying Iraq and destroying it. Nowadays, a popular US blame-the-victim theory is "Islamofascism." There is a growing media movement portraying Arabs and Muslims as fascists. Muslims are being portrayed as the modern day followers of Hitler and Mussolini. Jihad is being equated with terrorism. National resistance in Palestine, Iraq, and Lebanon is confounded with the organized crime of the Al-Qaeda world.

Arabs and Jews are Semites, and yet hate crimes against Arabs are not considered a form of anti-Semitism. US Christian scholars have anointed themselves as experts on Islam. Islam is increasingly being connected with end-of-time American Christian theology. The difference between Islamic and Christian chauvinism has disappeared.

In the Middle East Arabs engage in a similar process of demonization of the West, especially America. Arab anti-American and anti-Jewish bashing is obscene. But there is a difference of some significance between Arab and American prejudice. Biased Arabs tend to see the devil in America, as a political system, not in Americans as people. In contrast, Americans see the devil in Arabs, not in their political systems. The implications of this difference for policy planning are important.

At the roots of prejudice are ignorance and fear. I am amused how culturally distant American experts are from the Middle East. Their ignorance shows in cultural basics. Take for example the symbolic and irritating mispronunciation of Arab names. When talking about "Eye-raq" experts mean Iraq. When referring to "Eye-ran" they mean Iran. This is especially true among military consultants who tend to show little sensitivity to culture in politics.

More on language and policy. Iraq was an ailing but unified state before our invasion. Now Washington experts describe Iraq as territory of "rival Shiites, Sunnis and Kurds." US occupation fragmented Iraq by undermining its security and sovereignty. Our policy makers wonder about the causes of Iraqi ethnic and sectarian fratricide. Civil wars are political phenomena. They are not caused by sociometric differences among communities. No society is too strong to divide tribally when the economy is shattered, national security is eliminated, and systems of law and order are abolished.

Americans want to learn the facts about the Middle East but the political establishment is threatened by inconvenient realities. The popular Arabic Channel Al Jazeera launched its English language program in Washington DC last month to express the voice of Arabs in the US. Regrettably, Al Jazeera is having a hard time airing its programs on American cables. The embargo on Al Jazeera is phenomenal. Even Israel allows Al Jazeera to broadcast its programs on its soil, but the US media empires consider this Arab Channel too dangerous for Americans.

Experience counts a lot in policy planning. US policy makers tend to have minimal experience in the Arab world. America invaded Iraq with a goal to democratize it by force. But Americans had little knowledge about its language, history, culture or sentiments. US experts do not know Arabic, they have few friends in the region, and when they visit the Middle East they are sheltered in first class hotels or in US embassies that look like military camps.

American policy makers seek biased advisors who tell them what they want to hear. Neo-conservative Christian Arabs explain Islam to them. Jewish advisors tell them how Arabs feel and think. The few Americans who have solid knowledge and insight about Arabia are labeled "Arabists".

Arabists are now marginalized. The Iraq Study Group is trying to revive the Arabist role in US politics but the chances of that happening are slim. In only two weeks the

Baker-Hamilton Report (ISG) has been marginalized by a hostile US media campaign that portrays the region as a jungle, its politicians as unreliable and its culture as violent. If the Arabist Baker says let us talk to representatives of the region in Syria, Iran and Turkey, the neo-cons are alarmed: How can we talk to people who are crazy and criminal? The White House rebuked Congressman Nelson for his recent fact-finding visit to Syria. Former President Jimmy Carter is being targeted daily to discredit his revelations about American policy in the Middle East in his book "Palestine: Peace not Apartheid."

Political perspective on Iraq helps people screen the flood of information they receive daily. Many Americans still see the Iraq war as a victory in the making. They believe that it is just a matter of time before Iraq is straightened out. President Bush says additional troops are needed to do the job. Those who disagree with Bush believe that intervention in Iraq was a big US mistake and the US should pull the forces out. But still few Americans consider the US invasion and occupation as a crime against the human rights of a people and culture.

Until Americans realize the depth of the Iraq debacle and the root causes of US hegemony around the globe, the range of reflection on the Iraq tragedy will remain narrow and superficial. The view of the Middle East from Washington is out of focus.

Chapter Three

How the World Evolves

How Arabic Learning Enlightened Europe
By William Dalrymple

1.

SOMETIME IN THE EARLY 1140S A SCHOLAR FROM northern Italy made an arduous crossing of the Alps and the Pyrenees and eventually arrived in the newly reconquered Spanish town of Toledo. There Gerard of Cremona was given the position of canon at the cathedral, formerly the Friday Mosque, which had recently been seized from the town's Muslims.

Before the rise of Islam, Toledo had been the capital city of Visigothic Spain, and its capture by Alfonso VI of Castile was an important moment in the Christian *reconquista* of the land known to Islam as al-Andalus. Many of the Muslims of the city had, however, chosen to stay on under Castilian rule, and among them was a scholar named Ghalib the Mozarab. It is not known how Gerard and Ghalib met and became friends, but soon after Gerard's arrival the two began to cooperate on a series of translations from Toledo's Arabic library, which had survived the looting of the conquering Christians.

As Richard Fletcher points out in *The Cross and the Crescent: Christianity and Islam from Mohammad to the Reformation*, Gerard and Ghalib's mode of translation was not one that would be regarded as ideal by modern scholars. Ghalib rendered the classical Arabic of the texts into Castilian Spanish, which Gerard then translated into Latin. Since many of the texts were Greek classics that had themselves arrived in Arabic via Syriac, there was much room for error. But the system seems to have worked. In the course of the next half-century, Ghalib and Gerard translated no fewer than eighty-eight Arabic works of astronomy, mathematics, medicine, philosophy, and logic, branches of learning that underpinned the great revival of scholarship in Europe sometimes referred to as the Twelfth-Century Renaissance.

Other translations from the Arabic during this period filled European libraries with a richness of learning impossible even to imagine a century before. They included editions of Aristotle, Euclid, Plato, and Ptolemy, commentaries by Avicenna (Ibn Sina), and astrological texts by al-Khwarizmi, encyclopedias of astronomy, illustrated accounts of chess, and guides to precious stones and their medicinal qualities.

It was a crucial but sometimes forgotten moment in the development of Western civilization, the revival of medieval European learning by a wholesale transfusion of scholarship from the Islamic world. It was probably through Islamic Spain that such basic facets of Western civilization as paper, ideas of courtly love, algebra, and the abacus passed into Europe. Meanwhile the pointed arch and Greco-Arab (or *Unani*, from the Arabic word for Greek/Ionian) medicine arrived in Christendom by way of Salerno and Sicily, where the Norman king Roger II—known as the "Baptized Sultan" —was commissioning the Tunisian scholar al-Idrisi to produce an encyclopedic work of geography.

Some scholars go further. Professor George Makdisi of Harvard has argued convincingly for a major Islamic contribution to the emergence of the first universities in the medieval West, showing how terms such as having "fellows" holding a "chair," or students "reading" a subject and obtaining "degrees," as well as practices such as inaugural lectures and academic robes, can all be traced back to Islamic concepts and practices. Indeed the idea of a university in the modern sense—a place of learning where students congregate to study a wide variety of subjects under a number of teachers— is generally regarded as an Arab innovation developed at the al-Azhar university in Cairo. As Makdisi has demonstrated, it was in cities bordering the Islamic world— Salerno, Naples, Bologna, Montpellier, and Paris—that first developed universities in Christendom, the idea spreading northward from there.

The tortuous and complex relationship of Western Christendom and the world of Islam has provoked a wide variety of responses from historians. Some, such as the great medievalist Sir Steven Runciman, take the view (as he wrote at the end of his magisterial three-volume history of the Crusades) that "our civilization has grown" out of "the long sequence of interaction and fusion between Orient and Occident." Runciman believed that the Crusades should be understood less as an attempt to reconquer the Christian heartlands lost to Islam than as the last of the barbarian invasions. The real heirs of Roman civilization were not the chain-mailed knights of the rural West, but the sophisticated Byzantines of Constantinople and the cultivated Arab caliphate of Damascus, both of whom had preserved the Hellenized urban civilization of the antique Mediterranean long after it was destroyed in Europe.

Others have seen relations between Islam and Christianity as being basically adversarial, a long-drawn-out conflict between the two rival civilizations of East and West. As Gibbon famously observed of the Frankish victory at the Battle of Tours in 732 AD, which halted the Arab advance into Europe,

A victorious line of march had been prolonged above a thousand miles from the Rock of Gibraltar to the banks of the Loire; the repetition of an equal space would have carried the Saracens to the confines of Poland and the Highlands of Scotland: the Rhine is not more impassable than the Nile or the Euphrates, and the Arabian fleet might have sailed without a naval combat into the mouth of the Thames. Perhaps the interpretation of the *Quran* would now be taught in the schools of Oxford, and her pulpits might demonstrate to a circumcised people the sanctity and truth of the revelation of Mahomet. *["Mohammad" in contemporary usage, Ed.]*

Richard Fletcher's *The Cross and the Crescent* broadly belongs to Runciman's camp and emphasizes the fact that Muslim–Christian relations, while plagued with ignorance, mutual misunderstandings, and long periods of outright aggression, have never just been a story of conflict. Instead he shows how medieval Western civilization was profoundly cross-fertilized by the learning and literature of Islam.

Bernard Lewis, by contrast, sees the relationship of Islam and Christianity in more confrontational terms. His latest work, *From Babel to Dragomans: Interpreting the Middle East*, is a diverse collection of essays written over more than half a century. Underlying most of them, however, is the assumption that there are two fixed and opposed forces at work in the history of the Mediterranean world: on one hand Western civilization, which he envisages as a Judeo-Christian block; and on the other hand, quite distinct, an often hostile Islamic world hellbent on the conquest and conversion of the West. As he writes in one essay, "The Roots of Muslim Rage,"

> The struggle between these rival systems has now lasted for some fourteen centuries. It began with the advent of Islam, in the seventh century, and has continued virtually to the present day. It has consisted of a long series of attacks and counterattacks, jihads and crusades, conquests and reconquests.

It was this essay that contained the phrase "the clash of civilizations," later borrowed by Samuel Huntington for his controversial *Foreign Affairs* article and book.

Lewis's trenchant views have made him a number of enemies, notably the late Edward Said, who wrote in *Orientalism* that Lewis's work "purports to be liberal objective scholarship but is in reality very close to being propaganda *against* his subject." In the aftermath of the Islamist attacks on America, Lewis's reputation has, however, undergone something of a revival. Not only have two of his books —*What Went Wrong?* and *The Crisis of Islam* —been major US bestsellers, Lewis's ideas have largely formed the intellectual foundations for the neoconservative view of the Muslim world. Lewis has addressed the White House, and Dick Cheney and Richard Perle have both been named as disciples.

A series of prominent polemical pieces in *The Washington Post* and *The Wall Street Journal*, reprinted in this collection, gives an idea of the sort of advice Lewis would have offered his fans in the White House. For Lewis used the attack on the World Trade Center to encourage the US to attack Saddam Hussein, implicitly making a link between the Al-Qaeda operation and the secular Iraqi Baathist regime, while assuring the administration that they would be feted by the populace who "look to us for help and liberation" and thanked by other Muslim governments whose secret "dearest wish" was an American invasion to remove and replace Saddam.

Lewis has had such a profound influence that according to the *The Wall Street Journal*, "the Lewis doctrine, in effect, had become US policy." If that policy has now been shown to be fundamentally flawed and based on a set of wholly erroneous assumptions, it follows that for all his scholarship, Lewis's understanding of the subtleties of the contemporary Islamic world is, in some respects at least, dangerously defective.

2.

Richard Fletcher is a historian of early medieval Europe. He is particularly interested in relations between Christians and Muslims in Moorish Spain, about which he has written two books, one of which, *The Quest for El Cid*, won both the Los Angeles Times History Prize and Britain's Wolfson Prize. *The Cross and the Crescent* is, if anything, even better than his Cid book, a work of judicious compression and effortless erudition. Beautifully written, often witty, and eminently readable, it is as good an introduction as I have read to the history of medieval Islam and its relations with the Christian world.

Throughout, Fletcher highlights points of contact between the two worlds. He emphasizes how the Prophet Mohammad did not think he was "founding a new religion," so much as bringing "the fullness of divine revelation, partially granted to earlier prophets such as Abraham, Moses or Jesus, to the Arabs of the Arabian Peninsula." After all, Islam accepts much of the Old and New Testaments and obeys the Mosaic laws about circumcision and ablutions while the *Quran* calls Christians the "nearest in love" to Muslims, whom it instructs in Surah 29 to dispute not with the People of the Book [that is, Jews and Christians] save in the most courteous manner... and say, "We believe in what has been sent down to us and what has been sent down to you; our God and your God is one, and to him we have surrendered."

Fletcher also stresses the degree to which the Muslim armies were welcomed as liberators by the Syriac and Coptic Christians, who had suffered discrimination under the strictly Orthodox Byzantines:

> To the persecuted Monophysite Christians of Syria and Egypt, Muslims could be presented as deliverers. The same could be said of the persecuted Jews... Released from the bondage of Constantinopolitan persecution they flourished as never before, generating in the process a rich spiritual literature in hymns, prayers, sermons and devotional work.

Recent excavations by the Jerusalem-based archaeologist Michele Piccirillo have dramatically underlined this point. They have shown that the conquest of Byzantine Palestine and Transjordan by the Arabs resulted in an almost unparalleled burst of church-building and the construction of some remarkable Hellenistic mosaics, implying that under the rule of the Umayyad caliphs of Damascus religious practice was freer and the economy flourishing.

Early Byzantine writers, including the most subtle theologian of the early church, Saint John Damascene, assumed that Islam was merely a heterodox form of

Christianity. This perception is particularly fascinating since Saint John had grown up in the Umayyad court of Damascus—the hub of the young Islamic world—where his father was chancellor, and he was an intimate friend of the future Caliph al-Yazid. In his old age, John took the habit at the desert monastery of Mar Saba, where he began work on his great masterpiece, a refutation of heresies entitled *The Fount of Knowledge*. The book contains a precise critique of Islam, the first written by a Christian, which John regarded as closely related to the heterodox Christian doctrine of Nestorianism. This was a kinship that both the Muslims and the Nestorians were aware of. In 649 a Nestorian bishop wrote: "These Arabs fight not against our Christian religion; nay, rather they defend our faith, they revere our priests and saints, and they make gifts to our churches."

Throughout the medieval period, Christians and Muslims continued to meet as much in the business of trade and scholarship as they did on the battlefield. The tolerant and pluralistic civilization of Muslim al-Andalus allowed a particularly fruitful interaction. A revealing moment highlighted by Fletcher was when, in 949, a Byzantine embassy presented the court of Cordoba with the works of the Greek physician Dioscorides:

> There were no scholars in Spain who knew Greek, so an appeal was sent back to Constantinople in answer to which a learned Greek monk named Nicholas was sent to Spain in 951. A Muslim scholar from Sicily with a knowledge of Greek was also found. Together these two expounded the text to a group of Spanish scholars. This group was a most interesting one. It included native Andalusian Islamic scholars such as Ibn Juljul, who later composed a commentary on Dioscorides; a distinguished Jewish physician and courtier, Hasday ibn Shaprut; and a Mozarabic bishop Recemund of Elvira [who had been sent as the Caliph's ambassador to the German Emperor Otto I], who was himself the author of the so-called *Calendar of Córdoba*, a work containing much agronomical and botanical information. It was a truly international and interdenominational gathering of scholars.

Throughout the Crusades, the Venetians and other Italian trading cities kept up a profitable trade with their Muslim counterparts, resulting in a great many Arabic words surviving in Venetian dialect and a profound Islamic influence on Venetian architecture. Even Christian clerics who cohabited with Muslims in the Crusader kingdoms came to realize that as much bound them together as separated them. As William of Tripoli reported from Acre in 1272: "Though their beliefs are wrapped up in many lies and decorated with fictions, yet it now manifestly appears that they are near to the Christian faith and not far from the path of salvation." At the same time the Muslim traveler Ibn Jubayr noted that despite the military struggles for control of Palestine, "yet Muslims and Christian travellers will come and go between them without interference."

There was of course no shortage of travelers on both sides who could see no good in the infidels among whom they were obliged to mingle, and deep tensions often existed between Muslim rulers and the diverse religious communities living under their capricious thumb. By modern standards Christians and Jews under Muslim rule—the *dhimmi*—were treated as second-class citizens. But there was at least a kind of pluralist equilibrium (what Spanish historians have called *convivencia*, or "living together") which had no parallel in Christendom and which in Spain was lost soon after the completion of the Christian *reconquista*. On taking Grenada on January 2, 1492, the Catholic kings expelled the Moors and Jews, and let loose the Inquisition on those—the New Christians—who had converted. There was a similar pattern in Sicily. After a fruitful period of tolerant coexistence under the Norman kings, the Muslims were later given a blunt choice of transportation or conversion.

3.

Bernard Lewis's collection of fifty-one essays, *From Babel to Dragomans: Interpreting the Middle East*, can be read as an account of the end of an affair, Lewis's growing irritation with a culture and a people that once thrilled and fascinated him. The book's contents range from erudite lectures and specialist scholarly essays to light belles-lettres and some stridently polemical journalism. Over the years, however, one can see Lewis's enthusiasm for matters Muslim slowly but steadily giving way, from the late 1950s onward, to an increasingly negative, disillusioned, and occasionally contemptuous tone. *From Babel to Dragomans* certainly highlights the complexity of Lewis's strange love-hate relationship with the Islamic world he has studied since 1933.

At his best, Lewis can be witty, playful, and polymathically erudite. The title piece is a short history of interpreters and translation from the Book of Genesis to the United Nations, stopping off en route in the company of Pliny, Plutarch, "Bertha the daughter of Lothar, queen of Franja," various Ottoman sultans, Ibsen, Hans Christian Andersen, and Ismail Kadare. A wonderful piece on "Middle East Feasts" gives him full opportunity to show off his astonishing linguistic range, and we learn the reason why, for example, the American fowl we call a turkey is known as *hindi* (Indian) in Turkish and in Arabic as either *dik habashi* (the Ethiopian bird) or *dik rumi* (the bird from Rum, i.e., Byzantium): "All these words simply mean something strange and exotic from a far and unknown place."

Compared to the sophistication of such pieces, Lewis's recent newspaper polemics read with much less subtlety, as he trenchantly argues for invasions and the toppling of unappealing regimes, and implies that the only language "they" understand is brute force. The Muslim world, he generalizes at several points, does not respect weakness and believes "that the Americans have gone soft." Across the Islamic world, Lewis argues, people are praying for the US to liberate them from their tyrannical governments: "One is often told that if we succeed in overthrowing the regimes of what President

Bush has rightly called the 'Axis of Evil,' the scenes of rejoicing in their cities would even exceed those that followed the liberation of Kabul." It is here that Said's charge of Lewis acting as a propagandist against his subject rings most true.

In several places Lewis argues that Islamic hostility to America has less to do with American foreign policy in the Muslim world, notably American support for Israel, than a generalized Islamic "envy" and "rage" directed against its ancient cultural rival. This he claims derives from "a feeling of humiliation—a growing awareness, among the heirs of an old, proud, and long dominant civilization, of having been overtaken, overborne, and overwhelmed by those whom they regarded as their inferiors."

The idea that the Islamic world has been humiliated by a West it once despised and ignored, and that it has never come to terms with this reversal, is a thesis that links Lewis's historical work and his journalism, and has come to form his central theme. For a thousand years, argues Lewis, Islam was technologically superior to Christendom and dominated its Christian neighbors; but since the failure of the Ottoman siege of Vienna in 1683, the Muslim world has been in retreat. Militarily, economically, and scientifically it was soon eclipsed by its Christian rivals. Failure led first to a profound humiliation, then an aggressive hatred of the West:

> This is no less than a clash of civilizations—the perhaps irrational but surely historic reaction of an ancient rival against our Judeo-Christian heritage, our secular present, and the worldwide expansion of both.

It is a thesis that Lewis first formed in his *Muslim Discovery of Europe* (1982) and developed with a more contemporary spin in *The Crisis of Islam* and *What Went Wrong?* (2002). The idea reappears in various guises in no fewer than five essays in *From Babel to Dragomans*.

Lewis believes that during the sixteenth and seventeenth centuries in particular there was a crucial and fatal failure of curiosity about development in Europe. In the conclusion to *The Muslim Discovery of Europe*, Lewis contrasts the situation in Britain and Ottoman Turkey during this period:

> The first chair of Arabic in England was founded by Sir Thomas Adams at Cambridge University in 1633.
>
> There, and in similar centers in other west European countries, a great effort of creative scholarship was devoted to the ancient and medieval languages, literatures, and cultures of the region... All this is in striking contrast to the almost total lack of interest displayed by Middle Easterners in the languages, cultures, and religions of Europe... The record...shows that, until the latter part of the eighteenth century, [the information compiled by the Ottoman state about Europe] was usually superficial, often inaccurate, and almost

always out of date.

Lewis mentions a few exceptions to this conclusion and he adds that there were some changes in the eighteenth century, such as the adoption of European-style diplomacy and military techniques. But he argues that it was only in the early nineteenth century that there was substantial change in Muslim attitudes. In an essay entitled "On Occidentalism and Orientalism" Lewis writes:

> By the beginning of the 19th century, Muslims, first in Turkey and then elsewhere, were becoming aware of the changed balance, not only of power but also of knowledge, between Christendom and Islam, and, for the first time, thought it worth the effort to learn European languages… It is not until well into the 19th century that we find any attempt in any of the languages of the Middle East to produce grammars or dictionaries which would enable speakers of those languages to learn a Western language. And when it did happen, it was due largely to the initiative of those two detested intruders, the imperialist and the missionary. This is surely a striking contrast [to the situation in Europe] and it has prompted many to ask the question: why were the Muslims so uninterested?

By then it was too late. During the course of the nineteenth and twentieth centuries the colonial West imposed itself by force on Muslim countries from the Middle East to Indonesia, "a new era in which the Muslim discovery of Europe was forced, massive, and, for the most part, painful."

Lewis emphasizes that until the nineteenth century there was little question of Muslims going to study in Europe. As he writes in the essay "Europe and Islam": "The question of travel for study did not arise, since clearly there was nothing to be learnt from the benighted infidels of the outer wilderness." Again and again, Lewis returns to his idea that the awareness of Muslims that they belonged "to the most advanced and enlightened civilization in the world" led to the lack of a spirit of inquiry that might otherwise have propelled them to explore the non-Muslim world:

> Few Muslims travelled voluntarily to the lands of the infidels. Even the involuntary travellers, the many captives taken in the endless wars by land and sea, had nothing to say after their ransom and return, and perhaps no one to listen… A few notes and fragments…constitute almost the whole of the Muslim travel literature in Europe…

Such a view was tenable when there was only vague awareness of what Islamic libraries actually contained, but discoveries over the last thirty years have shown that this apparent lacuna was more the result of lack of archival research on the part of

Lewis and other scholars than any failing by Muslim writers. Lewis's findings, while always well argued, now appear somewhat dated. It is true that the Muslim world fell behind the West, and that (as Fletcher nicely puts it) the "cultural suppleness [and] adaptability" shown by the early Muslim states that absorbed the learning of Byzantium and ancient Persia "seemed to run out in later epochs"; but it is not true that the reason for this was a lofty disdain or a generalized hatred for the West, or that Muslims failed to take an intense and often enthusiastic interest in developments there.

Perhaps the best counterblast to this central strand of Lewis's thought are three remarkable books by Nabil Matar, a Christian Palestinian scholar based at the Florida Institute of Technology who has spent the last three decades digging away in archives across the Islamic world.

The first two, *Islam in Britain, 1558–1685* (1998) and *Turk, Moors, and Englishmen in the Age of Discovery* (1999), show the degree to which people from the Islamic and Christian world mixed and intermingled during the sixteenth and seventeenth centuries, while the most recent, *In the Lands of the Christians: Arabic Travel Writing in the Seventeenth Century* (2003), directly counters Lewis's idea that Muslim interest in the West really began in earnest in the nineteenth century. Here a succession of previously unknown seventeenth-century travel narratives unfold in English translation, with Arab writer after writer describing his intense interest in and excitement with Western science, literature, music, politics, and even opera. As Matar emphasizes in his introduction:

> The writings in this volume reveal [that] travelers, envoys, ambassadors, traders, and clerics were eager to ask questions about *bilad al-nasara* ("Lands of the Christians"] and to record their answers—and then turn their impressions into documents. They all wrote with precision and perspicacity, producing the most detailed and empirically based information about the way in which non-Europeans viewed Europeans in the early modern period. No other non-Christian people—neither the American Indians nor the sub-Saharan Africans nor the Asiatics —left behind as extensive a description of the Europeans and of the *bilad al-nasara*, both in the European as well as the American continents, as did the Arabic writers.

Recent research in Indian Muslim and Iranian archives has revealed a similarly inquisitive fascination with the developments in the West in the early modern period.

4.

Matar's work is full of surprises for anyone who believes that Christian–Muslim relations have always been confrontational. In *Turks, Moors, and Englishmen in the*

Age of Discovery we learn for example that in 1603, Ahmad al-Mansur, the King of Morocco, was making a proposal to his English ally, Queen Elizabeth I. The idea was a simple one: that England was to help the Moors colonize America.

The King proposed that Moroccan and English troops, using English ships, should together attack the Spanish colonies in America, expel their hated Spanish enemies, and then "possesse" the land and keep it "under our [joint] dominion for ever." There was a catch, however. Might it not be more sensible, suggested the King, that most of the future colonists should be Moroccan rather than English?

> Those of your countrie doe not fynde themselfes fitt to endure the extremetie of heat there…, where our men endure it very well by reason that heat hurtes them not.
>
> After due consideration, the Moroccan offer was not taken up by Her Majesty.

Such a proposal might seem extraordinary today, but at the time it clearly raised few eyebrows. After all, as Matar points out, the English were close allies of both the Moroccans and their overlords, the Ottomans—indeed the Pope regarded Elizabeth as "a confederate with the Turks." The English might have their reservations about Islam, but these were nothing compared to their hatred and fear of "Popery." As well as treaties of trade and friendship this alliance led to several joint expeditions, such as an Anglo-Moroccan attack on Cadiz in 1596. It also led to a great movement of people between the two worlds. Elizabethan London had a burgeoning Muslim community, which encompassed a large party of Turkish ex-prisoners, some Moorish craftsmen, a number of wealthy Turkish merchants, and a "Moorish solicitor," as well as "Albion Blackamore," the Turkish "Rope-daunser."

If there was a small but confident Muslim community in London, then larger numbers of Englishmen could be found living across the Ottoman Empire, as Matar shows in *Islam in Britain, 1558–1685*. British travelers regularly brought back tales of their compatriots who had "crossed over" and were now prospering in Ottoman service. One of the most powerful Ottoman eunuchs during the sixteenth century, Hasan Aga, was the former Samson Rowlie from Great Yarmouth, while in Algeria the "Moorish Kings Executioner" turned out to be a former butcher from Exeter called "Absalom" (Abd-es-Salaam). When Charles II sent Captain Hamilton to ransom some Englishmen enslaved on the Barbary Coast, his mission was unsuccessful because they all refused to return. The men had all converted to Islam and were now "partaking of the prosperous Successe of the Turks," living in a style to which they could not possibly have aspired back home. The frustrated Hamilton was forced to return empty-handed: "They are tempted to forsake their God for the love of Turkish women," he wrote in his report. "Such ladies are," he added, "generally very beautiful."

There is a serious point underlying such anecdotes, for they show that throughout history, Muslims and Christians have traded, studied, negotiated, and loved across the porous frontiers of religious differences. Probe relations between the two civilizations at any period of history, and you find that the neat civilizational blocks imagined by writers such as Bernard Lewis or Samuel Huntington soon dissolve. It is true that just as there have been some strands of Christian thinking that have always been deeply hostile to Islam, so within Islam there have been schools of thought that have always harbored a deep hostility toward Christians, Jews, and other non-Islamic religions and civilizations, notably the Wahhabi and Salafi schools dominant in modern Saudi Arabia. Until this century, however, the Wahhabis were a theological movement of only localized significance and were widely regarded by most Muslims as an alien sect bordering on infidelity—*kufr*. It is the oil wealth of modern Saudi Arabia that has allowed the Wahhabis to spread their narrow-minded and intolerant brand of Islam, notably by the funding of extremist Wahhabi, Salafi, and Deobandi madrasas across the Islamic world since the mid-1970s, with the disastrous results we see today.

What is most interesting about the early modern cases described by Matar is how the tolerant and pluralistic brand of Islam dominant at the time overpowered foreigners as often by its power of attraction as by the sword. Indeed the English ambassador Sir Thomas Shirley pointed out that the more time Englishmen spent in the East, the closer they moved toward adopting the manners of the Muslims: "conuersation with infidelles doeth mutch corrupte," he wrote. "Many wylde youthes of all nationes...in euerye 3 yeere that they staye in Turkye they loose one article of theyre faythe." In 1606 even the British consul in Egypt, Benjamin Bishop, converted and promptly disappeared from the records. It was a similar situation in India where up until the mid-nineteenth century substantial numbers of Britons were taking on aspects of Mughal culture, marrying Mughal women, and converting to Islam.

In one matter, however, Matar demonstrates something that will surprise no one: that English cooking, then as now, left much to be desired. For while English society was thrilled to taste Turkish cooking when the Ottoman ambassador presided over a feast *à la Turkeska* at his residence, the Moors proved rather less impressed by English fare. This emerges from the story of one unfortunate English captive who was captured in a sea battle and taken to Algiers, where he was put to work as a cook. This proved a mistake for everyone involved. Unused to the exotic ingredients of the region, the Englishman found himself producing such "mad sauces, and such strange Ragoux that every one took me for a Cook of the Antipodes." Worse was the reaction of his master. He declared that the food "hath the most loathsom taste," and ordered that the cook should be given "ten Bastonadoes" and returned to the slavemarket. As far as the King was concerned, the English, it seems, made better galley slaves than gourmets.

The Muslim Impact on Religious Thought in the Middle Ages
by Richard Nenneman

Most Americans do not know the role played by Muslim scholars in the religious ferment of the Middle Ages.

Protestants in general, to the extent that they have any historical perspective at all, tend to think of Protestantism as something that arose to clear the air both of abuses within the Church and some doctrinal errors, after a quiescent period following, let us say, St. Augustine in the fifth century. For a thousand years, nothing of note happened in Christian religious thinking, according to this simplified outlook, until Martin Luther nailed his ninety-five theses on the wall of the church in Wittenberg in 1517 and Henry VIII defied the Roman church in 1534 because it denied him a divorce. In actual fact, those thousand years were as full of religious history as political, but the textbooks we all study in school talk mainly about politics and culture.

What might be of particular interest are the various ways in which the theologians and philosophers of all three major monotheistic faiths tried to develop their concepts of God in the period from about 1100 to 1300 CE. First of all, this was a period of intense communication among the religious "elites" of that day. Muslim scholars had translated the works of Plato and Aristotle from Greek into Arabic, and their acquaintance with Greek philosophy impelled them to try to reconcile the ideas of God in Islam with the Greek philosophic ideas of deity.

The Muslims controlled Spain, and for a long period the Jewish community in Spain lived in close harmony with the Muslims. Then the knowledge of Plato and Aristotle spread from Spain into France, where their philosophies were translated into Latin. Moreover, the theologians who discussed these ideas had a mutual knowledge of the positions taken by others, so there was a genuine respect for each religion. (Maimonides, the best known Jewish philosopher of the period, eventually left Spain and served as the physician for the sultan, who was Muslim, in Cairo.)

Some of this intercommunication would have occurred without the Crusades, which lasted roughly from 1090 into the 1200s. But the Crusades acted as another "enabler" of the spread of religious ideas. In his book *A History of Christian Thought*, Paul Tillich says the Crusades were not important politically or militarily, but "because they brought about the encounter of Christianity with two highly developed cultures, the original Jewish and the Islamic cultures. One could perhaps even say that a third culture was encountered at that time, namely, the classical culture of ancient Greece, which was mediated into the medieval world by the Arabian theologians. The fact of an encounter with another, if it is serious enough, always involves a kind of self-reflection." Thus, "Christianity began to reflect on itself in a much more radical way."

There are some important names in the period that deserve to be memorized and remembered as much as those of any of the kings or popes. Among the Muslims, two philosophers stand out: Avicenna (Ibn Sina—980-1037) and Averroes (Ibn Rush—

1126-1198). Among the Christians, there are Anselm of Canterbury (1033-1109) and Peter Abelard, a Frenchman (1079-1142). The Muslim and Jewish philosophers are of interest because of the ways in which they thought God could be conceived of, or known.

The confrontation with Greek philosophy challenged these medieval thinkers to reconcile their concept of God with the Greek notions of deity. The most important point here is that they had to identify the means by which man can come to know God: through human reason, the way of the philosophers; or through revelation, which may come to only a few, such as the Hebrew prophets, Jesus, or Mohammad; or through a personal revelation that can come to anyone prepared to receive it. This latter way is the way of the mystics, and every major religion has within it groups of people who are more able practitioners of the mystical approach than the average man or woman seems to be.

None of these people questioned whether God exists—whether there is a God. But they wanted to know more about him, or it, and the methods they pursued and the answers they got were diverse. The Muslim thinkers who tried to reconcile reason with the *Quran* were called Faylasufs. Educated for their day, part of the scientific advances taking place in the Muslim world of 1000 CE, they felt that religion should not be relegated to a separate sphere. They believed that the entire universe is rational—therefore the human mind should be able to arrive at the same knowledge of God that had come through revelation.

It was Avicenna whom we remember as the most important exponent of this point of view. Karen Armstrong summarizes his thinking this way: "Something must have started the chain of cause and effect. The absence of such a supreme being would mean that our minds were not in sympathy with reality as a whole. That, in turn, would mean that the universe was not coherent and rational. This utterly simple being upon which the whole of multiple, contingent reality depended was what the religions called 'God.' Because it is the highest thing of all, it must be absolutely perfect and worthy of honor and worship."

Avicenna turned more toward mysticism in his later years. Yet he stands as a prime example of the attempt to reconcile the type of reasoning the Greek philosophers had used with the intuitions of the "religions of the book" that come through revelation.

An opponent of this approach to God was al-Ghazzali (1058-1111). He spent a good part of his life learning the approach of the Faylasufs and then rejecting them. He then spent ten years living as a Sufi (mystic) and became convinced that their way led to an intuitive knowledge. As Armstrong puts it, al-Ghazzali concluded that the mystical experience of the Sufis "was the only way of verifying a reality that lay beyond the reach of the human intellect and cerebral process."

The approach of the Faylasufs found support mostly from Averroes, who lived a couple of generations after the time of al-Ghazzali. His commentaries on Aristotle were translated into Hebrew and Latin, and it was through Averroes that this attempt to reconcile Greek thought, particularly that of Aristotle, with Christianity, spread to northern Europe. Its influence made itself felt most, during the thirteenth century, in the work of Albert the Great (1200-1280) and Thomas Aquinas (1225-1274).

At the same time that there was ferment in the religious thought of Muslims and Jews in southern Europe, there was a stirring going on among some individuals in the Christian North. This would become stronger with the founding of the first universities in leading centers of the continent. But for the moment, consider two persons of this period who had thoughts that resonate and can challenge thinkers today—Anselm and Abelard.

Anselm became the archbishop of Canterbury in 1093. However, he fell out of favor with the English king over several issues and spent much of his time in exile in Rome. He is interesting here because, like some of the Muslim thinkers, he also thought considerably about the relationship of faith and reason. He said he wrote in the spirit of *fides quaerens intellectum*, or "faith seeking understanding." Like the Muslims, he did not think he had to prove the existence of God, which he took for granted, but he wanted that faith to be one that did not contradict his human reason.

In developing his concept of God, he used the following argument: Since we see varying degrees of goodness in the world, there must be some standard of goodness. Similarly, we see varying degrees of perfection, suggesting that there must be some absolute perfection. Finally, we see that effect follows cause. Therefore there must be some ultimate cause. Therefore, for a Christian, the word God means "the highest good, the original cause and the infinite perfection." These proofs for God could be argued against, of course, and they were, even at the time. But the terms of the discussion show that for these thinkers, God was a more universal, spiritual concept than could be conveyed by the popular conceptions of a God made in the image of human beings.

As for Anselm's "faith seeking understanding," what he appears to believe becomes clearer from the translation of the Latin words *Credo ut intellegum*—I believe in order to understand. The word *Credo* at the time meant not a passive belief in some doctrine, but an intellectual grappling with it, or grasping it, since only in the grasping or taking hold of it was it possible to understand.

Another continental thinker of the period was Abelard (1079-1142). He is described by one religious scholar as being "usually rather conventional" in his theological views, but David Chidester calls him "the most controversial scholar of twelfth century Europe." (He is also remembered in literature because of his early love affair with Eloise and its disastrous consequences.) What may have caused Abelard the most trouble was his work on a treatise called *Sic et Non* (Yes and No), a work in which he contrasted some of the statements of faith attributed to the early Church fathers. This seemed to show that there had been disagreement early on over some matters of faith. Abelard fell into disfavor with St. Bernard of Clairvaux, who was perhaps the most prominent French churchman of the century. He was called before a Church council, at which he was vehemently attacked by Bernard. Abelard, already not well, is reported to have collapsed at the council. He died a year later.

Besides Abelard's work in analyzing the early Church fathers, the kind of work that was the beginning of stirrings within the Church that would increasingly cause it to examine itself and its teachings, Abelard rejected the Augustinian doctrine of original sin descending from Adam's disobedience. He maintained that Jesus came neither to pay a ransom for the rest of mankind nor to save humans from the devil. He held, instead, that Jesus' life was "the embodiment of perfect Love" and that by setting this example for mankind he had become its savior.

A World without Islam
by Graham E. Fuller

IMAGINE, IF YOU WILL, A WORLD WITHOUT ISLAM. admittedly an almost inconceivable state of affairs given its charged centrality in our daily news headlines. Islam seems to lie behind a broad range of international disorders: suicide attacks, car bombings, military occupations, resistance struggles, riots, *fatwas*, jihads, guerrilla warfare, threatening videos, and 9/11 itself. "Islam" seems to offer an instant and uncomplicated analytical touchstone, enabling us to make sense of today's convulsive world. Indeed, for some neoconservatives, "Islamofascism" is now our sworn foe in a looming "World War III."

But indulge me for a moment. What if there were no such thing as Islam? What if there had never been a Prophet Mohammad, no saga of the spread of Islam across vast parts of the Middle East, Asia, and Africa?

Given our intense current focus on terrorism, war, and rampant anti-Americanism— some of the most emotional international issues of the day—it's vital to understand the true sources of these crises. Is Islam, in fact, the source of the problem, or does it tend to lie with other less obvious and deeper factors?

For the sake of argument, in an act of historical imagination, picture a Middle East in which Islam had never appeared. Would we then be spared many of the current challenges before us? Would the Middle East be more peaceful? How different might the character of East-West relations be? Without Islam, surely the international order would present a very different picture than it does today. Or would it?

If not Islam, then what?
From the earliest days of a broader Middle East, Islam has seemingly shaped the cultural norms and even political preferences of its followers. How can we then separate Islam from the Middle East? As it turns out, it's not so hard to imagine.

Let's start with ethnicity. Without Islam, the face of the region still remains complex and conflicted. The dominant ethnic groups of the Middle East—Arabs, Persians, Turks, Kurds, Jews, even Berbers and Pashtuns—would still dominate politics. Take the Persians: Long before Islam, successive great Persian empires pushed to the doors of Athens and were the perpetual rivals of whoever inhabited Anatolia. Contesting

Semitic peoples, too, fought the Persians across the Fertile Crescent and into Iraq. And then there are the powerful forces of diverse Arab tribes and traders expanding and migrating into other Semitic areas of the Middle East before Islam. Mongols would still have overrun and destroyed the civilizations of Central Asia and much of the Middle East in the 13th century. Turks still would have conquered Anatolia, the Balkans up to Vienna, and most of the Middle East. These struggles—over power, territory, influence, and trade—existed long before Islam arrived.

Still, it's too arbitrary to exclude religion entirely from the equation. If in fact Islam had never emerged, most of the Middle East would have remained predominantly Christian in its various sects, just as it had been at the dawn of Islam. Apart from some Zoroastrians and small numbers of Jews, no other major religions were present.

But would harmony with the West really have reigned if the whole Middle East had remained Christian? That is a far reach. We would have to assume that a restless and expansive medieval European world would not have projected its power and hegemony into the neighboring East in search of economic and geopolitical footholds. After all, what were the Crusades if not a Western adventure driven primarily by political, social, and economic needs? The banner of Christianity was little more than a potent symbol, a rallying cry to bless the more secular urges of powerful Europeans. In fact, the particular religion of the natives never figured highly in the West's imperial push across the globe. Europe may have spoken upliftingly about bringing "Christian values to the natives," but the patent goal was to establish colonial outposts as sources of wealth for the metropole and bases for Western power projection.

And so it's unlikely that Christian inhabitants of the Middle East would have welcomed the stream of European fleets and their merchants backed by Western guns. Imperialism would have prospered in the region's complex ethnic mosaic—the raw materials for the old game of divide and rule. And Europeans still would have installed the same pliable local rulers to accommodate their needs.

Move the clock forward to the age of oil in the Middle East. Would Middle Eastern states, even if Christian, have welcomed the establishment of European protectorates over their region? Hardly. The West still would have built and controlled the same choke points, such as the Suez Canal. It wasn't Islam that made Middle Eastern states powerfully resist the colonial project, with its drastic redrawing of borders in accordance with European geopolitical preferences. Nor would Middle Eastern Christians have welcomed imperial Western oil companies, backed by their European viceregents, diplomats, intelligence agents, and armies, any more than Muslims did. Look at the long history of Latin American reactions to American domination of their oil, economics, and politics. The Middle East would have been equally keen to create nationalist anticolonial movements to wrest control of their own soil, markets, sovereignty, and destiny from foreign grip—just like anticolonial struggles in Hindu India, Confucian China, Buddhist Vietnam, and a Christian and animist Africa.

And surely the French would have just as readily expanded into a Christian Algeria to seize its rich farmlands and establish a colony. The Italians, too, never let Ethiopia's

Christianity stop them from turning that country into a harshly administered colony. In short, there is no reason to believe that a Middle Eastern reaction to the European colonial ordeal would have differed significantly from the way it actually reacted under Islam.

But maybe the Middle East would have been more democratic without Islam? The history of dictatorship in Europe itself is not reassuring here. Spain and Portugal ended harsh dictatorships only in the mid-1970s. Greece only emerged from church-linked dictatorship a few decades ago. Christian Russia is still not out of the woods. Until quite recently, Latin America was riddled with dictators, who often reigned with US blessing and in partnership with the Catholic Church. Most Christian African nations have not fared much better. Why would a Christian Middle East have looked any different?

And then there is Palestine. It was, of course, Christians who shamelessly persecuted Jews for more than a millennium, culminating in the Holocaust. These horrific examples of anti-Semitism were firmly rooted in Western Christian lands and culture. Jews would therefore have still sought a homeland outside Europe; the Zionist movement would still have emerged and sought a base in Palestine. And the new Jewish state would still have dislodged the same 750,000 Arab natives of Palestine from their lands even if they had been Christian—and indeed some of them were. Would not these Arab Palestinians have fought to protect or regain their own land? The Israeli-Palestinian problem remains at heart a national, ethnic, and territorial conflict, only recently bolstered by religious slogans. And let's not forget that Arab Christians played a major role in the early emergence of the whole Arab nationalist movement in the Middle East; indeed, the ideological founder of the first pan-Arab Ba'ath party, Michel Aflaq, was a Sorbonne-educated Syrian Christian.

But surely Christians in the Middle East would have at least been religiously predisposed toward the West? Couldn't we have avoided all that religious strife? In fact, the Christian world itself was torn by heresies from the early centuries of Christian power, heresies that became the very vehicle of political opposition to Roman or Byzantine power. Far from uniting under religion, the West's religious wars invariably veiled deeper ethnic, strategic, political, economic, and cultural struggles for dominance.

Even the very references to a "Christian Middle East" conceal an ugly animosity. Without Islam, the peoples of the Middle East would have remained as they were at the birth of Islam—mostly adherents of Eastern Orthodox Christianity. But it's easy to forget that one of history's most enduring, virulent, and bitter religious controversies was that between the Catholic Church in Rome and Eastern Orthodox Christianity in Constantinople—a rancor that still persists today. Eastern Orthodox Christians never forgot or forgave the sacking of Christian Constantinople by Western Crusaders in 1204. Nearly 800 years later, in 1999, Pope John Paul II sought to take a few small steps to heal the breach in the first visit of a Catholic pope to the Orthodox world in a thousand years. It was a start, but friction between East and West in a Christian

Middle East would have remained much as it is today. Take Greece, for example: The Orthodox cause has been a powerful driver behind nationalism and anti-Western feeling there, and anti-Western passions in Greek politics, as little as a decade ago, echoed the same suspicions and virulent views of the West that we hear from many Islamist leaders today.

The culture of the Orthodox Church differs sharply from the Western post-Enlightenment ethos, which emphasizes secularism, capitalism, and the primacy of the individual. It still maintains residual fears about the West that parallel in many ways current Muslim insecurities: fears of Western missionary proselytism, the perception of religion as a key vehicle for the protection and preservation of their own communities and culture, and a suspicion of the "corrupted" and imperial character of the West. Indeed, in an Orthodox Christian Middle East, Moscow would enjoy special influence, even today, as the last major center of Eastern Orthodoxy. The Orthodox world would have remained a key geopolitical arena of East-West rivalry in the Cold War. Samuel Huntington, after all, included the Orthodox Christian world among several civilizations embroiled in a cultural clash with the West.

Today, the US occupation of Iraq would be no more welcome to Iraqis if they were Christian. The United States did not overthrow Saddam Hussein, an intensely nationalist and secular leader, because he was Muslim. Other Arab peoples would still have supported the Iraqi Arabs in their trauma of occupation. Nowhere do people welcome foreign occupation and the killing of their citizens at the hands of foreign troops. Indeed, groups threatened by such outside forces invariably cast about for appropriate ideologies to justify and glorify their resistance struggle. Religion is one such ideology.

This, then, is the portrait of a putative "world without Islam". It is a Middle East dominated by Eastern Orthodox Christianity—a church historically and psychologically suspicious of, even hostile to, the West. Still riven by major ethnic and even sectarian differences, this Middle East possesses a fierce sense of historical consciousness and grievance against the West. It has been invaded repeatedly by Western imperialist armies; its resources commandeered; its borders redrawn by Western fiat in conformity with the West's various interests; and regimes established that are compliant with Western dictates. Palestine would still burn. Iran would still be intensely nationalistic. We would still see Palestinians resist Jews, Chechens resist Russians, Iranians resist the British and Americans, Kashmiris resist Indians, Tamils resist the Sinhalese in Sri Lanka, and Uighurs and Tibetans resist the Chinese. The Middle East would still have a glorious historical model—the great Byzantine Empire of more than 2,000 years standing—with which to identify as a cultural and religious symbol. It would, in many respects, perpetuate an East-West divide.

It does not present an entirely peaceful and comforting picture.

Under the Prophet's Banner
It is, of course, absurd to argue that the existence of Islam has had no independent

impact on the Middle East or East-West relations. Islam has provided a unifying force of a high order across a wide region. As a global universal faith, it has created a broad civilization that shares many common principles of philosophy, the arts, and society; a vision of the moral life; a sense of justice, jurisprudence, and good governance—all in a deeply rooted high culture. As a cultural and moral force, Islam has helped bridge ethnic differences among diverse Muslim peoples, encouraging them to feel part of a broader Muslim civilizational project. That alone furnishes it with great weight. Islam affected political geography as well: If there had been no Islam, the Muslim countries of South Asia and Southeast Asia today—particularly Pakistan, Bangladesh, Malaysia, and Indonesia—would be rooted instead in the Hindu world.

Islamic civilization provided a common ideal to which all Muslims could appeal in the name of resistance against Western encroachment. Even if that appeal failed to stem the Western imperial tide, it created a cultural memory of a commonly shared fate that did not go away. Europeans were able to divide and conquer numerous African, Asian, and Latin American peoples who then fell singly before Western power. A united, transnational resistance among those peoples was hard to achieve in the absence of any common ethnic or cultural symbol of resistance.

In a world without Islam, Western imperialism would have found the task of dividing, conquering, and dominating the Middle East and Asia much easier. There would not have remained a shared cultural memory of humiliation and defeat across a vast area. That is a key reason why the United States now finds itself breaking its teeth upon the Muslim world.

Today, global intercommunications and shared satellite images have created a strong self-consciousness among Muslims and a sense of a broader Western imperial siege against a common Islamic culture. This siege is not about modernity; it is about the unceasing Western quest for domination of the strategic space, resources, and even culture of the Muslim world—the drive to create a "pro-American" Middle East. Unfortunately, the United States naïvely assumes that Islam is all that stands between it and the prize.

But what of terrorism—the most urgent issue the West most immediately associates with Islam today? In the bluntest of terms, would there have been a 9/11 without Islam? If the grievances of the Middle East, rooted in years of political and emotional anger at US policies and actions, had been wrapped up in a different banner, would things have been vastly different? Again, it's important to remember how easily religion can be invoked even when other long-standing grievances are to blame. Sept. 11, 2001, was not the beginning of history. To the Al-Qaeda hijackers, Islam functioned as a magnifying glass in the sun, collecting these widespread shared common grievances and focusing them into an intense ray, a moment of clarity of action against the foreign invader.

In the West's focus on terrorism in the name of Islam, memories are short. Jewish guerrillas used terrorism against the British in Palestine. Sri Lankan Hindu Tamil "Tigers" invented the art of the suicide vest and for more than a decade led the world in the use of suicide bombings—including the assassination of Indian Prime Minister Rajiv Gandhi. Greek terrorists carried out assassination operations against US officials in Athens. Organized Sikh terrorism killed Indira Gandhi, spread havoc in India, established an overseas base in Canada, and brought down an Air India flight over the Atlantic. Macedonian terrorists were widely feared all across the Balkans on the eve of World War I. Dozens of major assassinations in the late 19th and early 20th centuries were carried out by European and American "anarchists," sowing collective fear. The Irish Republican Army employed brutally effective terrorism against the British for decades, as did communist guerrillas and terrorists in Vietnam against Americans, communist Malayans against British soldiers in the 1950s, Mau-Mau terrorists against British officers in Kenya—the list goes on. It doesn't take a Muslim to commit terrorism.

Even the recent history of terrorist activity doesn't look much different. According to Europol, 498 terrorist attacks took place in the European Union in 2006. Of these, 424 were perpetrated by separatist groups, 55 by left-wing extremists, and 18 by various other terrorists. Only 1 was carried out by Islamists. To be sure, there were a number of foiled attempts in a highly surveilled Muslim community. But these figures reveal the broad ideological range of potential terrorists in the world.

Is it so hard to imagine then, Arabs—Christian or Muslim—angered at Israel or imperialism's constant invasions, overthrows, and interventions employing similar acts of terrorism and guerrilla warfare? The question might be instead, why didn't it happen sooner? As radical groups articulate grievances in our globalized age, why should we not expect them to carry their struggle into the heart of the West?

If Islam hates modernity, why did it wait until 9/11 to launch its assault? And why did key Islamic thinkers in the early 20th century speak of the need to embrace modernity even while protecting Islamic culture? Osama bin Laden's cause in his early days was not modernity at all—he talked of Palestine, American boots on the ground in Saudi Arabia, Saudi rulers under US control, and modern "Crusaders." It is striking that it was not until as late as 2001 that we saw the first major boiling over of Muslim anger onto US soil itself, in reaction to historical as well as accumulated recent events and US policies. If not 9/11, some similar event like it was destined to come.

And even if Islam as a vehicle of resistance had never existed, Marxism did. It is an ideology that has spawned countless terrorist, guerrilla, and national liberation movements. It has informed the Basque ETA, the FARC in Colombia, the Shining Path in Peru, and the Red Army Faction in Europe, to name only a few in the West. George Habash, the founder of the deadly Popular Front for the Liberation of Palestine, was a Greek Orthodox Christian and Marxist who studied at the American University of Beirut. In an era when angry Arab nationalism flirted with violent Marxism, many Christian Palestinians lent Habash their support.

Peoples who resist foreign oppressors seek banners to propagate and glorify the cause of their struggle. The international class struggle for justice provides a good rallying point. Nationalism is even better. But religion provides the best one of all, appealing to the highest powers in prosecuting its cause. And religion everywhere can still serve to bolster ethnicity and nationalism even as it transcends it—especially when the enemy is of a different religion. In such cases, religion ceases to be primarily the source of clash and confrontation, but rather its vehicle. The banner of the moment may go away, but the grievances remain.

We live in an era when terrorism is often the chosen instrument of the weak. It already stymies the unprecedented might of US armies in Iraq, Afghanistan, and elsewhere. And thus bin Laden in many non-Muslim societies has been called the "next Che Guevara." It's nothing less than the appeal of successful resistance against dominant American power, the weak striking back, an appeal that transcends Islam or Middle Eastern culture.

More of the same

But the question remains, if Islam didn't exist, would the world be more peaceful? In the face of these tensions between East and West, Islam unquestionably adds yet one more emotive element, one more layer of complications to finding solutions. Islam is not the cause of such problems. It may seem sophisticated to seek out passages in the *Quran* that seem to explain "why they hate us." But that blindly misses the nature of the phenomenon. How comfortable to identify Islam as the source of "the problem"; it's certainly much easier than exploring the impact of the massive global footprint of the world's sole superpower.

A world without Islam would still see most of the enduring bloody rivalries whose wars and tribulations dominate the geopolitical landscape. If it were not religion, all of these groups would have found some other banner under which to express nationalism and a quest for independence. Sure, history would not have followed the exact same path as it has. But, at rock bottom, conflict between East and West remains all about the grand historical and geopolitical issues of human history: ethnicity, nationalism, ambition, greed, resources, local leaders, turf, financial gain, power, interventions, and hatred of outsiders, invaders, and imperialists. Faced with timeless issues like these, how could the power of religion not be invoked?

Remember too, that virtually every one of the principle horrors of the 20th century came almost exclusively from strictly secular regimes: Leopold II of Belgium in the Congo, Hitler, Mussolini, Lenin and Stalin, Mao, and Pol Pot. It was Europeans who visited their "world wars" twice upon the rest of the world—two devastating global conflicts with no remote parallels in Islamic history.

Some today might wish for a "world without Islam" in which these problems presumably had never come to be. But, in truth, the conflicts, rivalries, and crises of such a world might not look so vastly different than the ones we know today.

The Faith Line: On Building the Cathedrals of Pluralism
by Eboo Patel

THERE IS A LINE IN THE LATE WORK OF THE recently departed American writer Susan Sontag, "Whatever is happening, something else is always going on."

Reading that made me think of a woman I met at an interfaith conference in Australia a few months back, Gill Hicks. "She uses a cane," I remember thinking to myself when she walked into the room. "Strange for a woman so young."

I forgot about that as we got into a discussion of interfaith relations in Britain and America. I was struck by the depth of her knowledge of the Muslim community, the extent of her relationships. She spent her days meeting with Muslim leaders and her evenings organizing programs that brought people from different ethnic groups together to build bridges.

"What's your professional background?" I asked. "Were you trained in this?"

She laughed and said, "I'm an interior designer."

"So how did you come to do this work?" I prodded.

"I was on the London Tube on July 7. I lost my legs on the Piccadilly line."

I opened and closed my mouth a few times and finally stammered out, "What do you think of when you think of it now?"

"The same thing I thought of then," she said. "How good human beings can be."

I stared at her in disbelief.

"As I was almost bleeding to death, there were people making their way down into the tunnel, risking their lives to save me.

"I heard voices around me and felt someone touching my shoulder and shouting, 'Priority One.'"

"I awoke in the hospital with a wristband inscribed with words, 'One Unknown.' My medical intake sheet read, 'Estimated Female.' And I realized that the people who saved me had no idea who I was. They were from all different backgrounds themselves, and it didn't matter if I was richer or poorer than them, lighter or darker, if I prayed in the same way or a different way or not at all."

Listening to her, I thought back to my own reaction to the London Tube bombing, how angry I was—how angry the whole world was. I remember the newspaper headlines of how we were all becoming more suspicious of each other, how that was a natural reaction. I remember the calls to arms, the clouds hanging over groups that happened to share an ethnicity or religion with those four terrorists.

Who knew that there was another set of eyes on the matter? Who knew that Gill Hicks was lying in her hospital bed arguing with her fiancé about the menu for their wedding, determined to get married on the day that they had planned, resolved that this incident would only inspire her to learn more about other people, only commit her further to building bridges, to shining light, to loving fully. Who knew that one of the people who lay bleeding deep in the tunnel thought mostly of the strangers who were rescuing her rather than the strangers who had harmed her?

"Whatever is happening, something else is always going on."

In his new book, *Peace Be Upon You*, Zachary Karabell writes: "If we emphasize hate, scorn, war, and conquest, we are unlikely to perceive that any other path is viable…"

Hate, scorn, war, and conquest sound like a pretty good summary of our newscasts; it certainly seems like the dominant narrative of our times. And the soundtrack of violence these days appears to be prayer—in Arabic, in Hebrew, in Hindi, in various inflections of English.

There are many who are eager to divide humanity along a faith line: Sunnis vs Shias; Catholics vs Protestants; Hindus vs Buddhists.

I believe there is something else going on. I believe that the faith line is indeed the challenge of our century, but it does not divide people of different religious backgrounds. The faith line does not separate Muslims and Christians or Hindus and Jews. The faith line separates religious totalitarians and religious pluralists.

A religious totalitarian is someone who seeks to suffocate those who are different. Their weapons range from suicide bombs to media empires. There are Christian totalitarians and Hindu totalitarians, Jewish totalitarians and Muslim totalitarians. They are on the same side of the faith line: arm in arm against the dream of a common life together.

A pluralist is someone who seeks to live with people who are different, be enriched by them, help them thrive. Pluralists resonate with the Quranic line: "God made us different nations and tribes that we may come to know one another." Pluralists are moved by the image of the Reverend Martin Luther King Jr. marching together with the Rabbi Abraham Joshua Heschel in Selma. Pluralists love the words of the poet Gwendolyn Brooks:

We are each other's business
We are each other's harvest
We are each other's magnitude and bond

Near the beginning of *A People's History of the United States*, Howard Zinn hopes out loud that "our future may be found in the past's fugitive moments of compassion rather than in its solid centuries of warfare."

So many eyes went to the smoldering ruins of those subway trains on July 7 and saw only destruction, perceived only a victory for the totalitarians, imagined only the narrow inevitability of continuing violence.

But one woman was looking in a different direction. Her eyes went to the subway workers who rescued her, the nurses and doctors who restored her, the family and fiancé who never left her side. This was what it meant to be human.

Like Jane Addams, Nobel Peace laureate and founder of the US Settlement House movement, Gill Hicks began to imagine a "cathedral" for this humanity—a place where people from different backgrounds lived together in mutual trust and loyalty. And she left her career to follow that calling: to make the cathedral in her imagination a reality on earth—stone by stone, meeting by meeting, program by program.

We pluralists far outnumber the totalitarians. What if we let ourselves imagine? What if we began building? What if every city block were a cathedral of pluralism, every university campus; every summer camp and day care. There would not be enough bombs in the world to destroy all of our cathedrals.

I believe each one of us is born with that cathedral inscribed in our soul. Our imaginations know its architecture intimately. Our hands recognize the cut of each stone. As South African novelist and Nobel prizewinner J. M. Coetzee says, "All creatures come into the world bringing with them the memory of justice." We Muslims call it being born in a state of *fitrah*, naturally inclining towards that which is good, because God gave us the gift of his *ruh*, of his breath.

It is from breath that we get life, and from breath that we get song, and the most beautiful thing we do in cathedrals is sing.

Earth is not always an easy place to imagine cathedrals, or to build them, or to fill them with song. There are times when you will feel like there is a conspiracy against your clarity, like the loneliness is freezing and the darkness is deep and the silence is unbreakable. Go back to your breath. Know its source. Know its purpose. Know that sometimes the order is upside down—that instead of going from imagination to building to song, you have to begin by singing.

And as you get accustomed to the sound of your own voice, you may discover that it is not alone. You may discover that a group of strangers has gathered, and they are humming, harmonizing, taking your lead, singing along. You may realize that the darkness has been broken by a soft glow. You may wonder where exactly you are. You may look around and see stained glass, you may look up and find yourself staring into the forever spire of a majestic cathedral.

And then you will know the truth of the words of the Chinese-American poet Li-Young Lee: "You must sing to be found; when found, you must sing."

Economic Development in Three Muslim Countries
by Juan Cole

HERE ARE SOME TRENDS THAT I HOPE CONTINUE and deepen in 2008. Turkey and Indonesia are making strides as secular democracies in Muslim-majority countries, with impressive political participation on the part of the public, with elections that produce surprises for the powers that be, and with steady economic growth. The striking thing about both of them is that they did it mostly on their own. You have to contrast their success with Bush's two experiments in imposing democracy from the outside, both of which are having a rocky ride. A third good news story is Egypt, which has in the past few years seen impressive economic growth and foreign investment, though it has not significantly democratized.

Turkey weathered several major political crises and yet remained relatively stable and relatively democratic. The powerful Turkish military clearly did not want former Foreign Minister Abdullah Gul to become president, because he (although no fundamentalist) is too religious for their taste. Gul was nevertheless elected, and the military swallowed it. Turkey's democracy is fragile and the country has a number of objectionable laws that limit key freedoms, but it certainly is the most democratic state in the Muslim Middle East. The demonstration that secular elites will allow an Islamically tinged party like the AK Party of Gul to come to power could be an important lesson for other Muslim countries, e.g., Egypt.

Turkey's rate of population growth has slowed, a key requirement for economic progress. A package of changes in Turkish penal laws is being introduced by parliament as part of the attempt to harmonize Turkish law with that of the European Union (which Turkey wants to join). Turkey has been having strong economic growth for the past six years, in the range of 5% or 6%. That growth slowed in 2007, apparently mostly because of a drought that hurt agriculture and a slightly over-valued Turkish lira that hurt exports. While the ongoing crisis with Iraqi Kurdistan is worrisome, the OECD thinks that Turkey's economy will post good growth of 6% a year during 2008 and 2009. Turkey's tourist sector is expanding especially quickly, with lots of new airline routes to Istanbul and billions of dollars in foreign investment.

Democracy appears to be entrenching itself in Indonesia, which is a secular democratic state with a Muslim majority. Neither of the two major parties is interested in moving toward a theocracy. The country had a peaceful transition in the presidency in 2004 and weathered the devastating tsunami the following year. The economy is doing well, a 6.3% growth rate and a 10% increase in exports. The Jemaah Islamiyah, an affiliate of al-Qaeda, turns out to have no grass roots in the country, and the horrific Bali bombing of a nightclub was more an echo of the 1980s Afghanistan jihad than a harbinger of the future. Although there are Muslim parties that want to make Islamic law the law of the land, they are peaceful and small and are unlikely to get their way, at least any time soon.

Indonesia is the world's fourth-largest country, with a population of 234 million. It is also the largest Muslim country in the world (about 201 million are Muslim). While it has a fairly restrictive press law on government information, it is a genuine democracy by any measure, with some 800 newspapers that publish freely without government censorship. It is instructive that Indonesian newspaper editorials have seen Pakistan's current crisis as a result of military rule and have generally agreed that their country avoided such crises by democratizing from 1999. Tom Ginsburg argues that Indonesia is among a handful of "third wave" democratizations that have been success stories, and he notes that many of them (Taiwan, the Philippines, South Korea, and Mongolia) are in Asia. He contrasts Muslim Indonesia's success with the return to forms of authoritarianism in Russia and the rise of authoritarian populism in Latin America.

Egypt, which grew 7% in 2007, saw a drop in poverty levels and attracted $11 billion USD in foreign investment. Egypt was an economic basket case and turgid military dictatorship for so long that these numbers make my head spin (it has been growing five and six percent for the past few years). These changes have not passed without controversy. Some neoliberal policies have provoked labor strikes, by workers afraid that their job security will be lessened. Egypt's population growth rate is slowing, but it faces more problems from increased population than Turkey or Indonesia.

One explanation for Egypt's growth in the past half-decade is that the Gulf oil states are at last investing in local economies. The United States has made it unpleasant for Saudis and Qataris to come to the US, and investors like to be able to visit the places they park big capital. So, some of them are investing in Egypt, which has cheap labor, an increasing literacy rate, and expanding rates of internet use. Tourism generated $2 billion USD more in 2006 than it had in 2005, so Cairo is a pretty good place to own a five star hotel. If this theory is correct, and the vastly increased petroleum revenues in the Middle East are being put to use productively in the region itself, that could be an omen of big, positive changes.

Despite the Muslim Brotherhood's having won an unprecedented 88 seats in the lower house of the Egyptian parliament last year, the fact is that Egyptian elections are fixed and there is more or less a president for life. It seems to me unlikely that Egypt can maintain its current high growth rates unless it moves more quickly toward democracy. The perils of military rule in a growing economy with a restless but disenfranchised new middle class are obvious in Pakistan.

Chapter Four

Palestine / Israel

Growing Up in Al Quds
by Jacob Nammar

I WAS BORN ON MAY 16, 1941, IN MADINAT AL QUDS—The Holy City, the City of Peace, now known as Jerusalem. It is the holy city for the three Abrahamic religions of Judaism, Christianity and Islam. In my family, we were taught that we are all God's children and are all descendants of Abraham, who is the father of the three faiths. We believed in the biblical promise of the land to Abraham and his descendants. For centuries families of all three faiths had lived side by side, had shared the land, and had thought of themselves as one community.

We were a family of ten; my father, Yousef, my mother Tuma, four brothers and three sisters. We were all healthy, energetic and, I must admit, good-looking. Mihran was the oldest, followed by Fahima, Daoud, Suleiman, Wedad, Fadwa, Yacoub and Zakaria all about two years apart. Following the tradition in the Holy Land my parents gave biblical names for the boys and expressive names for the girls. My older sister Fahima's name in Arabic means understanding, Wedad means joy and Fadwa means patriotic—one who would die for a cause. My parents believed that "nothing was impossible" and hoped that the children would live-up to their name by example, faith and determination.

My extended family, the Nammars, also known as *Nammari* or *Al Nammuri* was one of the leading families in Al Quds with relatives scattered throughout the world. Our family owned several tracts of valuable property in the Old City near the Jewish quarter, including several houses near the *Al Nammari Suq Al A'ttarine*—spice market—a wholesale and retail market for the community. They owned several orchards near Jaffa and a large house where once a year they vacationed and helped in the harvest of citrus fruits. They also owned individual properties in the rich ancient historical city of Nablus, situated north of Al Quds, believed to be the biblical site of Jacob's well.

In addition, the Nammars owned agriculture farms in the villages of Yalu and Imwas for cultivation of grains, wheat, bulgur, and other produce. Each harvest we all received a large share of the yield to divide among all the extended family members. My oldest sister Fahima remembered that each year they came in a caravan of twelve camels riding for seven days and seven nights. While in town, the camels were sheltered in our large yard. On one occasion, Fahima noticed one camel crying in pain because he had a big nail in one foot. It took four men to hold him down to pull the nail out and bind the wound to save him.

In the mid-eighteen century Al Quds was primarily inside the Old City. It was surrounded by a large wall with eight gates, which were closed each night to protect the inhabitants. As the Old City became overcrowded, several wealthy families ventured outside the wall, including some of the Nammars who branched out by developing a new suburb west of the city in Al Baq'a. The relocation from the Old City to the West New City created an exclusive community named *Harat Al Namamreh* or *Al-Nammariyya*—the Nammars neighborhood. They built new palatial homes with unique spacious architectural designs for an upper class lifestyle. These *Qusur*—villas—were built from pure white/red stones with red tile roofs at a hill-top on both sides of a straight line which became known as the *Share'a Al Nammamreh*—Nammar Street.

Papa was handsome, a tall, dark man. He seemed a rock to me, powerfully built with authoritarian deep black eyes that could be stern but also gentle. He rarely used physical punishment. To discipline us all he needed was to give a stern look. His penetrating glance would make us shiver! We were always eager to welcome him home, not just because he brought us good news and gifts, but because the family seemed restored when he returned. On occasions we kissed his hand to show him our respect and love. In contrast to his strength, Mama was gentle, loving and tender. She was beautiful with fair skin and long hair. No wonder Papa fell in love with her in a romantic fairy-tale, "love at first sight."

Papa was born in Al Quds in 1900 and Mama was born in Deir Baker, Armenia, in 1910. When she was five, she witnessed her father, a judge, and her family massacred by the Ottoman Turks. Mama was rescued by Armenian nuns belonging to an underground resistance group. They transported her to Beirut, Lebanon, and placed her at a Christian convent.

During that time, Papa wore a *tarboush*—Fez Turkish hat—and drove a tourist bus throughout the Middle East's major cities. On one trip he was introduced to Mama in Beirut. He began to court her and showered her with gifts as is the traditional Palestinian custom. Papa had become a frequent visitor to this beautiful Mediterranean city and on each visit he became more attached and convinced she was to be his future wife. Unfortunately, the Nammar family did not approve of this courtship, since they had other plans for him. He was to marry one of his cousins as was customary in our extended family. But Papa's mind was made up and on one of his last trips to Beirut he got married by a civil Justice of Peace.

As it was illegal to cross from one country to the other, Papa daringly smuggled Mama in the bus luggage compartment to Al-Quds against not only the authorities but also against his own family wishes. As a result, for a while Papa was disinherited and isolated from his extended family. Several years later the Nammars gradually learned to accept our family. We moved to the *Harat Al Nammamreh* to live with my grandparents in their spacious home.

Mama was constantly busy taking great care of her eight children. All my brothers, sisters and I believed she was our living saint, which influenced my faith and gave me a deep moral upbringing. She was loved by everyone and was always positive. One day I accidentally broke one of her favorite water glasses. I felt awful. She did not scold me. All she said was, "You just broke the evil spell. Don't be hard on yourself."

Papa made trips throughout the Middle East, especially to exotic cities such as Beirut, Amman, Damascus, and Cairo—although, I did not know much about these beautiful places at the time. I remember a time when he was gone. I didn't know where. I knew only that he was away and it seemed as if he had been gone forever. Early in the mornings I would see Mama standing in front of the window, looking up toward heaven. A devout Armenian Christian, she always carried her little *Bible* with her. Regularly, standing at the window, she would raise her arms to pray in Arabic or Armenian. I knew then she was thinking of my Papa because sometimes when I stood before that same window I would be thinking of him too.

In the evenings when Papa was gone, Mama would tell us stories: the exciting adventures of King Sinbad the Sailor or the Forty Thieves of Baghdad or of the real-life Arab warrior Salah Al Din who defeated the Crusaders from Europe. Sometimes they were humorous, maybe the "tales of Juha," a popular Arab comic figure. But even as we listened raptly, all huddled together, or laughed together, sometimes falling on top of one another, we wondered where Papa was. And when he'd come home so we'd all be together.

One night while he was gone, I cuddled beside Mama as she told us a story. When she finished, I whispered to her, "Mama, when Papa returns, I want to be the one who takes his shoes." She kissed the top of my head. "Can I be the one who does that?" I implored.

"Isn't it enough to kiss his hand?" she asked.

"Please," I begged. "I want to take his shoes."

"Maybe," she said. "We'll see." What else could she say with eight children, all of whom would compete to take Papa's shoes? But as I lay waiting for sleep, I did not think about Shahrazad who needed every night to tell the king a story so fascinating that he would forget he intended to kill her in the morning and never could do so because she made sure to end the story only half told. I did not think of her. All I could think of was taking Papa's shoes.

Each morning Mama would wake me by kissing me on my forehead and telling me softly it was time to get ready for school. I would take bus number four from Al Baq'a to the Old City where everyone knew each other. Since my father was a member of the *Shareket Al Wataniya*, the national bus company, when he was at home he frequently took me with him sitting next to him on long journeys. So most bus drivers knew me, and when I proudly announced as I boarded the bus on my way to school that I was *Ibin Nammar*—son of Nammar—they gave me free rides.

After school each day returning to the bus stop I walked through the hubbub of an exciting shopping district past the *Suq Al-Attarine*, the open air spice market. I watched women, some flaunting their new western clothing with decorative hats, while most dressed in their traditional colorful hand-embroidered dresses and scarves. I noticed large bags of dried beans, bulgur, flour, sugar and an assortment of spices. The sweet and strong smell of cinnamon, allspice and cloves drew me to the center of the market where the merchant was sipping his strong coffee. I could hear the intense haggling going on between various merchants and customers which seemingly favored the customers. I was particularly fond of the store that sold *tahini*—sesame seed paste—and my feet always guided me there. Sometimes I would dip my finger to taste the rich smooth *tahini*. Oh, the aromas of that market! They would cling to me for the rest of the day.

Occasionally I could not resist the temptation of the beautiful fresh fruits display brought by the *falahin*—farmers, peasants who came each morning at dawn from the many small charming villages surrounding Al-Quds. My young taste buds were enticed by the pomegranates with their red seeds like rubies, sweet and juicy, but dearly guarded by the merchant. I found it easy to pick an apple and run. I knew it was mischievous but the owners never chased me. Only later did I learn that some of the stores in the *Suq* were owned by the *Al Nammar* family.

Often I walked by Gahwa, the coffee vendor, who carried his heavy coffee maker on his back, poor fellow. Or by Zuzu, a Sudanese peanut peddler, who had made Al Quds his home when he ran out of money after his pilgrimage to Mecca. To earn a living he roasted peanuts in a primitive fire pit. Approaching I would hear him call loudly, "*Fustuq suhun, fustuq suhun, mil wahad, mil wahad*"—"hot peanuts, hot peanuts, one penny, one penny," and I would smell that unmistakable aroma. Sometimes I stood in line waiting for him to roast a new batch to keep up with demand. When my turn came, I handed him a penny and for this he would place in the palm of my hand one full spoon of warm, delicious peanuts or drop them onto a piece of torn newspaper. And I would finally get to the bus stop, eating peanuts, wondering where my father was and when he would be coming home.

During the British Mandate period when I grew a little older, I became friends with Scottish soldiers who established camp in an olive grove. They liked to take pictures and allowed me to hold their rifles pretending I was shooting at enemies. The soldiers told jokes and my friends and I would make fun of the fact they wore kilts, which to us looked like skirts over bare bottoms! Late one afternoon a friend and I followed two of the soldiers into the *Al Nammar* forest. To our surprise we saw an attractive black woman following. They went to a hideout in the woods. We sneaked up on them and hid behind thick trees. Blissfully unaware of their audience, they undressed completely and—What we witnessed! Papa always insisted that Mama skip any story that included a hint of sex out of deference to my sisters. My friend and I swore that we would never tell what we had seen that day in the forest.

One afternoon, as I was playing with our dog after school, I noticed Laddie wagging his tail. I knew then that Papa was arriving home. I happily ran to greet him. Mama welcomed him with open arms. She quickly remembered and whispered to Papa,

"Yacoub will be honored to take your shoes and make you feel comfortable."

Papa sat in his overstuffed chair next to the window overlooking the vegetable garden. I promptly bent down and removed his faded shoes and worn socks from his tired feet. I immediately noticed the bunions on his two big toes, which became a trademark in our family. I slipped my small feet into his large shoes shuffling my way to his bedroom. Mama placed Papa's feet in a bucket of hot salted water to cleanse and relax them.

When I returned with Papa's slippers, I sat next to him. I could see in his eyes my bringing the slippers was as meaningful to him as it was for me. He then proceeded to tell us about his trip.

Al Quds was a city where religions coexisted happily together. I remember that every year, especially during the holidays, Christians, Muslims and Jews from all over the world made their pilgrimage and converged on the Old City. They greeted each other: "*Al salaam alaykum, Wa alaykum al salaam*"—"May peace be with you and upon you peace." Devoted visitors worshiped in their respective holy shrines.

Faithful Christians came from America and Europe during Easter and Christmas to pray holding their *Holy Bible* at the Church of the Nativity in Bethlehem, at the place where it was said Jesus Christ was born in the manger. They came to the Church of the Holy Sepulcher in Al Quds, known as Church of the Resurrection—traditional site of Jesus' burial. They also prayed at Golgotha, the scene of the crucifixion.

Muslim pilgrims came from as far away as the Philippines, Pakistan, China, Turkey, Sudan and Saudi Arabia. After they made their *Hajj* to Mecca they worshiped standing and kneeling together while reciting the *Holy Quran* at the *Haram Al-Sharif,* at the Dome of the Rock, the place from which the Prophet Mohammad ascended to heaven.

Devout Jews lined-up in front of the Wailing Wall, the last remnants of the Temple of Solomon, to pray with the *Holy Torah* while bowing and sticking small pieces of paper, messages to God, in the many holes in the wall.

Al Quds provided freedom, equality and schools for all multi-religious education. Since my parents placed great value on education and my mother, as the more religious, had me baptized and enrolled at French Catholic schools, which were the best private schools in the city.

Over the years, my parents managed our large family very well, teaching us the rules of life, independent thinking and the freedom to practice our religious beliefs. They emphasized the Ten Commandments and the traditional values of respect for others, irrespective of their religion, race or ethnicity. They taught us not to hate but to love everyone as children of God. We were strictly forbidden—*haram*—to curse or use foul language. We were taught religious tolerance and often reminded that "God will help those who help themselves."

It was a time of happiness. I grew up with multi-religious and cultural teachings and prayed in the city's holiest churches. Al Quds shaped my spirit, religion, heritage, identity and earthly consciousness. I sensed the presence of God always with me. It was the golden place—"Heaven on Earth"—the envy of the rest of the world. I felt loyal to my family and the City of Love and Peace. I was connected to the land and cherished my rich culture with its revered traditions and strong values.

The Israel I Was Fighting For
by Amitai Etzioni

SIXTY YEARS AGO, WHEN I WAS FIGHTING FOR Israel during its war of independence, I won a lot of respect. Now many of my liberal colleagues, including Jewish ones, raise their eyebrows. They hoped for an Israel that is citadel of individual rights, a land in which social justice prevails as laid out by the Prophets, and a peace-making nation—a sort of a Switzerland in the Middle East, only more enlightened.

These liberals are ready to trade land (that is, Israeli land) for peace, a fine idea—if peace can be had. They claim that they "know" (especially if they toured the Holy Land for a week or more) that when Hamas states that it seeks the destruction of Israel, this is merely rhetorical stance and nothing more than posturing to improve its hand in the forthcoming peace deal. They are sure that if Israeli leaders would only agree to sit down and talk with Hamas (and Syria and maybe even Iran), differences could be worked out. If not, they maintain, the US must "lean" more on Israel.

About the last thing my colleagues want to hear about is 1948, when seven Arab armies invaded the day-old Israel. They know little about the large numbers of Israelis killed during the War of Independence and the still larger number who were maimed and wounded. (My Pal Mach unit started with eleven hundred members and end up with four hundred).

During the Six Day War, when Israel again repelled its attackers with great courage and sacrifice, my colleagues still congratulated me. They still could take some pride in victorious Jewish fighters. Today, Israeli incursions into Gaza, the oppressive occupation of the West Bank, the killing of innocent Palestinian civilians, are viewed as akin to Bush's invasion of Iraq, or worse. When I now recount the days in Jerusalem when Jordanian tanks were closing in and we had nothing that could stop them and suggest that the same holds now for the missiles Syria, Hezbollah and Iran are readying, my many liberals are quick to suggest that if Israel would make peace with the Palestinians, all the other nations in the Middle East would fall in line. "The road to Tehran [Beirut, Damascus, Riyadh] runs through Jerusalem" is their favorite cliché.

Above all, they want for Israel to withdraw to the 1967 borders, not merely to stop the oppressive occupation but also to ensure that Israel will remain a democratic state. They hold that as long as Israel contains within its borders a large and rapidly multiplying Palestinian population, to become a majority in the near future, Israel will be forced to give up either its democratic nature—or its Jewishness. Given that they were never subject to a mortar barrage, or had to take out a machine gun nest, my colleagues pay little attention to the small number of days—or should I say hours?—

that Israel would survive if the West Bank would become a much extended version of rocket-launching Gaza.

Moreover, for many liberals, withdrawing to the 1967 borders is but the first step. Their next concern, very much echoing other multicultural agendas, is for Israel to cease being a Jewish state, to become a state in which the Arab citizens of Israel (about 17% of the total population) have exactly the same rights as Jews—and the state is culturally neutral. Never mind that as it is Arabs in Israel already have many more rights—*de jure* and *de facto*—than they have in any Arab state. Israeli Arabs vote freely and are represented in the Knesset by their elected officials. Muslim religious functionaries are free to arrange all personal matters (marriage, divorce, burial, etc.) as they wish, just as Jews are.

Still many liberals want to strip Israel from any remaining Jewish features. They are so inclined because in their mind this is what a full respect for the rights of Arab-Israelis commands and because these liberals are mainly secularists and deeply offended by the fundamentalist Rabbis who do command undue influence and a bunch of privileges in Israel. These liberals ignore that separation of state and religion is largely a French-American ideal, not established in most democracies, and that all nations have some kind of cultural identity, indeed often one that has a religious tinge. (For instance, in many democratic countries, only Christian holidays are national holidays).

All this makes me reexamine what I did fight for (and would again), why my son volunteered to serve in the Israeli Air Force, and why my granddaughter just completed her basic training. The need for Jews to have their own state is not smaller today than it was in 1948, given the very widespread anti-Semitism in the four corners of the earth. Moreover, by my light, Jews have the same rights as other ethnic groups all over the world, from Romanians to Indonesians, from Jamaicans to the people of East Timor, to embed their community in state, and for the Jewish state to maintain some, already very attenuated, cultural identity.

I strongly favor the kind of peace deal with the Palestinians that Ehud Barak championed and for which Yitzhak Rabin died. However, such a deal must entail stopping attacks on Israel and threatening its very existence. If not, I fear, and I know what I am writing about, there will be many more casualties on both sides, all God's children, all people who deserve to live in peace.

A Gift to My Elementary School in Gaza
by Ramzy Baroud

I COLLECTED THREE HUNDRED DOLLARS TO SEND TO my old elementary school in the Nuseirat refugee camp in Gaza. The purpose of the gift, as I outlined to my fifth grade English teacher, Zaki, was to honor the pupils of the barely standing refugee school. "To honor students with good grades?" my teacher proposed. "No," I said, "all the students."

I knew too well that the amount of money could hardly repair one damaged wall in the tattered school, still run by the United Nations Relief and Works Agency (UNRWA). I knew that three hundred dollars would even fall short of obtaining brand new chairs for only one of the classrooms, with battered roofs that block neither rain nor sun. But I didn't have the heart to exclude any of these young, tired faces from a possible smile of joy or happiness the three hundred dollars could bring, however little it might be.

Over two decades have passed since my "graduation" and entry to the Middle School, also run by UNRWA. Separating the two schools was a wall, which the students eventually toppled over to make an easy escape route for the first and second graders during Israeli army raids.

It's unfortunate that most of the images that crowd my memory, despite the passing of time, are of some reference to soldiers, military jeeps, bullets, teargas, and the dark smoke from burning tires. Strangely, I managed to forget the names of some of my best friends in the first grade, but remember too well the first army attack on our school. A few soldiers crept in from the least popular corner of the school, near an old orchard, and began firing teargas into the schoolyard. I knew I was suppose to run, but didn't know where exactly, since my tears, fear, and the unbelievable pain in my throat left me nearly paralyzed.

Unluckily for us first graders, the raid was initiated from our end of the school. We ran in circles screaming for our mothers. Some of us managed to escape. Others like me fell on the sand. I fell on my giant schoolbag, since I had no sense of direction. It was then that the sixth graders came to our rescue, some distracting the soldiers and others escorting the rest of us out. I didn't know that this was to be expected. But I later learned that it was an old school tradition. It was also a sad tradition for the parents to flood the school in a panic, some still in their pajamas, looking for their children.

I ran home to tell my mother all about it. The tears, snot, and sand covering my face were enough to tell it all. But as I began visualizing the glorious story I was about to tell in my head, and as I pictured her hugging me and running to get me a falafel sandwich to ease my pain, I spotted her running toward the school herself, looking for me, full of dust, tears, and shouting my name.

So much for my original story of grandeur, narrating my heroic encounter with the soldiers.

Later, I learned that the sixth graders played the role of protectors of the school. It was indeed "cool" being a sixth grader. I couldn't wait for this rite of passage, when I could repay the favor. And I did, more times than I ever hoped for.

But one particular memory managed to find its way through the dust, smoke, and crying children: the day when the UNRWA truck came with our school's ration of balls. The UNRWA truck used to come on the first week of each school year. The driver would step out, as hundreds of little eyes gazed at him, calculating every move he made until he would enter the "Teachers' Room." A few minutes later, it would be official: the United Nations didn't fail us, they delivered three balls: a soccer ball, a volleyball, and a basketball. But since we had to share these three balls between hundreds of students, all three balls were used for soccer. Only the strongest kids played soccer with the basketball. Now that was a challenge.

Mohamed Diab, our art, geography, history, and math teacher was also our physical education teacher. He was like a father to all of us, and like my father, he had no patience, especially when two or more classes had a PE session at the same time. Eventually, he would throw the balls into the crowd of students and let scores of students kick the ball around in any direction they wished. No rules, no referees, and no questions. He would then leave us for a badly needed smoke and a pitch-black cup of tea. I hardly participated in that deadly game of soccer. To satisfy my eagerness to kick something, anything, I used to kick whatever can of soda was lying around. My soccer can game would only catch on toward the end of the year when the three balls were either busted or stolen.

Now I look back at these days to realize how hard life was and still is for Palestinian refugees, for my classmates, then and now. Many of my friends made it to universities and failed to find a decent job afterward. Others were killed by the Israeli army. Some joined resistance groups. Many were imprisoned. And the rest are still in the camp, fighting for survival while holding onto the dream of return to Palestine, from where their parents were forced to flee over fifty years ago.

My fifth grade teacher, Zaki, who was the first to show me how to write my name in English, is supposed to call me with a proposal of how to use the three hundred dollars. Maybe I should ask him to purchase dozens of soccer balls, so that no student is ever forced to kick a rusty can of soda for six years. Maybe I should have him buy special thank you presents for all the sixth graders who have continued to protect the younger ones all these years.

But with all honesty, I don't wish for the roofs to be repaired. I loved it when birds flew into the classroom to feed their young. It was a pleasant distraction from a boring math lesson, to watch the baby birds, as they would sing whenever their mothers returned, carrying a tiny piece of bread. It always reminded me of my own mother, who I saw too often, running to the school, distressed and sometimes barefoot, calling my name. I wish I had the chance to tell her how much that meant to me. God bless her soul.

What's the Deal with Arabs and Jews?
by Stephen Fife

NOT LONG AGO, I WAS DRINKING WITH THE playwright/actor Sam Shepard in a midtown Manhattan watering hole when he turned to me and asked, "So what's the deal with the Arabs and Jews? Don't they ever get tired of killing each other?"

It was an odd question, to say the least. I'm a playwright, not an expert on the Middle East. My only qualification to answer that question was that I happened to be Jewish. Which I guess was why Sam (extremely not-Jewish) had posed the question.

Anyway, my response went something like: "Man, if I knew the answer to that, I'd be in Sweden accepting the Nobel Prize, not hanging out in a bar with you and your long-legged groupies."

Sam had pondered this for a moment, furrowing his cowboy brow, before he downed his drink, ordered another, and moved on to the subject of horse-breeding, its challenges and travails. (See, I told you that he wasn't Jewish.)

This interchange comes back to me now as I do my own brow-furrowing, trying to formulate an answer to what is basically the same conundrum that Sam posed:

What *is* the deal with the Arabs and Jews?

This never was a simple question. (Never mind judging the exploits of guerilla leaders/statesmen like Menachem Begin or Yassir Arafat. Try going all the way back to the unbalanced equation of Abraham, Sarah, and Haggar the handmaiden.) But now this question has become so complex, so many-layered and deeply tribal and drenched in blood and tears, that the mind reels in the face of it. It has become the diplomatic equivalent of Pi, a problem so incalculable, so unsimplify-able, that gelding horses does indeed start to seem like a pleasant way to pass an afternoon.

We can't give up that easily, though, if only because the world is too small and this hatred too big for anyone to be satisfied with simply ignoring it. By "we" and "us" I mean the reasonable people—Jews, Christians, Muslims, Hindus, whomever—who would like to see Reason triumph, who need to find a way for people to live in Peace, or at least some reasonable facsimile of such. We don't care who "wins." We don't care who has the last word. We just want the killing to stop. And we want that to happen ASAP. (Or so we wrote in our memo to Hamas. You got a copy, didn't you?)

The problem is that all sides of this argument have been increasingly co-opted (as they have been in Iraq, Somalia, and other political hot-spots) by the loudest and most polarizing voices. You know exactly what I mean, right? The Professional Jews ("Israel will not be a victim!"), the Professional Arabs ("Our people have been victims long enough!"), the actual victims, the refugees, the opportunists, the revenge seekers. By the time the reasonable people try to chime in, how can their voices ever be heard?

I experienced a taste of this when I went to a July 4th pool party in Orange County, California. It was the height of the war in Lebanon between Israel and Hezbollah—a war that I was (and am) frankly appalled by, first for its violence toward innocent civilians, second for its abject stupidity. While I'm no fan of modern warfare, I will admit to a sneaking admiration for the Israeli Six Day War and the other conflicts that the Israelis have been able to win quickly, with a minimum of casualties. But here the Israelis were dropping cluster bombs on civilian targets and even using phosphorus bombs, which horribly scar their victims with chemical burns. And they didn't even get the two soldiers back who had been captured by Hezbollah! How could this ever be justified?

Well, one of the guests at this party was a visitor from Israel, a man in his 20s who had served in the Israeli army. He had no problem with his country's acts of aggression. In fact he was excited by them. "What do you do when someone pushes you and pushes you and won't stop pushing you, no matter how many times you ask them to stop?" he said. "You have to push them back hard—so hard that they won't try to push you around anymore."

I pointed out that even if one subscribed to this line of reasoning (which in general I didn't; it sounds good in theory, but so do many rationales for mass-murder), the people who were mostly being pushed here were the Lebanese, who weren't the ones doing the original "pushing." The Israeli man dismissed this objection. "All the Lebanese are with Hezbollah, they hate the Jews," he claimed. "I won't shed any tears for them, no more than they would shed tears for me."

Ah, that good old Hamurabic Code, "an eye for an eye," etc. Hasn't that brought us to a wonderful place, with its satisfyingly tribal sense of justice? This is not to say that the man's words didn't come from a deep and sincere place, but they reminded me in a chilling way of a phrase I'd heard uttered several times over the years, mostly by older Jewish men. "Bomb those Arabs back to the stone age!" they said. "Just herd them all together and pow! Back to the stone age."

What can one say to such people?

Sometimes I reminded them of the Nazi Holocaust, where the Jews were indeed "herded together." Sometimes I mentioned that the Arabs and Jews are half-brothers, sharing the same progenitor (Abraham). Once I even brought up Hiroshima, and the devastating consequences that everyone paid (and is still paying) for that "victory."

In this case—after arguing myself hoarse about how the Israelis had been tricked into going to war and were now paying the price—I simply stripped down to my bathing suit and jumped into the water, swimming away from the young Israeli, who carried on his argument with others.

As it happened, this pool was made to look like a grotto, composed of large stones. I swam as far away as I could, until the shouting voices were more like a soothing hum, a sort of background music. Yes, he is Jewish, and I am Jewish, but that doesn't mean we see eye to eye or are ever going to have a meeting of the minds.

Is Irrelevance an Arab-American Goal?
by Hussein Ibish

WHAT WAS AMAZING IN THE RESPONSE TO THE much-publicized recent paper written by Steven Walt and John Mearsheimer on the influence of the pro-Israel lobby on American foreign policy was not the chorus of condemnations from Israel's supporters, but similar criticism from some on the Arab-American left.

The paper, a set of fairly obvious observations about the workings of one of the most influential centers of power in Washington, combined with a few debatable claims and a couple of minor errors, should have produced little comment. But given the atmosphere of intimidation in political and academic circles regarding Israel, its publication created a firestorm.

The response from the pro-Israel right was predictable. "There is no Israel lobby" one noted pundit thundered. Another called it "worse than the 'Protocols of the Elders of Zion.'"

The preposterous argument offered by some pro-Israel commentators is that hundreds of millions of dollars, innumerable man-hours and relentless organizing at every level of society, over many decades, has had no significant role in producing the staunchly Israel-centric American policies of recent years - allegedly no more than natural expressions of Americans' love of Israel. An insult to one's intelligence, this proposition holds that the intended effect was not produced by its putative cause.

If this were true, then the American Israel Public Affairs Committee (AIPAC) is not a great political force but a remarkable fraud and confidence trick: millions of unsuspecting Jewish Americans and their friends have been bilked by unscrupulous grifters continuously begging for money on the false pretense that it is needed to consolidate the US-Israel relationship. Call the cops!

But surely no serious person would believe that. Would they?

Enter some Arab-American commentators, stage left. Joseph Massad of Columbia University and Asaad Abu Khalil of Californian State University, Stanislaus, have dismissed the Walt-Mearsheimer paper and agree that the pro-Israel lobby is basically irrelevant.

In a widely-circulated article in Al-Ahram Weekly, Massad argued that the real problem was the "imperial policies" of the United States, which exist independently of the influence of the pro-Israel lobby. There are surely American imperial interests that have been pursued in very damaging ways in the Arab and post-colonial worlds. But Massad does not attempt to explain how, why, or by whom these interests are defined, except that he is sure the lobby has virtually no role in it.

Such arguments are deterministic, ahistorical, and profoundly disempowering. This thinking has led the Arab-American community to largely exclude itself from the political system, ensuring its own irrelevance in shaping political behavior, while also granting the pro-Israel lobby an open field without any substantial opposition.

One finds here a profound ignorance of, or more precisely complete disinterest in, the process of American policy-making as it actually takes place. There is no sense that the US government is the sum of its constituent parts that vie for influence in a system designed precisely to be lobbied if any faction seeks to effect policy and law.

In place of these mundane realities are the amorphous "imperial policies" described by Massad in the language of a divine absolute, floating above a Kabuki-show political fray. His is a simplistic version of American politics in which power is exercised in an automatic and irresistible manner by an imperial hidden hand—a caricature of the old Marxist idea of a social superstructure.

This argument cannot account for the development of American policy toward Israel, unless one accepts that American interests in the Middle East have independently evolved in almost perfect concert with the growing size, competency, and entrenched power of the pro-Israel lobby.

Take Israel's forced withdrawal from Suez in 1956, followed by its French-supported victory in the 1967 war, the development of a military technology-transfer regime with the Nixon administration, the closer embrace under President Ronald Reagan, and the almost complete convergence of US and Israeli policies under President Bill Clinton and his successor George W. Bush; is the movement toward the later developments better accounted for by changes in the international climate than by the gradual and painstaking development of political influence thanks to the efforts of a highly focused ethnic lobby and its allies? Did the removal of a number of key legislators in the late 1970s and early 1980s and the defeat of President George H.W. Bush, who confronted Israel over settlements, (all major scalps claimed by AIPAC) mean nothing? Is the adoption in recent years of Israel as the main issue for a well-organized fundamentalist Christian right irrelevant?

As the Walt-Mearsheimer paper points out, Arab-Americans have, for the most part, sat on the sidelines rather than engage the political system, unlike the pro-Israel lobby. After all, why would any politician care what a group that doesn't seriously participate, or contribute its time or money in a substantial or coordinated way, have to say?

If Walt and Mearsheimer are right, then Arab-Americans have been a big part of the problem by opting out of the give and take of politics and refusing to challenge their opponents or provide cover for and support their friends. If, on the other hand, Massad and Abu Khalil are right and American policies are not the products of the social forces brought to bear on political institutions, but instead follow the dictates of an ineluctable and ineffable imperial imperative, then what's the point?

And here, surely, lies the appeal of this analysis beyond the confines of the ultra-left: it lets both Arabs and Jews off the hook, frees them from their rivalry, and places "the blame," as Massad puts it, on "the United States," an entity that bears no resemblance to the sum of its parts. It's very convenient as an argument, but also completely wrong.

We Arab-Americans have failed ourselves and our Arab brethren through self-imposed alienation from American politics. While substantial efforts are required and obstacles must be overcome, there is nothing preventing Arab-Americans from serious political engagement, or from having a major impact on US foreign policy, except a tradition of ignoring our own interests and being seduced by beguiling pseudo-revolutionary excuses.

The late Edward Said warned against "sitting back blaming 'the Arabs' since, after all, we are the Arabs," and we all play a role in defining our social and political condition. It is high time for Arab-Americans to embrace the fact that we are also, in exactly the same sense, "the Americans."

Far from blaming "the United States," we need to roll up our sleeves, assert the full spectrum of our rights as citizens within our political system, and take responsibility for helping to shape our government's policies.

Boston Yellow Cabs
by Nathalie Handal

I FEEL MOST AT HOME WHEN I AM SITTING in a Boston Yellow Cab. The ride from Logan airport to my apartment in that yellow cab brings me peace. It calms even the echoes of my breathing.

Every time I travel, I am comforted knowing I will be welcomed in a yellow cab. My addresses change, the concierge changes, the furniture changes, the bed sheets change, and even I change, but the yellow cabs are still yellow. I open those heavy doors, sit on those bouncing back seats, and feel a sense of relief. It's like trying to convince myself that if one day I am lost, at least, I'll find a piece of myself in one of these cabs. . . .

I was sitting in a yellow cab going to the airport to fly to Iowa. Isn't there always a time for Iowa? Maybe not. Most people I spoke to asked me with their eyebrows rising, their foreheads wrinkling, "Why are you going there?" To begin with, I was invited by my friend Nastasia, who is Bulgarian and happened to be working in Iowa City. And why not Iowa?

Nastasia picked me up at the airport in Cedar Rapids. She had been in Iowa one month and had already gotten used to driving there, not that one needed any real time to know one's way around. Anyhow, after driving in Beirut or Paris, where she had lived, pretty much anything was possible. We had met at a Lebanese Cultural Gala two years before, in France. Since then the two of us kept in touch. We had gone to where I am originally from, Palestine. Then we went to Boston, and now we were in Nastasia's Jeep Cherokee driving in the pig state.

Before the sun departed, it gave us a majestic golden orange horizon with red waves in the middle of the skyline. We were driving through Welds, and I felt like I was entering a yellow kingdom. I had never experienced such unity of earth and sky. As it grew darker, I also realized that I had never really been in the night. An absolute silence, a sense that all is resting or gone . . . when only stars and moon remain. It was so dark that I could hardly see the road. It was so quiet that I was afraid to listen to the whistling of the heater, afraid that my thoughts were too loud. Nights exist in Iowa.

At one point, I asked Nastasia where we were going. Iowa City was only thirty minutes from the airport, and we had been driving for an hour. She told me we were going somewhere else for the evening and that it was a surprise. I was impatiently waiting to see whether that somewhere had electricity or moonlight. She suddenly turned left into a slightly dusty, narrow road. We drove for about five minutes, and there, in the middle of emptiness, stood a house with lights. Nastasia parked in the front driveway, we walked to the house, she opened the door, and five people stood up. "Welcome, welcome," they all said at once. They spoke with a heavy Midwestern accent. I was a bit confused but relieved to have finally arrived. "It sure is good to be here," I said.

In Middle America, in a remote corner, surrounded by Welds, I met a Palestinian family. There were Nessim, his wife, Marie, and their three children. Nessim was born in Palestine and immigrated to America in the 1950s. He first lived in Michigan where he met Marie, who was a student. They eventually moved to Marie's home state, Iowa. After their marriage, Nessim got accustomed to life in America and didn't want to go back to the instability in the Holy Land.

Marie and the children had slight knowledge of the Middle East—only what they saw in the news, what they read in the newspaper, and what Nessim had told them. But he had been away for forty years. Time and circumstances had created a large space between him and his family in Palestine. His parents had passed away, and he didn't know where his only brother was. What was left of their Arabic heritage could be summarized in one word—food. They surely knew how to cook Arabic food.

While we ate, we talked. I told them of a land far away, yet close in the way it could still breathe around them, a memory, but a memory still strong enough to survive. I played the Arabic cassette I had with me. They loved the rhythm of the music. The youngest daughter was particularly excited. As Nastasia and I danced, she naturally followed. I observed Nessim, he was crying. They were lost tears, tears put away for many years that had finally found a window. I felt saddened by his expression. Was it regret or melancholy? The evening ended with the final note of the last song on my cassette. It was difficult to leave. There where hugs and kisses and a crying laughter which I didn't want to hear.

When I got to Boston I sat in a yellow cab and closed the heavy door. Once again, I had changed a little. I felt a void. My moment in that cab, however, remained the same. The yellow cab filled the empty corners of my heart. By the time I got to my apartment, my yellow ride had already helped me return, return but not forget.

Chapter Five

The Effect of 9/11

The Sikh Experience after 9/11
by Rajbir Singh Datta

W HEN I WAS ASKED TO CONTRIBUTE TO THIS book, the French ban on religious symbols was a growing problem for Sikhs, Muslims and Jews, and I reflected on how unique the post-9/11 experience for Arab, Muslim and Sikhs has been in the United States than in other nations around the world. The tradition of bringing together communities who are historically without, or with a limited, voice is uniquely American and is reflected throughout the post-9/11 political engagement experience.

Sikhism, the world's fifth largest religion and a faith distinct from both Hinduism and Islam, was founded in Punjab, India in the 15th century. With over 25 million adherents worldwide, and over 500,000 Sikhs in the United States, practicing Sikh men are easily recognizable, as they are required by their faith, to maintain their hair uncut and to wear a turban. Uncut hair, which includes the beard, is one of five articles of faith essential to the identity that Sikhs must maintain at all times. While Sikhs have been in the United States since the late-19th century, most Americans are unaware that the vast majority of men wearing turbans in the United States are Sikhs, not Muslims or Arabs.

In the days following the attacks on September 11, 2001, Sikh Americans across the United States were victims of violent attacks from New York City to Arizona. Due to their unique identity, Sikhs became "soft targets" for victimization. In towns across America, Sikhs were chased by mobs of ignorant citizens armed with pipes, knives and other makeshift weapons. Sikhs were murdered, pulled from trains and buses for being suspected terrorists, and Sikh youths were being harassed at alarming rates.

The time was unique, one marking impressive national unity against the perpetrators of the heinous and cowardly terrorist attacks while masking the unspeakable brutality against the Arab, Muslim and Sikh American communities. While the nation embraced this unprecedented unity, we all consciously masked the disgrace that it was hiding.

After the 9/11 attack, thousands of Sikhs were victimized throughout the United States and abroad. Mr. Sher Singh, a practicing Sikh from Boston, was traveling to Washington DC to ensure the safety of his family when he was forcibly removed from a train and detained by law enforcement personnel responding to a misguided allegation that he was a terrorist. Balbir Singh Sodhi, a Sikh American residing in Mesa, Arizona, became the first post-9/11 casualty when Frank Roque shot him twice in the back of the head. On August 4, 2002, less than a year after Balbir's death, his younger brother Sukhpal was shot to death while driving his taxicab in San Francisco, CA. While the murder remains unsolved, it is widely accepted within the community that Sukhpal was targeted due to his religious identity. Incidents such as this have become all too common for members of the community throughout the United States.

The first images the nation saw after 9/11 was that of Osama bin Laden, sporting a large turban and long flowing beard. Unfortunately, this image became the nation's introduction to individuals wearing turbans and beards. The media failed in the aftermath of the attacks in executing their responsibility to their constituency. They failed to do an adequate job of highlighting the challenges and victimization of Sikh Americans and there was virtually no reporting about the "domestic terrorism" that was taking place on street corners, businesses, homes, and religious centers across America.

The attacks continue to this day, with children and grandfathers alike falling victim to physical attacks. However, from the beginning, the community's response has been one of optimism. This is best summed up by Balbir Sodhi's son, Sukhwinder Sodhi, who experienced his father and uncle murdered: "What are you going to do with anger? We like peace and we are a peaceful people."

Instead of fear, the community saw this as a watershed moment and was empowered to engage themselves in the political, social and civic processes. The community sought to inform their fellow Americans about the fundamentals of our faith, our values, and our conviction to live up to Sikh principles and how they parallel those of America's Founding Fathers.

The Sikh American Legal Defense and Education Fund (SALDEF), a civil rights and advocacy organization founded prior to 9/11, increased staff capacity, developed more intensive educational programs and amassed the largest Sikh American network of attorneys to support our efforts. In the months following the attacks, meetings with key federal officials ensued to ensure that individual rights were not violated. This provided government officials with the ability to understand what the Sikh American community was experiencing.

This greater understanding often informs policymakers to develop better policies to represent our increasingly diverse nation. For example, the Federal Bureau of Investigation (FBI) now requires all new recruits to visit the United States Holocaust Memorial Museum in Washington DC in order to fully grasp the plight of the Jewish community during the early part of the century. Similar action should to be taken by other agencies as the needs arise within the United States.

Ultimately, the mainstay of all tragedies is the challenge to respect the religious and cultural differences within our community and to ensure that the violence does not repeat itself. Over the past decade, minority communities have started to move out of densely populated areas, such as cities, which historically are more diverse, and are moving into areas with historically smaller percentages of these populations.

The mutual engagement and participation of both law enforcement and the local community is critical to understanding different cultures and the security of our nation's communities. In the words of David Baker, Montgomery County Maryland Hate Crimes Coordinator, "The more we know about each other the safer we are going to be around each other and the more we are going to appreciate the differences and similarities and understand that we're mostly the same."

The Weekend After
by Nour Merza

"HUMMUS AND PIZZA, please."

Khaleh Mona took my plate and filled it up, like all Arabs do, with much more food than I could possibly handle in one sitting. She laughed at my objections and piled on a third scoop of *hummus* before giving the plate back to me.

"Ammo Munir made the hummus. It's his secret Syrian recipe. You won't regret it!" She waved me away to where the other kids were sitting at the side of the garden.

It was almost 7:00 p.m., and I had to pick my way carefully through the chairs and running toddlers to get to my seat next to Amir in the dark. He was gone for the moment, probably upstairs in his room getting the anime drawings he'd promised to show me. We were both fourteen years old and, like everyone else our age, obsessed with anime, or what Mama and Baba degraded by calling "Japanese cartoons."

The Hadadi's backyard was big. There was a barbeque area under the patio, a pool on the left, and an open area big enough to play tag in—or set out a few tables for dinner with some friends and neighbors. This was our weekly get-together here in Los Angeles, a time for us and our closest Arab-American friends to reunite like family after a long week of work and school.

But this week was different. Just a few days ago, the World Trade Centers in New York had been attacked. Every TV screen and radio station was broadcasting about it. And about how the attackers were Muslim. Arab-Muslim, at that. I picked at my *hummus* with some bread I stole off of my cousin Salma's plate. It *was* good – cool, creamy, and salty. Although my parents were Syrian, I was born in Saudi Arabia right before moving to the US. I'd never been to Syria. Did all food in Syria taste like this? I moved on to my veggie pizza, waiting for Amir to come back outside.

And come back he did, with a folder clutched under his arm. The pictures. But just as he was passing the adult's table, he stopped. I looked over at what caught his attention: the group of men and women I knew as *ammos* and *khalehs*, uncles and aunts. They were sitting around one of the tables, their faces barely visible by the candles and the dim patio light. They were talking softly and swiftly, their backs hunched as they all craned to get as close as possible to the speaker. It was Ammo Munir, who'd made the *hummus*. I grabbed my cup of Pepsi and made my way over to them.

"Who knows what'll happen?" Ammo Munir's big bespectacled eyes shown. "You're all watching the news. There's talk about government surveillance now!"

"Or internment," Azza, his 20-year-old daughter, cut in. "Just like they did with the Japanese during World War Two. They rounded people up and put them in camps for months, cut off from everything. Just because they were Japanese-Americans." She inched closer to Hamid after speaking, and he put his arm around her shoulder. I smiled. Their first anniversary was in three months. I always thought they looked like Snow White and Prince Charming. They even had their own little castle: a brand new flat in an apartment near UCLA, where they both studied.

"But they can't do that anymore," my dad shook his head. Baba was the expert of the group, a doctor of political science. I didn't really understand what that meant, but I knew that whenever he'd talk about politics, everyone listened a little more carefully than they would otherwise. "Things are different now. Taking all of the country's Arabs and Muslims into custody wouldn't work. It would cause an uproar. We're citizens. We have rights."

"What rights?" That was Khaleh Razan, Omar's mom. "Your house is under police protection, Bilal. If people believed in your rights as an American, you wouldn't have drunken men trying to attack your family at night. And you wouldn't be sleeping at your brother-in-law's house 'just in case' either." She nodded towards my uncle, Khalo Ahmad.

"But we wouldn't have police protection either," Baba said. "And the sheriff himself wouldn't have visited the Islamic Center last Tuesday."

I caught myself nodding.

"Hey, let's grab seats," Amir whispered.

We walked back to the kids' table. All the other kids were inside watching *Dexter's Laboratory* on Cartoon Network.

"Was school weird this week?" I asked, putting down my cup of Pepsi. Amir and I folded up a chair each.

"A little. But people can't tell that I'm Arab, so I'm safe," he grinned. "You're the one who must have had a hard week." He raised his eyebrows at my headscarf.

"Not from the school kids," I replied. "New Horizon's a Muslim school. But we did get two days off because we got a bomb threat."

"Yeah, I heard."

"But it was probably just some weirdo trying to be funny. What *was* annoying was that Baba wouldn't let me go to Tae Kwon Do practice all week. I missed four lessons!" I rolled my eyes. "And every time we rode in the car, he made me sit in the back so it would be harder for people to see me."

"Yeah, my mom's wearing a hat instead of a scarf whenever she goes outside. Azza won't do it though." He looked at his sister, who was talking again. "She keeps going on about how she has the right to dress the way she wants in her own country."

"Let's go back. Things sound like they're heating up!"

We scurried back to the adults. Azza was getting louder as we opened up our folding chairs and sat at the edge of the circle.

"But why should you plaster the American flag all over our house?" she asked. "Hardly anyone was doing it before. Now it's this big trend, and you have to paint yourself red, white and blue to prove you're American!"

"*Ya baba*, we're Muslim! We have to show we love our country!"

"Why?" Azza looked incredulous. "Of course we love America. You decided to leave the Middle East and come live here, didn't you? Isn't that enough proof that we love this place? All these flags and bumper stickers, they're just for show!"

"But, *ya baba*, this is a time of crisis. Like you said, everyone's doing it. It shows unity! And that reminds me, you need to take that 'Stop US aid to Israel' sticker off your car. Are you *trying* to get attacked?"

I saw Hamid grab Azza's arm.

"Oh god, not this again," Amir mumbled. He opened up his folder and started flipping through his anime drawings.

"See, that's the problem with our community!" Azza pushed Hamid's hand away. "We are so complacent with everything that's going on around us. We're getting harassed, racially and religiously profiled, and completely misrepresented in the news. And what do we do? Lay low, blend in! And we can't talk about issues that matter, not just to us, but to anyone who cares about human rights. That is *not* what being American is about. We're just a bunch of scared suck-ups." She crossed her arms and leaned back into her seat, mumbling. "We're house-slaves, that's what we are."

I waited for her to say more, not understanding. But Azza stayed silent.

"*Ya ammo*, you have to remember to keep things balanced," Baba was talking again. "You have a point about the community, but—"

"Hey, let's go inside," Amir whispered. "I'm sick of this." He got up from his chair.

I followed.

We walked into the house and upstairs into his bedroom, where we flopped down on the bed, the same way we did ever since we'd met at the age of eight. We stared at the ceiling in silence.

"Amir, what do you feel you are? More Arab or more American?"

Amir was silent for a moment. "I dunno. You?"

I sat up on his bed and looked around his bedroom. There was a huge poster of Harry Potter on the wall to my left. On the dresser in front of me, two piles of CDs flanked a giant black boom box. A brand new blue Mac computer sat on the desk on my right, next to an orange lava lamp and the plastic souvenir Kaa'ba we'd gotten him last year on our trip to Mecca.

"I'm both," I said.

"But your Arabic sucks," he laughed.

"Look who's talking! Yours is even worse!"

Amir snorted. "Okay, would you ever want to live in Syria?"

"I've never been there, how am *I* supposed to know?" I made a face at him.

"Exactly," he grinned. He paused for a moment, then went on. "If you could live anywhere in the world, where would it be?"

I thought about it, then sighed. "Here. In L.A."

"Yup!" Amir sat up. "You're American."

"And Arab!" I retaliated.

"Uh-huh."

"Shut up."

He laughed. "Come on, let me show you these cool pictures I found on the internet. We can try to draw them."

"Fine. But you have to help me. It's not fair, you're so much better at this drawing thing."

Amir moved to his desk and started googling "Tenchi Muyo" in the image search. Our favorite anime. I grabbed some sheets of paper from the drawing book on his floor and found two pencils in one of his desk drawers. I started doodling a picture of an anime girl in a headscarf flying over a forest, waiting for him to find the Tenchi pictures he'd told me about.

"Hey, you should make her scarf red, white, and blue." Amir was looking over my shoulder, holding back a laugh. "Or better yet, make it an American flag!"

"Oh my god, you loser." I shook my head. "You know, I'll be the first Arab American to make an anime series, and then I'll show you."

"Ha, you'll have to beat me first! And at the rate your drawing's going, I'll be done with my 10th series before you even start!"

"Nour!" Mama's shrill voice rang from the stairs. "*Yallah*! Start getting ready to leave!"

"Five more minutes, Mama!"

"Fine, but not more than that. We have to get back to your uncle's house before it gets too late!"

I rolled my eyes.

Amir gave me a look. "It sucks, not being able to go home, huh?"

"Whatever," I shrugged. "Come on, we have five minutes."

I grabbed my pencil to start copying the Tenchi picture Amir had printed out. My flying headscarf-girl caught my eye, and I hesitated for a moment. I narrowed my eyes at Amir, then drew tiny stars and stripes on the girl's scarf.

"*You* can color them in," I said.

He laughed and got up to get some crayons.

Old Rituals Give Way to New
by John Milton Wesley

Most of the rituals are gone now, although I still catch myself staring at the yellow Lands' End short jacket she hung on the closet door in the foyer before she left that Tuesday morning, Sept. 11, 2001. She was on her way to Dulles to board American Airlines Flight 77.

Perhaps it was an omen, a kind of warning for me to use caution in the days ahead. We were to be married Dec. 22. And maybe it was just a jacket she forgot in haste. It now hangs in my bedroom closet, not in among the rows of stuff but out where I can see it and be reminded that caution has now become one of the rituals I live by. Others I have learned to let go in order to heal.

Candles no longer burn 24 hours a day and family pictures are long gone from the walls up the stairwell.

Most of the clothes are gone from the closets; only sweaters remain, neatly folded on one shelf. Somewhere in Houston or New Orleans, survivors of Katrina are leaving new footprints with shoes once neatly stacked in boxes in the bedroom closet.

For some reason it was easier to give away the dresses and suits—so many colors and sizes 4-8, one couldn't remember them all. Well, I couldn't, but Sarah did; she had a system that helped her remember. Over the past five years, I needed a system to help me forget, so giving her clothes to people who could put them to good use also helped me heal.

The shoes were harder to let go; I knew them one by one. I knew every nick, scratch and stain, every bruised heel and scuffed toe. Polishing them was always more than just a Saturday night ritual; it was also a way to accrue Brownie points like breakfast in bed. That ritual is gone too; now I just polish the ones I am going to wear to church on Sunday, another ritual begun at her urging that continues. No, I didn't discover God because of 9/11—thankfully, I had done so years before. However, before Sarah was in my life, I spent most of my Sunday mornings for thirtysomething years either hiking the trails of the Patapsco State Park or walking the 17th-century labyrinth maintained by the Sisters of Bon Secours off Marriottsville Road. Sarah loved this park too, not for the hiking or the labyrinth but for the chance to play on the swings while I pushed. Now at the park, I miss the ritual of pushing her.

Now shirts hang neatly in rows where blouses once hung, and pants line a lower shelf once used for short skirts and tops. And on the bureau across from where I sit and write, her familiar smile no longer looks back at me from a photograph.

Before 9/11, rituals for me were autonomic, like always putting my pants on right leg first, or going downstairs each morning and grinding equal amounts of Southern pecan and vanilla coffee beans, and brewing four cups. My new rituals would help keep me alive, and though not autonomic, they somehow became just as important. Five years later, I can gauge the level of my healing by my ability to let them go or keep them.

In fact, the past five years for 9/11 survivors in particular and Americans in general have been all about letting go. If you lost someone close, such as a relative or friend with whom you were very close, the process began for you immediately.

You learned early on that despite the enormity and shock of the tragedy of 9/11, only by letting go could you begin to wrestle with the real-world issues of pain, media, DNA, wills, bills and memorials, and searching for remains, and autopsies, and briefings by the FBI, and CIA, and counterintelligence, and conspiracy theories and theorists, and computer generated re-enactments, and boarding gate videos, and yes, America, the one we all knew back when the only time we took our shoes off at the airport was to rest our feet.

Just as those of us who lost someone that day are finally able to let go of some of our rituals, collectively, as Americans, we are forced to learn new ones, and it is no easy task. Rituals are like that: They begin either out of necessity or expedience, and before we know it, difficulty and time become relative. Soon the ritual becomes second nature, and we take part unconsciously almost.

A year passed before I was able to fly. My first trip was to Mississippi to take part in my family reunion. Somehow, the fear of being on a plane vanished in the thought of standing on the land in Port Gibson that my great-great-great-grandfather bought in 1868 for $1,000. I knew that standing next to the fence where I stood in 1954, looking east toward where his Tennessee walking horses roamed, surrounded by his timber farm, would be a healing experience.

Going home again has become very important. Since 9/11, I have gone home to Mississippi more than I did in all the 33 years I have lived in Maryland. I have attended every family reunion since, and, like many other Americans, have come to experience and appreciate family much more. So I have added another ritual: keeping in touch. I keep in touch with Sarah's children, the ones she bore and the ones she taught.

For those of us who lost someone close on 9/11, with whom we shared a home, our daily lives changed not just because they were no longer with us, but also because we learned in their death just how much of who we had become was so much a part of them. Things we did "just because" were no longer necessary. Rituals, for a time, compelled us to continue to do them anyway, until one day we no longer had to. Soon the ritual became an afterthought, and we knew maybe, just maybe, we were finally getting better. Somehow the rituals helped fill the void between then and now.

Five years ago, there was so much I took for granted that now I hold sacred and in awe. As a black boy growing up in the Delta of Mississippi, I had known what it was like to learn to live in a society in which I was hated because of my color. I never imagined living in a world in which I would be hated because of my country, and that a new enemy would appear, not in white sheets but in robes and pajamas, stateless, without compassion and respect for life.

Like most other "survivors" who watched the boarding gate tapes, I knew this new enemy was different. We knew this right away. Like us, the hijackers saw the faces of the other passengers that morning as they boarded the planes. They saw the children and mothers with their babies, and old couples, and giddy teenagers fiddling with their electronic toys, and crew members pushing seniors in wheelchairs, and were undeterred in their mission of death. Five years later, I continue to search in the "new normal" for a ritual to erase this thought from my mind, but then to do so—to forget that such evil is possible—could put my country and my own life at risk.

A Year Later at Ground Zero
By Stephen Fife

Here's a 9-11 story I bet you haven't heard.

It's about a bearded guy in black nylon workout gear and sandals who just wanted to get a peek at Ground Zero on the first year anniversary and instead ended up shaking hands with Colin Powell, Condoleeza Rice, Mayor Bloomberg, George Pataki, Rudy Giuliani, and the Leader of the Free World himself.

"How did this happen?" you ask. "How did this guy with no credentials and no pretense to belonging in a restricted area (and a scruffy Democrat no less!) end up at the center of everything with the Power Elite?"

Well, thereby hangs a tale, and, boy, it's not a pretty one.

It all started innocently enough with a simple desire to pay tribute to a friend who had died in Tower One. I knew enough not to venture downtown in the morning, when the names of the dead were being recited. But the crowds were still huge at 1:30, and the closest I could get to Ground Zero was a break in the covered chain-link fence at the rear of the site, through which I could see the vast plaza of buildings surrounding the pit.

"Hey, you can't stand there," a policeman told me. I shrugged, not surprised. Then he added, "If you want to come in, just go down to the corner and go through the metal detectors."

"Thanks," I said, walking to the corner of West Street and Vecsey.

Again, I expected to be turned away when police found my name was not on any list. Instead, I was motioned forward, where a young man in an NYPD windbreaker ran a detecting wand over my clothing. I was subjected to a quick frisk, my crumpled newspaper was inspected, and I was allowed to enter.

"Wow, this is great," I thought, sauntering into the plaza. It was difficult to see much of Ground Zero because of the plastic barriers that had been placed approximately three feet inside of the metal fences that bordered the site. Still, there were indentations in the barriers where it was possible to gain a foothold. Standing that way, I could see the entire eastern half of the site. A small group of policemen wearing dress blues were huddled around the modest circular memorial to the victims. Soon these men were joined by a contingent of military men and civilians. The wind kept gusting fiercely, making it difficult to remain on my perch. Down in the pit, the wind took off a policeman's cap, and he went racing after it.

That's all I could see, and it was plenty. It was more than I had dared to hope for.

But just minutes later I noticed that the small crowd in the southern part of the plaza was being ushered toward a ramp. I followed, certain that I would never make it. Surely there would be a list here, surely I would be found out and escorted away. But no. When I reached the top of the ramp, a clean-cut man handed me a beige card with the lyrics of "America the Beautiful" on it, topped off by the Presidential seal. Then I marched past the Honor Guard of policemen and rescue workers lining each side of the ramp, and, yes, there I was in Ground Zero. I quickly found a place in the crowd circling the small makeshift memorial, careful not to kick over any of the wooden stakes topped by photos of the dead that dotted the landscape.

A short time later, President and Mrs. Bush came walking down the ramp, starkly alone. I knew he was coming of course (the small crowd spoke of little else), but I thought he would be giving a speech. Instead, he began shaking hands with the men and hugging and kissing the women. He was followed around the circle by his team of Remarkable Mourners. (I must confess to being most impressed by Governor Pataki, who genuinely seemed to be weeping. We're talking huge, heavy tears. On the other hand, the crowd was most awed by ex-Mayor Giuliani, whom they greeted like some kind of god.)

Of course I realized by this time that I was among a group of victims' relatives. I spoke with people, heard them talking all around me, "I lost my son, I lost my fiancee, I lost my sister, I lost my Dad..." I felt bad, I didn't belong here, I had only lost a friend. She wasn't even a close friend, just a lovely person who would occasionally provide care for my daughter, and whom I thought had deserved a better fate. In the hierarchy of grief, I wasn't sure if this even rated.

But then, that was the remarkable thing. As different as we all were—and there are, frankly, few people I feel more different from than these politicians—we all seemed united for the moment in grief. The United States of Grief. Republican, Democrat, black, white, Jew, Arab—for the moment none of that mattered. Standing around that modest memorial, in the bowels of this great pit, we had achieved that rare thing: a true democracy, all equal under the weight of our loss.

But then something happened.

After the Marine chorus had completed their rendition of "America the Beautiful"— a simple and touching rendition, I might add—people around me suddenly began passing their beige lyric cards forward for the officials to autograph. This had started with President Bush (a few hesitantly-proffered cards), but only caught fire when Colin Powell and Giuliani came by. Soon a demure blonde woman at the front of our section was holding a thick sheaf of cards, then passing them back once they were signed.

In short order this had escalated into a full celebrity sizzle, as survivors of victims broke ranks with our group and jumped into the circle, to have their photos taken with The Elite. Soon the demure blonde woman was standing between the president and General Powell, all three putting on eye-popping grins when the photo-taker said "Cheese!"

In that flashbulb moment, I felt like a veil had been lifted from my eyes, like I could finally see. All those feelings of transcendence I'd had before, that sense of being united in a common grief, were wiped away, replaced by something very different—much less kind perhaps, but I think far more accurate: eBay. That's what this was about. Amassing collectibles.

Perhaps that sounds unduly harsh, perhaps all that these relatives of the dead wanted was a keepsake to pass down through the generations to mark this event, this anniversary of a terrible day. Yet that's not what I saw in the eyes of many people around me. They were seizing an opportunity, a Photo Op, an access to power, in order to turn this into hard cash somewhere down the line. And the Famous Republicans were more than happy to oblige, because that's how they saw it as well. The United States of eBay. An eBay democracy. Where every emotion has a dollar value, and we are all equally entitled to be part of the bidding. (Though some may have a bit more money to play with than others.)

Then again, what do I know? I'm just a scruffy Democrat with no credentials who shouldn't have been allowed here in the first place.

Chapter Six

Ways of War

Foreign Occupation Produces Radical Muslim Terrorism
by Juan Cole

Fareed Zakariya argues that Bush got one thing right. Zakariya writes:

> Bush never accepted the view that Islamic terrorism had its roots
> in religion or culture or the Arab-Israeli conflict. Instead he veered
> toward the analysis that the region was breeding terror because it had
> developed deep dysfunctions caused by decades of repression and an
> almost total lack of political, economic and social modernization.
> The Arab world, in this analysis, was almost unique in that over the
> past three decades it had become increasingly unfree, even as the rest
> of the world was opening up. His solution, therefore, was to push for
> reform in these lands.

I don't use the phrase "Islamic terrorism" because "Islamic" refers to the essentials
of the religion, and it forbids terrorism (*hirabah*). But if Bush rejected the idea that
radical Muslim terrorism came out of religion or culture, he was right.

I disagree with the rest of the paragraph, though. Let's think about terrorism in
the past few decades in a concrete and historical way, and it is obvious that it comes
out of a reaction to being occupied militarily by foreigners. The Muslim Brotherhood
developed its Secret Apparatus and began committing acts of terror in the 1940s in
Egypt, which the British had virtually reoccupied in order to deny it to the Italians
and then Germans. The Brotherhood assassinated pro-British judges and pro-British
politicians (the British installed the Wafd Party in power). The Brotherhood had
grown to some half a million members by 1948. Some Brothers also volunteered to
fight in Palestine against the rise of Israel, which they saw as a colonial settler state.

After the Muslim Brotherhood assassinated Prime Minister Nuqrashi in 1948, it was
banned and dissolved. It was briefly rehabilitated by Abdul Nasser in 1952-1954, but
in 1954 it tried to assassinate him, and he banned it again. There was no major radical
Muslim terrorism in Egypt in the period after 1954 and until Sadat again legitimized

the Brotherhood in 1971, despite Egypt being a dictatorship in that period.

The intimate connection between foreign military occupation and terrorism can be seen in Palestine in the 1940s, where the Zionist movement threw up a number of terrorist organizations that engaged in bombings and assassinations on a fair scale. That is, frustrated Zionists not getting their way behaved in ways difficult to distinguish from frustrated Muslim nationalists who didn't get their way.

There was what the French would have called radical Muslim terrorism in Algeria 1954-1962, though the Salafis were junior partners of the largely secular FLN. French colonialists were targeted for heartless bombings and assassinations. This campaign of terror aimed at expelling the French, who had colonized Algeria in 1830 and had kept it ever since, declaring it French soil. The French had usurped the best land and crowded the Algerians into dowdy old medinas or haciendas in the countryside. The nationalists succeeded in gaining Algerian independence in 1962.

Once Sadat let the Muslim Brotherhood out of jail and allowed it to operate freely in the 1970s, to offset the power of the Egyptian Left, it threw up fundamentalist splinter groups like Ayman al-Zawahiri's al-Gihad al-Islami and Sheikh Omar's al-Gamaah al-Islamiyah. They were radicalized when Sadat made a separate peace with Israel in 1978-79 that permitted the Israelis to do as they pleased to the Palestinians. In response, the radical Muslims assassinated Sadat and continued to campaign against his successor, Hosni Mubarak. They saw the Egyptian regime as pharaonic and evil because it had allied with the United States and Israel, thus legitimating the occupation of Muslim land (from their point of view).

The south Lebanon Shiite groups, Amal and Hezbollah, turned to radical Muslim terrorism mainly after the 1982 Israeli invasion and subsequent occupation of South Lebanon, which is largely Shiite.

The radical Muslim terrorism of Khomeini's Revolutionary Guards grew in part out of American hegemony over Iran, which was expressed most forcefully by the 1953 CIA coup that overthrew the last freely elected parliament of that country.

Likewise, Hamas (the Palestinian Muslim Brotherhood) turned to terrorism in large part out of desperation at the squalid circumstances and economic and political hopelessness of the Israeli military occupation of Gaza.

The Soviet invasion and occupation of Afghanistan in the 1980s was among the biggest generators of radical Muslim terrorism in modern history. The US abetted this phenomenon, giving billions to the radical Muslim ideologues at the top of Pakistani military intelligence (Inter-Services Intelligence), which in turn doled the money out to men like Gulbuddin Hikmatyar, a member of the Afghanistan Muslim Brotherhood (Jami'at-i Islami) who used to throw vials of acid at the faces of unveiled girls in the Kabul of the 1970s. The US also twisted the arm of the Saudi government to match its contributions to the Mujahidin. Saudi Intelligence Minister Turki al-Faisal was in charge of recruiting Arab volunteers to fight alongside the Mujahidin, and he brought in young Osama bin Laden as a fundraiser. The CIA training camps that imparted specialized tradecraft to the Mujahidin inevitably also ended up training, at least at second hand, the Arab volunteers, who learned about forming covert cells, practicing how to blow things up, etc. The "Afghan Arabs" fanned back to their homelands, to Algeria, Libya, Yemen, Kuwait, Saudi Arabia, carrying with them the ethos that Ronald Reagan had inspired them with, which held that they should take up arms against atheist Westerners who attempted to occupy Muslim lands.

To this litany of Occupations that produce radical Muslim terrorism, Chechnya and Kashmir can be added.

In contrast, authoritarian governments like that of Iraq and Syria, while they might use terror for their own purposes from time to time, did not produce large-scale independent terrorist organizations that struck international targets. Authoritarian governments also proved adept at effectively crushing terrorist groups, as can be seen in Algeria and Egypt. It was only in failed states such as Afghanistan that they could flourish, not in authoritarian ones.

So it is the combination of Western occupation and weak states that produced the conditions for radical Muslim terrorism.

Democratic countries have often produced terrorist movements. This was true of Germany, Italy, Japan and the United States in the late 1960s and through the 1970s. There is no guarantee that a more democratic Iraq, Egypt or Lebanon will produce less terrorism. Certainly, the transition from Baathist dictatorship has introduced terrorism on a large scale into Iraqi society, and it may well spill over from there into neighboring states.

Morocco has been liberalizing for some years and held fairly above-board parliamentary elections in 2002. Yet liberalizing Morocco produced the al-Salafiyyah al-Jihadiyyah group in Tangiers that committed the 2003 Casablanca bombings and the 2004 Madrid train bombings.

Moreover, if democracy means majority rule and the expression of the general will, then it won't always work to the advantage of the US. Bush administration spokesmen keep talking about Syrian withdrawal being the demand of the "Lebanese people." But 40% of the Lebanese are Shiites, and 15% are probably Sunnis, and it may well be that a majority of Lebanese want to keep at least some Syrian troops around. Hezbollah has sided with Syria.

For true democracy to flourish in Lebanon, the artificial division of seats in parliament so that half go to the Christian minority would have to be ended. Religious Shiites would have, as in Iraq, a much bigger voice in national affairs. Will a Lebanon left to its own devices to negotiate a social compact between rightwing Christians and Shiite Hezbollah really be an island of stability?

I'm all for democratization in the Middle East, as a good in its own right. But I don't believe that authoritarian governance produced most episodes of terrorism in the last 60 years in the region. Terrorism was a weapon of the weak wielded against what these radical Muslims saw as a menacing foreign occupation. To erase that fact is to commit a basic error in historical understanding. It is why the US military occupation of Iraq is actually a negative for any "war on terror." Nor do I believe that democratization, even if it is possible, is going to end terrorism in and of itself.

You want to end terrorism? End unjust military occupations. By all means have Syria conduct an orderly withdrawal from Lebanon if that is what the Lebanese public wants. But Israel needs to withdraw from the Golan Heights, which belong to Syria, as well. The Israeli military occupation of Gaza and the West Bank must be ended. The Russian scorched earth policy in Chechnya needs to stop. Some just disposition of the Kashmir issue must be attained, and Indian enormities against Kashmiri Muslims must stop. The US needs to conduct an orderly and complete withdrawal from Iraq. And when all these military occupations end, there is some hope for a vast decrease in terrorism. People need a sense of autonomy and dignity, and occupation produces helplessness and humiliation. Humiliation is what causes terrorism.

The Islamic Way of War
by Andrew J. Bacevich

IN IRAQ, THE WORLD'S ONLY SUPERPOWER FINDS itself mired in a conflict that it cannot win. History's mightiest military has been unable to defeat an enemy force of perhaps 20,000 to 30,000 insurgents equipped with post-World War II vintage assault rifles and anti-tank weapons.

In Gaza and southern Lebanon, the Middle East's mightiest military also finds itself locked in combat with adversaries that it cannot defeat. Despite weeks of bitter fighting, the IDF's Merkava tanks, F-16 fighter-bombers, and missile-launching unmanned aerial vehicles failed to suppress, much less eliminate, the armed resistance of Hamas and Hezbollah.

What are we to make of this? How is it that the seemingly weak and primitive are able to frustrate modern armies only recently viewed as all but invincible? What do the parallel tribulations—and embarrassments—of the United States and Israel have to tell us about war and politics in the 21st century? In short, what's going on here?

The answer to that question is dismayingly simple: the sun has set on the age of unquestioned Western military dominance. Bluntly, the East has solved the riddle of the Western Way of War. In Baghdad and in Anbar Province as at various points on Israel's troubled perimeter, the message is clear: methods that once could be counted on to deliver swift decision no longer work.

For centuries, Western military might underpinned Western political dominion everywhere from Asia to Africa to the New World. It was not virtue that created the overseas empires of Great Britain, France, Spain, and the other European colonizers; it was firepower, technology, and discipline.

Through much of the last century, nowhere was this Western military pre-eminence more in evidence than in the Middle East. During World War I, superior power enabled the British and French to topple the Ottomans, carve up the region to suit their own interests, and then rule it like a fiefdom. Until 1945, European machine guns kept restive Arabs under control in Egypt, Iraq, Syria, and Palestine.

The end of World War II found the Europeans without the will to operate the machine guns and short on the money to pay for them. In the Middle East, Arabs no longer willing to follow instructions issued by London or Paris demanded independence. Eager to claim prestige and respect, these nationalists, Egypt's Gamal Abdel Nasser foremost among them, saw in the creation of large machine-age armies a shortcut to achieving their goals.

Placing an order for Soviet-bloc armaments in 1955, Nasser began an ill-fated Arab flirtation with Western-style military technique that did not fully end until Saddam Hussein's army collapsed on the outskirts of Baghdad nearly a half-century later. Throughout the 1960s and 1970s, Arab leaders invested in fleets of tanks, field artillery, and other heavy armaments, which they organized into massive formations supported by costly air forces equipped with supersonic jets. On the ground, bigger meant better; in the air, speed was thought to signify superiority.

All of these pricy exertions yielded only humiliation and indignity. Israel—a Western implant in the Muslim world—also adopted Western-style military methods but with far greater success, subjecting the Arabs to repeated drubbings. Designed on the Soviet model, the new Arab armies turned out to be ponderous and predictable but with little of the Red Army's capacity to absorb punishment and keep fighting. Taking the best of the German military tradition, the Israel Defense Forces placed a premium on daring, dash, and decentralization as they demonstrated to great effect in 1956, 1967, and 1973.

What was it that made the IDF in its heyday look so good? According to the punch line of an old joke: because they always fought Arabs. In 1991, the Americans finally had their own chance to fight Arabs, and they too looked good, making mincemeat of Saddam Hussein's legions in Operation Desert Storm. In the spring of 2003, the Americans looked good once again, dispatching the remnant of Saddam's army in a short and seemingly decisive campaign. In Washington many concluded that an unstoppable US military machine could provide the leverage necessary to transform the entire region.

The truth is that US forces and the IDF looked good fighting Arabs only as long as Arab political leaders insisted on fighting on Western terms. As long as they persisted in pitting tank against tank or fighter plane against fighter plane, Arabs were never going to get the better of either the Americans or the Israelis. His stupidity perhaps matched only by his ruthlessness, Saddam may well have been the last Arab leader to figure this out.

Well before Saddam's final defeat, others, less stupid, began to develop alternative means of what they called "resistance." This new Islamic Way of War evolved over a period of decades not only in the Arab world but beyond.

In Afghanistan during the 1980s, the Mujahadeen got things started by bringing to its knees a Soviet army equipped with an arsenal of modern equipment. During the so-called First Intifada, which began in 1987, stone-throwing and Molotov-cocktail-wielding Palestinians gave the IDF conniptions. In 1993, an angry Somali rabble—not an army at all—sent the United States packing. In 2000, the collapse of the Camp David talks produced a Second Intifada, this one persuading the government of Ariel Sharon that Israeli occupation of Gaza and the West Bank was becoming unsustainable. Most spectacularly, in September 2001, Al-Qaeda engineered a successful assault on the American homeland, the culmination of a series of attacks that had begun a decade earlier.

First in Afghanistan and then in Iraq, the United States seemed briefly to turn the tables: Western military methods overthrew the Taliban and then made short shrift of Saddam. After the briefest of intervals, however, victory in both places gave way to renewed and protracted fighting. Most recently, in southern Lebanon an intervention that began with Israeli Prime Minister Ehud Olmert vowing to destroy Hezbollah has run aground and looks increasingly like an Israeli defeat.

So it turns out that Arabs—or more broadly Muslims—can fight after all. We may surmise that they now realize that fighting effectively requires that they do so on their own terms rather than mimicking the West. They don't need and don't want tanks and fighter-bombers. What many Westerners dismiss as "terrorism," whether directed against Israelis, Americans, or others in the West, ought to be seen as a panoply of techniques employed to undercut the apparent advantages of high-tech conventional forces. The methods employed do include terrorism—violence targeting civilians for purposes of intimidation—but they also incorporate propaganda, subversion, popular agitation, economic warfare, and hit-and-run attacks on regular forces, either to induce an overreaction or to wear them down. The common theme of those techniques, none of which are new, is this: avoid the enemy's strengths; exploit enemy vulnerabilities.

What are the implications of this new Islamic Way of War? While substantial, they fall well short of being apocalyptic. As Gen. Peter Pace, chairman of the Joint Chiefs of Staff, has correctly—if perhaps a trifle defensively—observed, "Our enemy knows they cannot defeat us in battle." Neither the Muslim world nor certainly the Arab world poses what some like to refer to as "an existential threat" to the United States. Despite overheated claims that the so-called Islamic fascists pose a danger greater than Hitler ever did, the United States is not going to be overrun, even should the forces of Al-Qaeda, Hamas, Hezbollah, Iraqi insurgents, and Shi'ite militias along with Syria and Iran all combine into a unified anti-Crusader coalition. Although Israelis for historical reasons are inclined to believe otherwise, the proximate threat to Israel itself is only marginally greater. Although neither Israel nor the United States can guarantee its citizens "perfect security"—what nation can?—both enjoy ample capabilities for self-defense.

What the Islamic Way of War does mean to both Israel and to the United States is this: the Arabs now possess—and know that they possess—the capacity to deny us victory, especially in any altercation that occurs on their own turf and among their own people. To put it another way, neither Israel nor the United States today possesses anything like the military muscle needed to impose its will on the various governments, nation-states, factions, and political movements that comprise our list of enemies. For politicians in Jerusalem or Washington to persist in pretending otherwise is the sheerest folly.

It's time for Americans to recognize that the enterprise that some neoconservatives refer to as World War IV is unwinnable in a strictly military sense. Indeed, it's past time to re-examine the post-Cold War assumption that military power provides the preferred antidote to any and all complaints that we have with the world beyond our borders.

In the Middle East and more broadly in our relations with the Islamic world, we face difficult and dangerous problems, more than a few of them problems to which we ourselves have contributed. Those problems will become more daunting still, for us and for Israel, should a nation like Iran succeed in acquiring nuclear weapons. But as events in Iraq and now in southern Lebanon make clear, reliance on the sword alone will not provide a solution to those problems. We must be strong and we must be vigilant. But we also need to be smart, and getting smart means ending our infatuation with war and rediscovering the possibilities of politics.

Losing the Three-Front War
by Patrick Seale

I N A WORD OF WISE ADVICE TO PIG-HEADED political leaders, Denis Healey, a former British Defence Secretary, used to say, "When you're in a hole, stop digging!" The United States and Israel are in a deep and dangerous hole. They urgently need to stop digging before the hole swallows them up.

In July of 2006, they were fighting, and losing, on three fronts—Iraq, Lebanon and Palestine. It seemed that this was not enough for the more insane and hysterical among them who were clamoring to extend the war to Syria and Iran, and to the whole of what they like to call the "Islamo-Fascist" world. Israel denies it is involved in the Iraq war. But, in fact, it is as much part of that conflict as the United States is now part of the wars in Lebanon and Palestine. Israel participated in the strategic planning for the Iraq War, which was designed to remove any threat to it from the east. Its neo-con friends in Washington egged on America and fabricated the phony intelligence which persuaded a gullible President that smashing Iraq was necessary for America's security.

Three years later, the United States would find itself up to its neck in the Iraqi quagmire, squandering billions of dollars and losing men at the rate of about one a day, but without the good sense or the will to hoist itself out of the hole. And now, nearly six years after the war began, US casualties would be down but the cost of the war would continue unabated while political reconciliation that could form the basis of a stable, independent regime was nowhere in sight.

The wars in Iraq, Palestine and Lebanon are all inter-linked, as US abuses in Iraq provide a model for Israel's indiscriminate violence against civilians in the 2006 July

War in Lebanon and its breach of international humanitarian law. Israel is doing what the United States pioneered, when the world's superpower created conditions of international anarchy by destroying the checks and balances of the international system.

The pro-Israeli ideologues in Washington are still driven by the fantasy that the entire Middle East can be restructured by military force to suit US and Israeli interests—and in the summer of 2006 the President, worried about the looming mid-term elections in November, was too stubborn and too ignorant to call an early halt to the madness of Israeli combat in Lebanon.

The wars in Lebanon and Palestine in 2006 were US-Israeli wars, pre-planned jointly and waged in close strategic coordination. The Israelis do the fighting while the United States provides the funding, the weapons, and the political and diplomatic cover: delaying a ceasefire to give Israel time to "finish the job."

But the wars did not go their way. In both Lebanon and Gaza, Israel might have achieved some tactical gains—like the commando raid on Baalbeck—but a strategic victory was unattainable.

Hezbollah and Hamas are not conventional armies that can be wiped out on a battlefield, nor are they terrorist organizations with no claim to recognition or respect. They are national resistance movements deeply rooted in the local populations they represent, whose rights and lives they seek to defend against Israel's repeated aggressions.

In Lebanon, Israel's immediate aim appeared to be to drive Hezbollah and the local civilian population out of a 30 kilometer-wide stretch in the hope that an international force would then step in to disarm Hezbollah and protect Israel from further rocket attacks. This was a pipe dream.

Occupying south Lebanon will not protect Israeli forces from further guerrilla attacks—such as drove them out in 2000—and no country will send troops to fight Hezbollah on Israel's behalf. As the French have made clear, an international force can be deployed only with the consent of all parties, Hezbollah included, and only when peace is restored.

In the meantime, the villages of south Lebanon were being devastated by intense bombardment, while their panic-stricken inhabitants fled north as best they could—those that had not been buried in the rubble of their homes.

The moral and political cost to Israel of this ethnic cleansing and state terrorism has been exceedingly high. Israel's contempt for Arab life and the laws of war has eroded the legitimacy it managed to achieve in its brief 58 years of existence. Thousands, perhaps tens of thousands, of outraged and radicalized Arabs are itching to attack it.

This is the fundamental contradiction at the heart of Israel's policy. By seeking to restore its dented deterrent capability by brutal means—by demanding the freedom to attack its enemies while denying them the freedom to hit back—leaves it increasingly vulnerable to asymmetrical warfare.

The wider US and Israeli aim of destroying Hezbollah and removing all trace of

Syria or Iranian influence from Lebanon is an unattainable fantasy flying in the face of local realities. For historical, confessional and social reasons, because of a dense network of family and other ties, and because of shared strategic and security interests, Syria and Iran will always have far greater sway in Lebanon than Israel or the United States.

Following the July War in Lebanon, hatred for Israel and disillusion with America knew no bounds, while Hezbollah emerged stronger from the battle. By setting themselves impossible aims, Israel and the United States guaranteed their own failure.

The United States is now at an important crossroads in its dealings with the Arab and Muslim world. Will it sink deeper into hostility or can it find the wisdom to correct its aim? There are experienced advisors in Washington who know what needs to be—e.g., Brent Scowcroft, national security adviser to Presidents Gerald Ford and George Bush senior, and Zbigniew Brzezinski, President Carter's national security adviser—but their voices are not heard in George W. Bush's White House.

Bush's Global War on Terrorism and his unconditional support for Israel have made him a host of enemies. No US President in modern times has been more reviled. The United States even seems incapable of disciplining its unruly Israeli protégé, as Secretary Rice learned to her cost in July 2006 [July 31, 2006]. She thought Israel's Prime Minister Olmert had promised her a 48-hour ceasefire, but Israel continued its bombardment of Lebanese targets unabashed. She told Shimon Peres, Israel's deputy premier, that a ceasefire could be obtained in days, and he contradicted her publicly saying Israel needed weeks.

Where then is America's global leadership? It has been flushed down the drain in what Turkey's Prime Minister Recep Tayyip Erdogan has called a "culture of violence."

The choice facing President George W. Bush is stark. It is between continuing his backing for Israel's disastrous wars in Lebanon and Palestine—perhaps even extending the conflict to Iran and Syria—or calling a halt to such folly and asserting his leadership for peace.

This could be Bush's chance to rescue his presidency from failure. He must put America's great weight and his personal prestige behind a comprehensive regional settlement. It can be done and he has the time to do it. But to succeed, he will need to make a clean sweep of advisers who have put America in danger.

The problems of the region must be tackled frontally and together, because they are interlinked:

- The Israeli-Palestinian conflict must be resolved with the creation of an independent Palestinian state based on the 1967 borders.
- The Israeli-Syrian conflict must be resolved with the return to Syria of the Golan.
- Lebanon must be rebuilt with a massive injection of aid and international guarantees for its future security.

- The United States must start a bilateral dialogue with Iran aimed at restoring diplomatic relations and recognizing Iran's regional interests and security fears.
- Israel must give up its vain ambition to dominate the region militarily and should instead, safe within its 1967 borders, conclude peace treaties with the entire Arab world based on mutual respect and good neighborliness.
- Is this utopian vision the greatest pipedream of all? In the meantime the killing and the threat of killing goes on, and everyone is a loser.

Not Yet
by General James A "Spider" Marks

NOT YET. THERE IS NO DOUBTING America's commitment to Iraq is not yet complete. Frankly, I'm not sure that we can define with any certainty or clarity what a "complete" relationship with Iraq looks like. Much like any relationship you hope will have some permanence, the time horizon remains distant and shifting. The sacrifices of US soldiers and their families as well as Iraqi soldiers, their families, and Iraqi citizens have been considerable. We will not "return on success" until or unless success is measured and realized. We honor too many to depart too soon.

I just returned to Iraq for the first time in four years. The conditions are far different from the hopeful, early days of the summer of 2003. Following our incredible push into Baghdad, the collapse of Saddam's military, the confirmation of his brutality and the macabre levers of power under which his people suffered, and the unforgettable demonstrations of grace and civility of his newly freed citizens, we witnessed uncontrolled cathartic releases of mindless destruction. We reaped what Saddam had sown.

Back then as is always the circumstance, good guys and their families needed to be uplifted. They needed security, a precondition for the promise of hope and opportunity. However, security only comes at the butt end or the business end of a weapon delivered by a soldier. It is never hatched. It is always hard won. Security is not a promise. Security is a guarantee delivered over time. It yields confidence and certainty that today's routine will be tomorrow's. Sadly, in the summer of 2003, we did not have enough weapons or soldiers. We delivered neither confidence nor certainty. We should have surged then. But we didn't.

Last year, we finally made a course correction. The surge of US ground troops in Iraq that began in January 2007 has provided the necessary conditions for the hope and opportunity in the summer of 2003 to be a near possibility. Today, Iraq is close but is not quite there. Maturity in Iraqi self governance continues to grow. The pace is slow and deliberate but there is progress. A new normalcy is being achieved. It is not the desired end state of a new normal but it is legitimate and it sure beats the alternative: Saddam's brutality and Al-Qaeda in Iraq's objective to pursue murder and terror as methods of influence. Good news...the bad guys are losing.

Better news...the Iraqi people are winning. That grace and dignity of the Iraqi citizens so prevalent five years ago has, under pressure, been strengthened and has re-emerged in full blossom. Good things are happening across Iraq.

My daughter's fiancé serves in Iraq as a young lieutenant. He and his soldiers are helping provide power to the village where they serve. The villagers have never had power before. Commerce is returning to this sand-choked corner of Iraq. A renovated building will soon become the new school.

However, the pursuit of the new normal must be relentless. If nothing else, recidivism defines bad guys. They always repeat their criminal ways. My future son-in-law's job is to prevent recidivism. Encouragement is his weapon of choice, his primary means of influence. "I love handing out soccer balls to the kids," he says. "Their parents want to show me their soccer skills and, man, they sure get chatty while kicking that thing around." He played college soccer (and pretty well) so he is convinced he can evaluate their soccer skills. More importantly, however, as a trained soldier, I know he can evaluate good intelligence when the village males "get chatty."

Good intelligence drives his mission to help deliver on the new normal. He'd prefer to provide the soft touch of encouragement, but willingly and swiftly responds to punish recidivism. This is not his choice. It is the choice of those who intend violence and terror and those who tolerate it. In this part of Iraq, his is a simple plot line. Encourage growth and opportunity or provide solid evidence that you can and will teach those who won't. Some folks just learn the hard way. It is working. The school opening is on track.

As new normal spreads, it must be given time to take root. A family anywhere in Iraq must know with certainty that a new day brings a guarantee of a positive, enduring chance for good to emerge. It is a guarantee, not the promise, of choice. This is what is going on in Iraq today. Sure, kids must be free to walk to school without constant worry or worse. Schools and markets must be open and functioning. Learning must take place and goods must be available. The lights have to turn on. These successes are being hard won and re won every day. Episodic results today will, over time, deliver the new normal.

Not yet. As fair as it is to say we're not delivering on that new normal as a matter of routine, it is equally unfair to prematurely assess that Iraq, with the aid and nurturing support of the US, never will. Together we will persist. Over time, soccer playing Dads who so impressed a young lieutenant with their skills will never become angry recidivists with limited choices.

The Role of Homeland Security and Training
by Daniel W. Sutherland

THE DEPARTMENT OF HOMELAND SECURITY's front-line officers confront a vast array of complex missions every day. For example, Customs and Border Protection (CBP) officers encounter more than one million people every day who seek to enter our country. They inspect more than 70,000 truck, rail, and sea containers and more than 300,000 privately owned vehicles. Coast Guard officers track and intercept drug-running narcotics boats. Transportation Security Officers screen over two million people every day who want to board an airplane. Guards with the Federal Protective Service screen tens of thousands of people every day who seek to enter federal buildings, courthouses and other facilities under their watch. In all, employees of the Department of Homeland Security come into contact with more than three million people every day.

In these complex environments, training is a key component. DHS officers receive in-depth training on topics such as boating laws, the tactics of drug smugglers, Fourth Amendment search-and-seizure case law, agricultural products, customs and financial laws, and behavioral pattern recognition.

It is also essential that our officers have a clear understanding of the cultures, traditions, and values of the people they interact with. Obviously, the majority of people who cross our borders every day come from other countries, speak languages other than English, and have customs that are different than ours. Some may have medical conditions or disabilities. Therefore, training in what we call "cultural competence" is critical. Three examples will help to illustrate my point:

A CBP officer is doing a quick scan of the contents of a suitcase. He comes across a copy of the *Quran*, and suddenly freezes. How should he handle this book that is considered holy to that traveler? Can he set it down on the counter? What if it drops to the floor? Can he set any other contents of the suitcase on top of the *Quran*? He does not want to spark an incident that would be offensive to the traveler and costly to his mission.

A guard with the Federal Protective Service is securing a federal courthouse, when a member of the public approaches the checkpoint. The individual is a woman wearing a religious headcovering—a scarf that is covering her entire head. How should the guard proceed? Can he pat down the headcovering?

A TSO is standing at an airport security checkpoint when a traveler causes the metal detector to alarm. As the TSO approaches the traveler, she realizes that the individual has a prosthetic device on his arm, from the elbow down. Obviously, the metal in the prosthetic device has set off the alarm. How should the TSO talk to the traveler? How should she screen the traveler?

Because of situations like this, DHS officers are deeply interested in receiving cultural competence training. This training cannot be seen to be part of "political correctness" or labeled as "sensitivity training." We reject political correctness. As the Department's civil libertarians, we are, by design, contrarians! This type of training is helpful because it gives our colleagues the skills and abilities they need to do their jobs at the highest levels of professionalism and efficiency. In our view, this is how the training must be executed in order to be successful in reaching law enforcement and military audiences.

To meet these needs, the Office for Civil Rights and Civil Liberties (CRCL) has developed the "Civil Liberties Institute." The goal is to provide high-quality training on a range of the most important civil rights and civil liberties topics and deliver the training in a cost-effective manner to the widest possible DHS audience via advanced distributed learning (ADL) methods. These include both computer-based and web-based training, as well as the production of training aids. The best training is done in collaboration, as two sets of eyes are almost always better than one. CRCL has been assisted by the Department's Chief Learning Officer, many training and policy offices within the Department, the Training Leaders Council, and several outstanding professionals at the Federal Law Enforcement Training Center (FLETC) in Glynco, Georgia.

The Civil Liberties Institute "library" includes products such as the following:
- A training session for DHS personnel who interact with Arab- Americans, people from the Arab world, Muslim Americans, and people from the Muslim world. The training includes insights from four national and international experts— an Assistant United States Attorney who is a practicing Muslim, a member of the National Security Council who is a practicing Muslim, an Islamic Studies scholar, and the author of this publication. We have distributed thousands of copies of this training on CDs to colleagues throughout the country;
- Posters that provide guidance to DHS personnel on how to screen and, if necessary, search individuals who wear common Muslim and Sikh head-coverings;
- Online training that emphasizes certain elements of the National Detention Standards;
- An educational poster on how to screen those of the Sikh faith who carry a *Kirpan*, or ceremonial religious dagger;
- Training on how frontline officers should interact with people who are seeking asylum, including the complex struggles that a government official may have in communicating with someone who has recently been tortured or oppressed by a government official in his or her home country; and,
- A TSA training video that helps screeners to successfully interact with travelers with disabilities. TSA also developed a "Z card" of basic instructions for screeners as they interact with travelers with disabilities. The pocket-sized card provides quick reference points for screeners as they interact with travelers in wheelchairs, those with service animals, and travelers with various complex medical conditions.

Some of the training products in our library have been produced with the help of the author of this book, Nawar Shora. We have been very grateful for his willingness to share his expertise with the US Government.

Our goal is to build a DHS culture that respects civil rights and civil liberties. We are accomplishing this goal by reviewing DHS programs and policies, investigating concerns raised by the public and, through proactive training. A highly professional law enforcement agency with a reputation for respecting individual rights and basic human dignity will engender public cooperation and respect, allowing it to reach its highest level of effectiveness and professionalism.

Chapter Seven

Syria as a Case Study

Syria Is Not Iraq
by Martha Kessler

THE UNITED STATES HAS ISSUED MORE WARNINGS and threats to Syria in the past week than ever in the history of relations between the two countries. But Syria is not Iraq, and Americans should beware of those who try to make that case.

Syria lives in the same tough neighborhood that Israel, Kuwait, Jordan and others complain about—neighborhood in which military muscle and regional ambition characterize the tough players, the big players. Israel is the biggest, with military prowess beyond that of all the others combined. Iraq was one of them, and Egypt and Iran are two aspirants.

Syria is decidedly not one of them. Like most states in the region, Syria has had to survive in the neighborhood in one of two ways: find a powerful patron (as Jordan, Kuwait, Saudi Arabia and the Gulf states have found in the United States) or create a credible military deterrence and a network of relationships to allow for bobbing and weaving through the punches of regional politics.

During the Cold War, Syria tried the patron route with the Soviet Union. But since the Soviet collapse in the 1980's, Syria has worked the more difficult approach of surviving on regional alliances and deals to generate the necessary economic and political wherewithal.

It has been able to do little more than manage—manage its transition from a socialist to a more liberal economy, manage its factious, diverse and highly political society in a rapidly changing world, and manage its meager natural resources. Syria is poor, its military is deteriorating and it is behind even by regional standards in the chase for modern technology. It is not a large powerful, oil-rich regional player like Iraq.

Many, including several US presidents, have accused Syria of having broad regional ambitions, as Iraq had. But, in fact, here are the only credible circumstances that fit the charge: Since independence in the 1940s, Syrians have believed that the map drawn by British and French colonialists left individual Arab nations weak and set one against another because of border disputes, divided societies and, thus, divided political loyalties.

Syrians, like many other Arabs, promoted the notion of rising above Western-imposed national distinctions to support broad Arab goals. Hafez Assad, Syrian President Bashar Assad's father, mixed this pan-Arab ideology with a good deal of pragmatism, but he believed it until his death in 2000.

Syria led the charge to isolate Egypt after it signed its peace agreement with Israel in 1979; most Arab states joined Syria in shunning Egypt. The case Syria made against Cairo was that it had abandoned its Arab brethren, all but guaranteeing that those with territorial claims against Israel would never have sufficient strength to regain their patrimony.

Syrian troops were sent into Lebanon in the 1970s to try to end the civil war there. They were dispatched under the aegis of the Arab League. The US quietly accepted and, in some respects, welcomed the presence once it became convinced that Syria was the only power that could bring the bloody conflict to an end. This was not Iraq marching into Kuwait—not by any stretch of the historical facts. As a result of its influence in Lebanon, Syria has battled Israel indirectly through Lebanese surrogates—Hezbollah. Syria has also pressed Lebanon not to settle or "sell out" to Israel but to move in lock step with Damascus in negotiations with Israel. These actions have a name, but it is not regional ambition.

Syria has been likened to Iraq as an authoritarian regime that represses its people. Syria is not democratic, but then there are no democracies in the Arab world; there are only authoritarian rulers—some brutal, some enlightened, some pragmatic. The Assads of Syria fall mainly into the category of pragmatic.

A walk through Syria would not uncover plastic bags with dismembered human remains or young boys brainwashed and inducted into militant service of a personality cult. As for prisons, Syria's are relatively empty, and their dark interiors would be indistinguishable from those in Jordan, Egypt, Saudi Arabia, Morocco and much of the rest of the world.

The international community has suspected for decades that Syria developed chemical and biological weapons to serve as a "poor man's" deterrent to the arsenal of several dozen nuclear weapons Israel is reported to possess. This fairly stable standoff has existed between Israel and Syria for decades. Not until now has it ever been suggested that Syria intended to use this capability offensively, much less against the United States.

This is a country that fought with the United States to oust Iraq from Kuwait. This is a country that sat at the table with the United States for 10 years of negotiations, patiently accepting Washington's instruction and trusting its intention to fairness in finding a settlement between Israel and the Arabs. This is also a country that has helped the United States track down Islamic extremists, providing assistance that has surprised even its most determined critics. This is the Arab country that voted to accept Resolution 1441—the Security Council resolution under which the US justified the war on Iraq—thereby causing Washington a lot less trouble than some of its other friends.

When Americans hear talk of another war—this time in Syria—they need to remember that Damascus under the Assads has for years been committed to peace with Israel on the basis of the return of Syrian territory. To be sure, Syria has created complications for the United States right now. But there are no megalomaniacs in Damascus or threats to the United States.

Syria is not Iraq—not even close—and Americans should not allow themselves to be spun into thinking so.

They Visited Damascus
by Sami Moubayed

OVER THE LAST 200-YEARS A VARIETY of political, cultural, and 'revolutionary' celebrities have visited Damascus. Some came for tourism, others for work. All of them, however, came across with very favorable impressions of the capital of the Umayyads. Whether it was Damascus under the Ottomans, the French, or since independence in 1946, the city has never failed to inspire, impress, and enchant its visitors. The hall of fame of those who have come to Syria is a long and impressive one, which has never been studied in a proper manner. It includes, among others, three US presidents, Richard Nixon, Jimmy Carter, Bill Clinton, four French presidents, Charles de Gaulle, Valéry Giscard D'Estaing, Francois Mitterrand, Jacques Chirac, and two British prime ministers, Winston Churchill and Tony Blair. It also includes every Secretary General of the United Nations, from the first Trygive Lie to the current Ban Ki Moon. Here's a look at some of the 'who's who' in the long list of Syria visitors.

Mark Twain (1835-1910)
The internationally acclaimed American writer who authored timeless classics like *Adventures of Huckleberry Finn*, and *The Adventures of Tom Sawyer* came to Damascus in 1869. He described the city in his travel book *The Innocents Abroad* saying: "Damascus measures time not by days and months and years, but by the empires she has seen rise and prosper and crumble to ruin. She is a type of immortality." He adds, "In her old age she saw Rome built; she saw it overshadow the world with its power; she saw it perish. Damascus has seen all that has ever occurred on earth, and still she lives. She has looked upon the dry bones of a thousand empires, and will see the tombs of a thousand more before she dies. Though another claims the name, old Damascus is by right, the Eternal City."

Kaiser Wilhelm II of Germany (1859-1941)
The last German Emperor who ruled from 1888 until the end of World War I in 1918 came to Damascus to pay for the restoration of the tomb of Saladin [see glossary] with a marble sarcophagus in 1898. The municipality of Damascus underwent a massive administrative and reform program, beautifying roads, parks, and buildings, to prepare for his visit to Ottoman Damascus. While in Syria he stayed at the home of Tawfiq

Shamiyya, a city notable from the Greek Orthodox community who later became a prominent anti-French statesman during the years of the Mandate (1920-1946).

Gertrude Bell (1868-1926)

A renowned British writer and administrator, Bell lived and worked in the Arab World before, during, and after World War I. Along with T.E. Lawrence, she literarily co-created the Hashemite Kingdom of Jordan and after the war, incorporated three Ottoman vilayets into one, creating the modern State of Iraq. Along with Lawrence, she convinced Winston Churchill to appoint the former King of Syria Faisal I as the first monarch of Iraq. She moved to Baghdad and advised the new king, whom she had known from Damascus, on a variety of issues that included matters of tribal geography, appointment of ministers, and affairs of state. Her influence was so strong that her nickname in Iraq was "The Uncrowned Queen of Iraq." She found the job difficult, and before committing suicide in 1926, remarked, "You may rely upon one thing—I'll never engage in creating kings again; it's too great a strain."

Agatha Christie (1890-1976)

The most famous English crime writer in the 20th century, Christie is also referred to sometimes as "The Queen of Crime." She was listed in the Guiness Book of World Records as the best selling writer of all time, second only to William Shakespeare. She published 66 detective stories and 21 plays, which collectively sold 1 billion copies in English and another 1 billion in a variety of other languages, translated in 103 different countries. Her play *The Moustrap* began at the Ambassador's Theatre in London in 1952 and is still running as of 2007, with over 20,000 performances. Christie first came to the Middle East for adventure and holiday in 1932. She went from London to Damascus and then to Baghdad. Her journey to Damascus inspired her to write her classic "Murder on the Orient Express" in 1934. The cities of the East, including Damascus and Aleppo, were often described and mentioned in her novels. Her room at the Baron Hotel in Aleppo is still a major tourist attraction even today, more than 30-years after her passing.

T.E. Lawrence (1888-1935)

The British Army colonel who came to the Arab World during World War I and was forever remembered as "Lawrence of Arabia." He served in the Arabian Desert during the war and helped launch guerilla warfare against the Ottoman Empire. Lawrence had a commanding influence on Sharif Hussein, the commander of the revolt, and his two sons, Prince Abdullah (later king of Jordan) and Prince Faisal (later king of Syria, then of Iraq).

On October 1, 1918, Lawrence and his men marched into Damascus declaring the end of the Ottoman Empire and the liberation of the city from 400-years of Turkish control. The Syrians greeted him as a liberator. He spent quality time with Faisal in Syria, adopting local customs and traditions, and was often photographed wearing traditional Arab garb. Right after the war he worked at the Foreign Office and attended the Paris Peace Conference with the Syrian King in 1919, trying to convince the British government to grant the Arabs their independence, without success. In 1926 he published his widely acclaimed book on the Arab Revolt called *Seven Pillars of Wisdom*.

Winston Churchill (1874-1965)

The legendary Prime Minister of Great Britain during World War II. In 1911, as First Lord of the Admiralty, Churchill visited Ottoman Damascus. Four years later, the people of Damascus sided with the British during the Great Arab Revolt against the Ottomans. Churchill almost single-handedly shaped the new Middle East in the immediate post-war period, and returned to Arab affairs during WWII by meeting with King Abdul-Aziz of Saudi Arabia and Syrian President Shukri al-Quwatli. He helped the Syrians achieve global recognition by inviting them to be founding members of the United Nations in May 1945 and pressuring the French to evacuate from Damascus in April 1946. When meeting President Quwatli in 1945, Churchill commented on the people of Syria, whom he had first met in 1911, saying: "The Syrians are a great people, and you are worthy of leading a great people, Mr. President."

Charlie Chaplin (1889-1977)

One of the giants of the silent film era and one of the greatest performers of all times, Chaplin came to Syria in 1931 to attend the screening of his silent film *City Lights*. The Syrians were great fans of Chaplin's character "The Tramp" who is a vagrant with the refined manners and dignity of a gentleman. The character wears a tight coat, oversized trousers and shoes, a derby, carries a bamboo cane, and has a signature toothbrush moustache. In *City Lights*, he meets a blind girl selling flowers on the street and falls in love with her. She mistakes him for a millionare, and since he does not want to disappoint her, he continues with the charade.

Shah Reza Pahlavi (1919-1980)

The last Shah of Iran, whose relations were not too cordial with the Syrians during his years in power, visited Damascus as crown prince in March 1939. The Shah was greeted and courted by then-Foreign Minister Fayez al-Khury and granted an audience with President Hashem al-Atassi. After coming to power in 1941 and until his toppling by the Islamic Revolution in 1979, the Shah had only proper diplomatic relations with the Syrians due to his alliance first with the United States and, after 1948, with the State of Israel. The Syrians supported the Islamic Revolution in 1979 and have been strong allies of the leaders of post-Shah Iran.

Charles de Gaulle (1890-1970)

Charles de Gaulle came to Syria on July 27, 1942, in his capacity as leader of the Free French Movement during World War II. His troops, aided by the British, had just defeated those of Vichy France stationed in Syria. De Gaulle promised to liberate the Syrians from the hated Mandate system and toyed with restoring the nationalists to power. He even went to the city of Homs to meet with their leader Hashem al-Atassi, requesting that he return to power and complete what was left of his presidential term, which had been cut short by his resignation in 1939. Unable to convince the nationalists to collaborate with the Free French, due to France's record in the region, de Gaulle instead appointed a pro-French president. In 1945, his officers ordered the bombardment of Damascus.

Count Folke Bernadotte (1895-1948)
The Swedish diplomat had risen to fame during World War II for negotiating the release of 15,000 prisoners from Nazi concentration camps, and had received an offer of surrender from Heinrich Himmler. He came to Syria in 1948 to meet with President Shukri al-Quwatli and Prime Minister Jamil Mardam Bey. Right after the first Palestine War, Bernadotte was chosen by the UN to serve as mediator in the Arab-Israeli Conflict. He offered two plans. Both were rejected by the Israelis. Bernadotte was assassinated by the Jewish terrorist group Lehi, headed by future Israeli Prime Minister Yitzhak Shamir.

Prince Philip of Edinburgh (1921-)
After marrying Princess Elizabeth, the heiress to the British throne, Philip was given the title of Duke of Edinburgh by his father-in-law King George VI. In this capacity he visited Damascus on June 29, 1950, to meet with President Hashem al-Atassi. Atassi held a banquet in his honor, attended by senior politicians, diplomats, and army officers. There the Prince jokingly told them about how he had courted the future Queen of England. In 1952, Elizabeth became Queen and in 1957, Philip became the Prince of the United Kingdom.

Trygive Lie (1896-1968)
The Norweigan statesman served as the first Secretary-General of the United Nations from 1946 to 1952. He was a good friend of Syria's Prime Minister Faris al-Khury, who attended the founding conference of the UN in 1945. Lie came to Syria as part of a regional tour in 1950, to meet with President Hashem al-Atassi and Prime Minister Khaled al-Azm. As an illustrious guest, he was given the Medal of Honor of the Syrian Republic (Excellence Class).

Humphrey Bogart (1899-1957)
Described by the American Film Institute as the Greatest Male Star of All Time, Humphrey Bogart is most remembered for his classical performance in the timeless 1942 production *Casablanca*, opposite Ingrid Bergman.

Nine years later he came to Damascus to shoot *Sirocco*, directed by Curtis Bernhardt, about an American gun runner operating from Syria in the 1920s, selling the Syrians arms to use in their revolt against the French Mandate. Because critics compared it to *Casablanca*, the film flopped at the box office.

Eleanor Roosevelt (1884-1962)
Wife of US President Franklin D, Roosevelt and famous as the iron-willed First Lady of America during the difficult years of the Great Depression and World War II, Eleanor Roosevelt was the longest serving First Lady in US history, from 1933-1945. After her husband's death, Roosevelt became an internationally acclaimed author, newspaper columnist, and human rights activist. From 1946 to 1961 she was ranked #1 as the "World's Most Popular Woman." When touring the Arab World, she came to Syria in March 1953 to meet with President Adib al-Shishakli. Cameras and newspaper reporters from around the world came with her, covering her tour of Damascus and reporting on the city, its people, and politics to the American and Western media. Her picture signing the guestbook at the Presidential Palace in Damascus made world headlines.

John Foster Dulles (1888-1959)
US President Dwight Eisenhower's Secretary of State came to Damascus shortly after assuming office in 1953. He met with President Adib al-Shishakli, commended the Syrian leader's reform program, and deemed Syria eligible for US aid. During the Shishakli-Dulles meeting, student demonstrations filled the streets of Damascus, objecting to Dulles' visit, the first of its kind by a US Secretary of State to Syria. One of the demonstrators was Shishakli's son, a member of the Baath Party. According to Andrew Rathmell's *Secret War in the Middle East: The Covert Struggle for Syria,* Dulles demanded this condition: that US aid not be used to threaten Israel. Shishakli refused to accept the condition. After Shishakli's downfall in 1954, Dulles continued to follow Syrian affairs and even authorized two coup attempts against the Syrian government in the late 1950s, designed to curb communist influence in Damascus. These coups failed as did other of Dulles' attempts to isolate the regime of President Shukri al-Quwatli.

Dag Hammerskold (1905-1961)
The Swedish diplomat, second Secretary-General of the UN, came to Syria to meet with President Shukri al-Quwatli during the Suez Canal War of 1956. He created the United Nations Emergency Force (UNEF) to prevent further warfare between Israel and Egypt.

Helen Keller (1880-1968)
The world famous deaf-blind American author, activist, and lecturer came to Damascus to meet with President Adib al-Shishakli in 1953. Keller was known internationally, but particularly in the US, as a speaker, author, and advocate for people with disabilities, especially after setting up Helen Keller International, a non-profit organization for preventing blindness. Helen Keller had met every US President

from Grover Cleveland to Lyndon B. Johnson and was friends with many famous figures including Alexander Graham Bell, inventor of the telephone, Charlie Chaplin and Mark Twain. Her autobiography, *The Story of My Life*, had been translated into Arabic upon its release in 1903 and sold in Syria.

Jawaharlal Nehru (1889-1964)
The first Prime Minister of independent India, an associate of Mahatma Gandhi, and one of the most influential figures of the 20th century, came to Damascus twice in 1956 and 1961 as a proponent of non-alignment. Co-founder of the Non-Aligned Movement with President Gamal Abdul-Nasser of Egypt, Nehru was greatly admired by President Shukri al-Quwatli. Nehru visited Quwatli shortly after recognizing the People's Republic of China, prompting the Syrian leader to do the same, an act that greatly angered the Eisenhower White House. Quwatli was particularly impressed by Nehru's stance against Great Britain, France, and Israel during the Suez Canal War of 1956.

Che Guevara (1928-1967)
The Argentine-born Marxist revolutionary, medical doctor, leader of Cuban guerillas, one of the world's most famous cult figures, Che Guevara visited Syria in 1959 to meet with President Gamal Abdul-Nasser during the years of the United Arab Republic (UAR) in 1959. At the time, the Cuban revolution had just seized power in Havana.

Muhammad Ali (Cassius Clay) (1942-)
The World Heavyweight Boxing Champion, a 1975 convert to Islam, came to Syria to receive treatment for Parkinson's disease. He was supervised by Syrian doctors and met President Hafez al-Assad.

Jesse Jackson (1941-)
The American civil rights activist and twice presidential hopeful Jackson traveled to Syria to secure the release of the captured US Navy airman Lt. Robert Goodman Jr., who had been shot down over Lebanon while on a mission to bomb Syrian positions in that war-torn country. The White House opposed Jackson's visit. But after Jackson met with President Hafez al-Assad, Goodman was released. Both Goodman and Jackson were received at the White House by President Ronald Reagan on January 4, 1984. Jackson returned in August 2006 to meet with the Damascus-based leaders of Hamas to seek an exchange of Israeli prisoners with Palestinians ones. After meeting Hamas chief Khaled Meshaal, he visited the Umayyad Mosque, a synagogue, and Jewish school in Old Damascus.

Henry Kissinger (1923-)
The Secretary of State under President Richard Nixon, Kissinger came to Syria in the immediate aftermath of the October War of 1973 to conduct 'shuttle diplomacy'

between the Syrians and the Israelis. These were groundbreaking meetings because relations between both countries had been cut since the June War of 1967 and Hafez al-Assad had just taken power. When Kissinger told the Syrian leader he hoped they could become friends, Assad replied: "There can be no friendship for the moment since you have taken sides (with Israel). But at least we can work to eliminate differences." At first Assad hoped Kissinger could be an honest broker in the Arab-Israeli conflict and smiled, noting that roles can be reversed in life: professors (like Kissinger) can turn into politicians while politicians like Assad can turn into professors. Assad lectured the US Secretary on history, the Arab relationship with Israel, and the October War while Kissinger held forth on politics, the personality of world leaders, and relations between the White House and Congress.

Valéry Giscard d'Estaing (1926-)
The French President of 1974-1981 came to Syria in the late 1970s to meet with President Hafez al-Assad. He was the first French President to visit Damascus since the end of the Mandate in 1946.

Richard Nixon (1913-1994)
In June 1974, US President Richard Nixon made a tour of the Middle East and visited Syria. Large and friendly crowds greeted him on June 16 in Damascus and his visit was seen as an end to many years of US bias towards Israel. Nixon's Secretary of State Henry Kissinger did not welcome the Syria visit, fearing that President Hafez al-Assad would discuss regional affairs directly with the US President. Kissinger had based his entire Middle East policy on evading these questions, believing that it was essential to say one thing to Israel and another to the Arabs. According to Patrick Seale's *Assad: Struggle for the Middle East* (which quotes from Kissinger's memoirs) as Assad started asking questions, on the final borders of Israel and UN resolutions, Kissinger interrupted Nixon as he was about to reply: "Mr. President. We have to leave. Our time is up. The plane is waiting." Again Nixon tried to answer Assad but he was interrupted once more by Kissinger, prompting him to ask: "Henry, don't you want me to speak?" Kissinger nodded, saying that these issues should be discussed only in Washington DC. Less than one month later, under the threats of impeachment, Richard Nixon resigned from the presidency on August 8, 1974 and was replaced by Gerald Ford.

Jimmy Carter (1924-)
Before visiting Syria (which he did after leaving office), 39th US President met twice with its President Hafez al-Assad in Geneva. Writing in his memoirs, Carter recalled: "Little was known about his personal or family life, but former secretary of state Henry Kissinger and others who knew Assad had described him to me as very intelligent, eloquent, and frank in discussing the most sensitive issues. I invited the Syrian leader to come and visit me in Washington, but he replied that he had no desire ever to visit the United States. Despite this firm but polite rebuff, I learned what I could about

him and his nation before meeting him." Carter then added, ""During subsequent trips to Syria, I spent hours debating with Assad and listening to his analysis of events in the Middle East…he seemed to speak like a modern Saladin—as though it was his obligation to rid the region of foreign presence while preserving Damascus as the focal point of modern Arab unity."

Bill Clinton (1946-)

The 42nd US President visited Syria in 1994 to meet with Syrian President Hafez al-Assad. Both were heavily involved in peace talks regarding the occupied Golan Heights. A final meeting, which also failed to produce a peace deal, took place in March 2000, less than three months before the Syrian leader's passing. In his book "My Life" Clinton wrote: "I was impressed by his (Assad's) intelligence and almost total recall for detailed events going back more than twenty years."

Fidel Castro (1926-)

The Cuban leader, a good friend of Syria since assuming power in 1959 visited the country for the first time in 2001 to meet with President Bashar al-Assad. He had met Hafez al-Assad when he first came to power in 1970 at the Non-Alligned Conference in Havana.

Sean Connery (1930-)

The Hollywood star who rose to international stardom through the character of James Bond, starting with his first *Dr. No* (1962) and his last *Never Say Never Again* (1983), came to Syria in 2002, along with the Hollywood based Syrian director Moustapha al-Akkad. The Syrian director had produced two Hollywood classics, *The Message* starting Anthony Quinn about the early years of Islam, and *Lion of the Desert* about the Libyan resistance against Italian Fascist occupation (also played by Quinn). The two films had made Akkad a legend in the Arab world from the 1970s onwards, but back in the US, his name was best remembered for the horror flic *Halloween*. Akkad was striving for a comeback in the minds and hearts of the Arab and Muslim world, equally aimed at polishing the image of Arabs and Muslims worldwide after the 9/11 terrorist attacks.

The best way to do this, he reasoned, was to produce a breathtaking work about the Muslim leader Salaadin, showing a true image of Islam, starring a Hollywood legend like Sean Connery. The film was supposed to cost $800 million. Along with Akkad, Connery visited Damascus and Aleppo and called upon Ignatius IV Hazeem, the Patriarch of Antioch And All The East. The film *Salaadin*, much anticipated in the Arab and Muslim World, never materialized because Akkad was killed in a terrorist bombing in Amman in November 2005.

François Mitterrand (1916-1996)

The president of France (1981 to 1995), Mitterand came to Syria in December 1984 to meet with President Hafez al-Assad during the Lebanese Civil War.

Tony Blair (1953-)

The British Prime Minister came to Syria in October 2001 to meet with Syrian President Bashar al-Assad during the Anglo-American War on Afghanistan in the immediate aftermath of the terrorist 9/11 attacks on Washington DC and New York. Blair wanted Syria to join the US "war on terror," but the Syrians objected to the manner in which this war was being conducted. Assad said: "We cannot accept what we see every day on our television screens, the killing of innocent civilians. There are hundreds dying every day." He added, "We should differentiate between combating terrorism and war. We did not say we support an international coalition for war. We are always against war." The Syrian leader went on saying: "We, and I personally, differentiate between resistance and terrorism. Resistance is a social, religious and legal right that is safeguarded by UN resolutions." He linked the Palestinian groups, both those residing in Syria and the occupied territories, to European resistance fighters in World War II seeking to liberate their lands from Nazi occupation. Assad argued that in Europe the great symbol of resistance had been Charles de Gaulle. "Can anyone accuse de Gaulle of being a terrorist? No way." The Guardian claimed that Blair had been "dressed down" in Damascus

Pope John Paul II (1920-2005)

The Pope made history when he came to Damascus in May 2001 to visit the Umayyad Mosque with Syria's Grand Mufti Ahmad Kaftaro. Riding in his popemobile through the narrow streets of old Damascus, he waved to the assembled crowds that were chanting "We love you, John Paul II." They were a combination of Muslims and Christians. He went to the Qunaytra village, the principal town in the Golan Heights, occupied by Israel in 1967, and said: "We pray to you for the peoples of the Middle East. Help them to break down the walls of hostility and division and to build together a world of justice and solidarity. Lord, you create new heavens and a new earth. To you we entrust the young people of these lands." Probably most striking in the Pope's speech are the remarks: "In a special way we pray for the leaders of this noble land of Syria. Grant them wisdom, farsightedness and perseverance; may they never yield to discouragement in their challenging task of building the lasting peace for which their people yearn." John Paul II concluded in Quntaytra saying: "Salam! Salam! Salam! Amen! (See page 110 for the text of the Pope's remarks.)

King Juan Carlos I of Spain (1938-)

The man accredited with ending the dictatorship in Spain and leading the transition to democracy, Juan Carlos I came to Syria in October 2003. Juan Carlos and Queen Sophia were greeted with red carpets in Damascus, not only as official visitors of state, but as friends of President Bashar al-Assad and First Lady Asma al-Assad.

Editor's note: Sami Moubayed is a Syrian journalist / historian. The views expressed and the historical inferences drawn represent a Syrian point of view.

Women in Syria
By Scott C. Davis

When I tell Americans about Syria, the land, the monuments, the people—and the incredibly warm and resilient families—they are surprised and pleased. The greatest source of interest is in Syrian women, who definitely break the stereotype. Syrian women are not submissive creatures who live in the shadow of their men. It's true that some are especially religious, but they make their own choices. The women I have met in Syria are proud, independent, well educated, and resourceful. They decide to cover, or not. They choose: where to study; where to work; and whom to marry. Some of the women I have met work in government, others run their own businesses or have taken over the family business. Still others have served as elected officials. And my interest in art and writing has introduced me to a number of Syrian women who excel in these fields.

Americans don't understand the interplay among dozens of different cultural and political traditions and forces in the Arab world and in Syria that have precise bearing on the status of women. It's a complex world in which individual women must operate. To simplify, I can isolate three major elements: Arab tradition, Islam, and Arab Nationalism.

Traditional Arab culture comes with the Arabic language and with conventions and art that predate Islam. An example of Arab art is traditional Arabic poetry and Arabic calligraphy. Conventions include legendary Arab hospitality, courage in battle, tribal allegiance to a male sheikh, the authority of the male head of the family, and darker customs such as revenge and honor killing. All of these elements are mirrored to varying degrees in other traditional cultures in the Mediterranean and around the world and are independent of the Muslim, Christian, or other religious overlays. For example, some of the problems encountered by a woman in a traditional Syrian village in a predominantly Muslim society are strikingly similar to those faced by a woman in a traditional Armenian community in Central Asia or a traditional Catholic community in Sicily.

A second force in contemporary life that affects women is religion. Seventy percent of Syrians are Sunni Muslims. Within Islam, it may be useful to isolate three different elements that pertain to women: Quranic Islam, Islamic tradition, and contemporary practice. I think of Quranic Islam as instructions in the text itself as well as the faith as it was first practiced.

Islamic tradition includes interpretations, applications, and practices built up over the centuries and solidified during 400 years of Ottoman rule. Contemporary Islamic practice mediates Islamic tradition against Arab culture, Quranic Islam, and the different strains of secular life. Current day reformers, for example, argue that Quranic Islam is far more accepting of independence among women than the Islamic tradition.

Syria has long been a center where Muslims from all over the world come to study the faith and to learn Arabic. And modern communication has brought the diversity among Muslims to the fore—with the result that contemporary Syrians are exposed to many different ways to understand and to practice their faith. At any given time in Damascus you will have Muslims from countries such as Indonesia, Iran, and Somaliland studying and worshipping beside Syrians: four different races, four different native languages, four different cultural traditions—and four different ways of understanding the proper role and rights of women in the family and in society.

A third force in contemporary Arab life that affects women is politics and government, especially the Arab Nationalist philosophy of regimes such as Syria, Egypt, and Algeria that have a socialist cast and are secular in their thrust. In Syria, the Baath party came to power in 1963 and consolidated its grip on the country in 1970. The military officers who took power cultivated women as a base of support. In 1976, President Hafez al-Asad appointed Najah al-Attar Minister of Culture, a position she held for 24 years. She was the first woman cabinet minister in the Arab world. In Syria, women were recruited into the military. At one time, there was a parachute corps composed entirely of women. The secular and socialist-modernist thrust of the Baath cut against Arab and Islamic tradition and, in so doing, maintained a public posture of "open doors" for women in government, in universities, and in the workplace. In practice, however, the regime needed to give concessions to the families (Arabic tradition) and to the various religious communities (primarily Islam) in order to maintain power.

In 2000 women's literacy in Syria was about 60% (it doubled from 1980 to 2000), while men's was 87%. In Syria's national universities, women compose 40% of the teachers and students. They compose a third of the work force (as compared to 46% of the workforce in the US). In 2000, 4% of businesses were owned by women (a difficult statistic, since family businesses may be run by women, but not registered as "women-owned"). As private investment and a market economy emerge in Syria based on a new investment law in 1991 and a host of legal and administrative measures since 2000, opportunities for women-owned businesses are increasing, encouraged by Syria's Women's Chamber of Commerce.

The thrust of government administrative rules, national law, and the educational system have long been gender neutral. Since July 2000, when Bashar al-Asad came to power (and since December, 2000, when he married Asma al-Akras) the government has been refining law and administrative practice to improve the lot of women. In 2003, Syria accepted the Convention on the Elimination of All forms of Discrimination against Women (CEDAW) which was adopted by the UN as a "bill of rights" for women. In doing so, Syria agreed to "incorporate the principle of equality of men and women in their legal system, abolish all discriminatory laws, and adopt appropriate ones prohibiting discrimination against women." Following the adoption of CEDAW, Syrian women's non-governmental organizations identified discriminatory laws that have since been amended.

In 2005, Mouna Ghanem, head of the Syrian Commission for Family Affairs, announced the preparation of a national plan to eliminate violence against women and children. In 2006 the Syrian government welcomed a study conducted by the UN Development Fund for Women about violence against women effectively bringing a once taboo subject into the public arena. (The study concluded that 1 in 4 Syrian women suffer violence, on par with other traditional Middle Eastern and Mediterranean societies; this figure is also used in the US.)

Does it really matter if the subject is taboo, or not? Well, yes. Since the UN study, and spurred by a particularly sad urban honor killing in Damascus in 2006, Syria's grand mufti has recently called for legal reform to remove protections against male relatives who commit violence against women. Without the breaking of the taboo against public discussion of this issue, the grand mufti might well have remained silent.

In Syria, women are free to drive cars, to purchase property, or to own a business. Women keep their family name when they marry. The government does not restrict women's right to cover or not cover themselves in public. Many Syrian women pursue a discrete existence centered on work, school, home, family, and mosque. Yet others choose to participate in civic affairs and to entertain themselves in restaurants, theaters, sporting arenas, and night clubs—just as women do in Europe and the United States.

Syrian women have had the right to vote since 1949, three years after independence. And Syrians point out that Syrian women might have had the right to vote the same year as American women . . . if the French had not invaded in 1920 and scuttled the women's suffrage measure that was pending before parliament.

In the parliamentary elections in April, 2007 158 women ran for office and won 30 seats. They occupy 12% of the total seats in parliament. By comparison: political participation in the Arab world as a whole is 4.6%; international participation is 13.4%; in the US, 16% of the seats in the US House and Senate are held by women. Over 400 women serve in the Syrian security and police apparatus. Last year, Najah al-Attar (the former Minister of Culture) was named Vice-President, the first woman in the Arab world to rise to this position. Attar is a political independent who was educated at the University of Edinburgh, speaks fluent English, and whose father fought for independence against the French from 1925-1927.

Another high ranking woman is Buthaina Shaaban, a published feminist and former English prof, also British educated, who now serves as Minister of Expatriate Affairs. She is familiar to Americans, who have seen her interviewed on major American talk shows such as Charlie Rose where her logic and charm have been in marked contrast to the spin and bluster that Americans too often have heard from their own government.

Syria's first lady, Asma al-Akhras, was trained in computer science at Kings College in London and worked on Wall Street in New York and as a banker with J. P. Morgan in London and Paris. In 2001, she created the Fund for Integrated Rural Development of Syria (FIRDOS), Syria's first rural development non-governmental organization. A year later she initiated the first National Children's Book Fair, bringing together Syrian authors, artists, and publishers. Also in 2002, she created the first Mobile Information Center (MIC), designed to bring mobile high tech classrooms to remote villages. More recently, she became head of the innovative Syrian Development Trust, a results-oriented management umbrella that puts FIRDOS and other non-governmental organizations under a single regimen that uses benchmarks and financial controls to weed out ineffective projects and to focus funding on programs that work.

The contemporary women of Syria are easy to admire, and it turns out that they are the most recent in a long tradition of Syrian women with verve and savvy. One of Syria's national figures is Naziq al-Abid who, as a young Damascene in 1914, organized for women's rights against the Ottomans, then at the end of hostilities in 1918 advocated for women's suffrage to the new Syrian parliament. In July 1920, when French troops moved against Damascus, al-Abid marched into combat at the Battle of Maysaloun, stopping along the way to rip her veil off in front of the television cameras—well, in that day it was newspaper men scribbling on their note pads, no TV cameras, but the impact was the same. When the battle was lost, Syria's general lay dead . . . but Abid survived, went into exile, and returned in 1922 to devote herself to humanitarian and literary activities—for three years until the Syrians broke into open revolt against the French and Abid joined the rebels, smuggling guns and medicine to the Arab mountain in southern Syria to support the insurgency. In 1927, she escaped a French arrest warrant, married a notable in Beirut, and then devoted herself to years of humanitarian work.

Chapter Eight

Arabs in Media

Baba Ali: Fun, not Fundamentalist
by Krystina Derrickson

BABA ALI IS DISARMING AND CHARMING, comically schizophrenic, momentarily serious before launching again into another multiple-personality monologue on the cost of Muslim weddings or the ludicrous posturing of airport security guards. He is, among other technologically-savvy young Muslims, at the crest of a wave of motivated and charismatic transformers of both the public culture and personal practice of Islam. Though he acknowledges himself that he is no expert and is hardly qualified to perform *tafsir*, interpretation of the *Quran* or *hadith,* he is certainly an adept at something that makes him, according to his global fan base, worth listening to. He is a pious American-Muslim who is young, hip, and funny. He is something of a popular preacher-*cum*-comedian-*cum*-regular Joe, a model which combines dynamism, informality, and a likable fallibility. He presents himself as a friendly guy offering friendly advice.

Baba Ali and many other Muslim "edu tainers" such as Zarqa Nawaz, producer of "Little Mosque on the Prairie," Azhar Usman, a comedian of the tongue-in-cheek troupe titled "Allah Made Me Funny," Moez Masoud, the young Egyptian televangelist who uses Arabic slang to share a vision of brotherly love, and even country musician Kareem Salama, have much in common. First, they live an Islam that starkly contrasts with the assumptions that most Americans have about a religion they associate with scowling clerics and invisible women, and they are openly presenting it in their work.

Second, their piety appeals to young Muslims who, in the world of dubious celebrity icons, are receptive to alternative role models with whom their generation can identify. Certainly a component of their success is the ability to communicate their message in everyday language. Baba Ali, well-versed in street *patois* (for example, referring to worldly wealth as "rocks"), peppers his slang with Arabic religious phrases such as *alhamdu-lillah,* "thanks be to God." Ali's YouTube videos (also available on YouTube's Muslim counterparts, MuxlimTube or IslamicTube) are short, between five to seven minutes. In an Internet media marketplace whose currency is popularity, Ali is a star in a new era of possibilities for communication and education in the Muslim community. The bite-sized monologues are easy to watch, to share, to post to one's blog, to emulate, and to respond to. Long threads of video response debates trailing through YouTube suggest some of the constructive forums for informal communication between Muslims and non-Muslims on the Internet (although at other times they are little more than trails of slurs, anger, and fear).

The man behind Baba Ali is Ali Ardekani, a Los Angeles native of Iranian descent and an "unlikely internet celebrity" who is "treated like a rock star" during his speaking appearances. The project is one of several that Ardekani has undertaken since his self-described conversion to Islam at age 20. Others include a Muslim basketball league and a production company, Ummah Films, in each showcasing his ability to communicate to a young audience. Future projects revolve around the character Baba Ali, including a movie and continuation of the successful vignettes by incorporating further viewer "something I would ask my friends" questions. He purposefully avoids issues of overt political content and instead zooms in on the quotidian experiences and lifestyles of American Muslims, maintaining that "there's enough people talking about that," while basic issues of what he refers to as "Islamic sense" are generally ignored. Islamic sense is the fundamental ethics of a moral Islamic life, an ethics which is located in both the mundane and huge, the minor and major decisions that individuals make in their lives to follow, or not follow, a moral path. In one video he says, "these videos are nothing more than reminders, to remind everyone, starting with myself," to observe that those seemingly small decisions that Muslims make in their lives are what define them as moral human beings. By offering friendly advice packaged in comedy, he breaches people's defenses, allowing them to take a moment to consider their experiences, their choices, and their goals as Muslims. He even claims that some non-Muslims have converted to Islam after watching and reflecting upon his videos.

Baba Ali is an example of the flourishing of Islam in spaces of technological human creativity. Some make the claim that Islam runs counter to modernity or that Islam is against modern technology. And yet out on the Internet Islam has a real presence, and not just in terms of how the media have framed it, namely, radicals recruiting would-be terrorists in the shadowy alleyways of the Net. Matrimonial sites, message boards, question-and-answer sites, weblogs, video diaries, informal news sites, business directories, and *fatwa* databases are only a few of the examples that immediately come to mind. But it goes much further. Individuals with creativity and skill who feel that communicating their identity as Muslims is for them an important goal will continue to move Islam into the corridors of new media.

Much of this presence, whether on television, the Internet, on the stage, on YouTube or even on Facebook, is geared towards a younger generation of Muslims, including many second and third generation immigrants to Western nations who are comfortable with these media and receptive to the message. Baba Ali, as someone who has experienced life as a child and teen in Los Angeles, is well-poised to communicate to a generation at odds with their parents' perceptions of and desires for their lives. While some might view his message as conservative from a culturally Western standpoint (for example, no dating before marriage), "Baba" Ali Ardekani's gift is to provide a moral beacon, providing simple advice to youths living in a society where Islamic sense may be up against the confusing challenges of a frequently un-Islamic dominant culture.

Among others, Ali recognizes that Muslim youths, like all teens, live in a world that their parents tend not to understand. By providing opportunities to laugh at, and with, him as well as at a society that has yet to come to terms with shifting demographics in a post-9/11 world, he gives his viewers a few minutes of respite, camaraderie, and fun.

The Arab in American Cinema:
From Bad to Worse, or Getting Better?
by Dr. Laurence Michalak

This piece was originally published in 2002. At the end, the author has provided notes on the current-day situation.

A Fiction Stranger than Truth: The Cinema Arab

THERE IS A PROVERB THAT SAYS, "TRUTH is stranger than fiction." However, at least in the case of the Arab world, it's not really so. The real Arab world makes sense; it is the fictional Arab world—the world of novels, cinema, television, and other media—that is strange. It includes the desert sheik abducting white women, the sorcerer on the flying carpet, the Arab oil tycoon, the tyrannical potentate, the sensuous belly dancer, the fanatical Islamic terrorist, and more. These disturbingly negative images are deeply ingrained in American popular culture. We learn from such images that the Arab is fundamentally different from "us," and this has important consequences.

This short article will examine the stereotyping of Arabs in just one popular medium, albeit an important one —that of cinema. We will analyze the image of the Arab in the movies and how it has changed in recent years, offering some thoughts about the causes of these negative images, what (if anything) can be done about it, and what might happen in the future.

It might at first seem strange to be concerned with such images. However, cinema images are a powerful force in shaping our national worldview. Most Americans have never met an Arab —except through movies— and younger people in their impressionable years are the biggest movie fans. In 2001 there were 1.5 billion movie admissions in the US—up 5% from the previous year. Movies on video are watched even more. By the mid-1990s, Americans were making 4 billion video rentals per year, bringing in roughly $8 billion to $9 billion. Old movies never die; they just go from the movie theater to the video store, prime time television, and then late night television.

Cinema about Arabs: Succession of Genres
Cinema is undoubtedly the area of American popular culture that offers the richest

and most detailed picture of the American stereotype of Arabs throughout its historical development during the twentieth century and into the new millennium.

American cinema has been fascinated from its very beginnings with the idea of the Arab. Thomas Edison built America's first film studio in 1893 in West Orange, New Jersey, and one of his first films, designed for a coin-operated viewer-box, was "The Dance of the Seven Veils." Moving pictures later progressed from viewer-boxes to theaters, spreading throughout the world, especially throughout Europe and the United States. After World War I, with Europe in ruins, America moved into pre-eminence in world cinema, a position it has never relinquished.

In examining feature films about Arabs, we find a succession of different genres, or representations of the Arab—from desert sheik to international terrorist—which have emerged in American cinema at different historical moments.

The Sheik

Americans in the 1920s fell in love with exotic melodramas about sheiks, such as *The Song of Love* (1923), *A Cafe in Cairo* (1924), *The Arab* (1924), *A Son of the Sahara* (1924), *The Desert Bride* (1928), and others. The earliest and by far most famous of these is *The Sheik* (1921), in which Rudolph Valentino plays an "Arab" who abducts a white woman. This violates the established social order, under which European men can have native women, but native men, oversexed and lusting after white European women, must be thwarted. The conflict in the Valentino movie finally finds a racist resolution when we learn that the Sheik is not really an Arab, but a European separated from his parents as a child.

The Foreign Legion

Foreign Legion films are closely related to the sheik genre; in them, the European is pitted against the Arab in settings of colonial encounter—especially foreign legion outposts where French or English soldiers fight desert battles with the Arabs. The classic of this genre is *Beau Geste* (1926), about three English brothers who join the Foreign Legion. The most common scene in these movies is the one in which waves of hostile Arabs in flowing robes and on horseback attack the Foreign Legion outpost. The Europeans are outnumbered but win with their superior weaponry, and the mostly faceless and nameless Arabs die unmourned. The European perspective and the colonial ideology are taken for granted. We know in retrospect, however, that it is the Europeans who are the usurpers and the Arabs are struggling to take back their countries.

Fantasy and Magic

This genre includes movies such as *The Thief of Baghdad* (1924), *Kismet* (1920, 1930, 1944, 1955), and *The Wonders of Aladdin* (1961), which present the Arab world as a fabulous land of snake charmers, monsters, great wealth, half-naked women, harems, flying horses and the like. In this genre, "Baghdad" is a projection of American fantasies, a place where Western taboos are violated and where even the laws of physics are suspended for flying carpets, magical ropes and cloaks of invisibility. The thieves and adventurers who are the main characters of these magical movies are lazy, thieving, violent and oversexed, but handsome and not without charm. Did people believe that Baghdad was really like the movie? One reviewer wrote that Baghdad "might have been shot in the lands it is supposed to picture. That it is authentic is not questioned, for clever people have aided in its making and persons who have visited some of the far away regions agree the picture is beyond criticism in that respect." (Variety, 3/26/1924)

The Mummy

This sinister and fascinating genre was launched in 1932 with *The Mummy*. It offers another kind of story, premised on a struggle between European and Egyptian males with the white woman as trophy. A mummified, long-dead Egyptian male from the time of the pharaohs comes back to life and pursues a terrified European woman whom he believes is a reincarnation of his mate. The mummy is one of the great horror roles and several famous actors have specialized in monster roles. Boris Karloff was the original mummy, followed by Lon Chaney Jr., Christopher Lee and others who have sported memorable make-up jobs and turned in chilling mummy performances. The mummy and the European archaeologist are binary opposites. The mummy represents Oriental despotism, changelessness, decrepitude, decay, death, magic, miscegenation and forbidden sexuality; the Western archaeologist represents individualism, democracy, progress, youth, vigor, life, science, racial endogamy, and socially approved sexuality.

An Exotic Setting for Europeans

In the 1930s and 1940s, the cinematic Arab world became a popular setting for events and plots that are essentially European. For example, *The Garden of Allah* (1936), *Algiers* (1938), and *Casbah* (1948) are love and adventure stories about Europeans, in which Algeria only provides the scenery. The most famous film of this kind—and one of the most famous films of all time—is *Casablanca* (1942), which is peopled by Americans, French, Germans, and even Czechs, but where are the Moroccans? Apart from a somewhat sleazy Moroccan played by Sidney Greenstreet, there are none. In films of this kind, the Arab world is reduced to a playground for Westerners.

Buffoons and Tycoons

In both comedies and "serious" films throughout the 1900s, the Arabs are often portrayed as wealthy, powerful, but ultimately incompetent characters. As in the other genres, they are often obsessed with Western women whom they try to abduct for their harems. For example, in *Ali Baba goes to Town* (1937) a sultan with 365 wives (one for every day of the year) mistakes Eddie Cantor in disguise for a woman and wants him for his harem. In *Road to Morocco* (1942) Bob Hope and Bing Crosby poke fun at the bumbling Sheik Kacem, winning the lovely Moroccan women for themselves. More recent examples of the genre are *Protocol* (1984), in which Goldie Hawn plays a cocktail waitress in Washington, D.C. who is sent to an Arab country by the State Department as the concubine to a lecherous emir, and *Rollover* (1982), in which sinister Saudi bankers plot to ruin the world financial system.

The Arab-Israeli Conflict

In Hollywood's version of the Arab-Israeli conflict, the Arab is villain, the Israeli is hero, and the prize for which they struggle is the land of Palestine. The defining film of this genre is *Exodus* (1960), in which Paul Newman plays a Zionist leader who successfully smuggles a shipload of Jewish refugees to Palestine. There are only two kinds of Europeans in Exodus—those sympathetic to Zionism and anti-Semites. The only remotely sympathetic Arab, played by John Derek, is killed by the Arabs' Nazi German leaders. In the end the only good Arab is literally a dead Arab. Other popular films that glorify Israel and demonize the Arabs include *Judith* (1966) and *Cast a Giant Shadow* (1966). Not only the Arabs, but also the Israelis tend to be stereotyped in peculiar ways, as emotionally repressed Israeli men reject dark, large-busted Israeli women in favor of blonde gentile women. What these movies have in common is that they oversimplify a complex conflict into a melodrama of good versus evil.

The Terrorist

The most recent "Arab" genre is the Terrorist Movie. The first such film was *Black Sunday* (1977), about an Arab terrorist plot to kill spectators at the Superbowl— including the President of the United States—with a gigantic bomb in a blimp over the stadium. The technologically incompetent terrorists are aided by a mentally unstable American Viet Nam veteran, but they are ultimately thwarted by brave Israeli agents. Another example is *The Delta Force* (1986), in which American commandos rescue the passengers on a hijacked plane and kill evil Arab terrorists. The most interesting of these films are those that involve Arab terrorists attacking on American soil. Movies with incidental Arab terrorists include Libyans in *Back to the Future* (1985) who try to kill an eccentric professor and the Arabs in *Trenchcoat* (1983) who want to inject Margot Kidder with a huge hypodermic needle. *Back to the Future* was an enormously popular movie and one that many young Americans viewed over and over again. *True Lies* (1994) features Arnold Schwarznegger as a CIA agent who prevents a terrorist group called "Crimson Jihad" from detonating a nuclear bomb in Florida, and *Executive Decision* (1996) portrayed Arab terrorists, led by a sadistic, *Quran*-waving fanatic, hijacking a plane for an attack centered on Washington, D.C.

Beginnings of Respect at the End of the Twentieth Century

During the 1990s one begins to see glimmerings of respect for Arabs in American cinema, at first in the form of positive minor characters. One such character in *Robin Hood: Prince of Thieves* (1991) is Azeem, a Saracen warrior who returns with Robin from the Crusades to England, conducting himself with dignity. In *Escape from LA* (1996), set in an apocalyptic future, the hero meets an attractive woman who explains "I was a Muslim in South Dakota; all of a sudden they made that a crime;" then she dies. There is a competent Arab-American detective who plays a minor role in *A Perfect Murder* (1998). But, until nearly the end of the century, there is not a single mainstream Hollywood movie whose main character is a sympathetic Arab, Turk, Persian, or Muslim of any kind.

Just when it looked as if the 1900s would be a century of unrelieved anti-Arab stereotyping, in 1999 there appeared a movie called *The Thirteenth Warrior*—the first mainstream Hollywood move with a positive Arab main character. This is the story of Ibn Fahdlan, an Arab diplomat of the Middle Ages who traveled in the Volga River area of Europe. The movie, based on a book by Michael Crichton, was inspired by the real Ibn Fahdlan's journals, but Crichton and the filmmakers have spun it into an elaborate fantasy of swashbuckling Vikings and matriarchal snake-handling cannibals. Drafted into a company of warriors, Ibn Fahdlan is the most civilized figure in the story, a strong, handsome Muslim who shuns alcohol and prays before battle.

Also in 1999 Americans were surprised with a second major Hollywood film that positively portrayed Arabs. *Three Kings* is the fictional story of a group of American soldiers in southern Iraq in the aftermath of the Gulf War, attempting to steal a cache of gold that Saddam Hussein had earlier stolen from Kuwait and hidden in Iraq. There are indeed Bad Arabs in the film—the Republican Guards and their unseen leader, Saddam Hussein. But there are also Good Arabs. These are Shi'a villagers in southern Iraq who are portrayed with unusual depth, humanity and compassion. Even an Arab torturer in the film is a complex character who acts, not out of innate evil, but because his family was bombed and maimed by Americans. The American soldiers achieve such sympathy for the Iraqi villagers that in the end they give up their stolen gold to secure safe passage for them. This uplifting story of a journey from materialism to altruism and from greed to compassion is not only an honest portrayal of Arabs, but it is an excellent film, well-produced, well-acted, and thought-provoking. Not surprisingly, Arab-American scholar Jack Shaheen was involved as a consultant.

After these two milestones, subsequent films demonstrated that the negative stereotyping of Arabs was alive and well. A particularly egregious example is *Rules of Engagement* (2000), about a fictional anti-American riot in Yemen. An American Marine commander is court-martialed for giving the order to fire on a crowd, killing 83 Yemeni civilians, most of them women and children. Is he found guilty? No. We discover in the end that the Yemeni women and children in the crowd were wild-eyed, gun-wielding terrorists. The other Yemenis in the movie are liars or religious fundamentalists who preach "jihad." In the end, the Marine commander who exhorted his men to "waste the m***-f***s" is found to be an innocent hero. Jack Shaheen reports that former US Navy Secretary James Webb, now the junior senator from Virginia, wrote this screenplay for the movie and that the US State Department provided free assistance. This racist production was the most popular film in the

United States in early April 2000.

Analyzing the Arab Stereotype

What can we conclude from these films about Arabs? We should begin by recognizing that the same negative stereotype of Arabs applies to other Middle Easterners and Muslims generally. For example, the Turks in *Midnight Express* (1978), a film about an American in a Turkish prison, are all sadistic torturers, and the Turkish officer in *Lawrence of Arabia* (1962) is a pervert. The Iranians in *Not Without my Daughter* (1991), about an American woman who smuggles her daughter from Iran to the US, are all joyless, scowling fundamentalists. An Iranian friend of mine once wondered why, since the father of the girl is Iranian, the movie was not called "Not Without Our Daughter." And the Chechens in *Air Force One* (1997) are brutal Muslim terrorists who kidnap the American president and blackmail him by threatening to kill his wife and child.

Not all the movies of the last century present Arabs as entirely bad. In the films of the 1920s the Arab characters often have an element of the noble savage. In *Thief of Baghdad*, for example, Douglas Fairbanks played a character who was lazy and dishonest but rehabilitated through the love of a good woman. *Lawrence of Arabia* included a good Arab or two—and they even let a real Arab actor (Omar Sharif) play the part of one of the Arabs. A few of these "Arab movies" are bad but not too bad. For example, Disney's animated feature film *Aladdin* (1992) was deservedly criticized for an opening song which described the Middle East as "barbaric but, hey, it's home!" and it featured a sinister Arab wizard. But there were also Good Arabs in the movie—Aladdin and Princess Jasmine. In the end I rather liked Aladdin, especially after the offending lyrics to the song were changed for its release in video. However, I thought that the "Arab" setting of the movie looked more like the Indian subcontinent, with a Bengal tiger and a palace resembling the Taj Mahal.

However, with minor qualification, most of the twentieth century movies about Arabs can be categorized as "bad," "worse," and "worst." If there was ever any doubt about the overwhelmingly negative image of the Arab in American cinema, it was definitively dispelled when Jack Shaheen published *Reel Bad Arabs* (New York: Olive Branch Press, 2001), an alphabetically organized annotated filmography of nearly a thousand movies about Arabs, offering an appalling chronicle of systematic and almost unrelieved defamation.

Why are Arabs Negatively Stereotyped? Some Bad Arguments

Thus films about Arabs are a hodge-podge of genres presenting, for the most part, a dismal record of negative stereotyping. There are only a couple of bright spots, and they don't appear until nearly the end of the century. What is the cause of this? What does this dismal cinematic record mean? I will begin by rejecting some false answers, before moving on to what I think are more likely answers.

One possible response is, "Isn't it true?" Aren't there nomads in the Arab World? Yes, but fewer than 1% of the population. Aren't there kings and sultans? Yes, but most of the 22 Arab countries are republics.

Don't Arabs have oil wealth? A small minority of them do, but most Arabs have to import oil just like the rest of the Third World. Aren't Arabs undemocratic? Some are relatively undemocratic, but democracy everywhere in the world is a question of degree. For example, the Palestinian Authority has a president who took office with a majority vote in an election with high voter turnout—which is more than can currently be said for the United States.

Aren't Arabs bad? There are about 250 million Arabs in the world, and they are like anyone else. It should be obvious that negative generalizations about millions of people—any people—are nothing more than racism. Arabs are like any other group of people—no better and no worse.

Didn't Arabs commit a terrorist act against New York on September 11th? Yes, but can we generalize about all Arabs from the actions of a handful? Are there not also terrorist groups among Americans, Europeans and others? We should remember that Arab terrorism against America was invented by Hollywood in the 1970s, long before it existed in reality. From 1977 to 1993, the only Arab terrorism in America was on movie screens and in novels. The relentless stereotyping of Arabs as terrorists resulted in a situation in which any terrorist act was automatically attributed to Arabs. Thus the Oklahoma City bombing in April 1995 was almost universally attributed to Arab terrorists although the terrorist turned out to be an American. Similarly, when a TWA plane exploded near New York in July 1996, the disaster was again attributed to Arab terrorists. It later turned out that the culprit was faulty wiring in the fuel system. Following each of these tragedies, there were outbreaks of anti-Arab and anti-Muslim violence in the US.

Another interpretation of cinematic defamation of Arabs is that it is a Jewish plot. Hollywood is controlled by Jews, the argument goes. One can certainly point to instances in which Jewish pro-Israeli filmmakers have made biased films. *Exodus* was made by a pro-Israeli director and was based on a book commissioned by a public relations firm to promote a positive image of Israel. Several egregiously anti-Arab movies—as *Sahara* (1983), *Bolero* (1984), and *The Delta Force* (1986)—were made by Cannon (Golan-Globus films), a company created by an Israeli, Menahem Golan, who received assistance from the Israeli government in making his films. However, while Jewish support for Israel is a factor in some specific instances, I disagree that the stereotyping of Arabs is a Jewish plot. The negative stereotype of Arabs is much more widespread than cinema and far older than the conflict over Palestine.

Similarly, I reject the argument that Americans are inherently stupid or intrinsically anti-Arab. Negative generalizations about Americans (or Jews) are comparable to the negative generalizations about Arabs that we seek to explain. Americans are fundamentally no less intelligent and compassionate than anyone else.

Why are Arabs Stereotyped? Some Better Arguments

We have just reviewed some unlikely hypotheses for why there is a negative stereotype of Arabs. Let us now turn to some more plausible reasons for why this is.

European Heritage

Fear of Arabs and Turks is a European attitude brought to America by our European ancestors. Europe's rivals to the south and the east were, first, the Arabs, who conquered much of Southern Europe, and later the Ottoman Turks. Both of these civilizations were more advanced than the Europeans in many respects, including military prowess. The Arabs in fact ruled Spain for centuries and penetrated as far as central France, and the Turks ruled much of Eastern Europe for centuries and twice penetrated as far as Vienna. Thus rivalries with Arabs, Turks, and other Muslims were the basis of the negative European views of the Orient which can be seen, for example, in Orientalist painting, and which were transmitted to America.

Ignorance of the Middle East

Another reason is that, although Americans are not stupid, they are ignorant about Arabs and Middle Easterners in general. This is because America is made up of people from every part of the world, but very few from the Middle East. Those Arabs who did immigrate to America in the late 19th and early 20th centuries were primarily Christians who tended to suppress their culture of origin and assimilate to American ways. In the 1920s and 1930s, the part of the world about which Americans knew least was the Middle East. Thus the Middle East became a screen onto which moviemakers projected fantasies of exoticism and otherness. Also, until recently, there was no organized Arab community to speak out against the resulting defamation.

Stereotyping is Universal

Since not all of us can know everything about the peoples of the world, all of us stereotype. Just as Americans stereotype Arabs, so also Arabs stereotype Americans. Living in the Arab world for many years, I have encountered Arabs who think that Americans are rich, violent, and sexually promiscuous. However, in many cases the source of their stereotype is our own American movies and television programs, such as *Dallas*. A stereotype is a simplified image. It can be a first step to understanding, as one learns more about unfamiliar peoples and parts of the world and develops more complex understandings, but negative stereotypes lead only to misunderstanding and dehumanization.

The Simplest Story

Movies have plots, and one of the simplest and most compelling of plots is the Good Guy versus the Bad Guy. We encounter this plot not just in cinema, but in folktales, novels, television programs, and other forms of popular culture. Americans like the bad guy to wear a black cowboy hat, or have a waxy handlebar moustache, or be a hunchback with an evil laugh. Arabs and Turks and especially Persians also have dualistic traditions with Good-Guy-versus-Bad-Guy stories. Because television news operates under severe time constraints, complex situations are often reduced to little melodramas, to fit a 30-second time slot and make room for the commercials. The best groups to choose as ethnic Bad Guys in such stories are those who are least numerous, least organized, and least likely to complain.

American Foreign Policy

The media, including cinema, tend to take their cues from our political leaders, viewing the world in part through the filter of American foreign policy. Thus, in World War II we had movies that demonized Germans and Japanese. During the cold war we demonized Russians. Unfortunately, the nemeses of American policy more recently have been Arabs and other Muslims. Muammar Qaddaffy, Saddam Hussein and Yassir Arafat have all been cast in a negative light. Thus *Iron Eagle* (1986), and *GI Jane* (1997) have villains from Libya. *Iron Eagle II* (1988) offers a prescient post-Cold War scenario in which America and Russia unite to fight against Iraq, in a kind of comic book pre-figuration of Samuel Huntington's "Clash of Civilizations." There is an important political context for the choice of ethnic villains in cinema.

Arabs in a Larger Ethnic Context: The Rehabilitation of Defamed Peoples

Arabs are not the only group that has ever been negatively stereotyped in American cinema. Asians, Blacks, Russians, Germans, American Indians and others have all figured in Hollywood's "Rogues Gallery." Indeed, we can learn a lot about the stereotyping of Arabs by looking at the stereotyping of other minority groups and noting the similarities, differences, and historic patterns. In American cinema, I would argue, minority groups have tended to be negatively stereotyped and then "rehabilitated" in stages.

Stage One: They're All Bad

In early cinema, there is a tendency to represent certain ethnic and minority groups as uniformly bad. In early cowboy movies, for example, the Indians were all bad—like the Arabs in the Foreign Legion movies. The scenes of Indians attacking wagon trains are much like those of Arabs attacking Foreign Legion outposts. *Treasure of the Sierra Madre* stereotyped Mexicans as cruel bandits. For Asians, there was Ming the Merciless and the evil Fu Manchu. Dozens of movies made during WWII negatively stereotyped the Germans, and later the Russians invade America during the Cold War in *Red Dawn* (1984).

Stage Two: Good Guys and Bad Guys

Next comes recognition that there are both Good Guys and Bad Guys among the minority group. There may be both good and bad cowboys and Indians. The Bad Cowboys sell whisky and guns to the Bad Indians who do bad things, but the Good

Cowboy fixes the misunderstanding and prevents the cavalry from fighting against the Good Indians (often led by Jeff Chandler). Similarly, *The Siege* (1998) has both Good Muslims and Bad Muslims (but nobody in between). Such movies represent a slightly higher level of sophistication, but the minority group is often still presented as rather primitive and gullible.

Stage Three: They're All Good

The rehabilitation of the minority group often involves an inversion of the social hierarchy at some point. The dominant group becomes "bad" and the minority group becomes "good" in a rite of reversal. For example, in *The Karate Kid* (1984) a wise Japanese karate master battles a villainous white martial arts teacher. In *Lady Sings the Blues* (1972) black singer Billie Holiday becomes addicted to heroin because of a white drug pusher. Germans are the sympathetic characters in *Town Without Pity* (1961) and American Indians are the Good Guys in *Dances with Wolves* (1990). In *Gorky Park* (1983) the hero is a hardworking Russian policeman and the villain is an American fur-poacher. And Mexicans are rehabilitated in such films as *Stand and Deliver* (1988) and *Like Water for Chocolate* (1993).

False Positives

Sometimes cinematic rehabilitation is only superficial, and at a deeper level the minority group is negated. For example, the hero of *Cry Freedom* (1987) is not Steve Biko, but the white journalist Donald Woods, through whom we see the predicament of the South African Blacks. Similarly, we see the predicament of the Indian through the eyes of the white man in *Little Big Man* (1970). In *Lawrence of Arabia* the British may betray their promises of self-rule to the Arabs, but it is clear that the Arabs, with their tribal rivalries and tendency to violence (epitomized by Anthony Quinn's portrayal of Auda), are not yet ready for self-rule. As soon as Lawrence dresses like an Arab, he starts to become cruel and sadistic. And, of course, it takes an Englishman to lead the Arabs, who are presented as incapable of organizing themselves.

Stage Four: Minority Self-representation

The highest stage of the liberation of a minority group in cinema is when they can make their own films and portray themselves. One of the best examples is the work of Spike Lee, an African-American who makes films about African-Americans as in *Do the Right Thing* (1989). He does not simply reverse the American hierarchy, creating a Good Black and Bad White story, but makes complex films of social realism and ethnic self-criticism. *Smoke Signals* (1998) is a similarly sophisticated Stage Four movie by a Native American about Native Americans.

The closest thing to Arab liberation through self-expression in American cinema is two films by the late Syrian-American filmmaker Moustafa Akkad. *The Message* (1977) dramatizes the beginnings of Islam and the life of the Prophet Mohammad, and *Lion of the Desert* (1981) is about the Libyan resistance against the Italians. The latter film is especially sophisticated, in that Akkad resists the urge to demonize the Italian Fascists—much as Spike Lee resists negatively stereotyping the white proprietor of the pizza parlor that is trashed in *Do the Right Thing*. But neither of Akkad's films was made with American funding and neither was a mainstream American movie.

Conclusion: Are Things Getting Better?

Against this historical background and with reference to the pattern of ethnic rehabilitation in American cinema, where do we locate the Arab? What is the likely future of the Arab in American cinema? Do two positive films in 1999 suggest that Arabs are following the pattern of "rehabilitation," like other ethnic minority groups that were once reviled but have achieved a modicum of respect from Hollywood? Or does the reversion to type in *Rules of Engagement* suggest a more pessimistic conclusion? It is easier to analyze the past than to predict the future, but three cautious generalizations seem warranted.

First, much depends upon Arab-Americans and other Middle Eastern and Muslim Americans. Opposing defamation requires organization and collective action, and Arab-Americans have made considerable progress on this front. The National Association of Arab-Americans, the American-Arab University Graduates, the American-Arab Anti-Discrimination Committee, the American Arab Institute, and other organizations have come into being and have become steadily more active. Arab-Americans increasingly protest films that defame them. They now consult in some of the films that represent them. Arab-Americans are diverse in their national origins and religious and political affiliations, which makes collective decisions and collective action difficult, but the need to combat defamation is an issue around which it is easy to unite.

Second, the larger context of world events will undoubtedly play a role. September 11th was a disaster for the image of Arabs and Muslims in America. Arab terrorism in America began as fiction on movie screens in 1977 at a time when it simply didn't exist in reality. But on September 11th, Arab terrorism against America finally passed from fiction to reality. Some misguided scholars have used this tragic incident to argue that all Arabs and Muslims—including Americans of Arab origin—represent a danger. Others argue that Muslims are diverse and not especially different from Christians and Jews and that the rights of Arab- and Muslim-Americans must be respected. Much will depend upon what happens in the future and who wins the rhetorical battle to interpret what does and does not happen.

Finally, much depends too upon the future directions of American society. In the coming years we will learn more about who we are and who we will become as a nation. Presumably, we can all agree that negative stereotyping harms our society. In our schools and in public life, our teachers and leaders must educate for critical thinking, understanding, tolerance and multi-culturalism. Only then will negative stereotyping, not just of Arabs but of all groups, and not just in cinema but in all aspects of life, become a phenomenon of the past.

A Post-script: The Arab in American Cinema since 9/11

When I originally wrote this article, not long after the tragic terrorist attacks against the US, I feared a possible backlash against Arabs and Muslims. I also feared a possible proliferation of the terrorist genre which I described in the article—movies with violent Arabs and Muslims perpetrating terrible deeds with no apparent motives other than innate evil. I am pleased to report that this has not happened. True, there are still movies being made with negative Arab figures. However, they seem outnumbered by American movies with balanced portrayals, including positive Arabs and Muslim characters.

Since 9/11 there have been a number of positive films about Arabs. Several recent examples come readily to mind. In *Kingdom of Heaven* (2005), the Muslims, and especially their leader Saladin, are portrayed much more sympathetically than the Crusaders. *Syriana* (2005) is a complex movie with both good and bad Middle Easterners, including a progressive prince who is assassinated by Americans. Spielberg's *Munich* (2005) is a complex film about how revenge is not a viable solution to terrorism. *The Kingdom* (2007) has both bad and good Arabs, but the hero is a brave and honest Saudi policeman who dies and is mourned at the end of the movie. And *Rendition* (2007) offers a nuanced portrayal of Arabs, reserving its strongest criticism for the American practice of sending prisoners abroad to be tortured—including innocent people who have been unjustly accused.

Thus only two positive movies about Arabs were made throughout the entire twentieth century, but several have come out just in the past two years. Perhaps it is too early to tell, but I think this is a sign that America has progressed and is moving up the scale of sophistication about North Africa and the Middle East. After a century of ignorance and racist stereotyping against Arabs and Muslims in cinema and in other aspects of American culture, the tide may be turning.

The Arab Image
by Jack G. Shaheen

BEGINNING IN 1896, HOLLYWOOD BEGAN saturating world viewers with hideous feature films which portrayed Arab Muslims and their descendants as sub-humans —sand niggers, lecherous sheikhs, and terrorists. More than one thousand pre-9/11 Hollywood movies reveal that Arabs are the most maligned group in the history of Hollywood. Inherent in Hollywood's continuous demonization of all things Arab is this message: We Americans despise you and your religion!

Consider Hollywood's role in preparing the way for the war in Iraq. Image makers did not churn out overt propaganda, but helped condition audiences to perceive Arabs — and by extension all Muslims — as unrelenting enemies of Western values. In cinematic terms, America first went to war in Iraq in 1943; the movie *Adventure In*

Iraq features the US Air Force staging a "shock and awe" bombing of Iraq's pro-Nazi "devil worshipers."

Adventure In Iraq and other Hollywood movies continue to advance this other anti-Semitism in spite of the fact that Arabs, like Jews, are Semites sharing a common genetic make-up. I use the word "other" not because anti-Semitism against Jews is passe (it isn't), but because the most damaging films directed against Arabs were released in the last third of the twentieth century, at a time when Hollywood was eliminating stereotypical portraits of other groups such as Asians, Blacks, and Latinos. Regrettably, it remains acceptable to keep advancing anti-Semitism in movies provided the Semites are Arabs.

Declaring war on Iraq, said President George Bush and his advisors, was in direct response to the September 11, 2001, tragedy, Nineteen suicidal Arab Muslim terrorists attacked the Pentagon and destroyed the World Trade Center. The terrorists and their fanatic handlers slaughtered about 3,000 people from more than 60 nations. Now we are engaged in a force of arms war in Iraq as well as force of facts to crush the guilty. The administration has launched an information war, complete with government sponsored media campaigns designed to reinvent America in the eyes of 1.2 billion Muslims. The purpose of our government's PR campaign? To crush big-time the myths that this conflict has anything to do with Islam against Christianity, or Arabs against the West. Instead, this war, believes the President and his supporters, has everything to do with exterminating the lunatic fringe responsible for 9/11 and other terrorist actions..

Political leaders, image-makers and journalists must not allow themselves to fall into the stale trap—"seen one, seen 'em all." They should not attribute the actions of the lunatic fringe to the vast majority of peaceful Arabs and Muslims. No individual, no nation should cast judgement on an entire race, culture, nation or religion based on the heinous acts of some fanatics. These fanatics no more represents Muslims than the Ku Klux Klan represents Christians.

On a canvas far broader in terms of ethnic coverage than its title indicates, my book, *Reel Bad Arabs: How Hollywood Vilifies a People*, paints the dangers of rigid and repetitive stereotypes when we lump "those people" together indiscriminately. For a full century before September 11, 2002, America's bogeyman was the Arab. Both nationwide and globally — Hollywood's movies are exported to 150-plus nations — entertainment shows projected hate-filled images depicting an entire people as demonic and less-than-human. In the process of disparaging a people and their faith, defamation itself gained strength by impacting viewers in the Middle East, as well as extending its ruinous power far beyond the people it was defaming.

For instance, here at home, in spite of the impressive and responsible rhetoric of President George Bush and Mayor Rudy Giuliani not to target Americans of Arab heritage and American Muslims, we witnessed vicious outbursts against "look-a-likes," more than 700 hate-crimes and the killing of several innocents.

No doubt about it: image-making affects thinking and stereotypical profiling injures the innocent. For nearly three decades, I have studied how Arab peoples are depicted, giving special emphasis to "entertainment" images of television programs and motion pictures. My research offers convincing evidence that lurid and insidious portraits are the media's staple fare. Almost all of Hollywood's portraits of Arabs are dangerously threatening. From 1896 until 2001, *reel* Arabs have been repeatedly projected as the cultural "other" bent on terrorizing civilized Westerners. Film-makers have collectively indicted all Arabs as Public Enemy No.1. Movies display them as anti-Christian bombers, billionaires, buffoons, bedouin bandits, belly dancers, bundles in black, beasts of burden or black magic vamps. Rarely are Arabs seen as ordinary neighbors with families, people who practice law, drive taxis, heal the sick, or teach youngsters. Think about it. When was the last time you saw a movie or TV show depicting an Arab or an American of Arab heritage as a regular guy? The absence of positive, realistic images nurtures suspicion and stereotype.

Most Americans have difficulty distinguishing between Arabs and Muslims, The term "Arab" is essentially a linguistic category referring to about 265 million people from Arabic-speaking countries. "Muslim" is a purely religious distinction, referring to 1.1 billion Muslims, most of whom are Indonesian, Indian and Malaysian. Only 12 percent of the world's Muslims are Arabs. Yet, media images are almost always hostile when it comes to Arab Muslims. As a result, the Arab Muslim lacks a human face. For all the prejudice, during the Gulf War and following the terrorist attack on the World Trade Center, all Arabs, including some of the 3 million Americans with Arabs roots became "camel jockeys," "ragheads," and "sand suckers." Whenever there is a crisis in the Middle East Arab-Americans are subjected to vicious stereotyping and incidents of violence and discrimination.

I was sheltered from prejudicial portraits at first. My parents came from Lebanon in the 1920s; they met and married in America. Our home in the steel city of Clairton, Pennsylvania, was a center for ethnic sharing—black, white, Jew, and gentile. There was only one major source of screen images then, at the State movie theater where I was lucky enough to get a part-time job as an usher. But in the late 1940's, Westerns and war movies were popular; not Middle Eastern dramas. Memories of World War II were fresh, and the screen heavies were the Japanese and the Germans. But when I mimicked or mocked the bad guys, my mother cautioned me. She explained that stereotypes hurt; that they blur our vision and corrupt the imagination. "Have compassion for all people, Jackie," she said. Experience the joy of accepting people as they are, and not as they appear in films, she advised.

Mother was right. I can remember the Saturday afternoon when my son, Michael, who was seven and my daughter, Michele, six, suddenly called out: "Daddy, Daddy, they've got some bad Arabs on TV." They were watching that great American morality play, professional wrestling, Akbar the Great, who liked to hear the cracking of bones, and Abdullah the Butcher, a dirty fighter who liked to inflict pain, were pinning their foes with "camel clutches." From that day on, I knew I had to try to neutralize the media caricatures.

I believe most researchers…did not exist. My research focuses on television and motion pictures because visual impressions…may never wither away.

Investigating Hollywood's Arabs began as a solo effort. But, soon after I began working on my first book, *The TV Arab* (1984) family members, friends, and colleagues assisted me in many ways.

It hasn't been easy. Images teach youngsters whom to love, whom to hate. With my children, I have watched animated heroes Heckle and Jeckle pull the rug from under "Ali Boo-Boo, the Desert Rat," and Laverne and Shirley stop "Sheik Ha-Mean-ie" from conquering "the US and the world." I have read more than 250 comic books like the "Fantastic Four" and "GI Combat" whose characters have sketched Arabs as "low-lifes" and "human hyenas." Negative stereotypes were everywhere. A dictionary informed my youngsters that an Arab is a "vagabond, drifter, hobo, and vagrant." Whatever happened, my wife wondered, to Aladdin's good genie?

To a child, the world is simple: good versus evil. But my children and others with Arab roots grew up without ever having seen a humane Arab on the silver screen, someone to look up to or to pattern their lives after. To them, it seems easier for a camel to go through the eye of a needle than for a screen Arab to appear as a genuine human being.

In my new book, *Reel Bad Arabs*, I analyze upwards of 1,000 feature films, the vast majority of which bombard audiences with rigid, repetitive and repulsive depictions. From 1896 (*Fatima*) until 2001 (*The Mummy Returns*) film makers have failed to project *real* Arabs as normal, everyday folks. Instead, hundreds of movies collectively indict *reel* Arabs as Public Enemy #1, falsely implying that the *Holy Quran* and Islam, a faith embraced by more than one billion people, advocate violence.

Why is it important for the average American to know and care about the Arab stereotype? It is critical because the dislike of "the stranger" image, which the Greeks knew as xenophobia, forewarns that when one ethnic or racial or religious group is vilified, innocent people suffer. The onslaught of the reel Arab conditions how young people perceive themselves and how others perceive them as well. Explains one Arab-American college student: "The most common questions I was asked [by classmates] were if I had ever ridden a camel or if my family lived in tents. Even worse, I learned at a very young age [that] every other movie seemed to feature Arab terrorists."

I recently asked 293 secondary school teachers from five states—Massachusetts, North Carolina, Arkansas, West Virginia, and Wisconsin—to write down the names of any humane or heroic screen Arab they had seen. Five cited past portraits of Ali Baba and Sinbad; one mentioned Omar Sharif and "those Arabs" in *Lion of the Desert* and *The Wind and the Lion*. The remaining 287 teachers wrote "none."

Nicholas Kadi, an actor with Iraqi roots, makes his living playing terrorists in such films as the 1990 release *Navy SEALS*. Kadi laments that he does "little talking and a lot of threatening—threatening looks, threatening gestures." On screen, he and others who play Arab villains say "America," then spit. "There are other kinds of Arabs in the world," says Kadi, "I'd like to think that some day there will be an Arab role out there for me that would be an honest portrayal."

The Arab remains American culture's favorite whipping boy. In his memoirs, Terrel Bell, Ronald Regan's first secretary of education, writes about an "apparent bias among mid-level, right-wing staffers at the White House" who dismissed Arabs as "sand niggers."

At a recent teacher's conference, I met a woman from Sioux Falls, South Dakota, who told me about the persistence of discrimination. She was in the process of adopting a baby when an agency staffer warned her that the infant had a problem. When she asked whether the child was mentally ill, or physically disabled, there was silence. Finally, the worker said: "The baby is Jordanian."

To me, the Arab demon of today is much like the Jewish demon of yesterday. We deplore the false portrait of Jews as a swarthy menace. Yet a similar portrait has been accepted and transferred to another group of Semites—the Arabs.

The Civil Rights movement of the 1960's not only helped bring about more realistic depictions of various groups, it curbed negative images of the lazy black, the wealthy Jew, the greasy Hispanic, and the corrupt Italian. These images are mercifully rare on today's screens. Conscientious image makers and citizens worked together to eliminate the racial mockery that had been a shameful part of the American cultural scene.

It would be a step in the right direction if movie and TV producers developed characters modeled after real-life Arab-Americans. We could view a White House correspondent like Helen Thomas, whose father came from Lebanon, in a movie like *The American President* (1996), a heart surgeon patterned after the late Dr. Michael DeBakey on TV shows such as *E. R.*, a lawyer such as Ralph Nader on *Law and Order*, a Palestinian teacher like Columbia University's Edward Said in *Dead Poet's Society* (1989), or a heroic air force pilot, like Colonel James Jabbara, Korea's first jet ace.

As motion pictures are the most powerful teaching tools ever created, we need to examine how image-making affects thinking, and how insidious myths and stereotyping help shape policy. In the spirit of fairness, Hollywood should begin portraying all Arabs as neither saints nor devils, but as fellow human beings, with all the potentials and frailties that condition implies. Producers should recognize that Islam, Christianity, and Judaism are religions of peace, advocating that all humankind is one family in the care of God.

The time is long overdue for the industry to shift gears and start churning out movies that help enhance tolerance and unify people. In this hour of global crisis, image-makers should keep in mind that xenophobia and prejudice are the flip sides of harmony and togetherness.

3
Section Three

In the Reference section the reader will find resources to assist in mining the *Handbook* as well as features designed to set our discussion into historical and geographic context.

Contents (Section Three)

Glossary

Allah: (See page 32)

Al-Qaeda: An international terroristic Sunni Islamic movement founded under the leadership of Osama bin Laden. Al-Qaeda terror groups have attacked civilian and military targets in various countries, the most notable being the September 11, 2001 attacks on New York's World Trade Center, the Pentagon, and Shanksville, Pennsylvania. In response the US government launched a military and intelligence campaign against Al-Qaeda. Its central effort involved a war in Afghanistan to destroy Al-Qaeda's bases there and overthrow the Taliban, the country's Muslim fanatical rulers who harbored bin Laden and his followers. "Al-Qaeda" is Arabic for "The Base," referring to a database of followers.

Al-Qaeda terror techniques include suicide attacks and simultaneous bombings of different targets. These activities may involve members of the organization, who have taken a pledge of loyalty to bin Laden, or the much more numerous "Al-Qaeda-linked" individuals who have undergone training in one of its camps in Afghanistan or Sudan. Al-Qaeda's objectives include the end of foreign influence in Muslim countries and the creation of a new Islamic caliphate. Reported beliefs include that a Christian-Jewish alliance is conspiring to destroy Islam and that the killing of bystanders and civilians is Islamically justified in holy war. Its management philosophy has been described as "centralization of decision and decentralization of execution."

Al-Qaeda grew out of the Services Office, a clearinghouse for the international Muslim brigade opposed to the 1979 Soviet invasion of Afghanistan. In the 1980s, the Services Office—run by bin Laden and the Palestinian religious scholar Abdullah Azzam—recruited, trained, and financed thousands of foreign mujahadeen, or holy warriors, from more than fifty countries. Bin Laden wanted these fighters to continue the "holy war" beyond Afghanistan. He formed Al-Qaeda circa 1988.

Noting Al-Qaeda's diffuse nature, the July 19, 2008, issue of the Economist wrote: "Its core members may number only hundreds, but it has connections of all kinds to military groups with thousands or even tens of thousands of fighters. Al-Qaeda is a terrorist organization, a militant network, and a subculture of rebellion all at the same time." It continues: "Some [experts] describe it as a venture-capital firm that invests in promising terrorist projects. Others speak of it as a global 'brand' maintained by its leaders through their propaganda, with its growing number of 'franchises' carrying out attacks."

Arabic: The language of Arabs and Islam, included here because the differences between Arabic and English demonstrate the extreme differences between Arab and American societies. To the English-speaker Arabic sounds different, looks different, reads different. Arabic uses an entirely different script. That script is read from right to left, the reverse of our way, and books are read from what we would call back to front. In addition, the styles of expression of the two languages differ. Arabic is not easily translated and therefore the beauty and impact of the *Quran* are lost on people who read it in translation.

Classified as Central Semitic, Arabic is closely related to Hebrew and Aramaic and has its roots in a Proto-Semitic common ancestor. Modern Arabic is classified as a macro-language with 27 sub-languages spoken throughout the Arab world. Standard Arabic is widely studied and known throughout the Islamic world.

During the Middle Ages, Arabic was a major vehicle of culture, especially in science, mathematics and philosophy, with the result that European languages have borrowed numerous words from it. These include algebra, alcohol, alchemy, alkali, zenith, sugar, cotton and magazine.

Beheading: Islam in the time of Mohammad adopted many practices that were traditional to the Arab tribes of the day. Beheading enemies was a widely used form of execution in the era when Islam was being established. It's possible, given the modes of execution at that time, that beheading was one of the more enlightened and humane forms of it.

The modern-day beheadings, photographed for television, are clearly designed to terrorize opponents. The intention seems un-Islamic.

Caliph: The now-defunct title meaning the head of state in a caliphate (a territory governed by Muslims). This title designated the leader of the Islamic umma, an Islamic community ruled by Sharia law. The successors to Mohammad were called caliphs. After the first four caliphs (Abu Bakr, Umar, Uthman, and Ali), the title was claimed by succeeding dynasties: the Umayyads, the Abbasids, and the Ottomans. Most historical Muslim governors were called sultans or emirs, and gave allegiance to a caliph, but at times had very little real authority.

Chador: An outer garment or open cloak worn by some Muslim women in Iran and Pakistan. This is often an expansion on an attempt to be modest in Islam. Other Muslim women may choose to wear variations such as the abaya or in Afghanistan the burka. It consists of a full-length semi-circle of fabric open down the front, thrown over the head and held shut in front. A chador has no hand openings or closures but is held shut by the hands or by wrapping the ends around the waist. This is different from the simple veil that some Muslim women wear.

(For more, see "The Veil" in the Informed Views section.)

Change: We often ask: Why are Arab and/or Muslim societies so resistant to change? In considering this question, perhaps it's well to point out that 800 years ago, when Muslim civilization was at its height, that civilization was both the product of change and its engine in science and technology. In addition, Arab societies underwent extensive urbanization in the 20th century.

But it may also be useful to look at recent change in American society. Americans are accustomed to change; it's a fact of life in their culture. Change, innovation, originality of thought and diversity are all regarded as American values. Moreover, America's political system institutionalizes at least the possibility of change every four years.

In addition, the 20th century has been an era of unparalleled technological change in the West, beginning with movies, automobiles and telephones, moving through airplanes, television, space exploration and sophisticated weaponry to the internet. Due to these developments, the world for Americans has shrunk incredibly in size, speaking metaphorically. A society comfortable with change can accommodate these technological advances. There have also been extraordinary cultural changes: the extension of women's rights, civil rights and the greater acceptance of alternative lifestyles. The fluidity of migration has also caused changes in the US. People have not always adjusted easily to these changes as the rise of fundamentalism in America attests.

By contrast change and originality of thought are not as viable in present-day Islamic societies. The general political system in the Arab or Muslim worlds is strong man rule, well exemplified by Saddam Hussein. Dictatorships discourage change unless it is instituted by the regime. (The Shah of Iran discovered that change can develop a momentum of its own and lead to the overthrow of a regime.) At the beginning of the 20th century Arabs were ruled by the decadent Ottoman Empire, by tribal leaders (ibn Saud) or by English or French colonial regimes. None of these encouraged change. Moreover, adherence to tradition and the espousing of a social system and set of laws enunciated more than a thousand years earlier have impeded change.

While the Islamic empire responded successfully to change in previous centuries, it now finds itself very far behind a West that seems to it magnificent in power while being decadent in culture. How to contend with – and emerge from – this situation has been a perplexing question for both Muslims and the West. Some Arabs have questioned the relevance of Quranic teachings. Muslim fundamentalists have embraced them unreservedly, wishing to force their societies to return to a pure and purely Islamic way of life. This will require overturning governments in their own countries. Some fundamentalists see attacking the West as a first step in the process of doing this.

Crusades: A series of military expeditions waged by much of feudal Christian Europe with the goal of recapturing Jerusalem and the Holy Land from Muslim rule. They are seen by some as a flip side of the civilization conflict launched by Muslim extremists against the West most notably by the attacks of 9/11. During Europe's Middle Ages, Muslim civilization, although beset by rivalries, led the world in scientific discoveries and technological domination and was at the height of its influence.

Since the 8th century devout Christians had been making pilgrimages to the Holy Sepulcher, the tomb in Jerusalem where Jesus was supposed to have been laid to rest. The crusades were undertaken to permit Christians to continue making pilgrimages to holy sites by retrieving them from Muslim rule. They took place over a period of the two centuries, from 1095 to 1291.

The crusades were actually triggered by a call from the Christian Eastern Orthodox Byzantine Empire for help against the expansion of the Muslim Seljuk Turks into Anatolia (central Turkey). While ostensibly religiously motivated and sanctioned by the Pope, Christendom's supreme ruler at the time, they inspired masses of Europeans, some in armies, others as pilgrim adventurers, to wander across southeastern Europe, through Constantinople (now Istanbul which was sacked in 1204) and into Asia Minor. They succeeded in recapturing Jerusalem only to lose it to the brilliant and honorable Muslim general Saladin. The crusades spurred the transformation of Europe out of feudalism, but failed in terms of basic goals. Besides Saladin, crusaders best known to Americans are the English king Richard the Lion-Hearted and Francis of Assisi, later a saint.

The crusades, seen as an all-out Western attack on Muslim civilization, still provoke excited and hostile reactions among Muslims. The word itself can act as a red flag to some.

Cutting the hands of thieves: As a matter of sharia law, in accordance with the *Quran* and several hadith, theft is punished by imprisonment or amputation of hands or feet, depending on the number of times theft was committed and on the items stolen. Before the punishment is executed eyewitnesses must say under oath that they saw the person stealing. Without witnesses the punishment cannot be executed. Other requirements specify that the thief must be adult and sane and that the theft was not caused by hunger, necessity or duress. If the thief repents, the punishment is not imposed. As a result, the actual instances of hands being amputated are relatively few.

Fatwa: (pl. *fatawa*) A ruling on Islamic law issued by an Islamic scholar, essentially a religious declaration. In theory, to be valid, a *fatwa* must be in line with relevant legal proofs, deduced from Quranic verses and *hadiths*; issued by a person (or a board) having due knowledge and sincerity of heart; be free from individual opportunism, and not depending on political servitude; and be adequate with the needs of the contemporary world. Today, *Fatawa* do not always meet these criteria.

The obligation of individual Muslims in relation to them varies from place to place, from circumstance to circumstance. Scholar of religion Karen Armstrong reports, for example, that 44 out of 45 member states attending a meeting of the Islamic Congress condemned the fatwa of Iran's Ayatollah Khomeini against Salmon Rushdie as un-Islamic.

Female circumcision/female genital mutilation/female genital cutting: The excision or tissue removal of any part of the female genitalia for cultural, religious or other non-medical reasons.

Writes scholar of religion Karen Armstrong: "Feminists frequently condemn 'Islam' for the custom of female circumcision. This despite the fact that it is really an African practice, is never mentioned in the [*Quran*], is not prescribed by three of the four main schools of Islamic jurisprudence, and was absorbed into the fourth school in North Africa where it was a fact of life."

Fundamentalism: In recent years "fundamentalism" has come to refer to strong adherence to a set of conservative and traditional beliefs and practices, perhaps especially when the values they espouse have come under attack. Those values relate particularly to cultural or religious practices and appear to challenge the adherent's sense of identity.

The term "fundamentalism" originally referred to a set of beliefs—regarded as "religious fundamentals"—within the American Protestant community early in the 20th century. Their values were being challenged by modernism.

Fundamentalism is seen as a basically religious response to change and the strains it causes. Given the kind of change the world has experienced in the past 100 years (see "Change" above), it is not surprising that evidences of fundamentalism have sprung up around the world. In the US there are both Catholic fundamentalism and the Protestant variety. American fundamentalists are particular opponents of cultural change as represented by the now familiar sexual revolution, the abortion it condones, pressures to accept homosexual lifestyles and immigration.

Islamic fundamentalists feel rage and humiliation at the power and arrogance of the West, its military and economic power, its overwhelming cultural imports, and its colonial and post-colonial encroachments on their territory. They have felt lost and disoriented by their own political impotence and the secular lifestyle invasions of the West. Revolted by the future offered by the secular and impious West, disgusted by the seeming stasis of the present, Muslim fundamentalists pin their hopes on a restoration of the golden age of Islamic flowering at the time of Mohammad and his immediate successors thirteen hundred years ago. This strikes most Westerners as extreme folly, given the change that the world has experienced in the interim.

But how the West can help Muslims to find an accommodation with the modern world that works for them has so far eluded it. The West's lack of cultural sensitivity and curiosity, its hubris and its incompetence in waging both war and peace have immensely complicated the attempt.

Arab-American educator Audrey Shabbas offers a different perspective. She writes: "The Western term 'Fundamentalism' does not accurately describe the modern movement in Islamic countries to renew Islamic values in Muslim personal and public life. Muslims prefer the term 'revivalism' as a more accurate description of this renewal, whose manifestations include an increase in religious observance (mosque attendance, Ramadan fast, wearing traditional Islamic dress); revitalization of mystical orders; the growth of numerous religious publications and media programming; support for the implementation of Islamic law; and the growth and creation of Islamic organizations and movements."

Hadith: Oral traditions relating to the words and deeds of Mohammad. *Hadith* collections are regarded as important tools for determining the *Sunnah*, or Muslim way of life, by all traditional schools of the Islamic legal system.

Hajj: An ancient Arab ritual involving a pilgrimage to Mecca and its shrine, the Ka'aba, the heart of Islam. The *hajj* predates Islam and was considered ancient even in the time of Mohammad the Prophet. The Ka'aba was believed to have been built by Abraham and his son Ishmael, the father of the Arabs. A sanctuary surrounds Mecca in which no violence was to occur even in the days when Arabia was inhabited by contending nomadic tribes.

The *hajj* is one of the five pillars (requirements) of Islam. It involves making a pilgrimage to Mecca in order to perform a series of rituals. At the Ka'aba the pilgrim walks counter-clockwise around the cube-shaped building in the center of *Masjid Al Haram* mosque toward which all Muslims orient their prayers as Mohammad and millions of other pilgrims have done. The pilgrim walks or runs between the hills of Al-Safa and Al-Marwah (as the abandoned Hagar, Ishmael's mother, is thought to have done in seeking water for her son). The pilgrim stands in vigil on the plains of Mount Arafat, drinks from the Zamzam well (which sprang forth, according to legend, when Ishmael stamped his foot) and gathers pebbles at Muzdalifah and throws them at pillars at Mina in order to "stone the devil."

During the *hajj* male pilgrims wear a garment of two sheets of unhemmed cloth as Mohammad himself did when in 632 he led exclusively his Muslim followers on a *hajj* from Medina. This clothing demonstrates the equality of all pilgrims before God. After performing *hajj* rituals the pilgrims cut their hair, sacrifice an animal in order to feed the poor and celebrate the festival of *Eid ul-Adha*.

In recent years *hajj* pilgrims have numbered an estimated two million. Due to the multitudes some rituals have become stylized. Pebbles are now thrown at walls with catch-bins. Despite crowd-control techniques, pilgrims are still trampled in the crush and ramps occasionally fall due to the weight of pilgrims, causing deaths.

Harem: The women's section in a polygamous household. There women's quarters are enclosed and forbidden to men. An Arab *harem* does not necessarily consist solely of women with whom the head of the household has sexual relations (wives and concubines). It may also include their young offspring, female relatives and other women. A *harem* may be a palatial complex, as in romantic tales, in which case it includes staff (women and eunuchs). Or it may simply be women's quarters, in the Ottoman tradition (*harem* comes from the Turkish) separated from the men's *selamlik*, that portion of a Turkish house reserved for men. This practice no longer exists in today's Arab world except for a few scattered examples in select societies.

Hijab: In Western usage *hijab* usually refers to the headscarf worn by Muslim women to cover their hair and ears. In Islamic scholarship *hijab* denotes morality encouraged by modesty.

In Western countries wearing the *hijab* scarf serves not only as an act of respect to Muslim tradition, but also as a woman's way of declaring her identity as a Muslim and her solidarity with other Muslims. Because of this, Muslim girls (and also Sikh boys) in France were prohibited from wearing head coverings to school as a means of protecting the state school's secularist values.

Wearing the *hijab* is intended to be the woman's choice to cover up with the veil. Modesty is expected of both men and women.

Honor killing: The murder of a family member (almost always a woman) by a male relative in order to erase a real or perceived humiliation of the family as a result of the victim's behavior. The offensive behavior is usually sexual, sometimes immodesty, sometimes disapproved liaisons. Honor killings sometimes occur among Muslim tribes in Arab countries and Pakistan, some among Kurds and Sikhs.

An Amnesty International statement declares: "The regime of honor is unforgiving: women on whom suspicion has fallen are not given an opportunity to defend themselves, and family members have no socially acceptable alternative but to remove the stain on their honor by attacking the woman." The United Nations Population Fund estimates that worldwide honor-killing victims may number as high as 5,000 women each year.

Islamic religious authorities claim that extra-legal punishments such as honor killings are prohibited. They cite the killings as a pre-Islamic cultural practice which continues to shape Muslim actions. They contend that murderers of females use Islam to justify honor killing, but they claim that there is no support for the act in the religion itself.

Jihad: (See page 34)

Ka'aba: A shrine venerated from time immemorial, considered by Muslims to be the most sacred spot on earth around which has been built the Great Mosque of Mecca. Muslims turn toward the shrine during prayer as the symbolic house of God. They are encouraged to visit and walk around it seven times in the *hajj* pilgrimage, one of the five pillars of Islam. The Ka'aba is cube-shaped, constructed of gray stone and marble, its corners corresponding roughly to the points of the compass. During most of the year an enormous black cloth covers the Ka'aba, ornamented with Quranic sayings woven in gold.

Karen Armstrong's biography *Mohammad* offers this account by the Iranian philosopher Ali Shariati of the experience of circumambulating (walking around) the Ka'aba: "As you circumambulate and move closer to the Ka'aba, you feel like a small stream merging with a big river. Carried by a wave you lose touch with the ground. Suddenly, you are floating, carried on by the flood. As you approach the center, the pressure of the crowd squeezes you so hard that you are given a new life. You are now part of the People; you are now a Man, alive and eternal…"

Madrassa education: The Arabic word for any type of school, secular or religious, is *madrassa*. In common English usage the word has been taken to mean a school giving Islamic religious instruction.

Islamic schools typically offer two courses of study: memorization of the *Quran* (which is shorter than the *Bible*'s New Testament) and preparation to become an accepted scholar in the community. Students study Arabic, *Quran* interpretation, *sharia* law, *hadith*, logic and Muslim history. More advanced *madrassas* offer world history, science, English and foreign languages.

The concern about *madrassas* in the United States has been two-fold: first, how can Islamic education, predominant in the Arab world, prepare young Muslims to interface with a complicated world? Second, if some *madrassas* are fashioning Muslim fundamentalists, are they also training young men to be violent extremists and, if so, what can be done about it?

During the Afghan resistance against the Soviets Saudi Arabia financed the establishment of *madrassas* in Pakistan. Those *madrassas* teach the austere and rigid form of Islam called *Wahhabism*; they educated many Taliban. This did not concern Americans when the fundamentalists were fighting the Soviets. But today the fundamentalists are fighting against America—as a reconstituted Taliban in Afghanistan and as violent extremists in Iraq. Some observers say that an education in *Quran*-by-rote does not equip a person for the technical and linguistic skills a terrorist needs. Even so, say others, the training of fundamentalists with mistaken, prejudiced and uneducated ideas about the world and the West should concern Americans.

Mecca: The holiest city of Islam, site of the Ka'aba, a shrine which, legend says, was built by Abraham and his son Ishmael, father of the Arabs. The shrine is located at the Zamzam spring, the water source that created an oasis at Mecca. Situated between mountains, the city hosts an estimated two million Muslim *hajj* pilgrims each year; they visit the sacred mosque and perform rituals comprising one of the five pillars of Islam. People from other faiths are prohibited from entering the city.

Modesty of dress: Modesty of dress is expected of all Muslims, both male and female.

Moreover, clothing should not reveal body contours nor should it be eye-catching. Some Western Muslim women who dress in accordance with these requirements stress that they feel freedom, not confinement, inside Islamic dress. There are various interpretations of what modesty requires. Some Western Muslim women wear the headscarf; others dress in conventional Western styles.

The *Quran* states: "Say to the believing men and women that they should lower their gaze and guard their modesty: that will make for greater purity for them: And God is well acquainted with all that they do." [24:30]

Given this tradition of modesty and the general seclusion of most Muslim women, one can understand how American movies with their frequent nudity or near-nudity and their depiction of sex acts give offense to devout Muslims and are regarded by some as evidence of a decadent society.

Mohammad: One of history's extraordinary men, 570-632 CE.

Says the Encyclopedia Brittanica: "Founder of the religion of Islam and of the Arab Empire, initiator of religious, social and cultural developments of monumental significance in the history of mankind." Says Wikipedia: "the founder of Islam regarded by Muslims as the last messenger and prophet of God (Allah in Arabic). Muslims do not believe that he was the creator of a new religion, but the restorer of the original, uncorrupted monotheistic faith of Adam, Abraham and others. They see him as the last and the greatest in a series of prophets." Says scholar of religions Karen Armstrong: "a complex, passionate man who sometimes did things that it is difficult for us [in the West] to accept, but who had genius of a profound order and founded a religion and a cultural tradition that was not based on the sword – despite Western myth – and whose name 'Islam' signifies peace and reconciliation."

Mohammad lived at a time when Arab tribes were leaving their traditional nomadic way of life on the steppes and settling into towns. A married merchant resident in Mecca, Mohammad began to receive revelations at age 40. While on a religious retreat in the mountains outside Mecca, Mohammad was visited by an angel who told him, "Recite." Mohammad at first refused, but was so overwhelmed by the angel that he eventually began to verbalize messages that became the basis of the *Quran*, Islam's holy book. (Mohammad was probably illiterate. The recitations were later transcribed. The Arabic *Quran* (*Qu'ran*) means the Recitation.) When Mohammad continued to receive the revelations—the main message of which was that there was one only God—he began to share them first with his wife, then with clan members and eventually with his tribal brothers, the Quraysh who had been settled in Mecca, taking up a life as traders, for about two generations.

Although Mohammad's call for worshipping only one God brought him followers, it also caused him and his followers great difficulties with the powerful clans of the Quraysh. They were not ready to renounce the pagan gods of their fathers. The tensions and harassment of Muslims became so extreme that a large portion of the followers went to live in Abyssinia (now Ethiopia) in 616.

When the harassment continued, it became clear that Mohammad and his followers must look for another place to live. Just at this time two Arab tribes had settled in the oasis of Yathrib, north of Mecca, where Jewish immigrants were farming. Rivalry between the groups meant that they needed an outsider to mediate between them. Accustomed to the monotheism of their Jewish neighbors, the now settled tribes of Yathrib accepted Mohammad as their change agent.

Mohammad and his people thus took a significant modernizing step. They cut themselves off from the system of protection based on blood ties, a paramount value among the Arabs, trusting that those who agreed to protect and help them, known as the *Ansar*, would in fact do this. Mohammad's transfer to Medina in 622 CE—also termed his "flight" there—marks the beginning of the Muslim era and is called the *hejra*.

When the Quraysh of Mecca realized that Mohammad's people had been leaving in small groups, the tribal leaders decided that Mohammed, who waited behind in Mecca until all his people had gone, should be killed. A group of young men, one from each clan, thus avoiding a blood feud, was appointed to do the deed. But Mohammad escaped.

En route to Medina he and a companion (Abu Bakr, who later succeeded him as the first *caliph*) hid in a cave. One of the great stories of God's protection concerns this cave. When the Quraysh pursued Mohammad, who remained in the cave with Abu Bakr, they found a spider's web covering it as well as an acacia tree in front of it, with a rock-dove nesting in it sitting on her eggs.

Since his followers had no way of sustaining themselves at Medina, Mohammad instructed them to raid Quraysh caravans passing nearby. Learning that Mohammad intended to stage a caravan ambush at a place called Badr, the Quraysh sent out an army to liquidate him. But Mohammad's men won a seemingly miraculous victory, seen as divine intervention, a *furqan* or sign of salvation. Muslims liken this event to the escape by Moses and the Children of Israel from the Egyptians at the miraculous parting of the Red Sea.

Two years later, in 625, however, the Quraysh, intent on vengeance, massed for an attack on Medina.

Although Mohammad had great difficult rallying a unified force, his men met the Quraysh at Uhud, outside Medina. They were defeated. Trying to rally his retreating men, Mohammad was hit on the head. Supposing him dead, the Quraysh withdrew. Only stunned, Mohammad was able to regroup his men and chase the Quraysh back toward Mecca for three days. The defeat at Uhud, however, left the Muslims deeply discouraged and depressed.

In 627 the Quraysh again sought to rid themselves of Mohammad by taking the attack into Medina itself. Mohammad led his followers to build a series of trenches at places where the Quraysh might gain entry to the settlement. The trenches, which his adversaries had never seen before, thwarted attempts by horses and camels in enter Medina. The Quraysh besieged Medina. They had, moreover, begun to negotiate with a Jewish tribe, resident at Medina, the Bani Qurayzah, for entry into the city. Distrust forestalled the triggering of this betrayal. Mohammad got wind of it and after three weeks of siege the Quraysh pulled out. Mohammad's victory at the Battle of the Trenches (for so it was regarded) made him the most powerful man in Arabia. The tribal ethic of the time forced him to deal harshly with the traitorous Bani Qurayzah.

While the victory solved Mohammad's security problem, he was trying to build a new kind of society based on his revelations. This meant that the next challenge with the Quraysh was to achieve reconciliation. In early 628 Mohammad decided to subscribe to ancient Arab practice and lead a *hajj* to the Ka'aba, the holiest of Arab shrines, in the Quraysh city of Mecca. About a thousand supporters accompanied him. They wore the traditional garb of Arab pilgrims, two pieces of cloth draped one about the shoulders, the other about the waist, and carried no weapons. A sanctuary surrounding Mecca prohibited acts of violence.

By tradition, pilgrims were free to enter Mecca in safety. But the Quraysh refused to allow Mohammad and his people into the city. When they reached the edge of the sanctuary, however, tradition held that they could not be attacked. But would the Quraysh honor this tradition? In this dangerous situation Mohammad asked each of his followers to swear an oath of loyalty to him. Negotiations then began. Mohammad made concessions to the Quraysh with which many of his followers disagreed. But because they had sworn loyalty to Mohammed, he was able to retain their support. The treaty made at this time led to better relations with his old enemies.

Of this moment Karen Armstrong writes, "[Mohammad] had intuitively penetrated to a deeper understanding of the dynamics of change in Arabia, and events would vindicate his insight. From this point, now that he had saved the *umma* [his followers] from the threat of extinction, the *jihad* would become an effort of peace that demanded all his patience and ingenuity." Muslims speak of a "lesser *jihad*" (by which they mean warfare) and a "greater *jihad*" (which is the struggle for a better understanding of God and the building of a better society).

In 630 Mohammad returned to Mecca, vanquished pagan Quraysh who wished to fight and welcomed into Islam those who wished to be his followers. He smashed the pagan idols in the Ka'aba, consecrated it to God and issued a general amnesty. Within a few years pagan worship had ceased in Mecca.

As a result of his power, Mohammad was able to break the patterns of tribal alliances that had previously characterized Arabia. Increasingly nomadic tribes chose to ally themselves with him. They promised to renounce idolatry, furnish troops when needed, not to attack the *umma* and to pay the tithing and alms demanded of all Muslims as one of the five pillars of their faith.

Mohammad's exploits as a political leader can overshadow the significance of his greater work. This was the founding of a religion that grew dramatically after his death, demonstrating its validity to its converts; to encourage individual values and stress the individual's fate in a society that had been highly communal; to replace narrow tribal loyalties with those to the ever-growing *umma*; to create a community in Medina that served as an example to others and to codify in the *Quran* the precepts that had been revealed to him over the years.

Muslim: According to Arab-American educator Audrey Shabbas, "A Muslim is anyone who says publicly, 'There is no God but God, and Mohammad is the messenger of God.'"

She continues, "The term 'Mohammedan' is offensive to Muslims and should not be used. Muslims worship God, not Mohammad, who warned his followers: "Do not exceed bounds in praising me as did the Christians in praising Jesus, the Son of Mary, by calling Him God, and the Son of God... I am only the Lord's servant: Then call me the servant of God and His messenger.'"

Muslim Brotherhood: Officially known as the Society of Muslim Brothers, the Muslim Brotherhood is a multi-national Sunni Islamist movement and the world's largest, most influential political Islamist group. Founded by the Sufi schoolteacher Hassan al-Banna in 1928, the Brotherhood is the largest political opposition organization in many Arab nations, particularly Egypt.

Organized by cells, the Brotherhood spread rapidly throughout the Muslim world, establishing schools, small-scale industries and clinics. A decade after its founding it became increasingly political, espousing a return to Islamic purity, the establishment of a unified Muslim state, and rejecting Westernization, secularization and modernization.

Its credo is: " God is our objective. The Prophet is our leader. *Quran* is our law. *Jihad* is our way. Dying in the way of God is our highest hope."

Officially disbanded after the 1952 coup during which Mohammad Naquib and Gamal Abdel Nasser overthrew the Egyptian monarchy, the Brotherhood went underground. In 1954 it was outlawed following student disturbances which it fomented. It survives, nonetheless, repeatedly challenging Arab or Muslim governments with violence and demonstrations and suffering oppression.

Oppression of women in Islam: A Muslim view of this matter is that in Islam—in principle, if not always in practice—women and men are equal. However, they do have different natures, biologically, psychologically and physiologically, and therefore different roles. A significant difference between the rights of Muslim women and American women, contend some Muslims, is the manner in which those rights were conferred. In the US women had to struggle for rights, such as voting, and had to prove their capacities by extraordinary service in wartime, for example, in factory work. Muslim women were given their rights by God through revelation to the Prophet and these cannot be changed.

Interestingly, in Islam women have always had rights to own property and to have inheritances. These rights came to Western women much later.

Polygamy: A widespread practice throughout the ages, seen generally in the form of polygyny (one man having several wives) and much more rarely in the form of polyandry (one woman with several husbands). Polygamy occurred in many traditional societies, on one hand, because tradition required that all women be under the protection of a man and, on the other, because plural wives were a way of manifesting a man's wealth, a kind of conspicuous consumption, in societies with few material possessions.

In traditional tribal societies, like that of Arab nomads, raiding caused the loss of men. Polygamy was a way of restoring protection to women. In societies that practiced levirate, Biblical Hebrews, for example, a man inherited his dead brother's widow(s) if she had no sons.

In Islam a man may have up to four wives except where monogamy is enforced by law, as in Turkey. The *Quran* specifically states that polygamous men must treat their wives fairly, housing them equally, spending equal amounts of time with and money on each woman. Men who cannot do this in good conscience are advised to avoid multiple wives.

Arab-American educator Audrey Shabbas writes: "Today, polygamy is illegal in many Arab countries... Several Arab countries permit polygamy under certain conditions such as the approval of the first wife, the approval of the judge, financial ability to support two wives, or a medical document certifying that the first wife cannot bear children. Today polygamous marriage represents less than 5% of all marriages and is rapidly disappearing as these countries become more developed and literate."

Pre-Islamic past: All religions rise out of a social context and help adherents deal with the problems posed by that context. Islam rose in the harsh and hostile environment of the Arabian steppes, among people who had left behind——for only about a century—a nomadic life. The harshness of the steppes meant that people could survive only by forming closely-knit groups, tribes made up clans, held together by kinship ties where the needs of the group were paramount and individualism had no place. These tribalists developed a highly masculine ethic based on – to quote Karen Armstrong—"courage in battle, patience and endurance in suffering, and a dedication to the chivalrous duties of avenging wrong done to the tribe." Women had no rights and were treated hardly better than animals. These people were polytheists. They did not believe in an afterlife, but observed rituals at shrines, the chief of which was the Ka'aba at Mecca. There circumambulating (walking around) the Ka'aba had long been practiced in pre-Islamic times as Muslims do today in the *hajj*.

About 500 CE, a tribe called the Quraysh settled in Mecca, an oasis watered by the Zamzam well at the terminus of a caravan route. The Quraysh was comprised of some 14 clans, of which the Hashim, Mohammad's clan was in decline. Nomadic life had been strictly egalitarian. After the Quraysh settled in Mecca, however, people became more individualistic, more capitalistic, more concerned with material wealth, sacrificing concern for fellow tribesmen. As a result, the tribe's social fabric began to fray. Out of the tensions created, Islam arose.

Prophets: Prophets of Islam are male human beings who are regarded by Muslims to be prophets chosen by God. All prophets preached the same message: to believe in one God, forswear idolatry, follow God's word, refrain from sin. These prophets all came to preach Islam and to tell of the coming of the final prophet and messenger of God: the Prophet Mohammad.

Muslims believe the first prophet was Adam. Others include Nuh (Noah), Ibrahim (Abraham), Musa (Moses) and Isa (Jesus) who is, as in Christianity, the result of a virgin birth. The last prophet was Mohammad.

Muslims believe that God has sent over 124,000 messengers all over the world, but select few prophets of which Mohammad was the last.

Although Jesus fits the definition of a prophet ("a religious teacher or leader regarded as, or claiming to be, divinely inspired" *Webster's New World Dictionary*), Christians do not generally regard him as a prophet. In fact, the *Bible* says that "a messenger" (John the Baptist) was sent to preach the imminence of Jesus' arrival.

Qibla: An Arabic word for the direction of the Ka'aba in Mecca, the direction that should be faced when a Muslim prays. Most mosques contain a niche in a wall that indicates the *qibla*.

After emigrating to Medina, Mohammad and his followers faced in the direction of Jerusalem when praying, following the practice of the Jews. According to a tradition, Abraham abandoned Hagar and his son Ishmael, seen as the father of the Arabs, in the valley of Mecca. Later when he visited them, said the tradition, Abraham and Ishmael built the Ka'aba. One Friday while he was leading prayers (and facing toward Jerusalem), Mohammad received a revelation from God that henceforth he and his followers should pray facing the direction of the Ka'aba. Mohammad instructed his followers to face in that direction. They obeyed and have been doing so ever since.

The larger significance of this action is that Islam relinquished any dependency on the prophecies of earlier traditions and declared itself a religion.

Quraysh: The Arab tribe from which Mohammad descended. Formerly nomadic, the Quraysh, comprised of 14 clans, had been settled in the oasis of Mecca for about two generations at the time of Mohammad's revelations. When Mohammad began to preach Islam, the Quraysh rejected him. Mohammad was forced to battle them over most of a decade before achieving an accommodation with them.

Quran: The holy book of Islam. It contains revelations to the Prophet Mohammad offering divine guidance and direction for mankind. Muslims regard the original text in Arabic, said to have indescribable beauty and impact, to be the word of God. They see the *Quran* as God's final revelation to mankind.

The word *Quran* (*Qu'ran* in Arabic) means "recitation." Mohammad recited these revelations through his interactions with the Angel Gabriel, which were memorized by his followers or written down on whatever material (bark, stone) was at hand.

The *Quran* has 114 chapters of varying lengths, each called a *sura*.

Translating the *Quran* in a way that suggests the power of the original has proved problematic. Since Arabic words can have a variety of meanings depending on context, accurate translation has been difficult.

The *Quran* can be read online. Check out the recommended resources section for a good translation.

Qutb, Sayyid: An influential Islamic fundamentalist and extremist thinker and a leading Muslim Brotherhood advocate in the 1950s and 1960s. Sayyid Qutb could recite the *Quran*, which he had memorized, at age ten. After a university education and a period as an Education Ministry functionary, Qutb spent about a year in the United States, becoming completely disenchanted with it.

Returning to his native Egypt, he became an influential figure in the Muslim Brotherhood. Following an attempt by members of the Brotherhood to assassinate Nasser, its leaders were jailed. Qutb was tortured. Later, however, he was given the freedom to write and produced an extensive commentary on the *Quran*. It won him a reputation as an important radical Islamist. In a manifesto called "Milestones" he wrote that "the Muslim community has been extinct for a few centuries." He wished to see its revival. Freed from jail for a short time, he was later rearrested and executed.

A notable disciple of Qutb is Ayman al-Zawahiri, who joined the Muslim Brotherhood at age 14 and is now Osama bin Laden's deputy in Al-Qaeda.

Qutb is included here because he did the same thing about America—hated it without understanding it—that we hope readers of this book will not do in judging Muslims, Arabs and Arab-Americans. Qutb visited in the United States for a bit more than a year (1948-1950).

In "The America I Have Seen" he inveighed against American materialism, racism, individual freedom, its blatant sexuality and its lack of support for the Palestinian cause. Of women he wrote: "The American girl is well acquainted with her body's seductive capacity. She knows it lies in the face, and in expressive eyes, and thirsty lips. She knows seductiveness lies in the round breasts, the full buttocks, and in the shapely thighs, sleek legs—and she shows all this and does not hide it."

The American man's interest in violent sports disgusted him. He wrote: "This primitiveness can be seen in the spectacle of the fans as they follow a game of football...or watch boxing matches or bloody, monstrous wrestling matches... This spectacle leaves no room for doubt as to the primitiveness of the feelings of those who are enamored with muscular strength and desire it."

Ramadan: Originally a summer month in the pre-Islamic Arab calendar. The present Islamic calendar is lunar. Ramadan is the ninth month in the Islamic calendar. Its year is 11 to 12 days shorter than the solar year. As a result, Ramadan migrates throughout the seasons.

In 623 Mohammad led a force of caravan raiders to Badr where he intended to ambush a caravan headed for Mecca. The Quraysh of Mecca learned of his intentions and assembled a large army to defeat him and avenge the death of a fellow tribesman killed in an earlier caravan raid. Despite being significantly outnumbered, Mohammad's force overcame the Quraysh. This victory occurred early in the month of Ramadan and was regarded as a *furqan*, a sign of salvation. To commemorate the *furqan* Mohammad decreed that Muslims would fast during the month of Ramadan. It was first observed in 625.

During Ramadan Muslims who are able to fast during the daylight hours, neither eating nor drinking and abstaining from sexual intercourse and any vices. This fasting is one of the five pillars of Islam. The first three days of the next month are spent in celebrations, the Festival of Breaking Fast or *Eid ul-Fitr*.

Notes Arab-American educator Audrey Shabbas: "Ramadan is not only a month of 'moral abstinence.' It also has the social value of creating new bonds of understanding between all classes of people. The fast, practiced by the rich and poor alike, reminds the more fortunate members of society of the pangs of hunger which the poor suffer. Ramadan is especially a month of charity."

Sharia law: *Sharia* means "path to the water source" and refers to the body of Islamic religious law. *Sharia* forms the legal framework within which the public and some private aspects of life are regulated for those living in a legal system based on Muslim principles. *Sharia* deals with many aspects of day-to-day life, including politics, economics, banking, business, contracts, family, sexuality, hygiene, and social issues.

Sharia is less a strictly codified set of laws and more a system of devising laws, based on the *Quran*, *hadith*, consensus, analogy and centuries of interpretation, precedent and debate. Just as the *Quran* draws on non-Arabic sources, *sharia* shows traces of Bedouin law, commercial law from Mecca, agrarian law from Medina as well as Roman and Jewish law.

Shia: (See page 33)

Succession: It's generally agreed that the problem of succession to leadership in a body politic often places that body in a position of extreme vulnerability, particularly when there are rivals for power. This is what happened at the time of Mohammad's death. The Sunni/Shia split resulted.

After Mohammad's death the claimants included Abu Bakr, a longtime ally of Mohammad who was also the father of one of the Prophet's cherished wives, Aisha; Umar, an early Qurayshi foe of Mohammad who converted to Islam with a suddenness similar to Saul of Tarsus' conversion to become Paul, also the father of Mohammad's wife Hafsah; and Ali, a cousin and ward of Mohammad, husband of the Prophet's daughter Fatimah and father of his only surviving grandsons Hasan and Husayn. Abu Bakr was elected, but the Shia (Shiat Ali or partisans for Ali) resented the choice, contending that Mohammad had designated Ali, his cousin and son-in-law, as successor. For the sake of unity Ali agreed to Abu Bakr's election, but Mohammad's kinsmen were never happy with this result.

Abu Bakr served as *caliph* for two years (632-634) and was succeeded by Umar who organized and extended the Arab empire and served until 644 when he was fatally knifed by a Persian slave. Six electors again denied Ali as caliph and chose Uthman, a convert to Islam, member of an aristocratic Qurayshi clan and a former son-in-law of Mohammad. Uthman was murdered in 656. With the support of the distressed people of Medina Ali at last succeeded to the position of *caliph*. However, Aisha, now an influential widow of Mohammad, along with others from Mecca, accused Ali of complicity in Uthman's murder. She left Arabia in order to raise an army against him.

Contention between the two parties was launched. Any possibility of harmonizing matters with the Shia was lost when Ali's surviving son Husayn, along with most of the men of his family, was ambushed and assassinated near Karbala (now in Iraq) in 680. Today, there are still some tensions in certain arenas such as Iraq and Lebanon, but most Muslims coexist as simply that, Muslims.

Suffism: Sometimes called *Tassawuf* in Arabic is a mystical dimension within Islam that focuses on personal piety. A follower of Suffism is a Sufi. Derived from the word *Suf* which means wool, Suffis literally mean "wearer of wool," which in ancient times was associated with spirituality. Whirling dervishes, sometimes called Suffi spinning, are an attractive visible aspect within Suffism. Practitioners twirl for long periods of time in meditative focus only on God.

Sunnah: "the way of the prophet". The word *Sunnah* in Sunni Islam means those religious actions that were instituted by Mohammad during the 23 years of his ministry. Muslims initially received these through consensus of the companions of Mohammad and later through generation-to-generation transmission. Some Sunni regard the *sunnah* as those religious actions initiated by Abraham and later only revived by Mohammad.

Sunni: (See page 33)

Tribalism: Human beings' most basic—and most lasting—social structure, tribalism exists in many parts of the world. Tribes, formed of clans or lineages, are primarily based on blood- or kinship-ties, real or mythical. Even if these ties become highly attenuated, an ethnic or cultural bond remains strong. Often it is the sense of a common ancestor (e.g. the children of Israel). The smaller the group, the harsher the environment in which the tribe finds itself, the stronger the degree of loyalty that members feel to one another and the more group survival and community needs have primacy over individual needs. Tribes and clans are often egalitarian, without significant distinctions between members. Some primitive tribes have little tradition of individual ownership.

In the harsh environment of the Arabian steppes in the seventh century and before, life prospects were uncertain. Food was scarce and the competition for the necessities of life was intense. Since there was little chance that individuals or individual families could survive by themselves, nomads formed themselves into clans and tribes. Tribal membership demanded a rigorous and unquestioning loyalty to group and a commitment to defend—and avenge—other tribesmen. Individualism could not be accommodated. The ethic was egalitarian and goods and possessions were shared out equally. The tribal chief had responsibilities to take care of weaker members of the group. If tribesmen had obligations and codes to tribal brothers, these codes did not apply to members outside the tribe. The nomads' ethic was virile, masculine. Women were not highly regarded, but their reproductive power was prized: their bodies could produce other men. Since there was little in the way of material wealth, accumulating wives was a way of manifesting success and prestige.

As nomads adopted a settled life in villages, adherence to tribal obligations lessened. But the knowledge of tribal ties and connections remained. Even stronger were—and are—ties between family members. Here blood is certainly thicker than water.

Umma: Arabic word originally referring to the "community of believers." More recently it has come to mean the entire Muslim world or in terms of pan-Arabism the entire Arab world.

When Mohammad and his followers left Mecca and emigrated to Medina, most Arabian societies were formed of tribes and clans held together by ties of blood and kinship. Medina was somewhat exceptional, an oasis inhabited by two previously nomadic Arab tribes as well as some Christian and some Jewish. Mohammed's emigrants represented a third Arab tribe along with a few non-Arabs.

Mohammad wished to convert Medina residents to Islam and so proclaimed an entirely new kind of "tribe," one based not on blood or kinship, but on religion: the *umma* or community of believers.

Today most Muslims regard themselves as belonging to the *umma*. It's a concept that ties all Muslims together and gives them a link to something beyond nationalism. Also beyond anything Christians feel for they do not regard all Christians as forming a like-minded community of believers.

Veiling women: (See Hijab)

Wahhabism: (See page 30)

—Thanks to Frederic Hunter for providing the "Glossary."

At a Glance
Arab Countries - Important Muslim Countries

Arab Countries
Algeria

A North African country more than 3 times the size of Texas, Algeria has 33 million people, almost all of whom are Arab and/or Berber Sunni Muslims. Officially a socialist republic, the government does not encourage citizens to participate in the political process. Opposing political parties are allowed, but parties based on religion or ethnic identity are outlawed. Relations with the US since 2001 have been warm, while those with France, which colonized the country, fluctuate. Algeria achieved independence in 1962. Its gas and oil reserves are the economy's mainstay, although they have done little to ameliorate the country's high unemployment.

Bahrain

A small collection of islands in the Persian Gulf with a population of only 700,000, Bahrain is a constitutional monarchy dominated by its king. The November 2006 elections brought a Shiite majority to power in Parliament, but it is unclear whether King Hamad will allow the Parliament more than nominal legislative powers, and sectarian confrontations have increased since the elections. Bahrain's economy rests on its oil production and refining, although it is attempting to diversify into transport and services—particularly financial and media. Like most Gulf states, Bahrain has warm relations with the United States and Europe, and in July 2008 sent its first Jewish female ambassador to the United States.

Comoros

The Comoros is a small grouping of islands off southern Africa with just under 700,000 people, almost all Sunni Muslim. The country is a republic based on the confederated union of the islands, with the presidency rotating every four years to the elected president of one of the Comoros' three main islands and a unicameral legislature. The country is extremely poor, with a weak economy that depends heavily on agriculture and remittances from citizens working abroad.

Djibouti

A small African country on the mouth of the Red Sea, Djibouti has 490,000 people, the majority Somali and Afar, and the vast majority of whom are Sunni Muslim. Djibouti is a republic with a president and a unicameral chamber of deputies. The governing party currently holds all seats. The country's economy is heavily service-based, relating to its position at the intersection of the Red Sea and the Gulf of Aden. It has little in the way of natural resources and few exports. The country enjoys warm relations with France and the United States, which has opened a military base there.

Egypt

One of the larger countries of the Arab world, Egypt has 79 million people, mostly Muslim with a Coptic Christian minority. A titular republic, Egypt has been ruled by "president for life" Hosni Mubarak for twenty-five years under a never-lifted emergency law. Limited influence accrues to the elected People's

Assembly. Religious and ethnic political parties are banned, and since 2001 the government has been increasingly intolerant of any expression of opposition. Nonetheless, the Muslim Brotherhood remains the state's most powerful opposition group, and civil society groups remain active. Egypt's economy is privatizing, and exports are growing, but for the average Egyptian the economic picture remains bleak. While European countries have pressured Egypt to respect human rights laws and accelerate reforms, the United States views the country as a strong ally in anti-terror initiatives and treats it warmly.

Iraq

A medium-large country in the heart of the Arab world, Iraq has roughly 27 million people, who are mostly Arab, with a sizeable Kurdish and smaller Turkoman and Assyrian minorities. They are almost all Muslim, with Shi'a approaching two-thirds of the population. Iraq is technically a democracy, although the deep instability there makes the elected government's capacity for governance questionable. Religious parties are actively involved in politics although they tend to join with other parties when contesting elections. Today Iraq's economy depends on oil revenues and aid from the United States government. Relations with other countries in and beyond the region are greatly conditioned by the ongoing US occupation.

Jordan

Jordan is a medium-small, land-locked country, with a population of just under 6 million, most of whom are Sunni Muslim and many of Palestinian origin. Relations between Jordan's Palestinian and Bedouin populations, and between Jordan and Israel, have dominated the country's political realm, which is a king-dominated constitutional monarchy with an appointed cabinet and a weak bicameral assembly. Political parties are allowed, although the strongest opposition movement is the Muslim Brotherhood, which has a separate political party. The economy is weak. Jordan has few natural resources and has struggled with efforts to develop private and semi-private industry. Jordan is a major United States aid recipient and has enjoyed particularly warm relations with the US since the outbreak of the second Gulf war in 1990.

Kuwait

A small Gulf state made famous by the 1990 Iraqi invasion, Kuwait's 2.5 million people are a mixture of Kuwaiti, Arab, and Asian ethnicities. Roughly four in five are Muslim, of whom three in 10 are Shi'a. The rest are Christian or other religions—with most of these foreign workers rather than citizens. The country is a constitutional emirate, with a unicameral assembly whose capacity for meaningful governing activity has varied over time. No political parties are allowed, although identifiable interest blocs exist and there is an increasing tendency towards "Islamist" political activism. Kuwait's economy is heavily dependent on its oil exports. The country has few natural resources and limited industry. Kuwait's relations with European states and the United States are warm. It hosts the United States' major military base and Iraq staging area.

Lebanon

A small Levantine state on the coast of the Mediterranean, Lebanon's nearly 4 million people are a mix of ethnicities and religions, the vast majority Arab and six in ten Muslim. A titular republic, Lebanon's complicated political system dictates the religion of the president, prime minister, and speaker of parliament, with the unicameral parliament's seats also allocated by religion. Political "parties" tend to be short-lived groupings around individual leaders rather than sustained institutions. Lebanon's economy is increasingly service and remittance based, with a growing tourist sector—although the viability of any sector is in question after the 2006 war between Israel and the Lebanon-based Hezbollah and the political infighting since then. Lebanon enjoys warm relations with European states and the United States, with France and the United States each aligning behind particular figures and political movements.

Libya

One of the largest Arab world countries, Libya's 5.9 million people are located in the middle of North Africa. Almost entirely Arab and/or Berber Sunni Muslims, Libyans live in an idiosyncratic socialist republic created by Revolutionary Leader-for-life Mu'ammar al-Qadhafi nearly forty years ago. No political parties are allowed and there is little organized opposition. Libya's economy depends heavily upon its oil revenues, which are substantial but rarely reach the ordinary citizen. The government's economic reforms are only beginning to have a visible effect. After years on the United States' blacklist, Libya is now enjoying warm relations with the United States, following its agreement in December 2003 to halt its development of nuclear weapons.

Mauritania

A medium-large country in northwest Africa, Mauritania has nearly 3.2 million people, all Muslim and evenly distributed among mixed Arab/Berber and African ethnicities. Although technically a republic, Mauritania is currently under the control of a military council, and opposition and Islamist parties are banned. The country's economy is heavily agriculture based, although its rich iron deposits comprise its largest export category. Mauritania's long-standing economic woes are expected to be offset by its entry into oil production, although this has been delayed by the country's political instability. While not particularly close to the United States, Mauritania has successfully cultivated good relations with Spain and other European states.

Morocco

The westernmost country in the Arab world, Morocco also has one of the largest populations: 33 million people, almost all Arab and/or Berber Muslims. The government is a king-dominated constitutional monarchy with a weak bicameral parliament. Although Morocco has well-known Islamists, the primary organized opposition comes from workers' groups. While agriculture, industry and services all share similar percentages of the country's GDP, the economy itself is extremely weak, and many people suffer from poverty and unemployment. Morocco enjoys warm relations with the United States as well as France and other European states.

Oman

Another small Gulf state, Oman's 2.5 million citizens are a mix of Arab, Indian, and South Asian ethnicities, three-quarters of whom are Ibadhi Muslim and the rest Sunni, Shi'a, and some minority religions. The country is under a strong monarchy, with a bicameral parliament that plays only a consulting role. While the current economy is supported by oil and gas production, the government has made substantive commitments to liberalization, training and hiring initiatives to strengthen the Omani workforce and develop local industry. Oman's moderate politics have enabled it to enjoy cordial relations with its neighbors as well as other countries.

Palestine

A territory that currently enjoys a degree of self-governance under severe military, political and economic restrictions, Palestine today is technically not a country but rather a zone under Israeli military control. Its land is split into two non-contiguous blocks, with the Palestinian Authority currently controlling Palestine's land in the West Bank and Hamas governing the Gaza Strip. There are approximately 2.4 million Palestinians in the West Bank, and 1.5 in the Gaza Strip. The total Palestinian population worldwide is estimated to be between 10 and 11 million people, over half of whom are stateless refugees with no legal citizenship in any country. The vast majority of Palestinians are Sunni Muslims, although there is a significant Christian minority as well as several smaller religious communities.

Qatar

One of the Gulf's smaller states, Qatar perches at the tip of Saudi Arabia. Its 900,000 inhabitants include roughly 450,000 resident workers, most from India, Pakistan, and the Philippines, who have residency but not citizenship. Approximately nine in ten Qataris are Sunni Muslims and follow the conservative Wahhabi interpretation found in Saudi Arabia, while the rest are Shi'a. The country is an emirate, with a consultative council for which elections were last held in 1970. Qatar's economic strength rests upon its oil and gas production, of which it has the world's third largest reserve. Qatar enjoys good relations with European states and close relations with the United States, which has two military bases there. Al Jazeera, the well-known Arabic satellite television network, is based in Qatar.

Saudi Arabia

This massive country physically dominates the Gulf, although its harsh climate supports a population of only 27 million, of whom nearly 5.6 million are foreign workers. Saudis are mostly Sunni and largely Arab, with small Shi'a and African/Asian ethnic and religious minorities, many of whom have faced discrimination. The government is a strong monarchy, with a consultative council whose members are appointed rather than elected. The Saud family dominates the top echelons of government, occupying the major ministry, cabinet, and diplomatic posts. This effectively curtails private political activity. The government's primary opposition comes from Islamist groups. Saudi Arabia's economy is heavily dependent upon revenues from its massive oil reserves, although it has made efforts to develop related industries. The country enjoys warm relations with the United States despite the latter's 2003 military withdrawal, caused by popular protests within the Kingdom.

Somalia

A medium-large country in Eastern Africa, Somalia's roughly 8.9 million people are Sunni Muslim, with more than four in five Somali and the rest Bantu and other ethnicities. The country has suffered from internal disorder for years and is currently under the control of a disputed transnational government. The economy is divided among several autonomous regions, and generally dependent upon agriculture and livestock exports, as well as remittances from those able to work abroad. Somalia and/or its sub-divisions do not have substantial relations with the United States. Most state relations in recent years have related to efforts to stabilize the country, which have been primarily led by the United Nations and Kenya, or to economic activity, in which the United Arab Emirates and Saudi Arabia, whose ban on Somali beef exports has had a noticeable economic impact, have played the largest roles.

Sudan

Africa's largest nation, Sudan has over 41 million people, the majority African, nearly 40% Arab and the rest a mixture. Seven in 10 are Sunni Muslim, with most of the rest animist and a small minority Christian. The country is currently under a two-party national unity government, although great instability remains throughout much of Sudan. Political parties are allowed, but they have limited ability to exert any degree of power in a country where the rule of law is so contested. The economy is stronger than the country's long civil war would suggest, thanks to oil exports, but deep poverty remains. Relations with Europe and the United States are primarily linked to aid, crisis intervention (especially related to the western region of Darfur), and anti-terrorism initiatives.

Syria

A medium-sized country in the heart of the Middle East, Syria has nearly 19 million people, mostly Arab but with measurable Kurdish and Armenian populations. Nearly three in four are Sunni Muslims, with minority Muslim sects, Christians, and a sprinkling of Jews comprising the remainder. Technically a republic, Syria is governed as a one-party state under a socialist but authoritarian regime led by the Baath Party. Certain political parties are approved, although parties with ethnic or religious identities and those that do not meet Ba'ath Party approval are not. Opposition comes from several outside organizations as well as Kurdish, Islamist, and democratic groups inside Syria. The country's economy depends greatly on its oil revenues, but in the face of the imminent depletion of its oil reserves, the government has begun accelerating economic reforms. These reforms often have proven more unpopular with local private enterprise than government officials, and reduction of government subsidies on basic commodities has forced the largely lower- and middle-class population to confront inflation and a rising cost of living. The country has very cool relations with the United States and France while Britain, Germany, Russia and other countries maintain closer ties.

Tunisia
A medium small North African country, Tunisia has just over 10 million people, almost all Arab and Muslim. A titular republic, Tunisia is effectively a one-party state dominated by a president who has been in power since 1987, and whose Neo-Destour party dominates the bicameral parliament. While the government has passed laws supporting women's rights and other progressive measures, it punishes criticism and represses opposition. The economy relies on several sectors, including strong contributions from tourism and industry. Although the country has no oil, it does have considerable ore deposits. Government-led privatization efforts continue, making the economic picture for the average Tunisian brighter than those of his or her neighbors. Tunisia enjoys warm relations with France and the United States, and generally good relations with its fellow OIC states.

United Arab Emirates (UAE)
Another small Gulf state, the United Arab Emirates' seven emirates have 2.6 million inhabitants, of whom perhaps 500,000 are Emirati. Arabs, Iranians, and South Asians make up the bulk of the population. The overwhelming majority of the population is Muslim, with a measurable Shi'a presence, and a very small Christian and Hindu minority. The Emirates are a federation, with the president chosen from Abu Dhabi and the prime minister/vice president from Dubai. There is a unicameral consultative council made up of members appointed by each emirate, but Dubai and Abu Dhabi dominate. The Emirati economy depends heavily on its oil and gas exports, which keep the country's GDP high. Real estate investments and developments in financial and other services are notable in Dubai and Abu Dhabi. The UAE enjoys warm relations with Europe and the United States, despite the failed 2006 Dubai Ports deal.

Yemen
A medium-large state on the southern side of the Gulf, Yemen has nearly 21.5 million people, most of whom are Arab, with African-Arab and South Asian mixes. The population is largely Muslim, with measurable Muslim minority Shafi'i and Zaydi communities, as well as small Christian, Jewish, and Hindu populations. A republic was established after the 1990 unification of north and south; the president has also been in power since then. A bicameral legislature began sitting in 2001, and political parties are allowed. Yemen's weak economy depends largely on its minimal oil revenues and remittances from abroad. Government efforts to modernize the economy have done little to combat widespread corruption, leading to popular discontent. Relations with the United States have improved since the war on terror began.

Important Countries and Regions in the Larger Muslim World
Afghanistan
A large, landlocked country located approximately at the center of Asia, Afghanistan has served as a natural crossroads between the East and the West and an ancient focal point of trade and migration. With a population estimated at 31.8 million, overwhelmingly Muslim but ethnically mixed, it has religious, ethno-linguistic, and geographic links with its neighbors: Pakistan in the south and east, Iran in the west, Turkmenistan, Uzbekistan and Tajikistan in the north, and China in the far northeast. During its long history, the land has seen various invaders and conquerors. Since the late 1970s Afghanistan has suffered

continuous and brutal civil war, as well as invasions from the Soviets in 1979 and from the 2001 US-led coalition following Al-Qaeda's September 2001 attacks.

The Taliban government, which took control following the Soviet withdrawal, permitted Al-Qaeda training camps on its territory. The US-led invasion toppled this government. In late 2001 the United Nations Security Council authorized the creation of an International Security Assistance Force, composed of NATO troops that are involved in assisting the government of President Hamid Karzai. In 2005 the United States and Afghanistan signed a strategic partnership agreement committing both nations to a long-term relationship. In the meantime, billions of dollars have also been provided by the international community as aid for the reconstruction of the country. Despite gains against the Taliban and Al-Qaeda, the Taliban remains a presence in the country. Based now in mountainous, tribal areas of northwest Pakistan, it has regained strength and represents a significant military challenge to the Karzai government and its allies.

Bangladesh

A country in South Asia, Bangladesh was established by the partition of Bengal and India in 1947, when the region became the eastern wing of the newly-formed Pakistan. However, a distance of 1000 miles separated this eastern wing from Pakistan's larger, western wing. Although both have majority-Muslim populations, large ethnic differences separated the two halves of Pakistan. Political and linguistic discrimination as well as economic neglect led to popular agitations against West Pakistan, culminating in the war for independence in 1971 and the establishment of Bangladesh. Among the most densely populated countries in the world, with a population of 150 million, Bangladesh has endured famines, cyclones, tsunamis, monsoon floods and widespread poverty, as well as political turmoil and several military coups. The government is a parliamentary democracy. However, political rule has been suspended under the emergency law imposed in January 2007. According to the World Bank's July 2005 Country Brief, the country has made significant progress in human development in the areas of literacy, gender parity in schooling and reduction of population growth—but it continues to face significant challenges.

Indonesia

Indonesia, located in Southeast Asia, is composed of 17,508 islands. With a population of over 222 million, it is the world's fourth most populous country and the most populous Muslim-majority nation. Officially, it is not an Islamic state, but a republic, with an elected parliament and president. Following three and a half centuries of Dutch colonial rule, Indonesia secured its independence after World War II. Its history has since been turbulent, with challenges posed by natural disasters, corruption, separatism, a democratization process, and periods of rapid economic change. The country has been held together, nonetheless, by a shared identity defined by a national language, a majority-Muslim population, and a history of colonialism and anti-colonial opposition. However, sectarian tensions and separatism have led to violent confrontations that have undermined political and economic stability. Despite its large population and densely populated regions, Indonesia has vast areas of wilderness which give it the world's second highest level of biodiversity.

Iran

The world's 18th-largest country in terms of surface area, Iran is located in Central Eurasia and stretches to the northeastern shore of the Persian Gulf. Historically known as Persia, Iran has a population of over 70 million, which is Aryan or Persian, with small Arab, Armenian and Azeri Turkish minorities. Home to one of the world's oldest continuous major civilizations, with historical and urban settlements dating back to 4000 BC, Iran today occupies an important position in international energy security and the world economy because of its large reserves of petroleum and natural gas. After centuries of foreign occupation and short-lived native dynasties, Iran was reunified as an independent state in 1501 by a dynasty promoting Shi'a Islam as the official religion. This marked one of the most important turning points in the history of Islam, as Iran is the only Muslim country with a majority-Shi'a population.

For most of its history, Iran's government was a monarchy ruled by a shah. The Pahlavis came to power in the early 1900s as military leaders with no royal blood, but they adopted the title shah as well. The Iranian revolution marked the country's transformation into an Islamic republic, which happened officially on April 1,1979.

Iran's political system comprises several intricately connected governing bodies. The Supreme Leader of Iran, Ayatollah Ali Khamenei, is responsible for delineation and supervision of the general policies of the Islamic Republic. Next in line is the current president, Mahmoud Ahmadinejad, elected in 2005 for a four-year term.

The United States' relationship with Iran has been strained since the Islamic revolution, due partly to a series of pre-Revolution events. In 1951 Dr. Mohammed Mossadegh was elected Iran's prime minister and became enormously popular by nationalizing Iran's oil reserves. In retaliation Britain embargoed Iranian oil and sought American help in overthrowing Mossadegh. This was provided by President Dwight D. Eisenhower. Mossadegh was deposed and arrested. With American support Shah Mohammad Reza Pahlavi rapidly modernized Iranian infrastructure, but simultaneously crushed all forms of political opposition with his intelligence agency, SAVAK.

Ayatollah Ruhollah Khomeini became an active critic of the shah, publicly denounced the government, and was sent into exile. His return to Iran in the late 1970s triggered the Iranian Revolution, a popular movement that overthrew the Shah and brought Khomeini to power. Part of this revolutionary fervor was directed against the United States, which gave refuge to the deposed shah and his family. In November 1979 Iranian students seized US embassy personnel and held 52 of them hostage for more than 14 months.

Iraqi leader Saddam Hussein decided to take advantage of what he perceived to be disorder in the wake of the Iranian Revolution and its unpopularity with Western governments. In September 1980 the Iraqi army invaded Iran at Khuzestan, a region with a substantial Arab population as well as rich oil fields. Although Saddam Hussein's army made early advances, Iranian forces managed to push it back into Iraq. Khomeini sought to export his Islamic revolution westward into Iraq, especially on the majority Shi'a Arabs. The war continued until 1988, when Khomeini, in his words, "drank the cup of poison" and accepted a truce mediated by the United Nations. The total Iranian casualties of the war were estimated to be between 500,000 and 1,000,000. Almost all relevant international agencies have confirmed that Saddam engaged in chemical warfare to blunt Iranian human wave attacks.

Today, Iran is developing nuclear capabilities for domestic energy consumption, a move that has alarmed the United States and many members of the international community. Tensions between the two countries remain.

Malaysia

A country in Southeast Asia with a population of over 25 million, Malaysia consists of two regions, Peninsular Malaysia and Malaysian Borneo, separated by the South China Sea. Today comprising 13 states and three federal territories, Malaysia did not exist as a unified state until 1963. At that time several former British-ruled territories on the Malay Peninsula, which had been independent since 1957, joined forces with the territories of Sabah and Sarawak on the northern coast of Borneo.

Malaysia is a constitutional monarchy, nominally headed by a paramount ruler and a bicameral Parliament consisting of a non-elected upper house and an elected lower house. All Peninsular Malaysian states have hereditary rulers except those of Melaka and Penang. Those two states, along with Sabah and Sarawak, have governors appointed by the government.

Malaysia is an ethnically mixed country, with Malays forming the majority of the population. There are also sizable Chinese and Indian communities, as well as a small minority of Arab descent. Islam is both the largest and the official religion. With Malaysia being one of the three countries controlling the strategic Strait of Malacca, international trade plays a large role in the country's economy.

Pakistan

A country in South Asia with a population of 165 million, Pakistan is the world's sixth most populous country and has the world's second-largest Muslim population after Indonesia. It is located in the home of one of the world's oldest civilizations, that of the Indus Valley, where civilized life dates back at least 5,000 years. The area has seen invasions from the Persians, Greeks, Scythians, Arabs, Afghans, and Turks. The British later dominated the region.

The separation in 1947 of British India into the Muslim state of Pakistan (with West and East sections) and largely Hindu India was never satisfactorily resolved, and India and Pakistan fought two wars (in 1947-48 and 1965) over the disputed Kashmir territory. A third war in 1971, in which India capitalized on the marginalization of Bengalis in Pakistani politics by fostering opposition to Islamabad's rule, resulted in East Pakistan becoming the separate nation of Bangladesh. In response to Indian nuclear weapons testing, Pakistan conducted its own tests in 1998. The dispute over the state of Kashmir is ongoing, but discussions and confidence-building measures have led to decreased tensions since 2002.

While officially an Islamic Republic with scheduled elections for Parliament and the presidency, an October 1999 military coup brought to power General Pervez Musharraf who named himself president in June, 2001. Following the 9/11 attacks Musharraf made Pakistan a crucial ally in the US war on terror despite considerable internal sympathy for Afghanistan's Taliban government. Musharraf's serving as both president and head of the army caused challenges from the Supreme Court, but he managed to be re-elected president in November 2007 by reconstituting the court and resigning his military post. The strains between Musharraf and his supporters and the ousted Supreme Court justices and theirs, in addition to Musharraf's support of the US war on terror, have caused concern in Washington about Pakistan's internal stability. After a return to civilian government in early-2008, Musharraf faced the likelihood of impeachment and in August resigned the presidency. Shortly afterwards the coalition governing the country fractured seeming to justify fears of the country's political instability. In addition, a resurgent Taliban has used Pakistan's northwestern frontier areas, over which the central government has limited control, to launch renewed attacks into Afghanistan.

Turkey

A Eurasian country stretching across the Anatolian peninsula in western Asia into the Balkan region of southeastern Europe, Turkey's strategic location astride two continents has given its culture a unique blend of Eastern and Western tradition. A powerful regional presence in the Eurasian landmass with strong historic, cultural and economic influence in the area between the European Union in the west and Central Asia in the east, Russia in the north and the Middle East in the south, Turkey possesses considerable strategic significance. It is a democratic, secular, unitary, constitutional republic whose political system was established in 1923 under the leadership of Mustafa Kemal Atatürk, following the fall of the Ottoman Empire in the aftermath of World War I. Atatürk set the country on a strongly secular course, introducing wide-ranging social, legal, and political reforms.

After a period of one-party rule, the 1950 election victory of the opposition Democratic Party led to a peaceful transfer of power. Turkish democracy has been interrupted by intermittent military coups (1960, 1971, 1980), which in each case eventually resulted in a return of political power to civilians. In 1997, the military helped engineer the ouster of the then Islamic-oriented government. Questions about the military's intentions of enforcing the country's secular orientation arose in mid-2007 when the present government led by the Islamic-leaning Justice and Development Party of Prime Minister Recep Tayyip Erdogan sought to elect its candidate Abdullaah Gul as president and succeeded in doing so without military intervention.

Turkey is a member of NATO and is currently seeking membership in the European Union. A separatist insurgency begun in 1984 by the Kurdistan Workers' Party (PKK) has dominated the military's attention, claiming more than 30,000 lives. After the capture of the group's leader in 1999, the insurgents largely withdrew to northern Iraq. To resist incursions from this area, Turkey sent troops into northern Iraq in the spring of 2008.

"Kurdistan"

Not a country at all, but rather the dream of a country cherished by the Kurdish people who hoped that the end of the Ottoman Empire would give them a nation-state. Kurds live on an extensive plateau and mountainous area in the Middle East. It covers large parts of eastern Turkey, northern Iraq, northwestern Iran and smaller parts of northern Syria and Armenia. The national aspirations of the Kurds (estimated population: 25 to 30 million) have complicated the politics of those countries with large Kurdish populations.

The Kurds of northern Iraq have created a region which has gained official recognition internationally as an autonomous federal entity.

Today the majority of Kurds are Muslim, although their interpretation of Muslim faith and practice frequently differs from Arab and other forms. Their faith tends to be less assertive than that of Muslims in other areas. For example, Kurdish women do not cover their faces, their hijab is less restrictive, and they do not wear full-cover garments such as the Iranian chador or Arabic abaya.

The Sahel Region of Africa

The Sahel is a semi-arid tropical savanna ecoregion in Africa, which forms the transition between the Sahara desert to the north and the more fertile region to the south. It runs 2,400 miles from the Atlantic Ocean in the west to the Red Sea in the east, in a belt that varies from several hundred to a thousand kilometers in width. The countries of the Sahel include Senegal, Mauritania, Mali, Burkina Faso, Niger, Nigeria, Chad, and Sudan. Over the history of Africa the region has been home to some of the most advanced kingdoms benefiting from trade across the desert. Muslim traders brought Islam to the region. Significant portions of the population are now Muslim.

From the Caucasus across the Steppes of Central Asia

Muslim populations inhabit the vast area that lies between the Caucasus mountains and the Uighur areas of western China. In ancient times the Great Steppe of Central Asia, a valuable prize for invaders, including Attila the Hun, Genghis Khan and Tamerlane, was crossed by the Silk Road, the trade route that linked western Europe to China. Following the implosion of the Soviet Union, nation-states were created in this area: Kazakhstan, Turkmenistan. Uzbekistan, Kyrgystan, Tajikistan. They seem remote to us, but comprise a part of the Muslim World.

The Muslim Diaspora

In recent years the world has witnessed large migrations of people from the less developed parts of the world to those developed parts which offer the hope of jobs, education and higher standards of living. Large groups of Muslims have been part of these migrations: Pakistanis to England; Turks to Germany; Tunisians, Algerians, and Moroccans to France; Moroccans to Spain and the Netherlands. Earlier migrations in particular brought Syrians to the United States and Lebanese throughout the world. Accommodating these immigrants has severely challenged the receiving societies, especially when Muslim immigrants wished to take advantage of jobs and welfare benefits without any desire to change their lifeways. Dashed expectations, bitterness at the injustices and humiliation of prejudice and cultural misunderstanding have produced fertile ground for recruiting disaffected young Muslims as terrorists. Fortunately, most Arab and Muslim immigrants to the United States have been able to integrate into the larger population, enjoying relatively high standards of living relative to the population as a whole. As a result they have tended to minimize acts of racism and discrimination, not wanting to jeopardize their security by criticizing their adopted country.

—Thanks to Andrea Stanton for providing "At a Glance."

Timelines

Iran

Iran is the site of some of the oldest of the ancient civilizations, those of the Assyrians, the Babylonians, the Medes, and the Persians. Prior to the 1900s Iran's centuries-old history is a story of various groups conquering the territory and establishing dynasties which are subsequently replaced by later dynasties. Notable among the conquering hordes were the Seljuk Turks in 1045; Mongols first under Genghis Khan in 1219 and later under his grandson Hulagu Khan in 1258; then the Tartar army of Tamburlain the Great in 1384.

An event that still shapes Iran today occurred around 1500. At about this time a ruler called Ismail gained supremacy over most of Iran, establishing the Safavid dynasty. Claiming descent from Ali, the father of Shiism, and thus becoming a legitimate imam-ruler, Ismail capitalized on religious, economic and political factors to firmly implant Shia Islam in Iran. In doing this, he shaped an essential element of what has become modern Iran.

Again invasions. In 1805 Iran loses the first of two wars with Russia, giving up Armenia, Georgia, and Azerbaijan which had been part of the Iranian Empire since the Safavids. During most of the 19th century Iran falls increasingly victim to commercial and political penetration from the West. The British wanting to protect their interests in India and Russia wanting hegemony over its southern flank became rivals for influence.

1872 Shah Nasir ed-Din gives British Baron Julius de Reuter of news-agency fame, exclusive rights over Iran's economy in trade for a small down payment and royalty payments. British Foreign Secretary, Lord Curzon, describes this takeover as "the most complete and extraordinary surrender of the entire industrial resources of a kingdom into foreign hands that has probably ever been dreamt of, much less accomplished, in history."

1896 Shah Nasir is assassinated. His son, Muzaffar al-Din, continues his father's habits of corruption.

1914 Iran remains neutral during the World War I. She is occupied at various times by troops from Russia, Turkey, and Britain.

1921 Reza Khan, a domineering man from the Elborz mountains, leads three thousand Iranian Cossack troops into Tehran and arrests the entire Iranian cabinet.

1922 Ostensibly in control of the country, Reza Khan drives out the Bolsheviks.

1923 Reza Khan subdues the Kurds in the northwest.

1925 On October 31 the mullahs summon Reza Khan to Qom, the country's holiest city of Shia Islam, and encourage him to become Shah, an offer he accepts. Reza Khan becomes Reza Shah, establishing the Pahlavi Dynasty.

1936 In response to Reza Shah's curtailment of Shia Islam, protesters gather before the Grand Mosque in Mashdad and are gunned down by the Shah's soldiers.

1941 Having aligned himself with Hitler, Reza Shah is deposed by occupying British and Russian troops who seek to use Iran's national railway as a vital supply line to Russia. The British install Reza Shah's playboy son, Mohammed Reza, on the throne.

1949 Mohammed Reza survives an assassination attempt.

1950 Winston Churchill describes Iranian oil as "a prize from fairyland beyond our wildest dreams." Receipts for the sale of Iranian oil pour into the British Treasury from the tax on the British controlled Anglo-Iranian Oil Company (AIOC).

1951 Opponents of the AIOC form the National Front, the first popular party in Iran's history. At 70, Iranian statesman Mohammad Mossadeq, a longtime opponent of the Pahlavi family, is appointed its leader. On March 15 Mossadeq becomes Prime Minister of Iran and calls for complete nationalization of the AIOC. In June Britain recalls its embassy staff and set up a naval blockade of oil exports from Iran.

1952 Newly-elected president Dwight Eisenhower agrees to a CIA plan to oust Mossadeq. Code-named Operation Ajax.

1953 After a first failed coup, a CIA team under leadership of Kermit Roosevelt successfully engineers a covert operation in August that results in the fall of Mossadeq and the triumphant return of Mohammad Reza Shah from exile in Rome. Seemingly a victory for Anglo-American policy, this coup against an elected civil government critically affects future Iranian-American relations by re-installing the unpopular Shah Mohammad Reza Pahlavi, who institutes a pro-Western dictatorship. Originally viewed as a triumph of covert action), Operation Ajax is now considered a terrible legacy. A quarter century after the event Kermit Roosevelt authored Countercoup. It claimed that CIA staged the coup to prevent a takeover of power by the Iranian Communist Party (Tudeh) closely backed by the Soviet Union.

1954 Mohammad Reza Shah embarks on various American-backed reforms that include government reorganization, privatization, and emancipation of women.

1956 Mahmoud Ahmadinejad, one of seven children of a blacksmith, is born in Garmsar near Tehran.

1963 Reza Shah takes large land holdings from the aristocracy and the clerics and distributes them to the peasants. Poor food production ensues.

1970 The world oil crisis gives the Shah a cash bonanza, enabling him and his family to have an extravagant life-style. Iran's national security police SAVAK, termed the country's "most hated and feared institution," cracks down on ordinary citizens.

1977 Mahmoud Ahmadinejad gains his PhD in engineering at the prestigious University of Science and Technology in Tehran.

1978 An exiled Iranian cleric named Ayatollah Ruhollah Khomeini calls for an Islamic Revolution and the overthrow of the Shah. On September 8, known as "Black Friday," the Shah's army randomly fires into a crowd of demonstrators in Tehran, killing scores.

1979 January 16. Mohammed Reza, Iran's last Shah, flees the country. On February 1 Ayatollah Khomeini returns to Iran from his exile in Paris. He forms a new government called The Islamic Republic of Iran. On November 4 a large group of Iranian students breaks into the American embassy in Tehran and seizes 52 hostages.

1980 September 22. Amid Iranian civil discord, Iraq's leader, Saddam Hussein, launches a surprise military attack into Iran.

1981 January 20. After 444 days in captivity, highlighted by a failed Carter Administration rescue mission, the American hostages are released. Ronald Reagan is sworn into office on the same day.

1983 The US removes Iraq from the "terrorist list" and adds Iran to it. In addition, America provides Iraq with satellite images of Iranian military positions.

1985 Two members of America's National Security Council, John Poindexter and Oliver North, orchestrate a deal whereby America sells arms to Iran in exchange for Iranian help to free American hostages in Lebanon and cash. $48 million of this cash gets sent to the Nicaraguan Contras fighting to unseat the leftist Sandinista government there. During the Iran-Iraq war American aid went to both parties in the conflict.

1988 Khomeini agrees to a UN sponsored ceasefire to end the war. Three quarters of a million Iranians die in eight years of fighting.

1989 Khomeini dies. Iran nominates Ali Khameni as Supreme Leader; Ali Rafsanjani is chosen President.

1994 Having joined the Revolutionary Guard during the Iran-Iraq War, Mahmoud Ahmadinejad becomes Governor of Ardaibil province and impresses hardliners in the country with his ultra-conservative credentials.

1997 Elections. Moderate candidate Mohammad Khatami wins a surprise victory over hardliners for President. A "Tehran Spring" ensues.

2001 Khatami is reelected with 78 percent of the vote. Even so, hardliners in the Guardian Council veto nearly half of the reforms introduced by the Khatami government.

2003 Ahmadinejad becomes mayor of Tehran.

2004 Elections. The Guardian Council bans over 2,000 reformist candidates from standing. Conservatives sweep back into power.

2005 Ahmadinejad is elected President. In October Ahmadinejad tells cheering crowds in Tehran that "Israel should be wiped off the map."

2006 July. The UN Security Council passes a resolution which gives Iran 30 days to halt uranium enrichment.

2006 September. Ahmadinejad arrives in New York to address the United Nations. From his speech: "The question needs to be asked: if the governments of the United States and the United Kingdom, who are permanent members of the Security Council, commit aggression, occupation, and violations of international law, which of the organs of the UN can take them to account?"

2007 February. President Bush accuses Iran of undermining security in Iraq by providing improvised explosive devices to combatants of American troops inside Iraq.

2007 April. Ahmadinejad defiantly proclaims that Iran will press forward with its nuclear program.

Iraq

1914 World War I breaks out in July, pitting, among others, Britain against Germany. In October the Ottoman Empire which ruled Greater Syria, a part of which would become Iraq, allies itself with Germany and the other Central Powers. Within weeks British forces invade and occupy Basra, Abadan (on the Persian side of the Tigris), and Nasiriya.

1916 April. 13,000 British and Indian soldiers surrender to Turkish and German forces at Kut after a five month siege.

1916 June. Sharif Hussein of Mecca calls on the Arabs to revolt against the Ottoman Turks and their German allies, putting his faith in Britain promise of a great Arab kingdom.

1916 Negotiations between the French and British lead to the Sykes-Picot Agreement in which the two countries plan to divide up the Ottoman territories between them, creating respective zones of influence.

1916 British General Allenby allows a young intelligence officer named T. E. Lawrence to assist Sharif Hussein's son, Faisal, in leading Arab forces against the Turks.

1917 March. Under the leadership of General Stanley Maude, British forces navigate up the Tigris and take Baghdad by surprise.

1918 November. Armistice with Turkey is signed. The British occupy Mosul, violating the Sykes-Picot agreement in which the territory of Mosul has been reserved for the French.

1919 February. The French agree to the continued British occupation of Mosul on the condition that France be allowed to participate in oil exploration in the area.

1919 May. Mahmud, a Kurdish sheik, proclaims himself "King of Kurdistan" and takes Sulaimaniya. British forces successfully quell his revolt.

1920 April. A conference at San Remo, Italy, assigns a Mandate for all of Iraq to the British.

1920 July. Euphrates tribesmen rise up and revolt against the British. Pending reinforcements, the British suffer 2,000 casualties in fighting that lasts through October. Eventually prevail.

1921 March. Led by British Colonial Secretary Winston S. Churchill, a conference in Cairo decides that Prince Faisal, who fought with T.E. Lawrence in the Arab Revolt, should be the King of Iraq. This decision is supported by T. E. Lawrence and Gertrude Bell, a British writer and Arabist, an unsung force behind the success of the Arab revolt in World War I, but it is kept private so that Faisal does not appear to be the puppet of the British.

1921 June. Faisal arrives in Baghdad. A referendum gives the new king 96 percent of the vote.

1921 August. Faisal is crowned King of Iraq in the courtyard of the Serai.

1922 Iraqi nationalists foment unrest. The British send High Commissioner Percy Cox to wield power behind the weakening Faisal.

1922 October. The British and the government of Iraq sign the Anglo-Iraqi Treaty in which Iraq is permitted to open an embassy in London, but Britain is to represent Iraq elsewhere in the world.

1924 March. Constituent Assembly opens.

1925 March. Iraqi government signs Turkish Petroleum Company oil concession.

1925 December. League of Nations decides that Mosul should remain part of Iraq.

1927 An oil field of unprecedented size is discovered near Kirkuk.

1928 The Iraq Petroleum Company is constituted. France creates the Compagnie Francaise des Petroles and obtains 23.75 percent of future profits.

1930 June. A new Anglo-Iraqi Treaty is signed promising Iraqi independence.

1932 October. The League of Nations admits Iraq, thus ending the British Mandate.

1932 The Iraqi Army successfully crushes uprisings by the Kurds and the Assyrians who have settled in northern Iraq.

1933 September. King Faisal dies mysteriously in a Swiss hospital. He is succeeded by his son, Ghazi.

1934 Although educated in England, Ghazi bears a deep antipathy towards the British. Ghazi is forced to repress revolts by the Kurds and the Shi'ites.

1935 January. Official opening of Kirkuk-Mediterranean pipeline.

1936 October. General Bakr Sidqi, of Kurdish origin, leads a coup and becomes head of the army. King Ghazi allows the coup to unfold.

1937 August. Bakr Sidqi is assassinated.

1939 April. King Ghazi, whose sympathies for Germany and personal desire to absorb Kuwait into the Iraqi kingdom are well known, dies in a suspicious car accident. His son Faisal II, four at the time, ascends to the throne under the regency of Prince 'Abd al-Ilah.

1941 April. Rashid 'Ali al-Kailani engineers a military coup d'etat and forms a "Government of National Defense." Prince 'Abd al-Ilah flees Baghdad.

1941 May. British troops march on Baghdad. The government of Rashid 'Ali al-Kailani collapses.

1941 June. Prince 'Abd al-Ilah, the regent, returns from exile.

1945 The Arab Socialist Ba'ath Party is founded in Damascus to work in both Iraq and Syria as the original secular Arab nationalist movement to combat Western colonial rule.

1948 January. A new Anglo-Iraqi Treaty is signed in Portsmouth but is later abandoned because of mass protests in Baghdad.

1948 May. Jews issue Declaration of the Establishment of the State of Israel. Arabs reject new state. Six Arab nations—Syria, Jordan, Egypt, Iran, Lebanon, and Saudi Arabia—invade Israel on May 15. The UN does not condemn the war and encourages Arabs to leave Palestine. Israeli Defense Forces secure a border for the new country.

1948 May. Iraq sends an expeditionary force to Palestine (Israel).

1949 February. Iraqi army withdraws from Palestine.

1952 February. The Iraqi government agrees to a 50-50 share of profits with the Iraq Petroleum Company (IPC).

1952 November. Demonstrations erupt in Baghdad, known as "al-Intifada" (the uprising). It expresses dissatisfaction with the pro-British government of Nuri Said.

1953 May. King Faisal II, now 18, is enthroned, ending the regency.

1955 February. The United States sponsors the Baghdad Pact, an anti-communist alliance of certain countries near the Soviet Union.

1956 October. A force made up of British, French, and Israeli troops invade Egypt to maintain control of the Suez Canal. Riots ensue in Baghdad, Mosul, and Najaf.

1958 February. Egypt and Syria form the United Arab Republic; Jordan and Iraq form the Arab Union.

1958 July. The Hashemite monarchy is overthrown by army units headed by Free Officers, a fairly small group of military men who have been meeting secretly. The royal family and Nuri Said are executed. Brigadier 'Abd al-Karim Qasim becomes prime minister, defense minister, and commander in chief.

1958 September. Agrarian Reform Law is passed.

1959 October. Mustafa Barzani asserts his control of Kurdistan Democratic Party (KDP).

1959 December. The government of Qasim withdraws from the Baghdad Pact and establishes relations with socialist countries.

1961 June. Kuwait achieves independence. Qasim demands its integration into Iraq. To prevent this integration, Great Britain sends troops to Kuwait.

1961 July. Barzani demands substantial autonomy for the Kurdish region.

1961 September. Hostilities erupt between Barzani's forces and the Iraqi army.

1963 February. Ba'ath Party and Arab nationalist military officers engineer a successful coup d'etat. Qasim and his colleagues are killed.

1963 April. With the help of the CIA, the Ba'ath Party begins arresting thousands of communists and leftists, many of whom are tortured and executed.

1963 October. Factional disputes divide Ba'ath Party.

1963 November. President 'Abd al-Salam 'Arif and his military allies eject the Ba'athists from power.

1964 July. The 'Arif government nationalizes all banks, insurance companies, and large industrial firms.

1964 October. Kurdish autonomy talks break down. Fighting resumes in the area.

1965 April. A full scale war between the Iraqi and Kurdish forces erupts in Kurdistan.

1966 April. President 'Abd al-Salam 'Arif dies in a helicopter crash and is succeeded by his brother, 'Abd al-Rahman 'Arif.

1966 July. Barzani accepts Iraq's twelve-point plan on Kurdish autonomy.

1967 June. Arab forces attack Israel. Iraq sends a handful of troops to Jordan.

1968 July. The government of 'Abd al-Rahman 'Arif is overthown by Ahmad Hassan al-Bakr and a group of Ba'ath Party militants including Saddam Hussein and his brother, Barzan. 'Arif is sent into exile. Ahmad Hassan al-Bakr becomes president. A further coup organized by al-Bakr ousts non-Ba'athist allies.

1968 September. Al-Bakr continues to consolidate power with the help of Saddam Hussein. Saddam ably administers the Ba'ath militia and the state's security apparatus. Al-Bakr and Saddam Hussein issue the regime's first constitution, declare Islam to be the state religion, socialism its economic system, and the Revolutionary Command Council (RCC) the supreme political authority.

1969 June. The government forges an agreement with the USSR on Soviet assistance in exploiting Iraqi oil fields The regime also expresses its opposition to Britain (first and foremost), the United States, and its Middle East allies, Israel and Iran.

1969 November. Saddam Hussein is appointed to the ruling Revolutionary Command Council and becomes its vice-chairman.

1970 March. The regime reaches an agreement with Barzani and drafts a manifesto recognizing Kurdish nationality and language and establishing an autonomous region for the Kurds in northern Iraq.

1971 November. Relations between Iraq and Iran are severed.

1972 April. Iraq and the Soviet Union sign a Treaty of Friendship and Cooperation.

1972 June. The regime nationalizes the Iraq Petroleum Company.

1972 November. In spite of the earlier agreements, fighting resumes in northern Kurdistan.

1973 July. Al-Bakr and Saddam Hussein fend off a coup and reinforce their hold over Iraq.

1974 March. An Autonomy Law is announced for the Kurdish area despite continued continuing disagreements between the government and the Kurdish Democratic Party (KDP). Widespread fighting wages throughout Kurdistan.

1975 March. Saddam Hussein and the Shah of Iran reach an agreement whereby the Shah ends Iranian assistance to the KDP. The Kurdish revolt collapses and splits into two factions, the KDP-Provisional Leadership led by Masoud Barzani and the Patriotic Union of Kurdistan (PUK) led by Jalal Talabani.

1977 February. Nearly 30,000 Iraqis protest the government in what would be called the Safar "intifada." This event spurs the early activities of the Dawa Party. It supports Islamicization and Shia interests in contrast to the secular and Sunni orientation of the Ba'ath.

1978 November. The Baghdad Summit follows the Camp David accords in which Iraq bids for Arab leadership.

1979 July. In bad health, President al-Bakr announces his resignation and officially bestows supreme executive authority upon Saddam Hussein. Sworn in as president, Saddam begins to purge the Ba'ath Party to consolidate his power.

1979 January 16. In Iran Mohammed Reza, the country's last Shah, flees the country. On February 1 Ayatollah Ruhollah Khomeini returns to Iran from his exile in Paris. He forms a new government called The Islamic Republic of Iran. By August success of the Iranian revolution encourages Shia Islamist organizations to launch more active campaigns in Iraq.

1979 November. The KDP Congress elects Masoud Barzani as chairman and calls for continuing armed struggle inside Iraq.

1980 March. The government of Iraq passes a law for election of National Assembly.

1980 April. Ayatollah al-Sadr, a prominent Shia religious leader, and his sister are executed in Baghdad. Over 40,000 Shia Iraqis are expelled to Iran.

1980 September. Iraqi forces invade Iran.

1981 Fierce fighting in the Iran-Iraq war. Iraq captures Iranian territory.

1982 June. Iran's counteroffensive recaptures most of its territory.

1982 July. Ninth Regional Congress of the Ba'ath Party reasserts Saddam's absolute control over the country.

1982 October. Former president Ahmad Hasan al-Bakr dies.

1984 Amid escalation of the war in the waters of the Gulf, Iraq re-established diplomatic relations with the United States.

1985 The United States provides Iraq with military intelligence useful in its conflict with Iran.

1986 Using its vaster number of troops, Iran recaptures al-Faw peninsula.

1987 Iraqi government campaigns against the KDP and the PUK in Kurdistan.

1988 February. "Al-Anfal," a genocidal campaign against Kurds led by the Iraqi regime of Saddam Hussein, begins in Kurdistan.

1988 July. Iran accepts UN cease-fire resolution. Iran-Iraq war comes to an end.

1990 May. Kuwait refuses to cancel the vast Iraqi debt incurred with the war against Iran and keeps oil prices low by dumping large quantities of oil on the open market.

1990 June. Saddam requests Kuwait to letup on its economic hostilities towards his country. Kuwait refuses.

1990 July. Iraq deputy prime minister Tariq Aziz sends a letter to the UN complaining that Kuwait and the United Arab Emirates are flooding the market with oil in violation of OPEC production quotas.

1990 July. Saddam calls a meeting with US Ambassador April Glaspie during which Glaspie tell Saddam that the United States has "no opinion" about Arab conflicts like "the border disagreement with Kuwait." Saddam considers this a tacit reassurance that the US will not stand in his way. Glaspie is recalled.

1990 August. Saddam Hussein launches a military offensive against Kuwait. UN imposes sanctions and a total trade embargo against Iraq with only Cuba and Yemen abstaining.

1990 November. The United States pressures the UN Security Council to pass Resolution 678 authorizing the use of force to remove Iraqi troops from Kuwait.

1991 January. President George H.W. Bush forms a coalition of countries to support and pay for hostilities with Iraq. "Operation Desert Storm" begins with a massive air bombardment of Iraqi forces in Kuwait followed by a swift and seemingly successful ground campaign.

1991 April. UN Security Council Resolution 687 demands Iraqi recognition of Kuwait and destruction of all Iraq's non-conventional weapons. Resolution 688 calls on the Iraqi government to cease oppressing its own people. Kurdistan comes under allied protection.

1991 May. A weapons inspection team of the United Nations Special Commission on Disarmament (UNSCOM) visits Iraq.

1991 October. Iraqi armed forces blockade Kurdistan.

1992 May. Elections in the Kurdistan result in an equal split of power between the KDP and the PUK.

1993 May. UN Security Council approves demarcation of Iraq-Kuwait border in Kuwait's favor.

1993 June. US launches missile strike on the headquarters of Iraqi intelligence services in Baghdad in reprisal for an Iraqi plot to kill President Bush during his visit to Kuwait.

1994 May. Fighting erupts between the KDP and the PUK in Kurdistan.

1994 November. Iraq recognizes Kuwait as an independent state.

1996 February. Iraq accepts UN Security Council Resolution 986 allowing limited Iraqi oil sales for the purchase of vital civilian supplies.

1996 August. Iraqi government forces enter Kurdish region at the behest of the KDP and help capture Arbil from the PUK. The United States responds by extending the southern no-fly zone north to the 33rd parallel.

1996 December. Iraqi oil flows again through pipeline to Turkey.

1998 September. Washington Agreement ends fighting between KDP and PUK.

1998 November. The US Congress passes the Iraq Liberation Act, statement of policy calling for regime change in Iraq.

1998 December. US commences Operation Desert Fox, an air bombardment of country in retaliation for Iraq's failure to cooperate with weapons inspection.

1999 January. American and British planes begin a year-long, and what proves to be nearly a weekly-attack, on Iraqi planes challenging the southern and northern no-fly zones.

2000 March. Iraq defies UN ban on civil air flights and allows flights of pilgrims to Mecca.

2000 September. The Baghdad airport reopens to allow much-publicized flights to arrive from Russia, France, and Syria.

2001 January. Leaders of the KDP and the PUK meet for the first time in three years.

2001 June. The US and UK try and fail to persuade the UN Security Council to adopt a "smart sanctions" resolution.

2001 September. Nineteen hijackers, later affiliated with al-Queda, commandeer four American commercials airliners and crash three into pre-planned American targets; a fourth crash lands into the ground. Influential neoconservative Bush Administration officials suspect an Iraqi role in the attacks and urge military action of effect regime change there.

2001 November. UN Security Council Resolution 1382 renews six-month "oil for food" arrangement.

2002 January. US President George W. Bush identifies Iraq, Iran, and North Korea as an "axis of evil."

2002 March. Iraq reconciles with Saudi Arabia at Arab League Summit in Beirut.

2002 June. President Bush and his staff put the finishing touches on their plans to invade Iraq. Suspicions that the Iraq regime possesses weapons of mass destruction (WMD) is offered as a reason for pre-emptive war.

2002 October. US Congress passes a resolution authorizing use of military force against Iraq. Senator Joseph Biden raises questions as to whether a group of Iraqi "James Madisons" will suddenly emerge to bring democracy to that country.

2003 February. US and UK try and fail to obtain UN Security Council resolutions explicitly authorizing the use of force against Iraq.

2003 March. Operation Iraq Freedom is launched by the US, the UK, and other countries, known as the coalition of the willing, to overthrow Saddam Hussein. Saddam calls the pending hostilities "the mother of all battles."

2003 April. Basra, Baghdad, and Mosul fall to allied forces. Widespread looting results.

2003 May. Paul Bremer assumes civil control, heading the Coalition Provisional Authority (CPA).

2003 May. UN Security Council Resolution 1483 grants the US and UK power to govern Iraq and ends sanctions. The Ba'ath Party is dissolved. Iraqi armed forces are disbanded.

2003 July. CPA sets up Iraqi Governing Council with limited powers; US military command admits it is facing a serious insurgency.

2003 August. UN headquarters in Baghdad is blown up. The UN withdraws its presence from Iraq. Sectarian violence erupts across the country.

2003 December. American forces capture Saddam hiding in a hole in the ground and display a video in which the former dictator is being de-loused.

2004 March. The Iraqi Governing Council approves a draft provisional constitution.

2004 April. Fierce fighting erupts between US forces and insurgents in Fallujah; Mahdy Army forces clash in Najaf.

2004 June. CPA and IGC are dissolved and sovereignty is handed to an interim government headed by prime minister Ayad 'Allawi.

2004 November. US and Iraqi forces launch major offensive against insurgents in Fallujah.

2005 January. General elections are held for the transitional national assembly that is charged with drafting new constitution.

2005 April. Jalal Talabani elected president of Iraq.

2005 October. Constitutional plebiscite approves constitution by 78 percent.

2005 November. Trial of Saddam and his colleagues begins.

2006 February. Al-Askariyya mosque in Samarra is blown to bits, presumably by Al-Qaeda in Iraq. This action inflames sectarian violence.

2006 May. Nuri al-Maliki forms a new Iraqi government.

2006 October. National assembly passes law allowing groups of provinces to form federal states.

2006 Saddam Hussein is executed by hanging. The death toll of US forces reaches over 3,000.

2007 February. US sends 28,000 extra troops, described as "the surge," to implement new security plan for Baghdad.

Palestine / Israel

1908 "Young Turks" establish a constitutional government.

1911 Tenth Zionist Congress adopts what will be known as "synthetic" trend of Zionism, a movement expounded by Chaim Weizman.

1914 August. World War I begins.

1914 Turkey enters hostilities on the side of Germany and against Russia. Turks in Palestine start a "holy crusade" against the Russian czar and his subjects with the result that Russian Jews flee Palestine, mostly to the United States. Among these is Ben-Gurion.

1914 Jemal Pasha, the local Turkish ruler in Palestine, fears that Jews there might form a fifth column working with the British or the French. He orders that Jews be deported from Palestine to Syria, Jaffa, and Alexandria.

1915 Under the urging of Joseph Trumpeldor, a Russian war veteran, the British use the Jewish refugees deported from Palestine to fight the Turks at Gallipoli. This brigade is known as the Zion Mule Corps and is charged with transporting food and military supplies.

1915 Sarah Aaronsohn, daughter of a Jewish farming family from an early settlement in Palestine, sees thousands of Armenians being driven southward from Constantinople and fears Turks will do the same to Jews in Palestine. She forms the Nili spy ring.

1916 Remaining Jews inside Palestine inform British intelligence of Turkish troop movements.

1916 British intelligence officer T.E. Lawrence receives valuable information from Sarah Aaronsohn inside Palestine about the Turks. Later, Lawrence would dedicate his book, *The Seven Pillars of Wisdom* to "SA," thought to be her.

1916 The British and French enter into the Sykes-Picot agreement whereby the Middle East would be divided according to British and French interests.

1917 The Turks uncover the Nili spy ring. Sarah Aaronsohn kills herself after extensive torture by the Turks. She is twenty-seven.

1917 November. The British government announces its support for a Jewish Homeland in Palestine. British Foreign Secretary Arthur Balfour issues a declaration promising that Britain would "view with favour the establishment in Palestine of a National Home for the Jewish people..." The declaration also added: "it being clearly understood that nothing shall be done which may prejudice the civil and religious rights of non-Jewish communities in Palestine, or the rights and politcal status enjoyed by Jews in any other country."

1917 December. British General Sir Edmund Allenby defeats the Turkish forces and enters Jerusalem, thus ending four hundred years of Ottoman rule there.

1918 October. After final defeat of their forces in Syria, Turkey sues for peace and concludes an armistice with the allies.

1919 January. An agreement is signed at the Paris Peace Conference between Feisal, the chief Arab delegate, and Weizmann, representing the Zionist Organization. Known as the Weizmann-Feisal Agreement, its terms pledge the two parties to cordial cooperation.

1919 Many Arab leaders fail to support Weizmann-Feisal Agreement principally because Allied war pledges for Arab Independence are not met.

1919 August. President Wilson assigns a commission to investigate the problem of dividing territory and assigning mandates. The report of the King-Crane Commission, issued August 28, opposes unlimited Jewish immigration and a separate Jewish state in Palestine. The report is not considered by the Paris Peace Conference and is not widely published until 1922.

1919 September. A former corporal in the German army named Adolf Hitler, employed by the Munich District Command to investigate right wing radical groups, visits a small group known as the German Workers' party which calls for curbing Jewish rights. Hitler soon leads this organization.

1920 The Grand Mufti of Jerusalem rejects cooperation with the Jews and instigates riots against them.

1920 Sir Herbert Samuel begins his five-year term as British High Commissioner for Palestine.

1920 Arab leaders fail to support the British Mandate to rule Palestine, declare both the Balfour Declaration and the Sykes-Picot Agreement null and void, and object to the Mandate's numerous references to the "Jewish Community" while the Arabs in Palestine that make up ninety-percent of its population are referred to only as "the other sections."

1921 Third wave of Jewish immigration. Thirty-five thousand Jews enter Palestine.
1921 Britain partitions Palestine at Jordan River and recognizes Transjordan.

1922 The League of Nations approves and formalizes the British Mandate over Palestine. The League also approves the British Mandate for Iraq and Transjordan (present day Jordan).

1922 The League of Nations grants French Mandate for Syria and Lebanon.

1924 More Jews immigrate to Palestine. Two underground military groups, Irgun and Stern, begin campaigns against British and later Arab marauders.

1925 *Mein Kampf* is published by Adolf Hitler. A typical passage reads: "Vienna appeared to me in a new light. . . Was there any shady undertaking, any form of foulness, especially in cultural life, in which at least one Jew did not participate? On putting the probing knife to that kind of abscess one immediately discovered, like a maggot in a putrescent body, a little Jew who was often blinded by the sudden light."

1929 Arabs in Jerusalem riot over acquisition of land by Jewish immigrants.

1933 Jews from Nazi Germany begin a larger stream of migration to Palestine.

1935 Germany issues the Nuremberg Laws that among other things deny Jews German citizenship.

1937 British Royal Commission on Palestine, known as the Peel Commission, issues its report that describes Arab and Jewish positions as irreconcilable. The report recommends that Palestine be partitioned into Jewish, Arab, and British zones. Under the plan, the British retain Mandate power over Nazareth, Bethlehem, Jerusalem, and a corridor from Jerusalem to the coast.

1937 Palestinian Arabs and most Arab states reject Peel Commission Report and renew violence against Jews.

1937 August. Twentieth Zionist Congress agrees in principle to partition proposal but rejects proposed boundaries.

1937 November. Woodhead Commission reverses Peel Commission recommendations arguing that partition is impractical.

1938 March. The British government calls for a conference in London with Jewish and Arab representatives, but the conference fails in part because the Arab delegation refuses to negotiate directly with Jewish representatives.

1939 May. The British government issues a White Paper that extends British rule in Palestine for a ten-year period, placing limits on Jewish immigration and their land purchases. It further states that a Palestinian government would be established at the
end of ten years. Arabs find the British White Paper generally negative. Jews reject it completely.

1939 September. On the first day of the month, Hitler launches an invasion of Poland, the first battle of World War II.

1939 September. In Palestine, Ben-Gurion states: "We the Jews of Palestine shall fight the war against Hitler as if there were no White Paper, and we shall fight the White Paper as if there were no war."
1940 In the spring Hitler plans his invasion of the Soviet Union. German troops are issued a special "Commissar Order" instructing them that all political commissars of the Bolshevik party, guerrillas, partisans, and Jews will be eliminated.

1941 Palestinian Jews helps supply British armed forces for the North Africa campaign.

1941 Within Palestine, the Jewish Agency resists the British Mandate attempts to regulate land sales and arranges immigration of many Jewish refugees to Palestine.

1941 June. Hitler launches Operation Barbarossa, invading the Soviet Union. Special SS commando units, the Einsatzgruppen, accompany the troops and begin the wholesale murder of Jewish civilians.

1942 January. In the Berlin suburb of Wannsee a group of high ranking Nazis plan the physical extermination of the Jews.

1942 Auschwitz, Treblinka, and other death camps, "Vernichtungslager," expand operations.

1942 July. Deportations from the Warsaw ghetto to Treblinka begin.

1943 February. The battle of Stalingrad ends with a total German defeat. The war in the east turns against the Nazis.

1944 A 30,000-man Jewish Brigade fights in Italy and Germany.

1945 May. Germany surrenders. Official estimates of the number of Jewish victims of the Nazi extermination policy is 5,820,000, roughly 37 percent of the world Jewish opulation in 1939.

1945 July. The new Labor Government in Britain endorses the 1939 White Paper, eeking to limit Jewish immigration into Palestine and to block land purchases by Jews there.

1946 May. Anglo-American Committee of Inquiry report denounces 1939 White Paper and calls for immediate entrance into Palestine of about 100,000 European Jews, most of whom are stateless survivors of the Holocaust.

1946 July. Irgun, an underground Jewish military group, bombs the King David Hotel, killing many British officials and over 100 Arab and Jewish employees of the hotel.

1946 December. Twenty-second Zionist Congress designates Ben-Gurion as executive chairman and defense ministers of Jewish Agency.

1947 Great Britain turns Palestine issue over to the United Nations. In May the UN establishes United Nations Special Committee on Palestine (UNSCOP).

1947 November. The UN General Assembly adopts a partition plan that will create a Jewish state of 5,500 square miles to include 538,000 Jews and 397,000 Arabs. The UN also votes for partition plan that will create a Palestinian state; 4,500 square miles to include 804,000 Arabs and 10,000 Jews. Arabs reject the plan.

1948 May. Jews issue Declaration of the Establishment of the State of Israel.
1948 Arab reject new state. Six Arab nations—Syria, Jordan, Egypt, Iran, Lebanon, and Saudia Arabia— invade Israel on May 15. The UN does not condemn the war and encourages Arabs to leave Palestine. Israeli Defense Forces secure a border for the new country.

1949 January. Israel's first Knesset (parliament) election is held.

1949 March. David Ben-Gurion forms a government as the country's first prime minister.

1950 October. Ben-Gurion and his cabinet resign on the issue of religious education.

1950 November. Ben-Gurion forms a second government.

1952 October. Chaim Weizmann dies.

1952 November. Itzhak Ben-Zvi is elected president.

1952 November. Knesset passes World Zionist Organization Jewish Agency Status Law.

1952 December. Ben-Gurion and his cabinet resign yet again because of the same religious education controversy.

1952 December. Ben-Gurion forms a new government.

1953 August. Knesset passes State Education Law.

1953 December. Ben-Gurion resigns for personal reasons.

1954 January. Moshe Sharett forms a government as new prime minister.

1955 June. Sharett resigns in dispute with opposition on issue of Nazi trials.

1955 November. Ben-Gurion forms a new government.

1956 July. Egypt announces nationalization of Suez Canal.

1956 October. Israeli forces invade Sinai Peninsula and the Gaza Strip.

1956 November. British and French military forces land at Port Said. A cease-fire follows.

1957 March. Israeli forces withdraw from the Gaza Strip.

1957 October. Ben-Zvi elected to a second five-year term as president on the 28th of the month.

1958 January. Ben-Gurion forms a new government.

1958 October. Knesset establishes Land Development Authority to assume control of land owned by the state and Jewish National Fund, about 90 percent of total land area.

1959 August. Israeli government restricts Arabs in the three areas under strict military control.

1960 May. Prime Minister Ben-Gurion informs the Knesset that Adolf Eichmann, one of the principal architects of the Final Solution, has been kidnapped in Argentina by the Israeli secret service and brought to Israel. The government of Argentina objects to this action.

1961 November. Ben-Gurion forms a new government with a coalition that includes the National Religious Party.

1962 October. Ben-Zvi elected to a third five-year presidential term.

1963 April. Ben-Zvi dies.

1963 May. Zalman Shazar elected president.

1963 June. Ben-Gurion resigns as prime minister but remains in the Knesset.

1963 June. Levi Eshkol forms a new government and assume the office of prime minister.

1967 February. Israel engages in a steady escalation of clashes on the Israel-Syria and the Israel-Egypt border.

1967 May. Egypt warns that it might close the Suez Canal to some or all ships.

1967 June. Moshe Dayan joins government as defense minister.

1967 June. Beginning of six-day war, June 5. Israeli aircraft launches attack that destroys 400 Arab aircraft.

1967 July. US and other nations oppose and refuse to recognize Israel's annexation of the Old City part of Jerusalem.

1969 March. Golda Meir, age 71, becomes prime minister after the death of Eshkol.

1970 August. After nearly two years of undeclared war of attrition. Egypt, Israel, and Jordan accept a US-proposed 90 day cease-fire.

1972 September. Palestinian terrorists enter living quarters of Israeli athletes at the Olympic Games held in Munich. During the course of hostage crises, eleven of the athletes are killed. In a botched rescue, West German security forces kill five of the eight terrorists.

1972 September. Israel retaliates by launching air strikes against PLO bases in Syria and Lebanon. Golda Meir approves a clandestine plan to assassinate eleven Arab operatives.

1973 October. Egypt and Syria launch an attack across the 1967 cease-fire borders. Israel pushes back on both countries. A cease-fire is declared on October 24.

1974 April. Golda Meir, aged seventy-six, resigns as prime minister. Yitzhak Rabin forms a new government.

1976 July. After a seven-day ordeal, Israeli commandos free 110 hostages held at Entebbe Airport in Uganda by terrorists allied with the Popular Front for the Liberation of Palestine (PFLP).

1977 May, Menachim Begin's party, Likud, emerges as the country's largest political party. Begin forms a new government.

1978 American President Jimmy Carter negotiates a peace treaty between Israel and Egypt at Camp David; Arab states expel Egypt from Arab League.

1981 Israel destroys atomic reactor in Iraq.

—Thanks to Steven Schlesser for providing "Timelines."

Acknowledgements

SINCERE THANKS TO ALL THOSE WHO advanced this project with their time, dedication and suggestions: my brother and his wife Kareem and Lorie Shora; Hanaa Rifaey for her balanced editing; Gabriel Swiney and Christie Flournoy for research assistance; Gwen Hubbard and Cassie Chandler for their steadfast support from the beginning; Maria Osman-Thakar for her candid reactions and Tony Kutayli for his technical support. Many thanks to Linda Pritchard for her quick edits.

Heartfelt thank yous to colleagues and mentors for their support: "Coach" Jack Shaheen, Daniel Sutherland, Professors David Cole and Juan Cole, Hussein Ibish, Laila Al Qatami, Eboo Patel, Maz Jobrani, General James "Spider" Marks and Rajbir Singh Datta.

Many thanks to the Cune Press team: publisher Scott C. Davis who believed in my vision for the *Handbook;* Ali Farzat who expressed my concepts eloquently in illustrations; Mamoun Sakkal who designed the cover and provided interior calligraphy; Frederic Hunter for invaluable effort and assistance; Dan Watkins; and all the other kind souls who made this project a reality. Cune wishes to thank the Seattle chapter of The World Affairs Council for their help in enlisting volunteers.

My gratitude to my parents Waseem and Zayada Shora. Their devotion, counsel, and perhaps genes have formed the man I am.

Sincere gratitude to my wife Camille. Her encouragement, support, and guidance have been the inspiration for me to achieve. And I thank God for giving me the motivation and energy to take on this project which is part of the bigger equation to conquer ignorance and hate.

The Calligraphy of Mamoun Sakkal

MAMOUN SAKKAL, THE COVER ARTIST (front cover inset; background calligraphy; section pages) of this handbook, is a leading Arabic calligrapher who has won international competitions for his calligraphic and typographic work. Sakkal has designed typefaces that adapt Arabic to the requirements of computer text and modern commerce. His creations include a computer typeface for Uighur, the Turkic-derived tongue of a Muslim minority in remote Western China. Sakkal has adapted Kufic (an angular Arabic script) as a decorative element for architectural design and even as a building form. The following samples are from Sakkal's work-in-progress: *The Principles of Square Kufic Design.* For more: www.sakkaldesign.com.

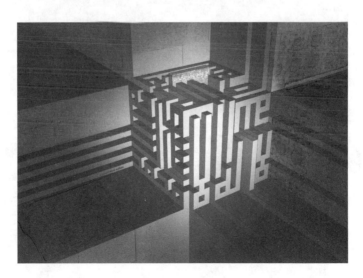

The Political Cartoons of Ali Farzat

ALI FARZAT, THE ILLUSTRATOR OF THIS HANDBOOK, is the leading Arab political cartoonist. He serves as head of the Arab Cartoonists' Association and publishes widely in Arab and European publications. The BBC is currently developing animations based on Farzat caricatures. Characteristically, Farzat cartoons appear without captions. The following caricatures are from Farzat's book: *A Pen of Damascus Steel: The Political Cartoons of an Arab Master*. For more: www.alifarzat.com.

"Informed Views" Writers

Devon Alisa Abdallah, PhD, a Pacific Northwest native, is a fourth generation Arab-American. Devon serves on several boards and has spoken on numerous panels, workshops, and forums on civil rights. She holds a masters degree from the London School of Economics and a PhD from Alliant International University.

Barbara Nimri Aziz is a veteran anthropologist, journalist and founder and host of the weekly broadcast "Tahrir: Voices of the Arab/Muslim Community Here and Abroad" over Pacifica's WBAI-NY and www.RadioTahrir.org. Her latest book, *Swimming Up the Tigris: Real Life Encounters With Iraq*, is published by U Press Florida.

Andrew J. Bacevich is professor of history and international relations at Boston University. A graduate of West Point and a Vietnam veteran, he received his PhD in American diplomatic history from Princeton and has also taught at West Point and Johns Hopkins. His books include *The Limits of Power: The End of American Exceptionalism* (2008), *The New American Militarism: How Americans Are Seduced by War* (2005), and *American Empire: The Realities and Consequences of U. S. Diplomacy* (2002).

Ramzy Baroud (www.ramzybaroud.net) is an author and editor of PalestineChronicle.com. His work has been published in many newspapers and journals worldwide. His books include *The Second Palestinian Intifada: A Chronicle of a People's Struggle*. He is the editor of *Searching Jenin: Eyewitness Accounts of the Israeli Invasion* (Cune Press, Seattle).

Bill Bazzi attended Fordson High School in Dearborn Michigan and enlisted in the US Marine Corps at age 18. He earned a Bachelors and Masters in Aeronautical Engineering from Embry Riddle Aeronautical University. He has worked for Boeing, currently works as a research engineer, and is on active reserves with the Marine Corps.

Susan Burton has worked as an educator for 17 years and is a parent of two transracially adopted children. She has a masters degree in counseling and personnel services and has served for eight years as director of the United Methodist Seminar Program on National and International Affairs.

David Cole is a professor at Georgetown University Law Center, the author of numerous books on terrorism and human rights, and a volunteer attorney with the Center for Constitutional Rights.

Juan Cole is an American professor of modern Middle Eastern and South Asian history at the University of Michigan. As a commentator on Middle East affairs, he has appeared in print and on television, and testified before the United States Senate.

Lauren Connolly writes and lectures on the political-cultural issues surrounding the image of Islamic women in the West. Her research interests include women's literature from the Middle East and North Africa. Lauren has spent time in Israel, Palestine, and most recently, Morocco and Tunisia, meeting women writers and educators exploring the issues.

William Dalrymple is author of *From the Holy Mountain: Travels Among the Christians of the Middle East* and *White Mughals: Love and Betrayal in 18th-Century India*.

Rajbir Singh Datta is the former National Director; Sikh American Legal Defense and Education Fund (SALDEF).

Scott C. Davis is a freelance writer and book publisher, based in Seattle. His book, *The Road from Damascus: A Journey Through Syria* is based on his many travels in Syria. In 1994 he and the calligrapher Mamoun Sakkal started Cune Press, which is now a leading publisher of trade nonfiction on Syria and the Levant. For more: www.scottcdavis.com | www.cunepress.net.

Krystina Derrickson recently received her master's degree in socio-cultural anthropology from Tulane University. She has lived on four continents. Fascinated by the Muslim world, Krystina hopes to continue her research on Islam, the Internet, and virtual environments. She currently works at the Middle East Youth Initiative at the Brookings Institution.

Hanna Eady is a Palestinian-American actor and playwright best known for co-writing *Suhmata*, a play about the destruction of the Palestinian village of Suhmata, near Acre in what is now northern Israel. Born in the Palestinian village of Buqu'ya in the Upper Galilee region of Israel, Eady earned a BA in social work from the University of Haifa, and then worked as the artistic director of a theater in Israel. He founded the New Image Theater Company in Seattle.

Amitai Etzioni, the author of many books, was a Senior Advisor to the Carter White House; taught at Columbia University, Harvard Business School, University of California at Berkeley, and is the first University Professor at George Washington University, where he directs the Institute for Communitarian Policy Studies. He served as the President of the American Sociological Association and founded the Communitarian Network.

Stephen Fife is an award-winning playwright, journalist, and author. His plays have been produced in New York City at The Jewish Repertory Theatre, Playhouse 91, Primary Stages, Circle Rep, La Mama, Theater for the New City, and the Samuel Beckett Theater. *This is Not What I Ordered*, his evening of short comedies, is published by Samuel French. *Savage World*, a multi-layered drama about African-Americans and Jews, was recently produced in Hollywood. His memoir of a production, *Best Revenge: How the Theater Saved My Life and Has Been Killing Me Ever Since*, was published by Cune Press in 2004.

Graham E. Fuller is a former vice chairman of the National Intelligence Council at the CIA in charge of long-range strategic forecasting. He is currently adjunct professor of history at Simon Fraser University in Vancouver, British Columbia, and author of numerous books about the Middle East, including *The Future of Political Islam* (New York: Palgrave Macmillan, 2003).

Jamal Gabobe is a scholar and poet who was born in Somaliland and is now based in Seattle. His book of poetry is titled, *Love & Memory* (Cune Press).

Nathalie Handal has lived in Europe, the United States, the Caribbean, Latin America, and the Arab world. As a writer-director-producer, Handal has been involved in over twenty productions worldwide. She is author of two poetry CDs, two poetry books, most recently, *The Lives of Rain*. She is currently working on the feature film, *Gibran*. Visit her website at www.nathaliehandal.com.

Frederic Hunter, a playwright and screenwriter, was a US Information Service Officer in Belgium and the Congo and served as the Africa correspondent of *The Christian Science Monitor* in the 1960s, an era when African independence was new and untested. Cune Press published his short story collection,

Africa, Africa! Fifteen Stories. Fred edited the *Arab-American Handbook* and compiled its Glossary.

Hussein Ibish is executive director of the Hala Salaam Maksoud Foundation for Arab-American Leadership and senior fellow at the American Task Force on Palestine.

Maz Jobrani is an Iranian-American comedian and actor. He is a founding member of the "Axis of Evil Comedy Tour," and was in *The Interpreter*, *Friday After Next*, and *13 Going on 30*. His work can be viewed on his website at www.mazjobrani.com.

Mohja Kahf is professor of English Literature at the University of Arkansas and the author of a collection of poetry (*E-Mails from Scheherazad*, U Press Florida) and the novel *Girl in the Tangerine Scarf* (Carroll & Graf Publishers). She is a regular contributor to www.MuslimWakeUp.com.

Martha Kessler, a former senior Middle East analyst with the CIA, is the author of *Syria: A Fragile Mosaic of Power.*

Lisa Suhair Majaj is a Palestinian-American writer and scholar. Born in Iowa, she grew up in Amman, Jordan, studied in Beirut, and lived 19 years in the US before moving to Cyprus. She is co-editor of the collections *Going Global: The Transnational Reception of Third World Women Writers*, Intersections: *Gender, Nation and Community in Arab Women's Novels*, and *Etel Adnan: Critical Essays on the Arab-American Writer and Artist.*

Major General James A. "Spider" Marks, (US Army, retired), served as the senior intelligence officer for the ground force invasion of Iraq. He is the former president and CEO of Global Linguist Solutions, providing over 8,000 linguists in support of military and humanitarian missions to rebuild Iraq.

Nour Merza is an Arab-American writer and poet, influenced, thanks to her family's globetrotting, by residence in Saudi Arabia, Chicago, Los Angeles, and the United Arab Emirates. Between reading every book within reach and exploring Dubai with friends, she enjoys attempting to make sense of her various social and cultural identities. She is currently studying International Relations at the American University of Sharjah.

Dr. Laurence Michalak is a Tunis-based cultural anthropologist with extensive experience in the Middle East and North Africa and director of the Center for North African Studies (CEMAT) in Tunis. He is the editor of two books and has published numerous articles and reviews about North Africa and the Middle East.

Sami Moubayed is a Syrian political analyst, journalist, and author based in Damascus, Syria. His articles on Middle East affairs have appeared in a variety of newspapers, including *al-Ahram Weekly*, *Gulf News*, *The Daily Star*, and *Asia Times*, and an online panel with *The Washington Post*. He is the author of *Steel & Silk: Men and Women Who Shaped Syria 1900 - 2000* (Cune Press).

Jacob Nammar lives with his wife in San Antonio, Texas, and is the father of three adult children. At the creation of the state of Israel in 1948, Jacob and his family were moved from their home. He, his mother, and six siblings were placed under guard in a concentration camp, separated from his father and oldest brother who were interned elsewhere. After two-and-a-half years the family was reunited and, in 1964, moved to the US. Jacob received degrees from North Dakota State University and the University of Wisconsin. His professional career was in the field of international relations.

Richard A. Nenneman, former editor in chief of *The Christian Science Monitor,* was also author of *Persistent Pilgrim: The Life of Mary Baker Eddy* as well as *The New Birth of Christianity: Why Religion Persists in a Scientific Age.* His third book, *A Spiritual Journey,* from which the *Handbook's* excerpt was taken, received posthumous publication in 2008 shortly after Nenneman's death.

Eboo Patel is the founder and executive director of the Interfaith Youth Core. An Ashoka fellow and Rhodes scholar, Eboo was named by *Islamica Magazine* as one of ten young Muslim visionaries shaping Islam in America. He is the author of *Acts of Faith* (2007) and writes "The Faith Divide," a featured blog on *The Washington Post.*

Laila al-Qatami is the former Communications Director for the American-Arab Anti-Discrimination Committee (ADC). She serves as an editorial consultant for documentaries and educational programs about Arabs, Arab-Americans, Islam, and civil rights in the US. Al-Qatami is a member of the National Board of Directors for the American Civil Liberties Union (ACLU).

Sara Rashad is a writer, actor, and cinematographer who lives in Los Angeles and Cairo. Her short film *Tahara* has received wide recognition. She has also won awards for the short films *Life is a Sweet* and *Through Thick and Thin.* She has earned an MFA in film production from USC and a BFA from Cornish College of the Arts. For more: www.taharafilm.com.

Ghassan Rubeiz is a Lebanese-American Middle East analyst and former professor with special interest in political sociology, social justice, and democracy.

Patrick Seale, a leading British writer on the Middle East, is author of *The Struggle for Syria; Asad of Syria: The Struggle for the Middle East;* and *Abu Nidal: A Gun for Hire.*

Jack Shaheen is the acclaimed author of five books and a media critic who defines crude caricatures, explains why they persist, and provides workable solutions to help shatter misperceptions.

Daniel W. Sutherland, a civil rights attorney throughout his legal career, served fourteen years with the Civil Rights Division of the US Department of Justice and co-authored *Religion in the Workplace,* published by the American Bar Association. From 2003 through 2008, he served as the Department of Homeland Security's officer for civil rights and civil liberties.

John Milton Wesley is a poet and essayist based in Columbia, Maryland. He grew up in the Mississippi delta in the heyday of the civil rights movement in Ruleville, Mississippi, under the tutelage of his "God Mother" Fannie Lou Hamer. Wesley, a 9/11 survivor, now supports himself as a journalist and public relations professional. For more: www.johnmiltonwesley.com.

Index

N AWAR SHORA IS A HIGHLY SOUGHT-AFTER public speaker who has given lectures and seminars to thousands of people over the past decade. In March 2010, as reported in the *Washington Post,* he was selected to serve in the Transportation Security Administration as a "senior adviser for its office of civil rights and liberties."

In his public events, Nawar speaks about Arabs and Muslims—their norms, mores, cultures, pop culture, history, current events as well as the public perceptions and misperceptions of individuals belonging to or thought to belong to these groups.

Nawar has participated in two federal government training videos as a subject matter expert. Shora has spoken to federal, state, and local law enforcement groups. His private sector appearances include churches, interfaith groups, and major corporations.

He has also served as a guest lecturer at numerous universities and academic institutions, the Federal Law Enforcement Training Center (FLETC), and the FBI Academy. Nawar's efforts have been recognized with awards from the Department of Homeland Security (DHS), Federal Bureau of Investigation (FBI), the Washington, DC Metro Police Department, and many others.